HEROES AND VILLAINS

HEROES AND VILLAINS

Creating National History
in Contemporary Ukraine

David R. Marples

C E U PRESS

Central European University Press
Budapest • New York

© 2007 by David R. Marples

Published in 2007 by
Central European University Press

An imprint of the
Central European University Share Company
Nádor utca 11, H-1051 Budapest, Hungary
Tel: +36-1-327-3138 or 327-3000
Fax: +36-1-327-3183
E-mail: ceupress@ceu.hu
Website: www.ceupress.com

400 West 59th Street, New York NY 10019, USA
Tel: +1-212-547-6932
Fax: +1-646-557-2416
E-mail: mgreenwald@sorosny.org

Cover photograph: Lubomyr Markevych

ISBN 978-963-7326-98-1 cloth

Library of Congress Cataloging-in-Publication Data

Marples, David R.
Heroes and villains : creating national history in contemporary Ukraine / David R. Marples. –
1st ed.
p. cm.
Includes bibliographical references and index.
ISBN 978-9637326981 (cloth : alk. paper)
1. Ukraine–History–1921-1944–Historiography. 2. Ukraine–History–1944-1991–
Historiography. 3. Orhanizatsiia ukraïns'kykh natsionalistiv–History. 4. Ukraïns'ka
povstans'ka armiia–History. 5. Historiography–Ukraine. 6. Nationalism–Ukraine. 7. Collective
memory–Ukraine. I. Title.

DK508.833.M367 2007
947.7'0842–dc22

2007030636

Printed in Hungary by
Akaprint

In memory of a good friend,

David W. J. Reid (1930-2006)

CONTENTS

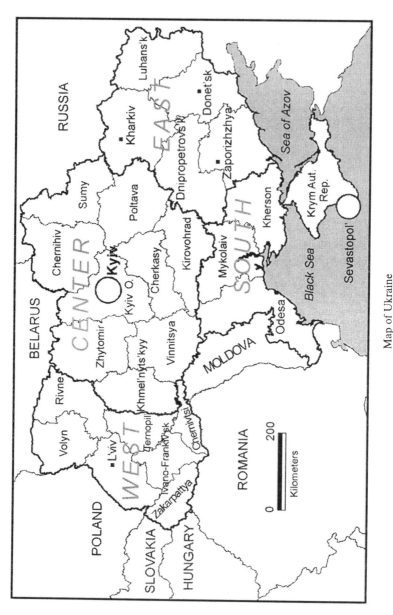

Map of Ukraine

Source: Clem, Ralph S., Craumer, Peter R. "Shades of Orange: The Electoral Geography of Ukraine's 2004 Presidential Elections," *Eurasian Geography and Economics*, Vol. 46, No. 5 (July–August 2005), p. 368. Reproduced with permission of V. H. Winston and Son, Inc.

PREFACE

Independent Ukraine emerged in August, 1991, and was ratified by a national referendum in December of this same year. However, the roots of the modern state are to be found in the period of Perestroika, under Mikhail S. Gorbachev, when civil society first began to emerge. Ukraine began the process of building a new nation, accepting the existing borders as "inviolable" and eventually agreeing to be a non-nuclear state with its own currency and constitution. The latter suffered a few crises, and at the time of writing, Ukraine appears to have opted for a parliamentary system over a presidential one, though the ramifications of that change—effective in 2006—have yet to be seen. Several scholars have offered analyses of the newly independent Ukraine and the respective presidencies of Leonid Kravchuk (1991-1994) and Leonid Kuchma (1994-2004), leading up to the mass uprising in Kyiv in November-December 2004 known as the Orange Revolution.[1] In January 2005, when Viktor Yushchenko became the third president, he announced his intention to have Ukraine join Euro-Atlantic structures such as the European Union and NATO, which implied—to what degree is a moot point—a move away from the Russian orbit. Ukraine's grassroots population had demonstrated its resistance to what was perceived as corruption, authoritarianism, and the restrictions on the media by the government of the day. But it has also appeared to support a fundamental change of direction from the Soviet period, some fifteen years after acquiring independence.

This book examines a question related to the concept of nation building, namely the construction of a national history. Arguably, there are several national histories and several interpretations of the past, and it may not be possible to determine which particular version is in the ascendancy. However, in Ukraine's case, the version in place—the Soviet narrative—has clearly been superseded and is obsolete. Yet that interpretation has remained influential in certain regions, particularly those of the east and south, and continues to sway the way residents of Ukraine perceive their state. By the mid-1990s, Mykhailo

Hrushevs'kyi's magisterial *History of Ukraine* could be found in Kyiv book-stores, offering a sweeping interpretation of some ten centuries of history that refuted the Soviet version of Kyivan Rus' as the birthplace of modern Russia, to the exclusion of the other East Slavic peoples: Ukrainians and Belarusians. Instead, it provided a Ukrainian conception of Ukrainian history, ostensibly for Ukrainians. The merits of this version need not be debated here, nor even the symbolic importance of such pre-20th century heroes as Bohdan Khmel-'nyts'kyi, Ivan Mazepa, or even the "true" founder of the modern Ukrainian state, the bard Taras Shevchenko, whose statue is now almost as common as that of V. I. Lenin used to be in times past. Instead, the focus is limited to the 20th century, and what I consider to be the most formative period, the leader-ship of Stalin (1928–53) and its impact on what was then termed the Ukrain-ian SSR and independent Ukraine. This period represents the most tragic era in the history of Ukraine, and one of the most profoundly influential in the formation of contemporary thinking about the modern nation and its relation-ship to the past. For it is in this period that Ukraine suffered its most dramatic and tragic experiences: the Famine of 1932–33, the Purges, the impact of the Nazi–Soviet Pact that saw its western territories incorporated into the USSR; the German invasion; and the bitter fighting as a result of national insurgency in the western regions that saw conflicts between several players: the retreat-ing Germans, the advancing Red Army, the local Polish population, and the local Ukrainians.

How are these events portrayed in contemporary Ukraine? That question forms the backbone to this monograph because the *raison d'être* of the mod-ern state seems predicated on the way it views its past. This perspective intro-duces two common elements of Ukraine's association with the past: glorifica-tion and victimization. The former was also a hallmark of Soviet writing and has simply been emulated, but the objects of glorification have changed radi-cally. In the case of the victimization, Ukraine is portrayed as a pawn of the Soviet regime, and more specifically of a Russian government based in Mos-cow. In turn, victimization implies an element of suffering. The argument in the modern context might run something like: because of our past suffering under a Moscow-based regime, we are now entitled to an independent state. The suffering has permitted the prevalence of a national conception of history that perceives and isolates Ukraine's past as a lengthy struggle against foreign oppressors, principally Russians and Poles, but also for a time Germans as well. It is simplistic in that the residents of the territory that currently com-prises Ukraine included many groups,[2] and the towns in particular were noted for the virtual absence of ethnic Ukrainians, at least until the Soviet period.

One could argue, however, that the victimization theory adds both legitimacy and propriety to the modern state. Levko Luk'yanenko, Ukraine's first ambassador to Canada, recently compiled a lengthy list of foreign repressions in Ukraine in an article that claimed in essence that the leaders of the former Soviet Union were largely members of a single ethnic group, namely Jews.[3] His article can be considered an extreme form of this same theory of outsiders controlling Ukraine until recent times.[4]

Though it is postulated here that the defining moments for modern Ukraine may have occurred in the Stalin period—also the high point of persecution and suffering—there were other events which could be fitted into the general pattern. These include a general phenomenon in the USSR of the 1960s and 1970s, i.e., Dissidence, which took numerous forms including national, religious, and scientific.[5] Dissidence was limited, however, in that it did not seek to replace the Soviet state, but only to ensure that it abided by the Constitution. Nevertheless, as discussed in Chapter 5, the Dissidents to some extent were the successors of the wartime generation of Ukrainians, some of whom fought a lengthy campaign against the Soviet occupants in the western areas for more than a decade after the "Great Patriotic War" ended. Also significant was the Chornobyl (Chernobyl) disaster in the Gorbachev era—an event that likewise affected Belarus. Chornobyl was also perceived as a result of the operation of outside forces, this time Moscow-based ministries and officials who ran nuclear power stations in Ukraine.[6] It could therefore be appended to the chronology of Ukraine as victim. Chornobyl was also a precursor of the modern Rukh movement, which like the Popular Fronts in the Baltic States was linked closely to concern over environmental issues. Though the uproar over Chornobyl and especially official secrecy about the aftermath soon died down, it should not be forgotten that the mass demonstrations that ensued and the political formations that resulted—such as the Green movement and Green Party—played an important role in undermining the Soviet regime.[7] Chornobyl also united several republics that suffered its consequences, most notably Belarus and the Baltic States.

Lastly, a key factor for Ukraine has been the maintenance of certain perceptions of the past outside the country by a large and politically active Diaspora that arrived in its new homes during or immediately after the Second World War and whose life experience and outlook were conditioned by their experience of the 1920s–1940s. For the most part these new arrivals emanated from the Halychyna (Galicia) region of Western Ukraine, a population with no experience of Soviet rule prior to 1939, but with very firm views on the events that had affected their compatriots in Eastern Ukraine, particularly the Famine of 1932–33, the Purges, and the Soviet occupation of 1939–41 and post-1944. Notably, the interpretation of the Famine as genocide[8] was initiated in the North American Diaspora, whence it emerged in Ukraine after Perestroika opened up contacts between Ukrainians and their relatives abroad—we will explore this issue in more detail below. Similarly, journals such as *Suchasnist'* provided national interpretations of organizations such as the OUN (Organization of Ukrainian Nationalists) and the UPA (Ukrainian Insurgent Army), and the émigrés who left Ukraine during or after the Second World War, though often politically divided, provided a plethora of works about the tyranny of the Stalin regime, the Famine, etc. On a more academic level, institutions like HURI and CIUS[9] have issued numerous publications about critical events, many of them by émigré political scientists, historians, and economists but others by scholars of non-Ukrainian background.[10] The result has been the elaboration of a national history (and other disciplines) outside Ukraine that could be taken up as part of the contemporary state and its official past following the collapse of the Soviet regime and its own version of history, with Russia as the benevolent elder brother and friend of Ukraine. The new histories issued in Ukraine virtually all take up these émigré themes and interpretations to a greater or lesser degree. For a time, after independence, Ukrainian schools relied completely on textbooks by Western academics such as Orest Subtelny, whose book, *Ukraine: a History*, published originally in 1988, became an international best seller. More recently, however, domestic historians have provided a broad variety of new histories of Ukraine geared to all levels of the population. The latter part of this study examines some of these histories in more detail in order to discuss their contents and omissions.

Any monograph that concentrates on discourse and narratives about events, rather than the "reality" of what actually occurred will face some criticisms. It is necessary to be selective—which discourses, and why? Are some sources more important than others? Conceivably the historian could study interpretations almost endlessly without coming to a conclusion or even approaching the end of the sources themselves. And what sort of time period should be imposed? The earliest writings on the Stalin period that attempted serious revisionism, as opposed to Khrushchev's reinterpretation of Stalin's crimes, occurred in the late 1980s after Gorbachev's decision to deepen "de-Stalinization" throughout the Soviet Union by allowing discussion in the official media. In Ukraine's case, some newspapers and journals proved very dilatory about changing long-held views, particularly the two central Kyiv newspapers: *Pravda Ukrainy* and *Radyans'ka Ukraina*. However, such obduracy was also instructive in demonstrating the influence of hard-line Soviet interpretations during a period of change. It seemed logical to begin around 1987–88, when the media in Ukraine began to open up to new debates, often pushing the limits of what could be discussed to new levels, but at a time when the Famine, for example, had just been acknowledged by the party leadership, thus signaling discernible progress in dealing with "blank spots" in Ukrainian history. Thus this book monitors the media, journals, and monographs, and offers an illustrative survey of school textbooks from 1987–88 to the present (2005–06).

In what ways was the study to be restricted in terms of content? My decision was to focus on those events that were most crucial and most controversial in terms of the construction of a new national history in the modern state. Two key issues stood out above all. The first was the Famine of 1932–33, known to one school of analysts as the *Holodomor* and an act of genocide against the Ukrainians as a nation, and to another as more a reflection of the ruthlessness of the regime but without a national component per se. While this study was being researched, on the 70th anniversary of the event several international governments recognized the Famine as genocide and issued acts or laws to say so.[11] Accepting the Famine as an act of genocide would also sever irrevocably the history of the Soviet state centered in Moscow from Ukraine, with its then capital of Kharkiv and, from 1934, Kyiv. Like no other event, it would portray Ukraine as a victim of a foreign nation and an outsider on Ukrainian territory. The inclusion of the Famine was thus self-evident, and the question is examined in detail in Chapter 2. The second event covers a much longer period and is more complex in its evolution, namely the development of integral nationalism in Ukraine, and its interwar and wartime formations in the shape of the Organization of Ukrainian Nationalists, and later the Ukrainian Insurgent Army, often simplified in Soviet and post-Soviet works by the acronym OUN-UPA. OUN-UPA in general occupies the bulk of this book, and significantly it has been evoked by Viktor Yushchenko as an organization whose members merit rehabilitation and full recognition as veterans of the Second World War.

The emphasis on OUN-UPA embraces several topics and the debates surrounding them. Chapter 3 examines the OUN from its formation in 1929 to the period immediately following the 30 June 1941 Act of Independence in L'viv, covering personalities, as well as the immediate impact of the Nazi-Soviet Pact. Chapter 4 looks at the various attempts to "heroize" OUN-UPA in the wartime period, and the changing portrayals of the way the UPA conducted warfare, as well as the thorny question of its alleged collaboration at various junctures with the German occupants. Chapter 5 continues chronologically by focusing on OUN-UPA after 1943, its sustained and brutal conflict with Soviet security forces, as well as the formation of the SS Division "Halychyna." This is followed in Chapter 6 with the period of "ethnic cleansing" of the Polish population in Volyn and Rivne regions, Operation Vistula, and the various academic and media debates that rose to a crescendo on the 60th anniversary of the dramatic events in Volhynia.[12] Chapter 7 then turns to the writing of new history textbooks in Ukraine and the attempts to rehabilitate OUN-UPA. It also provides a detailed focus on the efforts of the Yushchenko government to incorporate both the Famine and OUN-UPA into mainstream thinking as integral parts of the revised conception of Ukraine's national history. The final chapter looks at the Report by the Working Group to analyze the OUN and UPA and the degree to which its conclusions have been accepted. An analysis is provided as to how this revisionism of historical events relates to the current political changes that have occurred in Ukraine. The Conclusion offers an analysis of the current state of historical thinking on these complex events and a personal interpretation of them. It is hoped that the Conclusion will in this way offer some opinion of the narratives, which might otherwise appear to be lacking consensus. My own perspective, it is fair to say, was added somewhat reluctantly, but constitutes a recognition that a readership requires more than the reflection of events through prevailing discourses.

Concerning the choice of sources, the intention has been to provide representative perspectives from the different regions of Ukraine, as well as to demonstrate the viewpoints in mainstream newspapers. The book has also tried to incorporate the perspectives of the different generations, with a special focus on the youth newspaper *Ukraina moloda* as well as the organs of World War II veterans' associations, or those propagating the views of veterans, such as *Za vil'nu Ukrainu*. Journals covered include the central *Ukrains'kyi istorychnyi zhurnal*, which might be perceived as the main arbiter of what is debated and acceptable in Ukraine today, but also a number of journals used for schools. In some cases the contents of the journal or newspaper were read but deemed unsuitable for this project, and the decision not to include the Purges as a key focus was also quite deliberate. It stemmed from the fact that the impact of the Purges on Ukraine, while devastating, may not provide many insights that did not apply to their effects on other regions of the former Soviet Union. The events are well known and have been studied in depth.[13] They also form part of a completely different debate as to whether residents of the Soviet Union in the 1930s lived in a state of terror. Finally, the Purges, after 1956, were not subjected to radical changes of interpretation, other than perhaps the question of national content—whether some republics suffered more than others, etc. They were subjected to official government inquiries, based on at least three congresses of the Central Committee of the Communist Party of the Soviet Union, namely the 20th, 22nd, and 27th. The Soviet leadership acknowledged that most of their victims were innocent and maintained that this cleansing of the party and society was unwarranted by the internal situation. Hence the Purges are no longer an event that has been in some way covered up or misinterpreted, deliberately or otherwise. They could of course be studied purely in their Ukrainian dimension, but to do so would require a separate study.

Lastly one must consider the question of context. My focus in this book is exclusively on Ukraine, but were the latter's experiences unique, either during the years covered in the narratives, or after 1991 as an independent state, attempting to comprehend the past and fit it into a national dimension through the rewriting of history? In general, what happened in Ukraine—the Famine aside—mirrors to some extent what occurred in Central Europe as a whole during the interwar period and the years of the Second World War. Like many of the national groups seeking statehood, and indeed those that already possessed it after the Paris peace treaties, many Ukrainians perceived that embracing democracy would not resolve their dilemma or improve their situation. Integral nationalism appears today an extreme political creed, but it was familiar to political activists of that era. Similarly, all the states of central Europe with the exception of Czechoslovakia could be described at the least as authoritarian. That statement is not to condone the preeminence of extreme political views but rather to understand them. This monograph may appear critical of some of the views expressed, for example, by the two wings of the Organization of Ukrainian Nationalists, but that is not to say that they were not fairly typical of the period. Moreover, the Ukrainians were perhaps the largest group not to emerge after the First World War with their own statehood (aside from a brief period following the Russian Revolutions of 1917). Worse still, the majority of Western Ukrainians who ended up in the restored Polish state were not treated as equals. By the end of the 1920s their position was not much better than that of an internal colony of Poland. At this time there was even envy of their brethren in Soviet Ukraine, then reaching the peak of an indigenization program (though also on the verge of extensive repressions).

The Second World War was perhaps the most significant and most discussed cataclysm of the 20th century. Even in 2006 that debate has continued. As Norman Davies has demonstrated recently,[14] it is an event that has been written and interpreted principally by the victors. Because of this tendency, anti-Soviet Ukrainians, among others, have emerged with a rather bad press. Despite the fact that the Cold War that followed highlighted many of the darker sides of Soviet rule, Western analysts have tended to see those who joined the insurgency against the Red Army as ipso facto collaborators of the Germans or, even worse, as perpetrators of some of the worst atrocities that occurred in Eastern Europe. However, to take such a position is manifestly unfair. Ukrainians after all had experienced first-hand the worst excesses of Stalin and Stalinism. In what way could they assess the relative merits and defects of being ruled by Hitler or Stalin other than by what they had experienced? Thus for many in Ukraine, the date of 22 June 1941 was perceived as the day of liberation from a tyranny. On the other hand, some of the individuals and groups described herein may be said to have gone further, to have embraced some of the same policies as the German occupants and to have taken their enthusiasm at being "freed" too far. All one can say in an introduction is that the Ukrainians in all areas of Eastern Europe in which they lived were placed in a very difficult situation—between two of the most ruthless dictatorships ever devised, and with no prospect of neutrality or non-involvement.

Likewise, turning to the contemporary period, Ukrainians faced some familiar problems once they acquired statehood following the collapse of the Soviet Union in December 1991. Their views derived largely from their background and geographical location. For the more nationally conscious (Western) Ukrainians, independence was the culmination of long-term aspirations that began—at the least—in the early part of the century, and for others allegedly even earlier, perhaps back to the 17th century Hetmanate of Bohdan Khmel'nyts'kyi. The collapse of empires in the 20th century left behind many former colonies that struggled with national identity and often lacked the prerequisites of a modern state. The fall of the Soviet Empire cannot realistically be compared to, say, that of the British Empire, not least because of its disparate nature and the fact that its territories were contiguous. Some ten years after the end of the Soviet regime, all the new states were struggling to develop economically and in terms of establishing democracies, other than the three Baltic States of Estonia, Latvia, and Lithuania. In Central Asia, the rulers essentially had not changed from Communist times. In the Caucasus, there were severe problems between the titular nations and minorities over territory and rights to autonomy. Russia had been at war with one of its autonomous territories, Chechnya, albeit with an interruption, for twelve years.

On the other hand, perhaps Ukrainians, more than any other group, were attempting to come to terms with their recent past. In neighboring Belarus to the north, there seemed to be a consensus that the Soviet era had been a period of progress (at least economically), and those politicians who advocated national development toward Europe and away from Russia, or demanded that Belarusian should be the only state language, were regarded as extremists and failed to attract the support of more than one-fifth of the population during any election campaign. Ukraine was divided regionally and by language, though the importance of the latter is somewhat hard to measure. The various regions perceived the past quite differently, even though these perceptions were not necessarily static. Was the Soviet Union the epitome of evil or a benevolent and paternal master that saw the advancement of Ukrainians, as well as other non-Russian nations, in an egalitarian manner? For more than seventy years, residents of Eastern and Southern Ukraine had been subjected to one very specific interpretation of the past, particularly as applied to the 20th century. The alternative view was dismissed as being propagated by "bourgeois nationalists" in Western Ukraine, Ukrainians living abroad, as well as by imperialist powers such as the United States and Britain. It seems doubtful if any other post-Soviet republic emerged from the wreckage of the Soviet state with such ambivalent and diametrically opposed attitudes. In brief, residents of Ukraine did not know who they were because they had no overriding perception of the immediate past and what it had signified. The Soviet view was no longer relevant, but for many Ukrainians there was nothing with which to replace it.

Hence although one can offer a comparative approach, and suggest that what occurred in Ukraine formed part of a general experience that could be applied to other republics of the former USSR or the former Communist regimes of Eastern Europe, that statement would not really be accurate. Ukraine's experience was formulated by events of such magnitude as to defy comprehension. Only Belarus could lay claim to such a lengthy and brutal period of foreign occupation during the Second World War, and even this small neighbor to the north had not suffered the devastation of the Famine of 1932–1933. In addition, few republics were more diverse in territorial makeup. Ukraine's regions included lands that had been, in recent memory, under the sway of six different governments (Russia, Poland, Czechoslovakia, Hungary, Romania, and Nazi Germany), and the most Ukrainian of its cities, L'viv, had been part of the Austrian Empire and Poland in the first half of the century. Demographically, Ukrainians had not been an urban phenomenon until the 1960s and 1970s. For many years, both Soviet and non-Soviet-controlled areas had seen most Ukrainians devoted to agricultural pursuits, while other ethnic groups formed the majority in the towns. To Ukrainian peasants, urban dwellers represented "the other" regardless of any ethnic divisions. Urban Ukrainians are a relatively recent phenomenon and for that matter a Soviet phenomenon. Soviet education and propaganda managed in the eastern regions to inculcate views held by the Soviet elite, and to some extent those opinions are still in place.

All these factors make the present book more complicated than it might at first appear. Ukraine's past is often assessed by Western standards, just as much of present-day world politics reflects a Western dimension, from the Internet upward. That is one reason why, in my view, it is unwise to be too judgmental about some of the polarized attitudes toward the recent past or the failure to construct a viable and united state based on the sort of principles that would be acceptable in Washington, D.C. or London. On the other hand, what this monograph has tried to do is to examine the narratives from a distance, without necessarily offering critiques of views that might seem outrageous to the Western observer or for that matter to those who have condemned what is termed "the Ukrainian nationalist perspective." It is sometimes said that Eastern Ukrainians lack national consciousness or that they have been Russified so heavily that they no longer know their own language and culture. But who defines that culture? Who is to determine whether a worldview is misguided or weaker than an alternative view that may accentuate national attributes or virtues? Is a Ukrainian, for example, who thinks that the Red Army liberated Ukraine in 1943–44 backward or of an antediluvian mindset? Conversely, must citizens of an independent Ukraine accept the view of a relatively small and fanatical liberation movement against the Moscow regime that maintained, first and foremost, the need to end Russian control over Ukraine that dated back several centuries? It was with such questions in mind that I began this study.

Notes

1   Taras Kuzio and Paul D'Anieri, ed., *The Dilemmas of State-Led Nation Building in Ukraine* (Westport, Connecticut: Praeger, 2002); Taras Kuzio, *Ukraine: Perestroika to Independence* (New York: St. Martin's Press, 2000); Andrew Wilson, *Ukraine's Orange Revolution* (New Haven, Connecticut: Yale University Press, 2005); Bohdan Nahaylo, *The Ukrainian Resurgence* (Toronto: University of Toronto Press, 1999); and Marta Dyczok, *Ukraine: Movement without Change, Change without Movement* (Amsterdam: Harwood Academic Publishers, 2000).

2   See, for example, Kate Brown, *A Biography of No Place: from Ethnic Borderland to Soviet Heartland* (Cambridge, Massachusetts: Harvard University Press, 2004).

3   Levko Luk'yanenko, "U lystopadovi zhalobni dni," in M. V. Drodets'ka ed., *Komu buv vy-hidnyi holodomor?* (Kyiv: Telesyk, 2003), pp. 3–17.

4   A dissenting view is offered by political scientist Mikhail A. Molchanov, who comments on Ukraine's victimization in the past as follows: "Though denied their national state, Ukrainian aristocracy actively participated in medieval Lithuanian and Polish–Lithuanian states of the fourteenth and fifteenth centuries and Ukrainian clergy—in the building of the Russian Empire since the 1700s. Ukrainians, as no other people, were intimately connected with the structures of power in Moscow Czardom, the Russian Empire, and the Soviet Union... Communists never lacked Ukrainian representation in the party's apex, not only in Ukraine proper, but also in Moscow and other parts of the Soviet Union. Ukrainians constituted the weighty proportion of the Red Army brass; a KGB career starting in Ukraine and ending in Moscow was not exceptional either." Mikhail A. Molchanov, *Political Culture and National Identity in Russian-Ukrainian Relations* (College Station, TX: Texas A & M University Press, 2002), p. 39.

5   The most famous literary example of Ukrainian dissidence was the treatise by Ivan Dzyuba, *Internationalism or Russification: a Study in the Soviet Nationalities Problem*, 3rd ed. (New York: Pathfinder Press, 1974).

6   The nuclear power industry in Ukraine was described by one observer as the thoughtless expansion of atomic power stations in densely populated regions. Yurii Shcherbak, *Chorno-byl'* (Kyiv: Dnipro, 1989), p. 221.

7   See, for example, D. J. Peterson, *Troubled Lands: the Legacy of Soviet Environmental Destruction* (Boulder, Colorado: The Westview Press, 1993), pp. 210–211.

8   The term comes up regularly in discussions of twentieth-century Ukraine. How should it be defined? According to the definition adopted by Resolution 260 (III) A of the United Nations General Assembly on 9 December 1948, Article 2 stipulates that: "In the present Convention, genocide means any of the following acts committed with intent to destroy, in whole or in part, a national, ethnical, racial or religious group, as such: (a) Killing members of the group; (b) Causing serious bodily or mental harm to members of the group; (c) Deliberately inflicting on the group conditions of life calculated to bring about its physical destruction in whole or in part; (d) Imposing measures intended to prevent births within the group; (e) Forcibly transferring children of the group to another group."

9   HURI refers to the Ukrainian Research Institute at Harvard University; CIUS is the Canadian Institute of Ukrainian Studies at the University of Alberta. Both were founded through contributions from local Ukrainian communities in the 1970s.

10 Most notable was the book commissioned by HURI: Robert Conquest, *Harvest of Sorrow: Soviet Collectivization and the Terror-Famine* (Oxford: Oxford University Press, 1986). CIUS Press authors who were born in Ukraine but migrated to Europe or North America include Iwan S. Koropeckyj, Borys Lewytzkyj, and Peter J. Potichnyj.

11 On 28 November 2006, the Ukrainian Parliament passed a bill, which described the Famine of 1932–33 as genocide against the Ukrainian people. A previous draft had termed it genocide against the Ukrainian nation. The vote total, however, was 233–1, a bare majority in the 450-seat parliament (the remaining MPs abstained from voting). It has been speculated that these 200 deputies either did not wish to offend Russia or were concerned about the sentiments of their own constituents. The motion received support from President Viktor Yushchenko and some 70% of the general population. See *CBS News*, 29 November 2006.

12 I have used the term Volhynia throughout to refer to the north-western territories of Ukraine that today are comprised by Volyn and Rivne *oblasts* (provinces). Strictly speaking, in terms of the transliteration system applied, the correct spelling should be Volhyniya. However, the familiarity and use of "Volhynia" are such that I have applied this spelling throughout.

13 See, for example, Robert Conquest, *The Great Terror: a Reassessment* (New York: Oxford University Press, 1990); Robert W. Thurston, *Life and Terror in Stalin's Russia, 1934-1941* (New Haven, CT: Yale University Press, 1996); J. Arch Getty, *Origins of the Great Purges: the Soviet Communist Party Reconsidered, 1933-1938* (New York: Cambridge University Press, 1985); J. Arch Getty and Roberta Manning, ed., *Stalinist Terror: New Perspectives* (New York: Cambridge University Press, 1993); and J. Arch Getty and Oleg V. Naumov, *The Road to Terror: Stalin and the Self-Destruction of the Bolsheviks, 1932-1939* (New Haven, CT: Yale University Press, 1999). On Ukraine specifically, see, for example, Yurii Ivanovich Shapoval', Volodymyr Prystayko, and Vadym Zolotar'ov, *ChK-HPU-NKVD v Ukraini: osoby, fakty, dokumenty* (Kyiv: Abrys, 1997); and V. M. Danylenko, H. S. Kas'yanov, and S. V. Kul'chyts'kyi, *Stalinizm na Ukraini: 20-30-ti roky* (Lviv: Lybid, 1991).

14 Norman Davies, *Europe at War 1939-1945: No Simple Victory* (London: Macmillan, 2006).

ACKNOWLEDGEMENTS

The research for this book was generously funded by a major grant from the Social Sciences and Humanities Research Council of Canada, 2003–06. The author would like to thank the librarians and the staff of three repositories in particular: the Central Scientific Library, Kharkiv V. N. Karazin National University; the Kherson Honchar Oblast archives; and the European Reading Room at the Library of Congress in Washington, D.C., as well as Senior Slavic Bibliographer and longtime friend, Jurij Dobczansky. Nancy Popson, then at the Kennan Institute, generously sent me copies of various new texts on the history of Ukraine to supplement my own collection. The Stasiuk Endowment at the Canadian Institute of Ukrainian Studies, University of Alberta, also provided funding for some additional research assistance. My assistants provided invaluable aid and I would like to single out the following: Ilya Khineiko, Per Rudling, and Dr. Febe Pamonag. I would also like to acknowledge the help of my friend and colleague John-Paul Himka, who shares many of my interests in Ukraine and has produced his own revisionist accounts of many of the subjects discussed in this book, particularly on the Second World War. Special thanks go to Aya Fujiwara, a recently graduated PhD in history, who helped in a variety of ways, particularly with the analysis of recent writings on the issue of nationalism.

Materials and references were supplied by Terry Martin (Harvard University) and Mark Von Hagen (Columbia University). I have benefited from information gleaned from talks in the UK and Canada by Professors Yaroslav Hrytsak (L'viv) and Oleksii Haran (Kyiv). Taras Kuzio, Visiting Fellow at the German Marshall Fund of the United States, provided valuable information on the OUN after the Second World War. Svitlana Krasyns'ka, a Ukrainian now based in Los Angeles, was kind enough to read a draft version of the entire manuscript. My principal aides on this book, both natives of Ukraine (Kherson and Kharkiv, respectively) have been my former MA student and currently PhD candidate at the University of Toronto, Oleksandr Melnyk, an outstanding young scholar; and my friend Anna Yastrzhembska, recipient of a graduate degree in applied linguistics from Central European University, who provided the original idea for the study, carried out the editing of transliterations, and perused the entire text in depth, adding comments along the way. This is the first book I have published with CEU Press, cooperation with which has been exemplary. I would like in particular to thank Linda Kunos for her editorial work and assistance.

I recognize only too well the controversial nature of the events described herein and that some of the debates will not please everyone. Nonetheless, I have worked and communicated with the Ukrainian community of North America for over two decades. I trust that they will permit someone who is hardly an outsider to express views on their past that may be different from their own. It was largely through debates and discussions with its members on Internet discussion groups that the conception of this book developed. Scholars such as Peter J. Potichnyj, Taras Hunczak, and Roman Serbyn have authored dozens of articles and books pertaining to Ukraine in the Second World War. Dr. Potichnyj is also the editor of the multi-volume series entitled *Litopys UPA*, which can now be found in bookstores in the major cities of Ukraine. Concerning the Famine of 1932–33, no author can write today without acknowledging the writings of the late James E. Mace, who died prematurely in Kyiv in 2004, but remains a significant influence on current perceptions of that tragic event both in Ukraine and elsewhere. I owe a certain debt to all these scholars even if their views and my own do not necessarily coincide. The opinions expressed in this book, as well as any errors of judgement or fact, are mine alone.

David R. Marples
Edmonton, Alberta, Canada
April 2007

CHAPTER 1

INDEPENDENT UKRAINE REVIEWS THE PAST

Rethinking Perspectives in Ukraine

There are several general indications of changing perspectives in Ukraine after independence, a period when the government was preoccupied with elaborating its new relationship with Russia, with its autonomous region of Crimea, and with overcoming a serious economic crisis. Initially, there was some emphasis on taking revenge against the former Soviet regime in the form of an international tribunal. The situation was described by the president of the Kyiv branch of the Memorial association, Roman Krutsyk, who noted the disastrous consequences of Soviet rule in Ukraine. In 1989, when the contents of mass graves—victims of Stalin's terror—had been exhumed at Dem'yaniv Laz, Memorial activists gathered party cards from Communists disillusioned with the ruling party. He commented that the materials collected by Memorial were ready to be used as testimonies against the Communist Party of the Soviet Union (CPSU) at a new international tribunal. His organization had also facilitated the return to Ukraine of several families deported to the east. What were Memorial's main goals? They were to "hunt down" the perpetrators of Communist crimes, but the main task was to raise new citizens who would be aware of Ukraine's tragic past. With this goal in mind, the association intended to create a museum that would document Communist crimes and organize a Nuremberg-type trial for Communist criminals.[1]

Stanislav Kul'chyts'kyi, an historian who will enter these pages frequently, is deputy director of the Institute of History with the National Academy of Sciences in Ukraine. In the spring of 1992 he wrote an insightful article about the state of the historical discipline in Ukraine, noting that in the wake of the disintegration of the Soviet Union, historians found themselves in a state of confusion. Because the writing of history in Soviet times was directed toward service to the regime, it frequently led to the falsification of the events of the 20th century. Historians often did not know the true picture, being limited to a "Communist" vision of the past. Kul'chyts'kyi himself was misled regarding past events, and writes that only in 1988 did he comprehend that there were no secret Trotskyite circles in the country. However, from the perspective of 1992, he maintains that historians could attain a better idea of historical processes through ridding themselves of censorship and mounting an all-out attack on archival holdings. He perceives several "blank spots" in Ukrainian history, including the government of the Central Rada after the revolutions of 1917, as well as OUN-UPA.[2]

Kul'chyts'kyi also urges caution when dealing with archival documents, as they are not completely reliable. As an example, he cites party documents— pronouncements of party leaders at official ceremonies. These statements, he notes, did not necessarily reflect the sentiments of the speaker, and it is better for the historian to use the testimony of simple people or official reports that reflect the real state of affairs, such as police reports on the mood of the population. He appears to ignore or be ignorant of the fact that unofficial sources can be equally as slanted as official ones, reflecting the values and outlook of their originators. He thus cites as a reliable example the memoirs of simple peasants, praising the work of the US Commission on the Ukrainian Famine, led by James E. Mace, precisely for collecting such valuable testimonies, and declaring that "The subjective element disappears when hundreds of people have to answer the same question."[3] The statement reflects a rather naïve view of the historical discipline, as such surveys might also be depicted as hundreds of subjective narratives rooted in past and present discourses. Kul'chyts'kyi also bemoans the fact that Ukrainian historians lacked methodology because they were completely oblivious to the ways in which Western historians carried out their discipline.[4] That comment is also revealing because it demonstrates an almost obsequious attitude to Western historians and the implicit need to emulate them, and that for several years at least, those working in the discipline would be over-reliant on works published in the West (see below) whose authors had much less access to archival sources than the admittedly slanted Soviet publications.

What might be considered an extreme example of how the national element could be inserted into the conception of the past was provided in a 1993 article by Petro Vol'vach. His article sets out to explain economic and social problems in contemporary Ukraine through references to the pernicious influence of the legacies of the Russian Empire and the Soviet Union. He writes that the wretched state of the Ukrainian economy and spiritual life should be sought in Ukraine's "lengthy colonial enslavement." This "enslavement," he maintains, is responsible for the low level of national consciousness and lack of national pride, opportunism, and patronage that is especially common in the southern and eastern regions of the country. He portrays expansionism as something that is inherent to the development of the Russian state, and draws a direct line from the 16th-century wars of Ivan the Terrible to the post-Second World War subjugation of Eastern Europe. Thus in 1492, "*Muscovia*" covered 24,000 square kilometers, but by 1914 the Russian Empire encompassed 23.8 million square kilometers. Thus Russia increased its total area by 80 square kilometers per day. Vol'vach offers the following chronology of "Ukrainian enslavement" in the modern period, which is worth citing in full as representative of an anti-Russian or Russophobic version of the Ukrainian past:[5]

1720—decree of Peter I prohibiting the printing of books in Ukrainian;

1729—decree of the Holy Synod concerning the confiscation from the population of elementary textbooks and church writings in Ukrainian;

1768—the conspiracy of Catherine II with Polish aristocrats about the subjugation of the Koliivshchyna rebellion;[6]

1768-1775—the destruction of the Ukrainian Cossacks in the Russo-Turkish war;

1775—the destruction of the Zaporozhian Sich;

1771-1783—the liquidation of the Hetmanate;

1811—closure of the Kyiv Mohyla Academy;

1816-1821—military occupation of Ukraine in the form of 500,000-strong military settlements;

1847—destruction of the Cyrillo-Methodius Brotherhood;

1854-55—the Crimean War, in which Ukraine was the major supplier of "cannon fodder";

1876—the Ukaz of Ems banning Ukrainian publications and resulting in the exile of several prominent Ukrainian cultural figures;

1877-78—Russo-Turkish war that brought huge economic and human losses to Ukraine;

1904-05—Russo-Japanese war that claimed the lives of tens of thousands of Ukrainians;

1907-08—post-revolutionary reaction in Ukraine and the closing of Ukrainian-language journals and newspapers;

1914-1917—the First World War, with heavy Ukrainian casualties;

1917-1920—the Bolshevik–White Guard assault on Ukraine and civil war;

1921-22 [sic!]—War Communism;

1928-32—collectivization and the destruction of prosperous peasants; deportations;

1932-33—the man-made famine to destroy the rebellious Ukrainian peasants;

1933—halting the process of "Ukrainization;"

1933-38—the total genocide of the Ukrainian people and the destruction of Ukrainian culture;[7]

1938—Stalin's decree about the obligatory study of the Russian language;

1939—Winter war [in Finland] with human and economic losses for Ukraine;

1919-40—Soviet annexation of Western Ukraine;

1941-1945—the Second World War;

1944-45—the preparation of the Stalin–Beria plan for the deportation of all Ukrainians (22 June 1944);

1946-47—famine in Ukraine;

1947—the Soviet–Polish Operation Vistula;

1944-49—the destruction of the UPA; deportations;

1954-59—the Virgin Lands program—3 million young Ukrainians moved to Kazakhstan;

1964-83—the Communist Party reaction in Ukraine; the struggle against the Ukrainian renaissance;

1983—the decree of the CC CSU about the obligatory study of the Russian language;

1986—the nuclear disaster at Chornobyl.

Vol'vach notes with regret that the ratio of Ukrainians in the total population of Ukraine has been declining, partly as a result of the influx of people of other nationalities which, he believes, leads to the destruction of the moral foundations of society and the loss of awareness of a common historical fate and culture.

In another contribution on this same theme, Vol'vach documents the experience of "genocide" suffered by the Ukrainian-speaking population of the Kuban in 1933-39. In 1932, he writes, there existed some 240 Ukrainian schools in this region, and 20 Ukrainian-language newspapers were in circulation, along with five journals. The radio also broadcasted in Ukrainian. Early in 1933, the process of Ukrainization in the Kuban was halted, because it did not correspond to the cultural needs of the population, in the Soviet view, and provided the "class enemy" with the legal tools to organize resistance to the Soviet authorities. Within three days, Vol'vach writes, Ukrainian-language broadcasts were terminated and the entire Ukrainian-language press reverted to Russian. Many Ukrainian writers and teachers in the Kuban were arrested. Collectivization in this region in 1933 led to a peasant rebellion that was subdued by the NKVD. Famine claimed the lives of many Cossacks. For many centuries, concludes the article, with reference to all Ukrainian territories, governments have given priority to the development of Russian culture in the national land of Ukraine. Independent Ukraine, as a member of the community of nations, is therefore entitled to demand from Russia and the international community adequate protection of the interests of Ukrainians on their own territory. Should such protection not be forthcoming (and it is unclear how it would be manifested, but presumably by preventing "foreigners" from taking up residence in Ukraine), millions of Ukrainians, who survived by a miracle throughout many centuries of genocide and warped assimilatory policies, will disappear and be dissolved into a "Russian sea" as had happened to millions in the past. Without resolving this pressing problem, the Ukrainian-Russian relationship will remain one-sided, and the current conversations of Russian "new democrats" about people's friendship and the spirit of internationalism will be the sequel to the treacherous Communist demagoguery.[8]

These articles can perhaps be dismissed as representing a polarized view of Ukraine's past and a contribution to what has been termed "the cult of competitive suffering." However, other observers have noted first that there are some "blind spots" in the approach to the past, and second, that there are problems in "harmonizing" the national histories of Ukraine and Russia as reflected in history textbooks. Kul'chyts'kyi remarks that some Second World War veterans remain convinced that there was no famine in Ukraine in 1932-33, that the secret protocols of the Molotov-Ribbentrop Pact never existed, and that the Katyn massacre was a fabrication of the German occupants of the Soviet Union.[9] Another writer, Yaroslava Muzychenko, cites the chair of Ukrainian Studies at the University of St. Petersburg, Tet'yana Lebedyns'ka, who decried the lack of dialogue between Ukrainian and Russian historians on the dramatic episodes of modern history. Lebedyns'ka recalled two conferences dedicated to the 1709 Battle of Poltava, one in Moscow and another in Ukraine. The Russian one cursed Ukrainians; the Ukrainian gathering cursed Russians; and there was no common ground. She suggested a Western approach through which authors present comments on historical events from a variety of political perspectives. The same article quotes a Ukrainian teacher, Viktor Rudii, who is convinced that history textbooks have to tell the truth, however unpleasant it might be. He is frustrated that students seem incapable of viewing historical events objectively: people from Western Ukraine are still referred to as "Banderites" in the eastern parts of the country, while easterners in the west are called Communists. The problem has arisen, in Muzychenko's view, because of the lack of a state policy directed toward the reconciliation of citizens.[10]

Another factor behind such disparate perceptions is reportedly the "propaganda of intolerance" emanating from Russia, which together with the lack of a state policy from Kyiv and increasing poverty in Ukraine contribute to the spread of ethnic intolerance in the contemporary state. Muzychenko has little time for "gung-ho patriots" who are afraid that Ukrainians will disappear from Ukraine. This attitude, she writes, is imperialistic, as Ukraine is a multi-ethnic state. However, the greatest challenge to the Ukrainian–Russian Commission, created to examine the interpretations of history, is "ethno-centralism." Russian historians have adopted the Great Imperial conception of history, whereas simple Russians enjoy the memoirs of people like Pavel Sudoplatov, who by modern standards would be considered an international terrorist. She cites Ukrainian historian Serhii Kot, who maintains that any commission is meaningless unless Russian society is prepared to grant Ukrainians or any other nation the right to a distinct historical development. However, she is fearful that Ukrainian "gung-ho patriots" will also be unwilling to accept the conclusions of a commission. This gives rise to the danger that Ukrainian historians will be unable to prepare their own conception of the past for common textbooks.[11] The same topic, albeit with reference exclusively to the situation in Ukraine, is the subject of a reflective article by Kul'chyts'kyi on the state of history as a discipline in Ukraine's schools and universities. He feels that the current state of affairs (he is writing in 2003) has its origins in the year 1988. At that time, with Perestroika reaching its culmination and the liberalization in public life, there spread a movement for the reform of the educational system in Ukraine and a desire to make it national in character. This movement, in Kul'chyts'kyi's view, was a reaction to the all-out Russification of the educational system. One of its manifestations was to be seen in the teaching of the history of the USSR, which was de facto the history of Russia, with the history of Ukraine relegated to a secondary status, with about 30 hours of the academic load.[12]

In Kul'chyts'kyi's view, during the Perestroika period, the Communists lacked the power to stem the national-democratic wave and therefore opted to hijack the movement and take charge of it. In October 1988, at a Plenum of the Central Committee of the Communist Party of Ukraine (CC CPU), party leader Volodymyr Shcherbyts'kyi announced that the teaching in the social sciences poorly reflected the needs of society, and the work for filling in gaps in history was not being carried out energetically enough. In February 1989 the CC CPU issued a resolution to formulate a republican program for the development of historical research and the improvement of how history was taught in Ukraine. It contained concrete measures, such as introducing a course on the history of the Ukrainian SSR in schools, colleges, and institutes, the training of teachers and the preparation of textbooks. However, says Kul'chyts'kyi, because of the difficulties of the transitional period in coming to terms with the recent history of the USSR no textbook could appear at that time. Ukrainians relied on the book by Canadian professor Orest Subtelny. Only by 1995-96 did the two-volume *History of Ukraine* based on archival study appear under the editorship of V. Smolii. By 1989-90, Ukrainian history had become an independent discipline and was taught parallel to the history of the USSR and general history in the upper four grades. At that point the lack of relevant materials to cover various topics was very keenly felt and the Ukrainian Ministry of Education asked the Institute of History (affiliated with the Ukrainian Academy of Sciences) to begin immediately to prepare appropriate material. Kul'chyts'kyi and Yurii Kurnosov had thus prepared a brochure on materials for studying the history of Ukraine for the ninth and tenth grades. These materials were subsequently used to replace some chapters in existing Soviet textbooks.[13]

Kul'chyts'kyi informs readers that in 1990-91, the Institute of History created a new program for the study of history and published a new textbook entitled *Istoriya Ukrainy*. At the same time the publishing house "Radyans'ka shkola" (Soviet school) changed its name to "Osvita" (education). When the new history appeared, however, it was hopelessly outdated because Ukraine had become independent. Therefore in the fall of 1991 the Ministry of Education radically reconfigured the structure of historical education in schools. Two independent courses were taught: world history and the history of Ukraine, with the latter being taught from grades 7 to 11. What place does history occupy in contemporary Ukraine? Kul'chyts'kyi believes that it is a critical discipline, the foundation stone that allows pupils to grasp the fundamentals of social developments, and which should take priority over other social sciences. Of all the humanities and social science subjects, only history *has* to be included on the list of comprehensive examinations at the end of high school. It should have two chronologically complete circles, Kul'chyts'kyi believes, with the first ending after the ninth grade and the second covering the tenth and twelfth grades so that for those students who decide not to go on to Grade 10, the history of Ukraine does not end in the nineteenth century. Further, Ukrainian history must be studied within the context of world history. Students must learn to develop pluralistic views in making historical assessments and be subjected to different methods of looking at history, rather than being confined to the traditionally predominant political narratives. The author concludes with a discussion of the contested harmonization of Ukraine's history with that of its neighbors: Poland and Russia. The point is not to place heavy focus on one's national history, but to ensure that the "other side's" textbooks are not fostering the spirit of hatred.[14]

Other writers have addressed themes similar to those raised by Kul'-chyts'kyi. Some recent problems were put into perspective by writer Kost' Bondarenko in the spring of 2002. Having noted the recognition of the rights of members of the SS Division "Halychyna" as equal to those of veterans of the Great Patriotic War by the Ivano-Frankivs'k city council, he observes that in a country in which no civil peace or consensus had been reached, local decisions such as this one would stir public opinion long after the last veteran of the Second World War rests in peace. He anticipates that the next stage will be a struggle over tombs and monuments. The key fact, he states, is that the overwhelming majority of the population "is absolutely historically illiterate." Worst of all, people are unwilling to fill in the gaps of their ignorance about the past, or even correct their misconceptions. Some are taking the side of the "exclusively correct" Soviet interpretation, recognizing the Red Army and CPSU as true heroes and condemning all those who stood on the other side of the barricade as traitors, enemies, and criminals. Others study history from textbooks published in the Diaspora and are interpreting everything linked to the Soviet Union as negative, and all that was directed against the Communist regime as positive. He cites a small group of intellectuals that has approved a recent attempt at a new evaluation of the past by L'viv historian Yaroslav Hrytsak. But they are a small minority since most of the population prefers easier reading.[15]

In October 2003, the newspaper *Den'* introduced in its weekly digest a discussion forum entitled "How to make the past your own. History as taught in schools: time to decide" compiled by writers from different parts of Ukraine and featuring several well-known Ukrainian historians. The premise for the debate was that the creation of a civil society in Ukraine that is founded on the basis of democracy and a market economy requires the proper education of community members in the history of their national past. This is partly in order not to repeat the same mistakes but also because members of society must recognize the significance of acquiring a free society and how much it is needed, as demonstrated "by the tragic and controversial history of their own country." The premise seems somewhat illogical from the perspective of the approach to history, in that if past history has already been pronounced "tragic" and "controversial" then to some extent the task of the historians has already been decided for them. In fairness, however, this does not necessarily denote adherence to what might be termed the Vol'vach school of thought cited above. Several authors from this discussion merit citation, as their comments are also relevant to the current volume and the reasons that lie behind it. One of the contributors is Professor Valery Stepankov, Chair of the Department of World History at Kamyanets'-Podil's'kyi State University. He points out that on television and radio, and in newspapers the following rhetorical question is being posed constantly: "Are our children and grandchildren taught the true history of Ukraine? Isn't this history falsified to fit the new ideological dogmas?" Much depends, Stepankov writes, on the quality of textbooks and the competency of the teaching staff. Regarding the former, authors had to write in very restricted conditions, when all facets of instruction were under the sway of the Great Russian conception of Ukrainian history, which brought about gross distortions and the lack of any real Ukrainian version. Thus Ukrainian writers first had to determine the scholarly inheritance of Ukraine and then start writing new textbooks. Now it is necessary to go through these new books and select the best ones, while at the same time avoid the writing of any textbooks jointly with scholars from neighboring countries, as this would result in a version of history that conforms only to the views of foreigners.[16]

The situation, however, has been exceptionally difficult in Ukrainian schools. A history teacher from an elementary school in Uzhhorod in Western Ukraine points out that the curricula have been extremely inadequate and students "are under a senseless academic burden." There are no teaching aids, such as maps or charts featuring the history of Ukraine, and those that do exist are prohibitively expensive. Schools lack a sufficient supply of textbooks, and no one can find information about the Ukrainian hetmans or books about "Ukrainian feats of arms" during the Second World War. The teachers themselves are part of the problem according to Taras Honcharuk, Chair of Ukrainian History at the Odesa National University. Only some 20% of graduates of his department become teachers, and as a result history is being taught by retired army officers or people well beyond pensionable age. These people have not studied Ukrainian history and know little about it, so their focus is on world history. This situation is occurring during a time when the supply of textbooks on the history of Ukraine is "excellent." On this topic, Kul'chyts'kyi notes, "we haven't been wasting time." The recent textbooks are an example of how far Ukraine has come in the teaching of a national history. Today's books are shorter than in the past, and Soviet stereotypes have been removed. All these new books are richly illustrated and have maps. Kul'-chyts'kyi comments that for the past decade he has participated in a Ukrain-ian–Polish commission to upgrade school history and geography textbooks, which has enabled him to compare the situation in Ukraine to that in Poland. Even though the Poles have a reputation for the quality of their books, the Ukrainians today—in his view—have caught up. Notably, in passing, Kul'-chyts'kyi comments that the history of the twentieth century in Ukraine needs to be learned "in greater depth than the recent past."[17] While the statement may reflect a personal bias, it adds credence to the view that the formation of a national history is based on the criterion of a tragic and "genocidal" past in the twentieth century.

The final comments came from Professor Volodymyr Panchenko, Vice-President of the Kyiv-Mohyla Academy National University. He remarks on the dangers of not knowing one's own history and advances what he calls a paradoxical fact, namely that the Russification of Ukrainian history is being carried out by Ukrainians, as exemplified by the closure of Ukrainian-language schools in Donets'k and Dnipropetrovs'k. He complains about the limited use of the Ukrainian language in literature, films, and television, which he refers to as a "suicidal act." It is essential, in his view, through the younger genera-tion, to avoid becoming a people without a memory—but in order to reach such a situation, much will depend on teachers of history. They in turn, will be reliant on adequate textbooks and reference materials. He provides a warning about two very different tendencies that have been occurring in the Ukrainian case. The first concerns what he calls "naïve myths" with reference to Ukrain-ian history, and figuratively speaking can be illustrated by the efforts "to prove that Jesus Christ was Ukrainian." On the other hand, there is the more tradi-tional tendency to examine the history of Ukraine from a foreign, i.e., Russian point of view. This may be applied to the history of Kyivan Rus', and the fact that in a textbook about Tsar Aleksandr II, one cannot find a mention of the Ems Ukaz prohibiting the use of the Ukrainian language. Ukrainian values, he says, are not the same as Russian ones, and there is a great demand for new literature, particularly works on popular history which should be promoted, including on the pages of *Den'* and in other formats.[18]

Some comments can be made about new historical writings. First, the writ-ers are to some extent stating the obvious when they reject the old traditional formats in which, essentially, Ukraine in the Soviet period did not have its own history. However, no distinction is made between Soviet and Russian writing, or between, for example, the writing of Soviet history and that of Rus-sian history. Are they the same? Or was the history of Russia submerged too, in which case the role of Russians in Ukraine's story might need revising? Second, Panchenko seems to make a vital point when he remarks that one does not need to prove that Jesus Christ was Ukrainian. In other words, one cannot glorify the past. One might add a third point, which is the modern tendency to regard the past unequivocally as an era of both glory and suffering: with Ukrainians as the perennial victims and Russians, Poles, or Germans as the persecutors. Most often it is the Russians who are placed in this position. Such a tendency (though not with Ukrainians as victims) is particularly marked in Soviet works and—paradoxically—writings of Ukrainians in the West. It may also take other formats. Thus in the Ukrainian Cultural Center in Detroit an entire room is taken up with an exhibit about the persecution of Ukrainians under Soviet rule, evidently with the assistance of historians from Ukraine. The same exhibit was then transferred to Ukraine and can be found today in Kharkiv and the historical museums of other cities. However, it is hardly an accurate reflection of the past because history cannot be written in this way. Why has this situation occurred, and why must Ukrainian history necessarily be written from the perspective of victims? Is it a result merely of the lack of statehood? It could be argued, and to some extent this monograph is a reflection of this tendency, that with the end of the Soviet period, Ukrainian historians lacked guidelines to construct a new history that included the main and tumultuous events of the 20th century. Until very recent times there had been no opportunity to examine many of these events. Even many occurrences during the Stalin period only came under review during the period of Gorbachev's leadership of the USSR. The result—and it is a very obvious point—was the magnification of the works of those writing Ukrainian history in the West, and particularly those historians, writers, politicians, or polemicists who were of Ukrainian background. What did the "Diaspora" think?

The Ukrainian Diaspora:
The Example of the Famine-Genocide

This focus on the "Diaspora"—and it is a point also raised by Bondarenko—was pertinent, and gives rise to the question of the impact of those of Ukrainian ancestry living outside Ukraine, particularly the generation that left the native land during or shortly after the Second World War. Included in the rather sweeping term Diaspora are also people who were born in DP camps in Central Europe but subsequently moved to North America, Australia, or Western Europe. By and large the productivity of scholars from this community has been considerable and in many ways it has come to dominate popular writing on Ukraine even while the various groups, such as OUN, brought many of their political squabbles to the West with them. One objective of such writing was to offer a perspective on Ukraine that differed from that propagated by the authorities, i.e., of Ukraine as a "little brother" of Great Russia, but bound to Russia in eternal friendship. Often, such writings could be categorized as overtly anti-Soviet, such as the *ABN Correspondence*, which allegedly monitored four serious revolts in Ukraine against Soviet collectivization between August 1930 and 1931, precisely in the areas in which famine later occurred, i.e., Kherson, Poltava, Dnipropetrovs'k, and Kharkiv regions.[19] A later example of a "Diaspora perspective" might be that provided by a Ukrainian from Australia, Mykhailo Horan, writing in the newspaper *Literaturna Ukraina* early in 2004. Horan writes that even though Ukraine has been "free" for more than twelve years, one cannot feel free. The culture of fear had developed over generations, destroying initiatives, free thought, and national pride, and turning people into meek, submissive, and complacent individuals. In order to ascertain the reasons behind such a phenomenon, he notes, it is necessary to know the history of Ukraine to answer the question why Moscow exploited Ukraine for centuries and now seems unwilling to do without her.[20]

Continuing in the same vein, Horan writes that the Russian Empire used Ukrainian labor to undertake various projects, from the building of Petrograd [sic!] to the development of the Siberian taiga, and many died as a result. With the creation of the Bolshevik regime, the "genocide" of Ukrainians entered a new phase. The artificial famine resulted in 8 million victims. In 1947, the authorities would not permit Ukrainians from the famine-infected eastern regions to migrate to the western areas because at that time Soviet forces were fighting Ukrainian insurgents. The terrorized and oppressed Ukrainian people were transformed into "homo sovieticus," a new form of spiritual slavery. In order to ensure that Ukrainians did not recognize their miserable lot, the authorities resorted to scaremongering tactics to keep them divided, using phrases such as "Westerners" and "Easterners" to ensure that they never joined forces against foreign occupants. Communist propaganda meanwhile disseminated the lie that OUN leader Stepan Bandera collaborated with the Nazis when in fact the Germans had issued a secret instruction to arrest Bandera on trumped-up criminal charges. Horan comments that the Ukrainian Diaspora is baffled by the apparent inability of Ukraine's officials to govern the country properly but appears oblivious to the fact that Ukraine is ruled, to a large extent, by people hostile to the Ukrainian state.[21]

The excerpt is instructive because it encapsulates what might be termed a more partisan Diaspora view of the recent past: that of the Ukrainian being duped, exploited, and oppressed by the regime based in Moscow. It also implies that if a regime does not adopt the perspective of what Horan perceives to be the Diaspora viewpoint, then it is not representing the interests of the Ukrainian people. A similar perspective can be found in the writings of American analyst Myron B. Kuropas in the New Jersey newspaper, *The Ukrainian Weekly*. Kuropas, writing in June 2005, bemoans the way Ukrainian history is taught in many US universities, noting that the Ukrainian Holodomor is not considered genocide and the OUN is seen as something initiated by the Nazis. He then goes on to write:

> What does the world really know about the Ukrainian Insurgent Army (UPA), that glorious group of dedicated freedom fighters who emerged during World War II to fight both the Nazis and the Soviets? Why is it that we rarely hear of their exploits outside our own community? ... The UPA story is one of unequaled heroism. These were men and women who were willing to put their lives and sacred honor on the line against brutal and merciless enemies.

Kuropas maintains that scholars have declined to examine available primary sources, such as the *Litopys UPA* collection, edited by Canadian political scientist Peter J. Potichnyj.[22] In fairness, what Kuropas is asking is that scholars should write a history of the UPA that corresponds to his particular viewpoint, which is not really writing history per se, but rather a polemic. Nevertheless, his article is instructive in offering a clearly delineated perspective of the UPA as heroes, one that eventually began to penetrate writing in Ukraine.

The impact of the Diaspora on changing interpretations of modern Ukrainian history can also be illustrated by a campaign, held during the commemoration of the 70th anniversary of the Famine-Holodomor, to demand that *The New York Times* should strip its former Moscow correspondent, Walter Duranty, of his Pulitzer Prize for his reporting from the USSR. The campaign was coordinated by the Ukrainian Congress Committee of America (UCCA), which declared that the year-long protest was part of a wide-ranging effort to counter "Holodomor deniers." Hundreds of letters were solicited from the community, as well as from residents of Ukraine. The UCCA initiative evidently coincided with and worked alongside a similar campaign by the Ukrainian Canadian Civil Liberties Association, which started a worldwide postcard campaign in April 2003 to the administrator of the Pulitzer Prizes, Sig

Gissler. Its claim was that Duranty had deliberately lied about the real situation in Ukraine by denying the existence of the famine, while at the same time collaborating closely with the Soviet authorities, even going so far as to venerate Stalin.[23] The late James E. Mace claimed that the campaign actually originated in Canada, when Lubomyr Luciuk, a geography professor at the Royal Military College of Canada, conceived the idea and secured backing from various Ukrainian organizations in Canada and the United States, which then deluged the Pulitzer Committee with postcards.[24] Evidently on Mace's initiative, the Ukrainian newspaper *Den'* (The Day) also sent a letter to *The New York Times*, which stated:

We highly appreciate the New York Times' glorious history and its unique role in the history of the American press. However, here in Ukraine, a newly independent state in the process of developing its own independent journalism, we believe that you should consider voluntarily giving up the Pulitzer Prize received by your correspondent Walter Duranty in 1932. His denying the 1932–1933 Holodomor Manmade Famine in Ukraine and acting as Stalin's apologist during the period for which he received this prize are evidence that, of the numerous prizes won by NYT journalists, this one only clouds the reputation of those honestly earning their award for the ideals championed by Joseph Pulitzer.[25]

This letter is somewhat unusual in that an American correspondent is writing on behalf of a Ukrainian newspaper, but it is illustrative of the way a demand for redress in North American could be transferred to Ukraine and then back again. That the *Times* limited itself to rebuking Duranty's stance without revoking the prize ultimately meant very little because the awareness of the issues generated by the postcards and the publicity around them alerted thousands to the controversy. The Diaspora campaign for the Famine to be recognized as genocide is likewise an illustration of rewriting history by publicity and pressure—the justice of the case notwithstanding.

Mace pointed out that the US Commission on the Ukraine Famine, which he headed for four years prior to moving permanently to Ukraine, had collected eyewitness accounts, and that to these had now been added thousands more from Ukraine. Their collective accounts, he noted, "cannot fail to move even the most scientific of historians."[26] Evidently though, it did. An editorial in *The Ukrainian Weekly* a year earlier had commented that it "may seem incredible" but "denial of the Great Famine continues to exist." The phrase signified not the occurrence of famine per se, but the denial of what this newspaper saw as its certain cause: the intention of the Soviet leadership to eliminate Ukrainians. It cited a discussion on the H-Russia Internet list in which two American scholars, Mark B. Tauger and Grover Furr, disputed the view that the Famine of 1932-33 was an act of genocide perpetrated against Ukrainians by the Stalin regime. Tauger had offered the perspective that the Famine developed out of a grain shortage that encompassed the Soviet Union in these years. The editorial demanded that the Famine deniers should "cease their repulsive activity" in the face of incontrovertible evidence that the event constituted one of the "most grisly episodes of genocide" ever known to the world.[27] Again, the emotional outpouring is understandable, but the continuing debate at the same time suggested that the evidence presented to that point had not convinced everyone, particularly the two scholars in question. Taras Kuzio, a prominent political scientist on contemporary Ukraine, pointed out that Tauger maintained that oral testimonies were unreliable. More controversially, Kuzio added that after the US Commission on the Ukraine Famine closed, Mace had been unable to obtain academic employment because "his cards had been marked" as a "biased Ukrainian nationalist émigré." Bohdan Krawchenko, a Canadian political scientist who moved to Ukraine after 1991, is cited in Kuzio's article as remarking that the entire discussion about the origins of the Famine was "absurd and fundamentally immoral" and a "total abrogation of the responsibilities of intellectuals."[28] Krawchenko did not elaborate on these comments, but presumably they can be taken to mean that it is no longer feasible to question how and why the Famine took place. Such discussions have also been featured frequently at academic gatherings in North America, such as panels at the annual conference of the American Association for the Advancement of Slavic Studies, in which Tauger, the late James Mace, and Robert Conquest offered their perspectives.

The Diaspora's contribution to the study of the Famine developed further during the 70th anniversary year. Though the debate on the Famine's origins continued, the community in North America launched several initiatives that had an impact on perspectives in Ukraine regarding the centrality and significance of this tragedy in national history. One was for the creation of a memorial complex that included an educational and research center in Kyiv to be established on the 75th anniversary (2008), an idea of an American public relations professional living in Kyiv, Morgan Williams.[29] On 19 June 2003, the Canadian Senate adopted unanimously a motion from Senator Raynell Andreychuk calling for the Canadian government to recognize the Ukrainian Famine-Genocide of 1932-33. The motion called for the condemnation of any effort to deny or distort "this historical truth" as being anything less than

genocide, and requested that historians, educators, and members of parliament should include the "true facts" in Canadian records and in educational
material.[30] Four months later, the US House of Representatives followed suit,
stating in Clause 2 of the resolution that "this man-made famine was designed
and implemented by the Soviet regime as a deliberate act of terror and mass
murder against the Ukrainian people." Clause 4 declared that

> the official recognition of the famine [as an act of genocide] by the Gov-
> ernment of Ukraine and the Verkhovna Rada represents a significant step
> in the reestablishment of Ukraine's national identity, the elimination of the
> legacy of the Soviet dictatorship, and the advancement of efforts to estab-
> lish a democratic and free Ukraine that is fully integrated into the Western
> Community of nations.[31]

The wording is significant in that it demonstrated the sentiments of many
in the Ukrainian community that the Famine was clearly linked to the formation of national identity in Ukraine. Moreover, in Canada and the United
States, the Ukrainian community successfully took the debate out of the
hands of historians and declared that no further discussion should take place.
But can debate be ended on historical questions in this way? And, if so, who is
to make such a decision, the community at large or professional historians?
And do such decisions render historical research in recently opened archives
in Ukraine, Russia, and elsewhere meaningless?

However, the response from Ukraine and other countries was initially quite
limited. In November 2003, Ukraine and 26 other nations signed a joint declaration of the United Nations "in connection with the 70th anniversary of the
Great Famine in Ukraine of 1932-33." The opening statements at once
broadened the impact of the Famine and suggested that it was a tragedy that
went beyond the borders of Ukraine: "In the former Soviet Union millions of
men, women, and children fell victims to the cruel actions and policies of the
totalitarian regime." Having noted that the Famine was a "national tragedy"
for the Ukrainian people, the declaration continued as follows:

> Honoring the 70th anniversary of the Ukrainian tragedy, we also com-
> memorate the memory of millions of Russians, Kazakhs, and representa-
> tives of other nationalities who died of starvation in the Volga river region,
> North Caucasus, Kazakhstan, and in other parts of the former Soviet Un-
> ion, as a result of civil war and forced collectivization, leaving deep scars in
> the consciousness of future generations.[32]

For some in the North American community, such comments were simply unacceptable in that the UN resolution declined to focus exclusively on Ukraine, probably in order to acquire the signatures of other nations such as Russia and Kazakhstan. On the other hand, within Ukraine, as is illustrated by examples in Chapter 2, there were a number of ethnic minority communities that were directly affected by the Famine and who suffered losses on a similar scale to those of the Ukrainians, most notably the Jewish community, the Mennonites, the Greeks, the Bulgarians and the Germans (the latter did receive some aid directly from Germany, a rare instance of Stalin's regime permitting aid from abroad). The question that arises therefore is whether these groups were incidental to the ostensible purpose of the government to strike at Ukrainians, or whether they were also included as part of a genocidal campaign. On the whole, however, the awareness of the international community about the 1932-33 Famine in Ukraine was heightened as a result of campaigns initiated by Ukrainian communities in North America, Australia, and elsewhere. Moreover, these campaigns intensified debates within Ukraine itself, as did contacts between Westerners and Ukrainians that had opened up since the late 1980s as a result of exchanges, travel, and a large coterie of prominent community members from the West who took up residence, either for the short or long term, in Ukraine.

Western Scholarship

The events dealt with in detail in the remainder of this book have all been subjected to research by scholars resident in the West. This brief survey will be limited to works that have appeared in English over the past 20 years, a period roughly equivalent to the time span of the interpretations cited in Ukraine in subsequent chapters. Throughout this monograph there are cited articles that deal with the question of nationalism and nationalist thought, and the term "nationalist" is frequently used without explanation. There is an extensive literature on nationalism and little consensus among those who perceive the nation as a "construct of imagination," those who insist that national and nationalism are a modern phenomenon, or those who stress the important role of historical continuity, and long-term attachment to culture and traditions. One of the most eloquent theorists, Anthony D. Smith, emphasizes the important role of memory, symbols, and history in the rise of nations and nationalism in offering an alternative perspective to the so-called modernists, represented by scholars such as Benedict Anderson and Eric Hobsbawm.[33]

Smith maintains that the latter have failed to recognize the "properties of territory and the role of ancestral homelands" in the construction of a nation. Nationalism is a process in which "the idea of an historic and poetic landscape" converges with "the culture and history of a group," signifying in his view that the link between people and territory must be analyzed. Special events contribute to the formation of experiences and memories, which develop over generations of a sacred land that encompasses myths of ancestors, memories, and symbols.[34] Hugh Seton-Watson makes a distinction between "national consciousness," "nationalism," and "the nation." The first is a state of mind when community members feel they belong to a nation, whereas nationalism is a political movement to promote the nation's interest. The nation is a community of people that has national consciousness and an elite group to lead them. Nation-building in turn is divided between "old nations" that emerge after state formation and "new nations" that form the state. Language and historical myths are far more important in new nations than in older ones.[35]

Applying nationalist theories directly to the former Soviet Union, Ronald G. Suny examines inter alia the case of the non-Russian peoples in tsarist Russia, including the Ukrainians. He perceives a gap between national and class consciousness among many groups. Ukrainian nationality often overlapped with membership of the peasant class, and in the 19th century, Ukrainians developed a distinct culture and language. By the early 20th century Galicia had become the center of Ukrainian popular nationalism, but national discourse had not yet surfaced. Suny notes the lack of agreement in assessing Ukrainian nationalism in the revolutionary period of 1917-18, with some authors maintaining that events in Ukraine reflected the initiative of the middle class, others focusing on the peasantry, and a third view being that the elite in Ukraine was supported by nationally conscious peasants in a single class movement. Suny's view is that the peasantry was not prepared for a sustained political movement and eventually went over to the side of the Bolsheviks. He maintains that the common dichotomy between class and nationality, the bourgeoisie and the peasantry, and town and country do not apply here as the categories were intertwined, fluid, and situational. The chances of success for the nationalist elite were enhanced when they could combine social reform with programs of self-definition, autonomy, or independence.[36] In the later Soviet period, under Gorbachev, Suny writes that the formation of nations occurred as a direct consequence of state-building through a pseudo-federal system or policies of nativization. He sees Soviet policies as being a direct cause of the rise of nationalism—as opposed to the idea that primordial nations were waiting to be emancipated.[37]

How do these post-Soviet states, involved in nation-building, view the past? In an article that focuses primarily on the question of whether Ukraine has a history, Mark von Hagen also pays attention to the issue of Ukraine's situation, caught between two powerful and dominant historiographies: that of the Germans and the Russians (Soviets). The postwar political order also served to reduce the significance of East and Central Europe in the academic world of North America. He maintains that the history of the region that includes Ukraine was linked with "nationalism, anti-Semitism, and ethnic irredentism," and that nationalism was demonized because of its association with collaboration with German National Socialism and Fascism. Two nationalisms thus emerged in the world: the good nationalism of the NATO countries and the bad nationalism equated with Eastern Europe (Ukraine) and the Third World. Ukraine's situation was also worsened by its secondary role within the former Soviet Union. After 1991, however, Ukrainian leaders began to turn to the past in a quest to "build legitimacy." One possibility was the adoption of the primordial and integral nationalist perspective that is espoused by the Diaspora, which links the struggle of the past to the present state, and perceives Ukraine as a victim of other nations in its quest for independence. Von Hagen seems rather perturbed by the fact that when independence did come, "the teaching staff remained almost entirely unchanged." In other words, the teachers of Marxism-Leninism could now become the instructors of a new national history. The problem is that Marxists had trust in a single version of "true history," and the black-and-white version of the past is now being repeated, but in reverse. Further, the evolution of anti-Stalinist views has resulted in the inclusion of the entire Soviet period as one of an occupation regime, and, from Ukraine's perspective, uniformly negative.[38]

Von Hagen's comments sparked several responses in the pages of the same issue of *Slavic Review*, two of which merit citation here as relevant to the topic under review. Yaroslav Isayevich (Iaroslav Isaievych) writes that he was educated in an environment in which "the term 'nation' meant exclusively an ethnic nation mostly... with a territory and not necessarily with a state." He feels that Von Hagen's implicit condemnation of party historians is too sweeping because they included a variety of people, some of whom have managed to combined patriotism with the duties of a historian. In a footnote, he says the following: "It is strange that authors who have forgiven so many contemporary democratic Ukrainian politicians for their communist past will not extend that forgiveness to historians who are now sincere and serious critics of totalitarianism." He feels that no matter which country is being portrayed, native historians will write, to some extent, a patriotic version of history (including the United States).[39] Isayevich's response is very defensive and overlooks the basic question of whether historians who have made a career out of writing propaganda have not retained some of that same methodology in a newer era. Serhii M. Plokhy, an historian who moved from Eastern Ukraine to Canada, feels that the triumph of the pro-independence forces in Ukraine in 1991 resulted from the success of two "historical myths": first, the notion that Ukraine was an old nation with a "glorious past" that had been denied its legitimate statehood by the Russian tsarist and Soviet Communist regimes; and second, that Ukraine was an economic power house, both in terms of being the "breadbasket of Europe" and a major industrial power. He points out accurately that the modern Ukrainian nationalism is not xenophobic and indeed that Ukrainians and Russians in particular share a well-developed Cossack mythology.[40]

Plokhy notes the portrayal of Ukraine as the main victim of the Soviet regime through events such as the Famine of 1932–33 and the nuclear accident at Chornobyl in 1986. The most important aspect of such depictions has been their all-inclusiveness, i.e., the view that all citizens of Ukraine, no matter what their background, were victims of the Communist government. However, after 1991, it became very difficult to develop an all-inclusive model of historical mythology. Nationalistic myths, such as the feats of the Ukrainian Insurgent Army, could not penetrate Eastern Ukraine, and the attempt by Ukraine's first two presidents, Leonid Kravchuk and Leonid Kuchma, to include the Great Patriotic War in an official conception of history did not meet with favor in Western Ukraine. Plokhy thinks that Ukraine needs a new historical myth in order to advance further, but it has run up against virtually unsolvable problems in interpreting the events of the Ukrainian Revolution (1917-1920) and the Second World War. He also brings up an important question that is frequently overlooked, namely the declining state of history as a discipline in independent Ukraine. Whereas Soviet historians were powerful figures, well-paid and often the arbiters of state ideology; post-Soviet historians are impoverished and of a lower social status. Outside the country Ukraine has faced the problem of a deeply entrenched perspective in the American scholarly community that has adopted the views of émigré historians from Russia. In addition, the fall of the Soviet Union brought about a sharp reduction in government funding and the collapse of what was known as "Sovietology."[41] Plokhy might have added a qualifying remark, namely that when a discipline is based on government funding then it contains an inherent political purpose; in other words it is not necessarily a bad thing for the writing of Ukrainian history that it is not sponsored by governments: East or West.

Andrew Wilson has written two books that deal with similar questions and are extensive in their scope. The first, published in 1997, was the more controversial because it deals with Ukrainian nationalism in the 1990s and argues that an ethnically based nationalism will never hold sway in many parts of Ukraine. It is a fairly negative view that attempts to incorporate historical events dating from the period of Kyivan Rus' to the present state, and posits that modern Ukraine is a deeply polarized society that may well face insuperable problems in the future if it tries to found the state on a conception of ethnic nationalism. Like some other scholars, Wilson attributes a large role in state-building to the issue of language, and he doubts whether the large group of Russian speakers in Ukraine (both Ukrainians and Russians) can ever be persuaded to adopt "modern ethno-nationalism."[42] This line of argument raises the question of whether state-building is exclusively the privilege of Ukrainian speakers or ethno-nationalists, and also leads to the question, whether, what can be termed rightist political thought in Ukraine today, is as pervasive as integral nationalism was in Western Ukraine in the 1930s and the war years. His second book also delves into the past, largely to debunk the notion of Ukrainian antiquity and the perspective that the Kyivan Rus' state could be described as the exclusive origin of modern Ukraine. Wilson does accept that the roots of the modern state are very old, but he adheres to the view that Ukraine evolved from a common experience of empire (under Lithuanian, Polish, and Russian rule). In the 20th century, he considers that there were different possible paths to statehood, and that it was not a foregone conclusion which would succeed. He cites the example of the "Skoropadsky Project," which attempted to form a state based on loyalty rather than on a linguistically Ukrainian population. More debatable is his analysis of contemporary political issues, because at times he seems to overstress the significance of ethno-nationalism in modern debates, such as when he states that Kuchma's victory in the 1994 presidential race was a result of "ethno-linguistic and geopolitical" rather than economic factors.[43] Overall the book contains many perceptive and even brilliant insights, and the reader gets the impression that Ukrainian statehood is a fairly recent phenomenon and by no means preordained. In this sense, and for our purposes, the direct link between the efforts to form an independent Ukrainian state in the war years and the current state can be seriously questioned.

Turning to more specific studies, early works on the Famine of 1932–33 were commissioned by the Ukrainian Research Institute at Harvard University (HURI) and the Canadian Institute of Ukrainian Studies (CIUS). In the case of the former, Robert Conquest, a senior scholar at the Hoover Institution at

Stanford University, produced the book (cited above) *Harvest of Sorrow*, a careful study of the Famine based mainly on documents available in libraries of the West,[44] with the assistance of James E. Mace, who had recently completed a PhD and published a book on a related topic.[45] Conquest argues that the Soviet leadership, and specifically Kaganovich, Molotov, and Stalin, were well aware of the severity of the Famine, even if it cannot be proved definitively that it had planned such an event.[46] Conquest estimates 11 million peasant deaths in the Soviet Union between 1930 and 1937, with a further 3.5 million arrested and dying in camps, or a total of 14.5 million victims. Of this figure, he writes, 5 million died in the 1932–33 Famine in Ukraine.[47] The Canadian production was a volume of essays on the famine, edited by Roman Serbyn and Bohdan Krawchenko, which also included Duranty's cover-up.[48] The US Commission on the Ukraine Famine also published several volumes of analysis and eyewitness testimonies upon the completion of its work in 1990. Thereafter there was little work that focused on the Famine specifically. Notably it was the US Commission, rather than Conquest, that first sought to establish that the Famine constituted an act of genocide.

A new study by Swedish scholar Johan Dietsch offers a very critical look at writings on the Famine. Specifically he uses the phrase "making facts fight" and argues that scholars such as Robert Conquest and James E. Mace have expanded the traditional role of the historian, which Dietsch describes as "essentially a scientific scholarly one, whereby the past is recorded as it happened by establishing historical facts." Once that job is completed, however, the historian takes on a new role of making moral judgements, and in the case of the new interpretations by Conquest and Mace the task was to use the Famine to illustrate the victimization of Ukrainians by the Soviet regime with explicit comparison with the Jewish Holocaust. In Dietsch's view, the description of Ukraine by Conquest as "one vast concentration camp" led others "engaged in the struggle" [!] to make a direct analogy with the Holocaust, which in turn undermined the image of Ukrainians welcoming German troops in the summer of 1941. He also maintains that the purpose of the new attention to the Famine that began among Ukrainian groups in the West from 1983 was, first of all, to make the subject known to a wider audience, but secondly, to strengthen the notion that the third-wave of emigrants had departed from Ukraine because of "political and cultural persecutions." Dietsch editorializes that "such an existential use of history simply confirmed an understood image of victimhood." Dietsch also believes that within Ukraine, the Holocaust and Jewish victimization per se has never received due attention, and he points out that this crucial event of 20th century Europe is mysteriously absent from

Ukrainian textbooks, which often provide a narrative on Ukraine in the Second World War without mentioning the assault on Jews. He attributes this omission not to some inherent anti-Semitism, but rather the issue of "opposing martyrdoms" and the fact that Ukrainian suffering would thereby be overshadowed by its Jewish counterpart.[49]

Two other works merit citation for their analysis of the Famine. The first is Orest Subtelny's *Ukraine: a History*, which first appeared in 1988, and was widely distributed in Ukraine in its Ukrainian translation.[50] It is discussed in context in Chapter 2, as is Terry Martin's *The Affirmative Action Empire*.[51] Neither work lays great emphasis on the Famine as an act of genocide, though Martin conducts a long discussion concerning the national element of the Famine, and the extent to which Stalin's campaign against peasants coincided with a campaign against Ukrainians as a national group. Those who reject the theory of genocide, overtly or implicitly, are led—at least in terms of output—by the aforementioned Mark B. Tauger, a historian at the University of West Virginia, who believes that the famine (he refers to it as the "famine of 1931-33") arose mainly from environmental factors.[52] The lengthy series on the economic history of the Soviet Union by E. H. Carr and R. W. Davies, and more recently by Davies and Stephen G. Wheatcroft, has included a recent volume entitled *The Years of Hunger: Soviet Agriculture, 1931-1933*, which emphasizes both food shortages and distribution problems as the main factors behind the famine.[53] The article on the topic published in 2005 by Michael Ellman, an economist based at the University of Amsterdam, declines even to engage the literature on the Famine as genocide (though he takes a more critical stance than Davies and Wheatcroft vis-à-vis the Soviet regime), and should be considered in the same category of genocide-rejection theory. It also extends the famine period from 1931 to 1934.[54] Thus from the field of academic historians working specifically on the Famine and basing their findings on former Soviet archives, only Conquest's work (indirectly) supports the genocide theory among the works that have appeared in English. Clearly there is a significant split between those who rely on eyewitness testimonies and those who prefer to focus on Soviet documents or Politburo correspondence from the period.

One can find similar disputes in English-language scholarship when it comes to OUN-UPA, a topic that covers a much longer period and a plethora of events, including a world war, a civil war, and a nationalist insurgency over a time span of more than 15 years. One of the earliest works in the field has retained its importance despite the passage of five decades since its first appearance, namely John A. Armstrong's book, *Ukrainian Nationalism*.[55] He focuses on the origins and structure of the OUN in a difficult period faced by a Ukrainian minority under Polish rule. Based primarily on OUN-M newspapers, he provides a detailed account of the collaboration between the two branches of the OUN and the Germans during the period of occupation. Concerning the nature of OUN's ideology, Armstrong notes how it modeled itself on German National Socialism and Italian Fascism, and that the leadership principle remained intact even after the Third OUN Congress (which some sources maintain resulted in the democratization of the organization with the adoption of more moderate views), and that its origins were fundamentally anti-democratic.[56] When the third edition of the book appeared in 1990, archives in the Soviet Union, as well as those of OUN leaders such as Mykola Lebed', were still unavailable to Western researchers. The most notable addition to the earlier editions was a postscript on the development of the OUN in the Diaspora since 1960. Perhaps the most glaring omission from Armstrong's magisterial book is a detailed discussion of the Volhynia massacres of 1943. A different perspective is offered by Taras Hunczak, who maintains that the OUN-B was in opposition from the very beginning of Operation Barbarossa. On June 30, 1941, its leaders were arrested following the declaration of an independent Ukraine in L'viv. The OUN was "a vibrant force which played a most important role in the Ukrainian resistance movement against the German occupation."[57]

Two younger scholars have offered new perspectives on the issues under discussion in this book. Timothy Snyder's *The Reconstruction of Nations* offers a fairly detailed account of the massacres of Poles in Volhynia by the UPA in 1943. The author is very scathing about UPA, and in attempting to bring the story into his narrative, he offers several critiques of the way its members operated. He states, for example, that UPA insurgents killed as many Ukrainians as they did their opponents, particularly members of the OUN-M. Through the UPA, ethnic cleansing was established, and its policies inspired Stalin, who completed the process that was begun during the war years to bring about states that were ethnically homogeneous. Since the UPA considered the Poles agents of both Hitler and Stalin, it felt justified in its attitude. Snyder indicates that Mykola Lebed' was one of the main architects of the policy of ethnic cleansing. He also depicts OUN-UPA as an organization that was far from popular among native Ukrainians—with the UPA a repository for many former collaborators with the German occupants. These emanated from an estimated 12,000 Ukrainian auxiliary police who reportedly assisted 1,200 German police in the destruction of the Volhynian Jews. Snyder estimates that 40,000–60,000 Poles were killed by UPA, which also conducted massacres of Jewish citizens who had survived the Holocaust.[58] The Dutch scholar, Karel Berkhoff, generally concurs with Snyder's interpretation, though his concentration is primarily on the German occupation regime. Berkhoff's documentation of the Volhynia massacres is drawn from a wide variety of sources, including UPA, Soviet, and German accounts. He emphasizes that both wings of the OUN sought out and killed Poles, and that few Ukrainians seemed willing to assist Poles or Jews. He also notes the internal conflicts of August 1943, when the internal security force—the Sluzhba Bezpeky (SB)—executed hundreds of UPA members. Like Snyder, he maintains that neither the Communists nor the Nationalists had mass appeal among the Ukrainian population.[59]

German scholar Frank Golczewski has also focused on the "incompatible pasts" of Poland and Ukraine from the perspective of historical narratives. He notes that "different discourse groups create their own reality." After 1991 in Ukraine (as elsewhere) it was theoretically possible to have a pluralism of positions. However, he feels, in reality what has occurred is adhesion to the view that there is only one possible "truth." Whereas Western historians dealt with a variety of approaches from Benedict Anderson's "imagined communities" and Eric Hobsbawm's "invention of traditions," in the new countries of Europe, more often, it was a case of making black white and white black. But the Second World War has proved particularly problematic in terms of producing new and "correct" narratives. It is manifested in new textbooks in Ukraine (see Chapter 7), which tend to combine Soviet triumphs along with the resistance of UPA, even though the two seem mutually contradictory. Since OUN-UPA is now identified with a liberation struggle of Ukrainians, Golczewski maintains, its collaboration with the Germans is either ignored or concealed. He focuses in particular on efforts to present the SS Division Halychyna as a Ukrainian movement that did not have close links with the Germans, commenting that historian Taras Hunczak portrays its members as heroes at the time (1943) when even the OUN felt obliged to moderate its views from its more rigid integral nationalism. He finds that the deconstruction of historical narratives is more advanced in Poland. In Ukraine, because of the difficulties entailed in combining the historical positions in Western and Eastern Ukraine (the former with a tendency to a nationalist perspective and the latter Soviet), negative aspects of the war years are omitted and some collaborationist acts are interpreted as "nationally positive."[60]

From the opposite perspective, political scientist Peter J. Potichnyj has authored or edited numerous works on UPA, including the multi-volume *Litopys UPA* series, which is widely available today in Ukraine. In an article written more than two decades ago, Potichnyj makes the case that the approach to the question of the Ukrainian underground in the West has been oversimplified. Its members were depicted as Fascists because of its creation by Nationalists, many of whom had been placed in military units linked to the Germans. Another thorny issue is UPA membership, because in Potichnyj's view, UPA members derived from "all organized nationalist groups." They included members of the Ukrainian police who had deserted, as well as members of the SS Division Halychyna defeated at the Battle of Brody by the Red Army. Consequently, "uninformed writers" in the West as well as Soviet propaganda organs worked to create the impression that the Ukrainian underground was a German-created body, intended for fighting the Soviet Union, and made up of numerous war criminals. In fact, Potichnyj writes, UPA's membership included even Red Army soldiers, and its leaders came from the regions that were controlled by the Soviet Union prior to the outbreak of war in September 1939. He cites the memoirs of former political prisoner Danylo Shumuk, who recalled that members of the Communist Party of Western Ukraine also found their way into UPA ranks. Few Ukrainians in German military units, Potichnyj reflects, were sympathetic to German racist ideology and most Ukrainian nationalists had one overriding goal: the creation of an independent Ukraine.[61]

In a later article on UPA and its relations with the German authorities, published in 1994, Potichnyj depicts the army's actions as independent from those of the Germans and downplays any links with the occupation regime. If there were such contacts, which developed during the final months of the German occupation, they were "sporadic and tactical in nature." Accusations of collaboration derived mainly from members of the OUN-M who attempted to denigrate the image of the UPA.[62] A collection of articles on the political thought of the Ukrainian underground, edited by Potichnyj and Yevhen Shtendera and issued in 1986, contains essays highly critical of Fascism, including one by an anonymous UPA publicist from 1946. There are no statements in this volume that could be identified as anti-democratic, and thus the impression gained of the Ukrainian underground is that it operated according to democratic principles. In one essay, for example, Ukraine as a whole is described as the "most dangerous opponent of Germany's imperialist plans."[63] This position is also emphasized in Volume 17 of the *Litopys UPA* series, which reiterates that there was no UPA collaboration with the Germans, but rather a determined struggle against them. The *Akt* of 30 June 1941 marks the beginning of this struggle and was an expressly anti-German declaration.[64] Potichnyj's position is explained by his McMaster University colleague, Howard Aster. Writing in 1996, Aster comments that Potichnyj adheres to the Diaspora view that there was a genuine democratic transition in the OUN-UPA in 1943–44. By studying the *Litopys UPA*, he adds, "one can secure the sources of the genuinely pluralistic, democratic Ukrainian society that [Potichnyj] values."[65]

John-Paul Himka, an historian based at the University of Alberta, has authored several articles that focus on what he has called a "blank spot in the collective memory of the Ukrainian Diaspora," i.e., the denial of war crimes, anti-Semitism among Ukrainian nationalist groups, and the anti-democratic nature of the OUN and UPA. In the case of the OUN, Himka does not believe that its nature changed in this regard, even after the end of the war. He argues that among the Ukrainian Diaspora, there is a marked preference for victimization, and the perception of Ukrainians as sufferers rather than as perpetrators of some of the misdeeds that occurred. In an examination of the wartime newspaper *Krakivs'ki visti*, Himka claims that this source exhibited a callous disregard concerning the maltreatment of Jews. The three main trends of the newspaper, in his view, were in fact a profound animosity toward Jews; the abnormality of their moral and political universe; and a failure to comprehend the magnitude and horrors of the Holocaust.[66] In a later article, he comments that the anti-Semitic stereotypes were particularly central to the ideology of the OUN-M, and that Volodymyr Kubiiovych and other leading nationalists published anti-Semitic materials and were well aware of the Holocaust. Again he focuses on the way the Ukrainians were consistently portrayed as victims within the Diaspora narrative, and that the perpetrators of crimes were Russians and Jews.[67] The central tenet of Himka's recent studies appears to be aptly represented in the following statement:

> I object to instrumentalizing this memory with the aim of generating political and moral capital, particularly when it is linked to an exclusion from historical research and reflection of events in which Ukrainians figured as perpetrators not victims, and when "our own" evil is kept invisible and the memory of the others' dead is not held sacred.[68]

Himka's case is an unusual example of a modification of earlier views and a rejection of what might be considered accepted views within the Ukrainian community of North America. Not surprisingly his articles and letters engendered a sustained debate on the pages of *The Ukrainian Weekly*.

Wilfried Jilge's study of the politics of history and the Second World War in contemporary Ukraine observes how the nationalist version of history is developed through discourse, rituals and symbols, using the past to establish political legitimacy and as a foundation for future actions. He discusses how the Soviet collective myth of the Great Patriotic War was rivaled by new national symbols after 1990, particularly in Western Ukraine where Lenin monuments were swiftly replaced by nationalist equivalents and streets were renamed after the heroes of the OUN and UPA. In July 1991, he notes, Viktor Koval' published a "sweeping apologetic view" of the history of the OUN and UPA, which linked national history with a correct version of the memory of the people of Ukraine. In similar fashion, the Grade 10 textbook for schools by Fedir Turchenko, *Novitnaya istoriya Ukrainy*, also portrayed the OUN and UPA as the only true standard bearers of Ukrainian culture and identity. In Jilge's view the issue of regional attitudes toward the OUN and UPA—which have always been very hostile in the east and south of Ukraine—are simply dismissed. He also takes issue with the view that OUN-B turned against the German invaders of Ukraine immediately after the German refusal to countenance an independent Ukrainian state in June 1941. He points out that the OUN-B's part in the *pogroms* that took place in Western Ukraine against the Jewish population in the summer of 1941 is excluded from the new textbooks, as is the fact that in 1940–41 anti-Semitism was a prominent part of the OUN platform. He maintains that in today's Ukraine there is a "fixation" on the state, which has rendered it feasible to include military formations that fought alongside the Germans within a tradition of a Ukrainian national army and as part of a nation-state perspective of history. UPA, for example, is depicted as maintaining the traditions of the Ukrainian Cossacks and is regarded as the "third force" in the war that equally fought both the Germans and the Soviet occupiers. Jilge acknowledges, however, that the Kuchma regime has tried to resurrect some of the traditions of the Soviet era, particularly with regard to the commemoration of the Great Patriotic War. This was linked to a watered-down version of the national-state view of the Ukrainian past. The Partisan movement was deployed in an attempt to unite the two polarized views of the war, but with limited success to date.[69]

This book is focused in part on the notion of creating a collective memory based on historical narratives, a topic that is dealt with in the now classic work of Catherine Wanner.[70] In a pioneering article devoted to the 1997 history textbook by Viktor Mysan, Nancy Popson remarks that this survey, produced for fifth-grade schoolchildren in Ukraine, reflects the version of events that is accepted by the Ukrainian elite: one that provides a vision of a nation that is broader than simple ethnicity, but which nevertheless assigns priority to the past of the leading ethnic group, i.e., Ukrainians.[71] Ukrainian history is taught earlier than world history, and in Popson's view will be perceived by pupils as "one's own" history. She notes that the textbooks in use in Ukraine have to be approved by the Ministry of Education, which along with several other agencies—including the National Academy of Sciences of Ukraine—runs annual competitions for new textbooks. Therefore regional variances do not have a major influence.[72] Popson discusses how Mysan's book, *Opovidannya z istorii Ukrainy*, discusses Kyivan Rus' (according to Hrushevsky's interpretation), the Cossack period, and then jumps immediately to the twentieth century, thereby omitting the pivotal nineteenth century and Ukrainian development under the empires of Russia and the Habsburgs. Popson maintains that in this way, the textbook is permitted to avoid the debates over the various types of nationalism. While the text reveres Ukrainian heroes such as Bandera and the Ukrainian Insurgent Army (UPA), and highlights Bolshevik tyranny, it omits the treatment of non-Ukrainian populations such as the Jews: "The history of the non-Ukrainian nationalities is not woven into the historical chronology."[73] While the history of other groups is not excluded, it is secondary. The author therefore sees this representative text as corroboration for her claim that the Ukrainian elite seeks to establish a "civic nation" along the lines suggested by the model of British scholar Anthony D. Smith, that is inclusive of all ethnic groups living in Ukraine, but in which the decisive role is played by ethnic Ukrainians:

> [As] long as *Opovidannia* continues to be used in fifth-grade classrooms across Ukraine, we can conclude that the message of the Ministry of Education stresses two characteristics of "nation": inclusiveness and the leading role of Ukrainian ethnic history, culture, and language.[74]

This brief survey of recent, as well as some older writings on the Stalin years in Ukraine reveals the disparate and widely conflicting views that have not been diminished with time. Indeed, the debates if anything seem more bitter and sustained today than in the past, despite—or perhaps because of—enhanced access to the archives and more detailed information. But throughout the polemics, it is possible to discern with ever more clarity the connections between the discussions and the nature and world-view of the current independent state in Ukraine. The link between the demands of the OUN in the 1930s, for example, the quest of UPA insurgents, and the more recent Rukh, as well as the onset of Ukrainian independence is stressed repeatedly. The conflict and differences of opinion lie in the legacy of the past, and the role played by people who on one hand are regarded as freedom fighters and on the other as collaborators and agents of the German occupation regime. Similarly, the Ukrainian Famine might be regarded as the pivotal example of the Soviet persecution of Ukrainians, *as a nation*, but is regarded by several Western scholars as reflective of difficulties in the countryside without reference to any national dimension. Just as the modern Ukrainian state's historical past was welded together ingeniously by nationalist historian Mykhailo Hrushevs'kyi, so there is a need to link the most recent past—the crucial and tragic events of the Stalin years—in the makeup and the conception of the modern state. It is a form of nation-building, and historical and political narratives are a critical component of that process. At the time of writing, about 18 years had transpired since the Gorbachev regime permitted new investigations into the Stalin years as part of an official program of de-Stalinization. These years can provide a profound reflection of the changing historical narratives, the differences in approach and conclusions, and an examination of how far Ukraine has come in its self-examination and construction of a national identity.

Notes

1 Mariya Bazelyuk, "Chy bude v Ukraini Nyurnberg-2?" *Ukraina moloda*, 12 May 2001, p. 4.

2 S. Kul'chyts'kyi, "Istoriya i chas: Rozdumy istoryka," *Ukrains'kyi istorychnyi zhurnal*, No. 4, (April 1992): 4-6.

3 Ibid., p. 7.

4 Ibid., p. 8.

5 Petro Vol'vach, "Kudy ta homu znykayut' ukraintsi na neosiazhnykh prostorakh imperii?" *Istoriya i natsiya*, 17 June 1993, p. 5.

6 The reference is to the last major Ukrainian peasant uprising against Polish lords. See, for example, Orest Subtelny, *Ukraine: A History*, 3rd ed. (Toronto: University of Toronto Press, 2000), pp. 192-193.

7 The author is presumably referring to both the Famine and the mass purges in Ukraine in the 1930s, which resulted in the elimination of the republic's cultural elite.

8 Ibid., 22 July 1993, p. 3.

9 S. V. Kul'chyts'kyi, "Nerozv'yazani problemy vykladannya istorii u seredni shkoli," *Istoriya Ukrainy*, No. 11 (1998): 1-2.

10 Yaroslava Muzychenko, "Pidruchnyky: istorychni chy isternychi?" *Ukraina moloda*, 18 September 2002, p. 12.

11 Ibid.

12 S. V. Kul'chyts'kyi, "Vitchyzniana istoriya v shkolakh i VNZ Ukrainy: stannie desyatyrichchya," *Istoriya Ukrainy*, No. 15, (2003): 1-6.

13 Ibid.

14 Ibid.

15 Kost' Bondarenko, "Istoriya, kotoruyu ne znaem ili ne khotim znat'?" *Zerkalo Nedeli*, 29 March-5 April 2002; [http://www.zn.kiev.ua/ie/index/387/].

16 Serhiy Makhun et al, "History as Taught in the Schools: Time to Decide," *Den', The Day Weekly Digest*, 14 October 2003; [http://www.day.kiev.ua/261121/].

17 Ibid.

18 Ibid.

19 Vasyl' Plyushch, "Genocide of the Ukrainian People: Artificial Famine in the Years 1931-1933," *ABN Correspondence*, Vol. 24, No. 3 (May-June 1973): 31.

20 Mykhailo Horan, "Chyya pravda, chyya kryvda? Publitsystychnyi rozdum," *Literaturna Ukraina*, 15 January 2004, p. 1.

21 Ibid.

22 Myron B. Kuropas, "UPA and the Ukrainian Identity Problem," *The Ukrainian Weekly*, 19 June 2005, p. 7.

23 *Ukrainian Congress Committee of America*, 28 October 2003, [http://ucca.org].

24 James Mace, "A Historic Motion," *Den'; The Day Weekly Digest*, 24 June 2003; [http://www.day.kiev.ua/260728/].

25 James Mace, "Remembrance and Justice," *Den'; The Day Weekly Digest*, 28 October 2003; [http://www.day.kiev.ua/261177/].

26 James Mace, "Is the Ukrainian Genocide a Myth?" *Den'; The Day Weekly Digest*, 25 November 2003; [http://www.day.kiev.ua/261343/].

27 Editorial, *The Ukrainian Weekly*, 14 July 2002, p. 6.

28 Taras Kuzio, "Denial of Great Famine Continues a Decade after the Collapse of the USSR," *The Ukrainian Weekly*, 7 July 2002, [http://ukrweekly.com/Archive/2002/270203/shtml].

29 Editorial, *The Ukrainian Weekly*, 7 July 2002, p. 6.

30 James Mace, "A Historic Motion," *The Day Digest*, 24 June 2003.

31 HRES 356 EH, 20 October 2003.

32 Morgan Williams, "Ukrainian issues joint declaration at the United Nations in connection with the 70th Anniversary of the Great Famine in Ukraine of 1932-1933," *The Action Ukraine Report*, 11 November 2003, http://www.artukraine.com/famineart/ukr_un_decl.htm.

33 Benedict Anderson, *Imagined Communities: Reflections on the Origin and Spread of Nationalism* (London: Verso, 1983); Eric Hobsbawm, *Nations and Nationalism since 1780: Programme, Myth, Reality* (Cambridge, UK: Cambridge University Press, 1990).

34 Anthony D. Smith, *Myths and Memories of the Nation* (Oxford, UK: Oxford University Press, 1999), pp. 49-50.

35 Hugh Seton-Watson, *Language and National Consciousness* (Oxford, UK: Oxford University Press, 1981), p. 13.

36 Ronald G. Suny, *The Revenge of the Past: Nationalism, Revolution, and the Collapse of the Soviet Union* (Stanford, CA: Stanford University Press, 1993), p. 79.

37 Ibid., especially pages 124-126.

38 Mark Von Hagen, "Does Ukraine Have a History?" *Slavic Review*, Vol. 54, No. 3 (Fall 1995): 658-673. The comments cited are mainly from pages 660-666.

39 Iaroslav Isaievych, "Ukrainian Studies—Exceptional or Merely Exemplary?" *Slavic Review*, Vol. 54, No. 3 (Fall 1995): 702-708. The citations are from pages 704-705.

40 Serhii M. Plokhy, "The History of a 'Non-historical' Nation: Notes on the Nature and Current Problems of Ukrainian Historiography," *Slavic Review*, Vol. 54, No. 3 (Fall 1995): 709-716. This citation is from page 711.

41 Ibid., pp. 712–715.

42 Andrew Wilson, *Ukrainian Nationalism in the 1990s: a Minority Faith* (Cambridge, UK: Cambridge University Press, 1997), p. 1.

43 Andrew Wilson, *The Ukrainians: Unexpected Nation* (Cambridge, UK: Cambridge University Press, 2000). The citation is from page 193.

44 Robert Conquest, *Harvest of Sorrow: Soviet Collectivization and the Terror-Famine* (Oxford: Oxford University Press, 1986).

45 James E. Mace, *Communism and the Dilemmas of National Liberation: National Communism in Ukraine, 1918–1933* (Cambridge, Mass: Harvard University Press, 1983). In this same year, 1983, Mace delivered the Shevchenko Lecture at the University of Alberta in Edmonton to commemorate the Famine's 50th anniversary.

46 Recently, Conquest has distanced himself from the "genocide" school of thought on the Famine of 1932–33. In a letter of September 2003 to R. W. Davies and Stephen G. Wheatcroft, he wrote that he did not believe that "Stalin purposely inflicted the 1933 famine. No. What I argue is that with resulting famine imminent, he could have prevented it, but put 'Soviet interest' other than feeding the starving first—thus consciously abetting it." Cited in R. W. Davies and Stephen G. Wheatcroft, "Stalin and the Soviet Famine of 1932–33: A Reply to Ellman," *Europe-Asia Studies*, Vol. 58, No. 4 (June 2006): 629.

47 Conquest, *Harvest of Sorrow*, pp. 306, 326. For a recent debate on the intent and the origins of the Famine, see Michael Ellman, "The Role of Leadership Perceptions and of Intent in the Soviet Famine of 1931–1934," *Europe-Asia Studies*, Vol. 56, No. 6 (September 2005): 823–841; as well as a response in R. W. Davies and Stephen G. Wheatcroft, "Stalin and the Soviet Famine of 1932–33: a Reply to Ellman," *Europe-Asia Studies*, Vol. 58, No. 4 (June 2006): 625–633. In the latter article (p. 628), the two authors state: "We have found no evidence, either direct or indirect, that Stalin sought deliberately to starve the peasants."

48 Roman Serbyn and Bohdan Krawchenko, ed. *Famine in Ukraine, 1932–1933* (Edmonton, Canadian Institute of Ukrainian Studies, 1986).

49 Johan Dietsch, *Making Sense of Suffering: Holocaust and Holodomor in Ukrainian Historical Culture* (Lund, Sweden: Department of History, Lund University, 2006), pp. 136–139, 144, 232.

50 Orest Subtelny, *Ukraine: A History* (Toronto: University of Toronto Press, 1988).

51 Terry Martin, *The Affirmative Action Empire: Nations and Nationalism in the Soviet Union, 1923–1939* (Ithaca and London: Cornell University Press, 2001).

52 Mark B. Tauger, "The 1932 Harvest and the Famine of 1933," *Slavic Review*, Vol. 50, No. 1 (Spring 1990); Mark B. Tauger, "Natural Disaster and Human Action in the Soviet Famine of 1931–1933," *Carl Beck Papers in Russian and East European Studies*, No. 1506, 2001.

53 R. W. Davies and Stephen G. Wheatcroft, *The Years of Hunger: Soviet Agriculture, 1931–1933* (London: Palgrave Macmillan, 2004).

54 Michael Ellman, "The Role of Leadership Perceptions and of Intent in the Soviet Famine of 1931–1934," *Europe-Asia Studies*, Vol. 57, No. 6 (September 2005): 823–841. In a book review in a later edition of the same journal, Ellman writes in parentheses: "The notion that Ukraine was uniquely victimized by Soviet famines is just a nationalist fantasy." *Europe-Asia Studies*, Vol. 58, No. 6 (September 2006): 986.

55 John A. Armstrong, *Ukrainian Nationalism*, 3rd ed. (Englewood, Colorado: Ukrainian Academic Press, 1990).

56 Armstrong, *Ukrainian Nationalism*, p. 163.

57 Taras Hunczak, "OUN-German Relations, 1941-1945," in Joachim Torke and John-Paul Himka, ed., *German-Ukrainian Relations in Historical Perspective* (Edmonton: CIUS Press, 1994), pp. 178-186. The quotation is from page 183.

58 Timothy Snyder, *The Reconstruction of Nations: Poland, Ukraine, Lithuania, Belarus, 1569-1999* (New Haven, Connecticut: Yale University Press, 2003), pp. 201, 203.

59 Karel Berkhoff, *Harvest of Despair: Life and Death in Ukraine under Nazi Rule* (Cambridge, Massachusetts: Harvard University Press, 2004), pp. 286, 305, 312.

60 Frank Golczewski, "Poland's and Ukraine's Incompatible Past," *Jahrbuecher fuer Geschichte Osteuropas*, Vol. 54, No. 1 (2006): 37-49.

61 Peter J. Potichnyj, "Ukrainians in World War II Military Formations: An Overview," in Yury Boshyk, ed. *Ukraine during World War II: History and its Aftermath* (Edmonton: CIUS Press, 1986), p. 65.

62 Peter J. Potichnyj, "The Ukrainian Insurgent Army (UPA) and the German Authorities," in Himka and Torke, *German-Ukrainian Relations in Historical Perspective*, pp 168-171.

63 Peter J. Potichnyj and Evhen Shtendera, ed. *Political Thought of the Ukrainian Underground: 1943-1951* (Edmonton: CIUS Press, 1986), p. 50.

64 Peter J. Potichnyj, ed. *English Language Publications of the Ukrainian Underground: Litopys UPA, Volume 17* (Toronto: Litopys UPA, 1988), pp. 140, 144.

65 Howard Aster, "Reflections on the Work of Peter J. Potichnyj," *Journal of Ukrainian Studies*, Vol. 21, No. 1-2 (Summer-Winter 1996): 226-227.

66 John-Paul Himka, "Krakivs'ki Visti and the Jews," *Journal of Ukrainian Studies*, Vol. 21, No. 1-2 (Summer-Winter, 1996): 89-92.

67 John-Paul Himka, "Ethnicity and the Reporting of State Violence: *Krakivs'ki Visti*, the NKVD Murders, and the Vinnytsia Exhumation," paper presented at the Holocaust Workshop, University of Alberta, 15 January 2005.

68 John-Paul Himka, "War Criminality: a Blank Spot in the Collective Memory of the Ukrainian Diaspora," *Spaces of Identity*, Vol. 5, No. 1 (2005): 13.

69 Wilfried Jilge, "The Politics of History and the Second World War in Post-Communist Ukraine," *Jahrbuecher fuer Geschichte Osteuropas*, Vol. 54, No. 1 (2006): 50-81 (my comments here pertain mainly to pages 51-67).

70 Catherine Wanner, *Burden of Dreams: History and Identity in Post-Soviet Ukraine* (University Park: Pennsylvania State University Press, 1998), pp. xxiv-xxv.

71 Nancy Popson, "The Ukrainian History Textbook: Introducing Children to the 'Ukrainian Nation'," *Nationalities Papers*, Vol. 29, No. 2 (2001): 325-350.

72 Not all scholars agree with this assessment of local variations. See, for example, Peter Rodgers, "Rewriting History in Post-Soviet Ukraine: Contestation and Negotiation of Ukraine's Eastern Borderlands," Paper presented at the International Graduate Student Syposium, Centre for European, Russian, and Eurasian Studies, University of Toronto, 17 March 2006.

73 Popson, "The Ukrainian History Textbook", p. 342.

74 Ibid., p. 346.

CHAPTER 2

THE FAMINE OF 1932–33

Introduction

For independent Ukraine, no event has greater significance in the history of the developing nation-state than the Famine of 1932–33. It brought about a period of intensive suffering on a hitherto unimagined scale. Yet, although the Famine is becoming part of Ukraine's new national history, its progress to that status has been uneven, littered with public disputes and academic dissension, and with no consensus among historians as to its scale or even its origins. In part, these disputes illustrate the continuing relevance of the Soviet period to life in Ukraine, despite the material and practical steps taken in forging an independent state. As noted in Chapter 1, the Famine has generated an emotional debate in the West, and no consensus has resulted. Ironically, the historians and economic historians who have worked most extensively on this period and published their results are much closer to the former Soviet perspective that emerged from the earlier period of silence on the Famine, namely that it was a result of environmental or climatic conditions rather than part of an official state policy aimed at eliminating Ukrainians as a nation. This chapter explores the genesis of the Famine debate in Ukraine, examining several different aspects and ending with the campaign in independent Ukraine for recognition of the Famine as genocide.

In the former Soviet Union, the Famine was a state secret for decades. Stanislav Kul'chyts'kyi has chronicled the background to the crucial decision to end this secrecy.[1] In 1966, Kul'chyts'kyi notes, the then Ukrainian party leader Petro Shelest reportedly gave permission orally for the Famine to be mentioned in an article to be published in the newspaper for Ukrainians abroad, *News from Ukraine*. However, Ukrainian journalists were fearful of taking such a step without explicit written permission from the authorities. Under Gorbachev, a new critique of Stalinism was initiated in the official media that included rehabilitation of the victims of the 1930s Purges, and formerly taboo subjects were increasingly challenged. On 16 July 1987, an article in the writers' weekly *Literaturna Ukraina* twice mentioned the existence of the Famine. On 11 October of this same year, Russian historian Viktor Danilov made reference to a famine of 1932-33 that had resulted in "huge losses," in the newspaper *Sovetskaya Rossiya*. The following month, demographer Mark Tolts wrote an article in *Ogonyok* about the banned 1937 census in the USSR, citing losses incurred during the 1933 Famine as the main reason for a reported shortfall of the population.[2] These three examples form the prelude to the official revelation about the Famine in Ukraine. It was first revealed publicly by Ukrainian Communist Party leader Volodymyr V. Shcherbytsky during a speech of December 1987, when he declared that it had been caused by a drought and a poor harvest. The catalyst for such a revelation from a party leader, hardly at the forefront of the *Glasnost* reforms, was the completion of work of the US Commission on the Ukraine Famine, which was about to release its findings. Shcherbytsky's speech therefore was intended mainly to pre-empt any information that might be forthcoming from Washington. The news that a major famine had indeed occurred followed some four years of intensive publicity work in Western countries, starting with the 50th anniversary of the Famine in 1933. Shcherbytsky's speech had the approval of Gorbachev, and provided Ukraine's historians with a green light to investigate the issue further, albeit with some caution.[3]

Soviet Revisionism, 1988-1991

In March 1988, Kul'chyts'kyi published a pioneering article on the Famine in the monthly *Ukrains'kyi istorychnyi zhurnal*. Part of his conclusions also appeared in abbreviated form in the media in the newspaper *Visti z Ukrainy*. The article was noticeably cautious and conservative in tone. He noted the "food difficulties" in various parts of the country in the early 1930s: Western Siberia, South Urals, North Kazakhstan, North Caucasus, the Kuban, the Volga region from Gorky to Astrakhan, Rostov, Tambov, part of Kursk Oblast, and the grain growing regions of Ukraine. In villages embraced by famine, the inhabitants moved to the cities, and by the end of December 1932, the authorities introduced a passport system for urban residents to restrict the migration process. At that point the refugees were effectively in an illegal situation. Kul'chyts'kyi then adds that the scale of the 1932-33 famine was relatively small compared to the catastrophic famine of 1921 and "nationalists" tended to downplay the scale of the Famine of 1932-33 in other areas of the Soviet Union in order to add weight to their key thesis, i.e., that ethnocide occurred only in Ukraine. This point, he adds, was encapsulated in the "pseudo-documentary" film *Harvest of Despair*, directed by Yurii Luhovyi and released in Canada in 1984, which maintained that the goal of the famine was to destroy a large portion of the Ukrainian nation because of its opposition to Socialism. He cites as an example of this misguided view the book "of the former Fascist collaborator" V. Hryshko, published in Canada in 1983.[4]

Kul'chyts'kyi also points out the importance of assimilation in the "loss" of the Ukrainian population between the census of 1926 and that of 1939 (a total decline of 3 million people—at that time the existence of the banned 1937 census was not known). He adds that the two peoples (Ukrainians and Russians) derive from a single ancient Rus' nationality, have similar languages and cultures, and an almost identical "psychic composition." Because of the colonization of large swathes of territory (Slobids'ka Ukraine, the Kuban, today's Kursk and Voronezh *oblasts*) by both national groups, a portion of the population that resided in these regions in the first decade of the 20th century was in an "ethnically transient state." The rise in the number of Russians in the USSR as a whole between 1926 and 1939, from 77.8 to 99.6 million, cannot be attributed to a natural increase, particularly when one notes that even representatives of Central Asia, which traditionally had much higher birthrates, could not match the increasing number of Russians. And whereas the 1926 census focused on place of birth, the census of 1939 gave more weight to nationality.[5] Thus only assimilation could explain the apparent demographic decline of Ukrainians and increase in those of Russian nationality. Much of the assimilation was about language issues, he continues, for it was because Ukrainians began to speak Russian more widely that their numbers in the North Caucasus dropped from 3.1 million in 1926 to 170,000 by the time of the 1959 census.[6]

Kul'chyts'kyi also describes how the collective farms in Ukraine were weak and badly organized, because the peasants were not convinced psychologically of the advantages of collective work over individual farming. In some instances peasants concealed property and destroyed their livestock before entering. However, the key factor, in the author's view, was that the introduction of "socialist consciousness" could only occur under conditions of an existing *kolkhoz* order. In short, the peasants were in almost all cases unwilling to join collective farms unless they had no land or livestock in the first place. The situation was exacerbated by the administrative structure in Ukraine, which in contrast to other areas of the Soviet Union lacked an oblast section, so that orders were transmitted directly from the center to the *rayon* (district level). Though *oblasts* were created between February and October 1932, they were not sufficiently organized to prevent anarchy in the collective farms. The situation was made worse by the incompetence of the republic's party organs. Ukrainian party leader Stanislav Kosior was cited as declaring that in several regions, especially on the steppe, fields remained unsown and about half of the harvest was lost at the time of threshing, and sabotage by the collective farmers was quite common.[7] To this point, Kul'chyts'kyi's analysis does not stray far from the official party line. However, on one issue, this historian already began to forge a new path.

Because of the failure of farms in Ukraine to fulfill grain procurement quotas, he comments, Stalin sent Extraordinary Commissions into Kharkiv, Rostov-on-Don, and Saratov, which led to repressions and confiscation of natural and seed funds. However, such methods did not produce the desired results because the new farms lacked supplies of grain. The Commissions established quotas based on so-called biological harvests of grain. When quotas were still unfulfilled, the explanation provided was that collective farms were exploiting the anarchy in order to take grain into their own homes. This statement, Kul'chyts'kyi writes, ignored the fact that the lack of order on the farms had led directly to harvest losses. The food requisitions only made the situation worse. On 19 January 1933, the Soviet government issued a new decree stipulating which part of the harvest would be for the farmers' own use and restored the concept of a flat tax. Also, in the winter of 1933, the state made an effort to help the peasants, and the Central Committee of the Communist Party of Ukraine (CC CPU) created a centralized fund for aid to children, but state resources were soon exhausted, and it was not possible to buy food abroad.[8] In short, the situation in the villages was now so critical that an emergency could not be averted.

Notably in this first detailed article about the causes of the Famine, the national question did not enter the discussion and the factors cited were basically economic and administrative issues, affecting the delivery of grain from the villages to the towns. In a similar vein, writing in the newspaper *Pravda Ukrainy* (July 1989), historian V. Savel'ev, in providing an overview of the main historiographical trends of the time, highlighted the significance of forced collectivization and the arbitrary nature of the administrative command system established under Stalin. He points out the difference of views between those who emphasized these factors and those—like Yurii Shcherbak[9]—who stressed the genocidal intentions of the all-Union leadership. Interestingly, Savil'ev supports his argument with citations from Western scholars writing on the USSR in this period, such as Alexander Dallin. He also cites American scholar Mark Tauger for what he terms the successful balance of a natural disaster with the human agency.[10] Both Savel'ev's and Kul'-

chyts'kyi's 1988 articles were understandably tentative. Historians had to test the ground to see what was acceptable and what would be considered presumptuous. However, more radical newspapers, like the L'viv *Za vil'nu Ukrainu*, were already publishing articles by Diaspora scholars and activists about the Famine and its consequences.[11]

Though many articles of 1989-90 had begun to criticize Soviet methods in the Stalin period, their chief focus was the inefficiencies of the administrative-command system and/or what was termed Stalin's criminal policy toward peasants. Writing in May 1990, Grigoriy Koinash, who experienced the famine, declares that the situation in 1932 was much worse than that in 1921. His family lived in Krivyi Rih and was well acquainted with peasants from nearby villages. The author recalls conversations of his father with peasants about the state of agriculture. He maintains that collectivization was unpopular in all quarters and everyone sympathized with the *kulaks* who had been deported to Siberia. Though one *kulak* in the region—a "bloodsucker"—merited such treatment, the same was not true for the other victims. Koinash also recalls the drought in 1932, noting that in this summer no rain had fallen, and the earth was covered with cracks. Children had to put on footwear in order not to burn their feet. Most of the harvest was lost to fires. By the summertime, residents in some of the neighboring villages were starving, and peasants no longer appeared in the town because they had nothing to bring to the market. Instead of coming to the aid of the peasants, the government persecuted them for stealing state property. What was the main cause of the famine, which reached its height in the spring of 1933? Koinash is unequivocal: [it arose because of] "the inhuman adventurist policy of the Stalinist leadership, drunk with plans for industrialization."[12]

By 1991 there were a number of plans in Ukraine to commemorate the Famine more appropriately. In the village Yaroslavka (Ruzhyn Rayon, Zhytomyr Oblast) residents decided in the spring to erect a memorial plinth to famine victims and a film about the events was in progress.[13] Serhii Dyachenko, a writer and scriptwriter and holder of the Shevchenko State Prize, already had a screenplay in mind for such a film, which would portray the famine through the eyes of a child. He had published a short essay about his plans and readers had responded with a flood of letters as well as R500,000 in contributions. The author promised to publish a script as a separate book.[14] Also involved in such work was the Vasyl Stus' Ukrainian Voluntary Historical-Memorial Association, which was founded in 1989. It organized actions such as the all-Ukrainian Memorial week for the victims of the Famine of 1932-33 and the Stalinist repressions, an International Symposium called "Holodomor-

33", and established the location of some of the mass graves of victims of Stalinism. A member from Ivano-Frankivs'k, P. Arsenych, noted that it was necessary to issue a decree concerning the establishment of a Book of Memory for all those who were victims of repression. Concerning the Famine, M. Lysenko of Kyiv proposed a monument in the center of Kyiv to the "victims of Communist terror," which should be located close to the former headquarters of the NKVD, the October Palace.[15]

By December 1991, however, with the dissolution of the Soviet Union, the Famine became a critically important issue for any analysis of the Stalinist past. Ukrainian historians, further, had a broader task to compose for the first time a non-Soviet version of Ukrainian history. For earlier periods they already had the 11-volume history written by Mykailo Hrushevs'kyi. But Hrushevs'kyi had died in 1934 at the very beginning of Stalin's assault on Ukrainian national culture and its political elite. The Famine quickly came to symbolize the period of Soviet rule at its cruelest, and Ukraine's persecution at the hands of a centralized Soviet regime based in the capital of Russia. In short time the national and political dimensions of the Famine became more critical than the economic chaos and upheaval caused by the introduction of mass collectivization in 1929–32, with its composite policy of grain procurements and attacks on real and alleged kulaks. In this respect the work of the late American historian James E. Mace has arguably been more influential than those of more established experts on the period of collectivization in the USSR, such as R. W. Davies and Lynne Viola. Whereas they have been hesitant to attribute the origins of the Famine solely (or at all) to the national question, the US Commission on the Ukraine Famine, chaired by Mace, concluded that the Famine was an act of genocide directed against Ukrainians as a nation—oddly, the statement was not the first or prime finding of the commission, it was listed 16th out of 19 major points.[16] In turn, this position signified that those persons responsible for the onset of the Famine were, by implication, non-Ukrainians.

The reanalysis of the Famine as a topic of history took place at a time of dramatic changes in the Soviet Union. The political circumstances posed some problems for Ukraine's historians. Kul'chyts'kyi has remarked elsewhere that he and his colleagues were heavily reliant on Orest Subtelny's book, *Ukraine: a History,* for several years.[17] Why was there such reliance on a scholar from the West? Subtelny points out that his colleagues in Ukraine, having witnessed the removal of the suffocating restraints of adherence to the official Soviet line, lacked both directions and guidelines. In addition, the teaching of the history of the USSR was de facto the history of Russia, with that of Ukraine limited to about 30 hours of the academic load. However, in the transitional period, prior to the issuance of new Ukrainian history textbooks and with the need to come to terms with the recent history of the USSR, Ukrainian historians had to turn to Western scholars of Ukraine for guidance. The work of the latter was elevated to a new authority, ironically perhaps given the inability of these same scholars to gain access to any primary source materials during most of the Soviet period. Thus it became the new practice in Ukraine to cite Western works to add credibility to any article.

Subtelny's book went through three Ukrainian editions between 1991 and 1993. However, what did Subtelny say about the Famine of 1932-33? The answer is: very little. The central point about the Famine, reports Subtelny, is that it was an event that did not have to happen. He cites the well-known quotation by Viktor Kravchenko in his book *I Chose Freedom*: "It's a struggle to the death... It took a famine to show who is master here. It has cost millions of lives, but the collective farm system is here to stay." Subtelny continues by commenting that because of the tradition of private land ownership, Ukrainians tended to resist collectivization more fiercely than Russians.[18] The introduction to an article on teaching history in schools in the Ukrainian newspaper *Den'* commented that Subtelny's book cannot be considered an academic work, but should be regarded rather as "an outstanding textbook of the Western type."[19] It could not satiate the need for more definitive studies of the Famine of 1932-33. It was thus left to Ukrainian historians to fill the requisite gaps by new investigations into the Famine. Foremost among them has once again been Kul'chyts'kyi, but there have been numerous others, writing in both in the academic milieu and in the popular press.

Gradually, Ukrainian writers and scholars began to delve more deeply into the events of the early 1930s. Kul'chyts'kyi, now recognized as Ukraine's senior scholar on the Famine, published several more articles. Here we will highlight another piece in *Ukrains'kyi istorychnyi zhurnal* in September 1991, entitled "Between two wars."[20] The article focuses on dekulakization, and the role of Stalin and his two main associates in the field of agriculture: Kaganovich and Molotov. He cites the loss of "hundreds of millions" of *poods* of grain at the time of threshing and delivery, which he claims was the result of the collective farmers' lack of interest in their work,[21] but he concentrates most closely on the establishment of the grain procurement commission under Premier Vyacheslav Molotov which was given extraordinary powers. In late January, P. P. Postyshev, a secretary of the CC CPSU was also sent into Ukraine with "dictatorial powers." Kul'chyts'kyi cites Molotov's insistence in November 1932 that a further procurement quota be placed on Ukraine that equaled in dimension the original quota for the period June–October. Reports about the lack of any grain were ignored because the focus was on the "struggle for grain." Because of the failure, even under these stringent conditions, to meet the required targets, Molotov's Commission took from Ukraine all available supplies down to the straw and chaff left after threshing.

In adopting such a policy, the requisition teams were guided by the decree of the Ukrainian government, accepted at the insistence of Molotov, "About measures to raise grain procurements," of 20 November 1932, which contained a clause about applying "natural penalties" of meat for shortfalls in grain. The inference, says Kul'chyts'kyi, is clear. The government was creating the conditions for the complete physical destruction of the rural population, including women and children. Archival documents and newspapers testify that in all localities of Ukraine searches took place for the confiscation not only of grain, but also of sugar, potatoes, beets, and lard as a punishment for "*kulak* sabotage" of grain procurements.[22] The "Holodomor"—Kul'chyts'kyi uses that term—was now in place, and the Soviet government refused all foreign aid for the starving, while Stalin placed police forces on the Ukrainian border to prevent peasants from crossing into areas that had some supplies of food. In addition, as was pointed out in an August 1991 article by Yurii Shapoval, the decree of 14 December, signed by both Molotov and Stalin, not only applied measures of extraordinary severity for failure to meet grain procurements in Ukraine, but also demanded that regional authorities "turn attention to the correct implementation of Ukrainization" and the removal of so-called "Petlyurites and other bourgeois nationalists from party and Soviet organizations."[23]

Transition of Interpretations, 1992–95

The change in tone and emphasis between Soviet-period and post-Soviet articles is evident as Ukrainian historians were now much freer to pursue independent research. They also benefited from direct collaboration with researchers from the West. In August 1992, for example, a world forum of Ukrainians was announced that would conduct a round-table discussion on "Genocide in Ukraine," with the participation of Robert Conquest, author of *Harvest of Sorrow*, and James E. Mace, as well as several well-known leaders from the Ukrainian Diaspora.[24] For the first time, Ukrainian scholars and publicists began to give free rein to the topic of victimization of Ukraine by the Soviet authorities, particularly in the influential literary weekly, *Literaturna*

Ukraina. This development is not surprising since the literary leaders of Ukraine were the initiators of the Ukrainian Popular Movement for Perestroika (Rukh) and had spearheaded the movement for autonomy and ultimately independence. The Famine now became the focal point of the early independence writing, which often took on literary and emotional forms.

An important article in this regard was written by Ivan Drach under the title "The Genocide of Ukraine" in the fall of 1992. Drach provides first of all the image of Chornobyl: "We are living on the ruins and have not been able to finish counting all our losses." Likewise the Famine "is hidden in our genetic depths" like some sort of nuclear monster and brings forth negative energy that leads to constant bickering and inability to comprehend even simple things among the Ukrainian people. Voices are sometimes heard, he writes, that complain about the "victim mentality" in the national discourse.

> The phenomenon of the nation-Christ, which is being crucified endlessly, with only the executioners and guards rotating at the site of the crucifixion has not been fully comprehended by mankind or us. Human civilization has yet to apologize to Ukrainians for their services paid in blood and flesh... This is the century through the main calamities of which—world wars, communism, fascism, nuclear energy—comes the main message of the new era: genocide against Ukrainians.[25]

Ukrainian losses in the 20th century, Drach continues, are numbered not in hundreds of thousands, but in millions and "dozens of millions." It is possible to lose track of the count because no one knows how many were liquidated by the White and Red guards or perished in the famines of 1921-22 and 1932-33, or how many were dispersed around Siberia. Stalin's plan for a "final solution" to the Ukrainian question cited by Khrushchev was just a symptom of this paranoia. Here in its most simplistic form is the victim theory of what might be termed the "permanent persecution" of Ukrainians. With the open communication with Western scholars about the Famine, it was now possible to develop a new interpretation of an event that had long been hidden officially from the Ukrainian public.

The first notable occasion for a commemoration was the 60th anniversary of the Famine in 1993. After decades of neglect, Ukrainian newspapers and journals could direct their focus to the event. An editorial in *Literaturna Ukraina* stated that it was now known that "millions upon millions" of Ukrainians and members of other nationalities had perished from hunger. Therefore every *oblast*, district, town, and village of the newly independent country should honor the sacred memory of the innocent victims of hunger. Crosses should be erected and mass gravesites properly maintained, and most important, young people and children should know and remember the "horrendous crime of the Communist clique" against the Ukrainian nation. Parents, teachers, and museum guides must be responsible for narrating the story of the Famine. Officially the occasion was to be known as Days of Sorrow and Remembrance. The editorial remarked that the horrific events of sixty years ago should serve as a warning what can happen when a "freedom-loving and industrious nation" lacks its own state.[26] Two days later, the editor of the same newspaper V. Kyryluk declared that the Famine was an attempt to "liquidate the Ukrainian nation" thus completing the "dirty work of Russian autocrats" through an unheard of genocide that had accounted for the deaths of up to 15 million people.[27]

The theme of Soviet persecution of Ukraine and Ukrainians was also taken up by Vasyl Mazorchuk, who maintained that the objective of Lenin and his associates in the Russian Revolution was to turn Russia (including Ukraine) into a source of cheap labor and mineral resources for the developed countries of the world. How did the Famine fit into this argument? The Bolsheviks believed that by using tractors in agriculture, they would be able to dispense with the large number of excess peasants. A food surplus would be created by reducing the number of consumers, which could then be exported. The famine in his view was the ultimate manifestation of racism, and one can perceive a historical parallel between the Ukrainian victims and the Native Americans who are victims of US government policies.[28] Racism is also the subject of an impassioned article by Ivan Drach, one of the founders of Rukh, who in a speech delivered at a conference on the 50th anniversary of the Famine, stated that the first lesson is that Russia in the past, present, and future has only a destructive and negative attitude toward Ukraine. Many Russians, he writes, "suffer from a fatal Ukrainophobia." At the present time, Drach laments, Russia is not considering any repentance for severing the Ukrainian nation in half over the past 75 years. He and like-minded Ukrainians would like the northern neighbor to turn its attention to the condition of Ukraine. The Ukrainian nation has survived and now demands of Moscow that it take responsibility for its misdeeds of the past, especially for the Holodomor of 1933, which brought losses of 8–12 million, double those incurred during the war of 1941–45.[29]

A more balanced analysis was provided by historian Vasyl' Marochko in a series of articles in the newspaper *Osvita*, also published to commemorate the 60th anniversary of the Famine. At the outset he counters claims that the

Famine constituted a war of one nation against another. Clearly it took on an anti-Ukrainian direction, but its real organizers—the Soviet political elite— were made up of different nationality groups. However, the Famine was man-made and consciously organized by the Soviet political leadership even though its purpose, in his view, was to physically exterminate the peasants of Ukraine. The Famine occurred, he states, as a result of "the forcible introduction of the Communist doctrine in agriculture, a doctrine that remained alien to Ukrainian peasants" since the latter were attuned to the tradition of individual farming.[30] Without doubt, he says, the Famine was genocide; a fact, he adds incorrectly, long established by foreign scholars. The actions of the authorities were illegal because they persecuted peasants who did not commit any crimes, but simply refused to join the *kolkhozes* and surrender their bread (of which frequently they had none). In the fall of 1933, following the famine, a large number of Belarusian and Russian peasants were settled in the empty villages of Ukraine. Marochko also provides his assessment of the number of victims of the Famine, arriving at the conclusion that losses in Ukraine amounted to around 2.9 million people, a very different total from that of Kyrylyuk cited above.[31]

Memoirs

In the early 1990s the Ukrainian press, and particularly informal newspapers, began to publish memoirs from those who had lived through the famine. Some of the stories are worth relating because they provide an indication of how the attempts to acquire knowledge about the Famine from official materials and documents were supplemented by eyewitness accounts that often provide harrowing stories of suffering and hunger. The memoirs also added weight to the very emotional outpourings of figures like Drach, and to the theory that the Famine was genocide perpetrated on the Ukrainians as a people by their masters in Moscow. Memoirs have sometimes been criticized as unreliable by Western scholars, and in turn defended by historians such as James E. Mace, who was one of the earliest collectors of such accounts as head of the US Commission on the Ukraine Famine in 1986-90. After the passage of sixty years and more, the memories of survivors are often less than clear (unless they kept diaries). There is also the added dimension of the way interviews are conducted, particularly if the goal is to chronicle past suffering or commemorate rather than analyze an event. However, in the case of the Famine in Ukraine, memoirs have provided some of the most significant impressions, resurrecting a tragedy that had long been concealed, denied, and then distorted.

An early post-Soviet memoir was written by Dmytro Brylins'kyi, who had lost his parents at the age of three and was raised, together with his sister, by his grandmother. He recalled the grain collection campaign in 1932 and how the family sometimes managed to find some rotten potatoes in the garden, as well as eating grass and weeds. His arms and legs began to swell from lack of food. He also describes instances of cannibalism. Though he survived the Famine, his teacher N. S. Shurovs'kyi was arrested as an enemy of the people because his wife received a letter from some relatives in Poland.[32] Another author related what he had heard from a retired teacher called Hryhorii Konovalenko, who was 18 years of age in 1932 and worked at an elementary school in the district of Reshetylivka. During the grain collection campaign, it was recalled, activists were walking about the village piercing the ground with special metal spikes looking for hidden grain. They took away everything, including the last handful of beans. Konovalenko survived thanks to the aid of a skilled fisherman who would share his catch. However, fish was not available on a daily basis. By the spring of 1933, villagers were adding grass to the ersatz flour they used to make bread. As a result many died from intestinal problems. By the end of the school year, out of a class of 83 school pupils, only 3 survived, all of whom came from the same family. The school was closed for lack of students and Konovalenko was transferred to a different school.[33]

The famine experience in the Cherkasy region was related by Yaryna Mytsyk, a famine survivor. The first collective farm appeared in her village of Vyshnopil in 1931, and some people joined voluntarily, whereas others joined because they had been robbed of all their possessions during the collectivization campaign. The 1931 harvest, she recalls, was so poor that her family had to switch to a diet of potatoes, along with borscht. In 1932 the harvest was worse, and potatoes were now in short supply, too. Frequently people had to roast beets and squash as well as some oil seeds. A type of cookie was manufactured from fragmented buckwheat, but usually the food surrogates were barely edible, and many people began to suffer from acute stomachache after eating them. The *kolkhoz* provided a cart for the transport of corpses to the cemetery, and as many were in an advanced state of decomposition, men would use pitchforks to lift them onto the cart. Mytsyk also relates some stories of cannibalism, particularly of a number of farmers who killed their children. In the spring, people ate whatever they could find, including a poisonous variety of mushrooms, which caused them to lose their senses before dying. The author cites the materials of a Famine Commission organized in 1983 by the Ukrainian Congress in Toronto, another indicator of the direct influence of events and pressure from outside Ukraine affecting the views of those within the country, including famine survivors themselves.[34]

A description of the famine in the Kyiv region cites one incident in which the members of the grain requisition commission left a small sack of grain upon discovering that the mother of the house was pregnant. This same eye-witness recalls a cart traveling down the street with a human leg sticking out of it. The cart took the corpses to the cemetery and deposited them in a pre-pared deep pit. Mad and hungry dogs jumped into the pits and tore the bodies to pieces, resisting the efforts of the gravediggers to drive them away. This source relates one horrific example of an old woman and her daughter who induced travelers to stay for the night, then killed them and used their bodies for meat. The article suggests that there were several people who indulged in acts of cannibalism in this fashion.[35] A similar report from the Cherkasy region begins with the de-kulakization campaign of 1930 and the establishment of a special commission headed by the chairman of the village council. Once the commission took grain from the village of Kozats'ke, many people chose to commit suicide rather than starve. Some tried to retake their former cattle from the *kolkhoz* but were met with gunfire. Over 600 people reportedly died in this village from hunger in 1932-33, and the writer's aunt warned him not to roam the village for fear that he would be caught and eaten. Communists and activists did not die, writes the author. They watched guiltily as other peasants died.[36]

More recent memoirs appear to elaborate rather than provide fewer details as one might anticipate with the passage of time. Kateryna Marchenko bases her account on the memories of her parents and grandparents, as well as her own. She outlines the historical context, starting with collectivization, the de-portation of the *kulaks*, and finally grain requisitions. The scale of the latter, she stated, was exceptionally high. It was carried out by lazy residents and drunkards, including in the village Kyshentsi, Uman district of the Cherkasy region, by two brothers with the name of Marochko. She remembers the so-called "red caravans" (several carts that took away the grain and which bore red flags). In her recollection, the harvest of 1932 was a good one—a state-ment contradicted by several other accounts—and she blames the famine di-rectly on the subsequent requisitions. Local women tried to prevent the red caravans from leaving the village and in one instance got into a brawl with the activists. Her father had died during the Russian Civil War, but her mother managed to preserve her family by exchanging some goods such as beads, handkerchiefs, and towels in return for grain. When spring came, the children would go into the fields and steal straw from the *kolkhoz*. They also collected bark from the trees, sought frozen potatoes in the fields, and consumed new shoots of grass. Many of her extended family died during this period: uncles, aunts, and cousins. In her opinion, the figure of deaths for the whole of Ukraine must have been around 14 million, a total she claims was corroborated by a number of historians, and the famine occurred because "Ukraine did not want to be in chains and put up with occupiers."[37]

This style of memoir may not be very convincing in terms of historical accuracy, but the detail of the description provides a counterweight to the depiction of a nation in chains. An even more detailed account from Tamara Ruchko reads like something out of a horror movie. It is worth recounting as an exceptionally emotive example of the Famine memoir genre. Ruchko's father had been a victim of the early purge in 1932, and when the famine occurred the family consisted of the mother and three children: Borys, Tamara, and Yurii. Tamara was taken to stay with an uncle and aunt because of the hardship at home. However, the uncle died shortly afterward. One day, she recalls, the aunt left her alone and forgot to lock the door. Suddenly the door opened and an emaciated man entered the house, with "glass eyes gleaming from inside their orbits." Assuming no one was present he began to search the house, drinking a jug of soup that had been left on the stove before collapsing in a heap on the floor. The young girl screamed once she realized he was dead and ran outside to seek help. Along the way she tripped over a dead woman. Later Tamara's aunt contracted typhus. The girl tried to barter some clothes for food but was attacked and beaten by two men who took her bundle. Later she was housed with her aunt's father who treated her brutally. However, she does provide some examples of neighborly assistance. She also recounts some narratives from others, such as the story of how in the neighboring village of Baryshivka, stray dogs and cats would be used for soup as also sometimes were children.[38]

Transition of Interpretations after 1995

The second half of the 1990s saw a plethora of new interpretations of the Ukrainian Famine, led once again by Kul'chyts'kyi, Ukraine's leading authority on this event. These studies concentrated on several specific aspects: the number of victims, the relationship between Stalin's collectivization campaign and the Famine, and the motives behind the tragedy. They varied in tone and quality, but in general by this period, historians in Ukraine were convinced of the malevolent nature of the tragedy, and that it was directed from above. However, it took longer to reach a consensus on whether the Famine was a phenomenon deliberately engineered to target Ukrainians as a nation, rather than as one of the most important grain growing regions of the country. The analyses benefited from the opening of Ukrainian archives in 1989, but according to Kul'chyts'kyi the demographic data from 1933 proved to be of extremely low quality and therefore statistics about the Famine had to be reconstructed using indirect methods. As in the earlier article, Kul'chyts'kyi also felt it necessary to take into account the migration processes as well as archival data for years other than the pivotal 1933 year. In turn, he considered that Western media and some local authors tended to exaggerate the number of casualties. According to his scientific deductions and based on the number of recorded victims each month, the losses on the territory of the Ukrainian SSR in the year 1933 amounted to 3–3.5 million.[39]

Once again, the focus of the research is on the activities of the Grain Commissions. The most severe grain procurements were imposed on those regions that had failed to fulfill the state annual targets. The "extraordinary commission" led by Molotov in Ukraine was unable to find any grain in the peasant households of most districts of Soviet Ukraine, and therefore began to confiscate other food products as a form of punishment. These policies were more severe than those introduced elsewhere, says Kul'chyts'kyi, particularly those of Postyshev in the Volga region, where only grain was confiscated. Harsher policies were also imposed in the North Caucasus and particularly the Kuban region by Kaganovich. By 1998, Kul'chyts'kyi had fallen into line with the theory of a "terror-famine"—the term used by Robert Conquest earlier—that had rendered the Ukrainian peasantry entirely obedient.[40] This theory, however, was still some distance from those who attributed the Famine solely to reasons linked to recalcitrant nationalism. One such example from this period is that of Mykhailo Hoyan, who relies heavily on the book *Holod-33* by Lidiya Kovalenko and Volodymyr Manyak, published in 1991. According to Hoyan, the famine was not a consequence of drought, flood, or epidemic, but rather caused by the evil designs of one group of people against another, i.e., Russians against Ukrainians. In a vitriolic attack on Russians, he claims that the "free world" has long understood that the mentality of the Muscovite is one of expansionism and that the Famine should be regarded in this context. However, some Ukrainians living in the eastern and southern regions of the country are ignorant of this fact because they do not know their own history, and thus hapless people sometimes still vote for traitors and "janissaries nourished by the bloody system of Lenin and Stalin." Hoyan calls for a tribunal to judge those who have damaged the "genofond" of the Ukrainian people and who are responsible for 7.5 million deaths.[41]

Generally, however, in these early post-independence writings, the Famine was attributed chiefly to policies of terror and retribution rather than an all-out attempt to eliminate Ukrainians as a national group. Many authors overtly debate such issues in trying to assess the status of the Famine in contemporary Ukraine. Some are downright muddled. Dana Romanets, for example, concurs that despite the efforts of some intellectuals to organize a Nuremberg-style tribunal for those who committed crimes against Ukrainians, the state cannot compensate victims so the only plausible recourse is to remember them. She believes that the Famine was genocidal because the state created the conditions in which the deaths of masses of people were inevitable. Because there was no drought in 1932, in contrast to the years 1921 and 1946 when famines also occurred, the Holodomor of 1933 was unique. However, the harvest of 1932 was low because the peasants lacked motivation to cultivate the fields in the wake of collectivization. Ostensibly this article tries to link the Famine of 1932–33 directly with the Purges of 1937, so one suspects that she is adhering to the line that the Famine was an act of terror. However, her conclusions could be interpreted in several ways, and thus they exhibit the lack of a clear thesis on the causes of the Famine.[42]

Similarly, Yaroslava Muzychenko's article, which tries to relate the Famine to the emergence of the new Ukrainian state, struggles to corroborate her conclusion, which is that the Famine was introduced to "teach Ukrainian peasants a lesson." She makes a clear demographic distinction between the suffering peasants and the relatively unaffected urban dwellers, going on to comment that because most peasants were of Ukrainian ethnicity, they were overrepresented among the victims, who included residents of Bulgarian, German, and Greek villages. Because they were city dwellers, Russians and Jews did not suffer unduly during this period. Though she claims to recognize that the Famine knew no ethnic boundaries, she is convinced that Ukrainians' situation was the most severe: "Only in Ukraine did severe terror accompany famine." She laments the lack of or superficial character of Famine commemoration in the new Ukrainian state, which is limited to laying flowers on the symbolic monument in Kyiv. She approves the idea of Roman Serbyn (a history professor from Montreal, Canada) to establish a research center for the Famine similar to the Yad Vashem Institute in Israel (for the study of the Holocaust) or the Polish Institute of Memory. But her appeal is weakened by the lack of a clear conception on the causes and meaning of the Famine. In particular, there is little discussion of what the Ukrainians did wrong in order to be the victims of punishment from the Soviet state. Unlike Romanets, she does not dwell on the national issue, restricting her argument to a few comments about the ethnic backgrounds of sufferers.[43]

Six months later, Muzychenko returns to her theme in an article that documents episodes of resistance to collectivization and the Famine, as well as contemporary attitudes of the public toward the commemoration of the past. Using oral testimonies of Ukrainians, she constructs a fairly unrealistic picture of universal resistance to the first collectivization campaign through her description of an opposition "band" in the Hadiach district of Poltava region. The group was led by Yukhym Shcherban who lived together with his brothers in the forest to avoid deportation. An informant maintained that Shcherban's band had been designated as rich peasants. By contrast the poor peasants donned leather jackets and became Communists and started to order people how to live their lives. The band reportedly tried to persuade collective farm members to abandon the enterprise but eventually all the bandits were killed. Muzychenko then goes on to portray the Famine as Stalin's attempt to subdue resistance, citing Kul'chyts'kyi's theory of Terror with Famine. Those peasants who took on the role of activists for the Soviet regime, she says, ate well in contrast to the rest of the village residents. She also comments on the concealment of the Famine by the authorities, arguing that if the Soviet leaders refused to divulge news about the event, then they must have been the ones to organize it—a statement that requires a leap in logic. She relies also on the work of the Diaspora to commemorate the Famine, citing the Commission for the Study of the Ukraine Famine in the USA, which delivered "30 volumes of documents" to the Ukrainian Parliament. One week before this article appeared, an all-Ukrainian conference on the Famine was held at the Interregional Academy of Personnel Management (MAUP) in Kyiv, which proposed to send a petition to the UN to acknowledge the Famine as an act of genocide. The problem is that Muzychenko's article failed to prove that point.[44]

A more scholarly paper of this same period pinpoints some signposts on the road to famine: forced industrialization at the expense of the countryside and collectivization marking the starting point. Collectivization in Ukraine, the author posits, was carried out faster than elsewhere, and was followed by confiscation of grain, livestock, and farm equipment. The main thesis of this article is that despite the official awareness of drought, low harvest, and famine in some localities, the central authorities still endorsed truly fantastic plans for grain procurements. The author cites specifically the activities of the

Molotov Commission, which in October 1932 managed to squeeze another 89.5 million *poods* of grain out of peasant households. The purge of the Ukrainian party and state apparatus took place simultaneously: in November and the first days of December 1932 the authorities arrested 340 *kolkhoz* chairmen and 140 book-keepers. Through the law for the protection of the harvest, over 20,000 people were imprisoned. Stalin and his associates were fully aware of the Famine but continued to ship grain abroad in order to promote the image of a Bolshevik paradise and to earn income to support the industrialization campaign. The author proposes a series of events, particularly in schools, to commemorate the Famine, including conferences and drawing competitions. This writer more explicitly endorses the theory of a Famine-Genocide, but does not elaborate on the possible reasons behind it, though he has explained clearly that Ukraine as a republic was singled out for very harsh treatment.[45]

The 70th Anniversary of the Famine

The 70th anniversary of the Famine in Ukraine was commemorated widely in 2003. It included official recognition of the Famine as an act of genocide by the government and parliament of Ukraine, as well as various foreign governments, including the Senate of Canada and the government of the United States. In contrast, the United Nations offered a watered-down resolution that offered condolences to various groups that suffered from starvation in the Soviet Union, including the Kazakhs and the Russians. In Ukraine also, a national day of mourning was recognized on the fourth Sunday of November. There were conferences, exhibits in museums, and lengthy discussions in academic forums and the media. By now, several clear trends could be delineated in world opinion about the nature of the Famine:

a) That of the academics, writers, and publicists of Ukrainian ancestry, who commemorated the Famine as an act of genocide (as indeed they had done for decades), using the term that Kul'chyts'kyi had applied in his article ten years earlier—Holodomor, or death by hunger. North Americans of Ukrainian ancestry had commemorated the Famine ten years earlier in significant fashion, including the commissioning by the Harvard Ukrainian Research Institute of the definitive work on the Famine to date by Robert Conquest, a historian based at the Hoover Institution, Stanford University, in 1986.[46] In 2003, the campaign benefited from increased awareness and knowledge of the Famine and the scale of the catastrophe engendered by the Conquest book, and the work of James E. Mace and his colleagues on the US Commission on the Ukraine Famine, which had published its findings in several volumes by 1990. It coincided also with a campaign discussed earlier, taken up by the Ukrainian Civil Liberties Association,[47] to persuade the *New York Times* to revoke the Pulitzer Prize it had awarded to its Moscow correspondent Walter Duranty in 1932 for his reporting from the USSR. This latter campaign, though never attaining its ultimate goal, resulted in a sustained effort that involved letters to the media and a number of editorials in various newspapers. Duranty, an admirer of Stalin, had misled readers over a period of several years regarding the nature of the Soviet regime, including the existence of the Famine of 1932-33.[48]

b) That of Western academics, not of Ukrainian ancestry, who still hesitated to delineate national motives to Stalin's collectivization and grain collection campaigns.[49] Key among them has been Mark Tauger of the University of West Virginia, who has maintained that the 1932 harvest was much poorer than believed hitherto.[50] Notably, Western academics were paying much more attention to the topic. In contrast to earlier works that never even cited the Famine—Moshe Lewin's *Russian Peasants and Soviet Power* being the classic example—new studies discussed the issue carefully. Most notable in this regard was Terry Martin's much heralded book, *The Affirmative Action Empire*, which argues that:

The Politburo's development of a national interpretation of their grain requisitions crisis in late 1932 helps explain both the pattern of terror and the role of the national factor during the 1932-1933 famine. The 1932-33 terror campaign consisted of both a grain requisitions terror, whose primary target was the peasantry, both Russian and non-Russian, and a nationalities terror, whose primary target was Ukraine and subsequently Belarus. The grain requisitions terror was the final and decisive culmination of a campaign begun in 1927-1928 to extract the maximum possible amount of grain from a hostile peasantry. As such, its primary targets were the grain-producing regions of Ukraine, the North Caucasus, and the Lower Volga, though no grain-producing regions escaped the 1932-1933 grain requisitions terror entirely. Nationality was of minimal importance in this campaign. The famine was not an intentional act of genocide specifically targeting the Ukrainian nation. It is equally false, however, to assert that nationality played no role whatsoever in the famine. The nationalities terror resulted from the gradual emergence of an anti-*korenizatsiia* hard-line critique combined with the immediate pressures of the grain requisitions crisis in

Ukraine and Kuban, whose particularly intense resistance was attributed to Ukrainization.[51]

In other words, the denationalization campaign came after the Famine rather than alongside it and when it did take place it affected Ukraine and Belarus more or less equally.[52]

c) The work of academics in Ukraine, led by Kul'chyts'kyi, Shapoval, Marochko, and Danilov, and also the writings of James E. Mace, resident in Ukraine for the last decade of his life. There remain subtle but very distinct differences in the interpretation of the Famine by historians in Ukraine. Kul'chyts'kyi, Mace, and Shapoval emphasize the importance of the 11 August 1932 letter from Stalin to Kaganovich, which complained about the weakness of the CPU and the presence within it of Petlyurites working in the interests of Polish leader Pilsudski. Though it seems reasonable to assume a fear of Ukrainian nationalism, oddly neither of them remark on Stalin's startling paranoia and fear of Poles, illustrated in this document most vividly. They also lay emphasis, correctly in my view, on the formation of an extraordinary commission under Molotov on 22 October 1932 (other leaders policed different areas: Kaganovich was sent to the North Caucasus and Pavel Postyshev to the Volga region) and the Molotov decree of 18 November 1932 extending requisitions for failure to meet the assigned grain quotas. Shapoval, as noted earlier, believes that the decision to abort the policy of Ukrainization of 14 December 1932 was tied directly to the grain requisitions policy. Mace notes that the problems were blamed on *kulaks* and wreckers in order to "unleash a reign of terror on party officials" (*The Day*, 25 November 2003).

According to Kul'chyts'kyi, in a March 2003 article in the journal *Istoriya v shkolakh Ukrainy*, the causes of the Famine are impossible to comprehend without a study of the nature of the Soviet social-economic transformation that occurred after 1929. After the abandonment of the New Economic Policy in 1928, the new political leadership under Stalin moved to the forced creation of the Communist order under slogans of socialist construction. The key goal was to transform the peasantry into an engaged work force that could labor through a command system on the collective farms. This drive was more successful than Lenin's attempt of 1918–21 and relied on three factors. First, says Kul'chyts'kyi, in the 1920s and 1930s the authorities proved stronger than the peasantry. The state prepared for several years for a campaign of full collectivization, having eliminated the *kulak* sector from the villages. The GPU organs made a list, and neutralized the most mutinous element among the peasantry. Second, Stalin introduced a policy change in March 1930. He refused to force peasants into Communes as demanded by Communist doctrine and switched to the "artel" form of collectivization, which was much looser. The logical result was the legalization of free commodity circulation in May 1932, which was prohibited by Communist doctrine. There thus arose a *kolkhoz* trade sector and the monetary form of wages was retained for workers and employees. The third factor was the use of terror, and the division of peasants into rich, middle, and poor, with the expropriation and deportation of kulaks. Such a fate befell all those who were hostile to collective farms.[53]

Kul'chyts'kyi also focuses once again on the Grain Commissions that began to operate from November 1932. He believes that these commissions functioned with unusual force and venom in Ukraine and the Kuban/North Caucasus, where two-thirds of the population was of Ukrainian ethnicity. Here, the commissions took not only grain. When they could not find any grain, a new penalty—the requisitioning of meat and potatoes—was applied to the peasantry. Those who were "in debt" for grain procurements thus saw the confiscation of all food supplies accumulated from the new harvest, such as sugar, fruits, onions, etc.[54] "Stalin acutely struck out at these 'debtors' in order to teach them a lesson," he continues, and the goal was not so much revenge as intimidation. This phrase "teaching a lesson" echoes a report of Ukrainian party secretary Stanislav Kosior in the spring of 1933 when he complained that the tempo of spring sowing in Ukraine was unsatisfactory and that the peasants needed to be punished. Kul'chyts'kyi goes on to note that once grain was taken from the village, the weakest farmers, with no other food supplies, were the ones to perish, whereas those with some food stored away might survive until the next harvest. But when all stocks of food were confiscated then death from starvation rose by "tens of times."[55]

Notable here is less a difference in interpretation than in emphasis. Kul'chyts'kyi chooses once again to highlight a "terror-famine" imposed by the Soviet authorities as a form of punishment, which together with excessive grain procurements ensured that Ukraine suffered large losses of its rural population. Stalin responded to the Famine as a phenomenon that never existed. The word was never used in party documents, but is found only in special papers that were not for discussion. This ban on use of the word was for strategic reasons, i.e., to avoid the necessity of organizing aid to the hungry. Internal military police were installed to prevent starving peasants from crossing the republican border. According to Kul'chyts'kyi, Western governments were aware of the Famine but chose not to intervene directly because they put their national interests first—in the case of the United States, because such an intervention would compromise the diplomatic recognition of the Soviet Union by Washington, and as a potential ally given the coming to power of Hitler in Germany. Many of the Soviet leaders, including Khrushchev, were reportedly unaware of the scale of the Famine, he writes. In summary then, Kul'chyts'kyi has used the traditional explanations of the collectivization campaign to explain how Famine occurred in Ukraine in 1932–33, adding emphasis on the punishment of Ukraine to his old 1988 explanation of how the Famine occurred. The national question as an issue is excluded from his analysis.

This theory is refined in an article Kul'chyts'kyi wrote in this same year in *Ukrains'kyi istorychnyi zhurnal*, which explores conditions in collectivized agriculture in 1930–31 with the goal of establishing a "genetic link" between all-out collectivization and the Famine. According to this paper, although the state successfully managed to coerce peasants into collective farms, in the years following it failed completely to organize effective management of the *kolkhoz* economy. Peasants also felt alienated from the results of their labor. The authorities bungled by moving to a two-tier form of administrative control of center-district, eliminating the middle sector of regions, which made it difficult to oversee operations. The result was administrative chaos. Two other factors are considered: first the 25,000ers, or urban volunteers who moved from towns to the villages to create the leadership cadres in the *kolkhozes*. Their results, says Kul'chyts'kyi, were mixed. The Machine-Tractor Stations, on the other hand, which were supposed to provide the collective farms with technical support during the sowing campaign, were a failure because they lacked skilled machine operators. Finally he describes the grain procurement campaign and highlights the discrepancy between the projected harvest and the actual yield.[56] Though detailed, one could advance an argument that there is little in Kul'chyts'kyi's explanation in this article that could not be applied to other republics subjected to collectivization, including Russia and Belarus. What was distinctive about the campaign in Ukraine, and was collectivization really the main cause of the Famine?

In a research paper delivered in Canada during the 70th anniversary period, Yurii Shapoval addressed the issue of the Famine through various primary documents, including exchanges between leaders and Stalin, letters, reports, and diary entries to emphasize the role of Stalinist leaders in the Famine, particularly Molotov and Kaganovich. He points out that at the third conference of the Communist Party of Ukraine, held during the summer of 1932, and attended by the two leaders in question, CPU leaders and local officials tried to draw the attention of the Kremlin to the catastrophic situation in Ukraine, but to no avail. Conversely, in his letter to Kaganovich of 11 August

1932—a letter recognized by several historians as pivotal to the issue—Stalin outlined his suspicions about the Ukrainian peasants and questioned the loyalty of the Ukrainian party leadership in Kharkiv. He believed that it was under the influence of the late Symon Petlyura as well as agents of the Polish leader Jozef Pilsudski. He was afraid that the Soviet Union might "lose" Ukraine and that it required prompt attention so that it could be drawn into the fortress of the USSR. Shapoval believes that the letter indicates Stalin's desire to squeeze the maximum grain out of Ukraine to feed the urban population, as well as his intention to conduct a purge at all levels of Ukrainian society to eliminate nationalists and other enemies.[57]

Shapoval's second major point is that what made the situation in Ukraine quite distinct from that in Russia was a sudden shift in nationality policy on 14 December 1932 by Stalin and Molotov who issued a resolution on behalf of the Central Committee of the CPSU that called for a decisive struggle against recalcitrant elements in Ukraine. Shapoval perceives this event as the end of official Ukrainization (the implementation of a national culture with a socialist content begun in the 1920s) and the beginning of purges directed against Ukrainians. Thus in 1933 a purge was introduced and Pavel Postyshev was appointed Second Secretary of the CPU with plenipotentiary powers. Documents demonstrate that party officials from Moscow, including Postyshev, took an active role in requisitioning grain from the Ukrainian villages. Later the purges became part of the Great Terror that encompassed the entire Soviet Union in 1936-38. Thus we have an added element to the outline provided by Kul'chyts'kyi and others, namely a terror-punishment that was linked to Soviet nationality policy. Evident from this account, but never explicitly stated by Shapoval or any other Ukrainian historian in the discussion to this point, is Stalin's fear of Poland and its intentions toward Ukraine, a holdover from the war of 1920-21, and reflected in Stalin's subsequent purge of the Communist Party of Poland, the Katyn massacre of 1940, and other events. Were Ukrainians feared because of nationalism or because they had allied in the past with Poles against the Soviet leadership? If the Poles are taken into account as a factor in Stalin's thinking, then what impact does that have on the theory of the Famine as genocide?

The national issue is given further emphasis in another article on the 70th anniversary by two well-known Ukrainian historians, V. M. Danylenko and M. M. Kuz'menko. They concentrate on Stalinist repressions against two groups in the period of 1929-33: the upper scientific intelligentsia and village teachers. The political aspects of the "terror-famine," they argue, are to be found not only in punitive operations of state organs against the peasants, but also in the attack by the party leadership on "national-cultural deviationism," i.e., the campaign for Ukrainization and the "socio-spiritual self-organization of Ukraine," particularly in the rural areas. In 1932–33, they point out, 1,649 Ukrainian scholars were purged. In reality, the accusations of nationalism lacked substance as Stalin was seeking scapegoats for his own errors—the Ukrainian intelligentsia had tried to sabotage collectivization and was thus responsible for the onset of famine. After the Famine was organized, the leadership, in the opinion of the two authors, began to be fearful of food riots and therefore embarked on further repressions and deportations. These repressions were soon extended to organizations with members who were prominent Ukrainian intellectuals, such as the Ukrainian Association of Cultural and Scientific Workers for assistance to Socialist Construction, as well as rank-and-file teaching cadres. By February 1933, the purge had extended to the People's Commissariat for Education and some 200 "nationalists," "enemies," and unreliable elements were removed. Teachers were linked to the events in the villages because by this time the economic support of teachers had become the responsibility of the collective farms.[58]

Aside from the example of teachers, however, Danylenko and Kuz'menko fail to explain the links between the Famine in the villages and Stalin's clampdown on intellectuals and the reversal of Ukrainization. That there was such a link seems plausible, but the authors fail to come up with any conclusions; and this article in Ukraine's most authoritative historical journal is unconvincing because it fails to deal adequately with the social situation and the relationship between the towns and the villages. Indeed, in general, despite the close attention to the subject of the Famine by 2003 and the plethora of published works, Ukrainian historiography is notable for its absence of clear conclusions or convincingly argued theories about why events took the course they did. The most important figure—at least as determined by standing and productivity—Stanislav Kul'chyts'kyi continued to seek economic explanations whereas others began to turn to the national question. Others still took a very narrow view that laid the blame on other ethnic groups, principally the Russians, thus perceiving the Famine purely in ethnic terms. As we have seen, some writers took this conception further, and sought explanations from hundreds of years of history, maintaining that Russian persecution of Ukrainians was a centuries-old tradition. That the Famine was a more complex issue was evident from the works of other writers who attempted to provide a portrait of how the Famine affected non-Ukrainian regions of the republic.

Famine in Non-Ukrainian Villages

Writings and discourses that maintain there was no ethnic element to the Famine are found infrequently in Ukraine in the period since 1988. Nevertheless, they are worth recounting briefly because they offer a new dimension to the topic that may eventually be explored more fully. It should be recalled that there were several large ethnic communities living in Ukraine during the Stalinist period, of which the German and Jewish communities were the most notable. Both of them suffered considerable losses during the years 1932-33. Very little has appeared on the Germans, but in a lengthy article on the causes and consequences of the Famine, Vasyl' Marochko asserts that the situation in the national districts essentially did not differ from the plight of Ukrainian villages. He observes that the only outside country that recognized the scale of the Famine was Nazi Germany, which organized broad assistance for ethnic Germans living in Ukraine. However, some Germans refused to accept this aid because they were fearful of Soviet reprisals.[59] Clearly, Hitler's regime may have had more selfish motives than aiding kin in the Soviet Union, and some Volksdeutsche offered a warm welcome to the invading forces of the Wehrmacht in 1941. A more detailed picture has emerged of the Jewish settlements, principally from Jewish regional newspapers in contemporary Ukraine.

Thus Yakov Konigsman contests the theory that the Famine in Ukraine was the deliberate policy of the Soviet government, which singled out Ukrainians for destruction—this theme represents the more extreme version of the genocide theory. He argues that the Famine affected different areas of the Soviet Union, such as Kazakhstan and the Volga region, and encompassed members of different nationality groups. His main thesis is that the Famine resulted from the criminal policies of Stalin's regime which, despite a relatively poor harvest, tried to requisition as much grain as possible from the villages for export. The Famine, in Konigsman's view, signaled the decline of Jewish settlements in Ukraine. The start of such habitation dated back to Imperial Russian times, and Russia's efforts to convert Jews to Orthodoxy by tying them to the land. By the late 19th century, he points out, only 3% of almost 2 million Ukrainian Jews, were working in agriculture, whereas 97% resided in towns and cities. The revolution and Civil War had a devastating impact on Jewish settlements, reducing the Jewish population by about half compared to the numbers in 1914. However, the years 1921–22 saw a revitalization of colonization efforts by Zionist activists, who favored settlement in the Ukrainian south and the Crimean peninsula. Zionist cooperatives received support from Jewish organizations in the United States. A number of such cooperatives emerged in Crimea and employed over 1,600 Jewish peasants by 1923.[60]

By August 1924, the Soviet authorities were overtly supporting the policy of settling Jewish working people, and as a result Jewish colonies began to develop in Crimea and South Ukraine, based on the administrative districts of Freifeld, Neufeld, Blumenfeld, Kalinindorf, and Stalindorf. Similar colonies appeared in other parts of the USSR, such as Belarus, the Smolensk region of Russia, and the Caucasus. Jewish settlers were hostile to collectivization and the upheaval it posed for their settlements. However, by 1930, 93 Jewish collective farms had been founded in Ukraine, with a population of 156,000 peasants, which was 10% of the entire Jewish community of the republic. Konigsman maintains that collectivization was a destructive process. People lacked motivation, and requisitions undermined the stability of the *kolkhoz* and brought famine to the Jewish regions. Some American Jewish organizations (Agrojoint, Komzet), upon learning of the outbreak of famine in the Kherson region, attempted to help the communities, but their support was not accepted by the Soviet authorities. Konigsman reports that starving Jews attempted to escape to the cities and even to the Jewish region of Birobidzhan in the Soviet Far East. By 1937, only 68 Jewish *kolkhozes* remained, and the number of peasants in them had fallen to 109,000, a decline of 30%.[61]

One memoir relates the Jewish experience of the Famine in Kherson region. The author is a native of the village Sudnyakove in Khmel'nyts'kyi region, but moved with her parents to Kherson as part of a Jewish colonization venture organized by Agrojoint in 1928. They settled in the village Rodonsk and the company built them houses. When the Soviet authorities collectivized the region, the settlers were deprived of their horses and tools, but retained their cattle. In 1932–33 the father received 30 *poods* of grain for his labor on the *kolkhoz*, and 22 *poods* were exchanged for some sheep. When requisitions began, the family had to make bread from mustard flour, the grandfather died, and the author became swollen from hunger, although she survived. The malnourished children received one meal a day at school—some thin soup with beans.[62] Another author takes issue with those who have maintained that the Famine in Ukraine was organized by Jews (see below) and argues that Jews suffered from the event as much as any other group. In Ukraine, she states, the death toll for Jews was second only to that for Ukrainians and Russians, because the Famine targeted people based not on national identity but on the region and class affiliation, i.e., peasantry. Mikhail Siganevich from Kalinindorf recalled that the harvest in 1932 was satisfactory. His family received 20 *poods* of grain, but this amount was requisitioned in the fall of that year. The village schoolteacher ordered all children to bring 5 kilograms of grain to donate to the state, and his mother was obliged to give up what grain remained. The family endured the winter eating rotten vegetables. Though the Siganevich family survived, many of the neighbors perished.[63] There is little to distinguish such stories from those of Ukrainian villages.

Another article by Marochko is worth citing as a final example in the category of non-Ukrainian victims during the Famine. Though the Famine was not limited to Ukraine, he remarks, starvation tended to affect primarily those areas in which many Ukrainians lived, such as the Kuban region, along the Don River, and Kazakhstan. Though members of other nationalities suffered, it was primarily because they were unfortunate enough to reside in Ukraine (Russians, Jews, and Germans). In 1932, he points out, there were 2.6 million Russians in Ukraine, and most Russian peasants lived in nine national districts. Like their Ukrainian counterparts, they resisted collectivization and by 1932 those in all the Russian national districts were starving. The 1932 famine was also unique in that it affected cities as well as villages. Thus various cities were facing crises: Kyiv, Berdyakhiv, Zhytomyr, Uman, Zaporizhzhya, and others. He challenges the perspective that Jews occupied the prominent party and government posts and played some role in organizing the Famine by observing that they were also sufferers, but also somewhat absurdly participates in this discussion by suggesting that Russians and Ukrainians occupied more of such positions than Jews.[64] This article overall seems to contradict his earlier contribution to the debate in that it suggests that the Famine may well have been directed primarily against Ukrainians, but affected other groups by the simple factor of geography; that these peoples happened to be in the locality and therefore suffered as well. On the other hand, a regime that intended to eradicate Ukrainians for their nationalist views, or for their potential alliance with the Poles, might have taken steps not to alienate other national groups living in the republic. In general, this question has received little attention from historians and requires a fuller treatment.

Anti-Semitic Tracts

The following section looks at some selected articles that are anti-Semitic in tone. Their inclusion does not denote such items as typical or representative of a prevailing view. However, they have been frequent enough to merit attention, and through institutions such as MAUP, publications and conferences in Ukraine sometimes contain a mixture of academic and virulently extremist articles that tend to target Jews.[65] The most notable example with regard to the Famine was a collection issued by MAUP from a conference on the Famine-Genocide, which included two overtly anti-Semitic articles within a generally scholarly and objective collection.[66] These papers were also issued as individual publications and distributed in bookstores in Ukraine's major cities at the time of the 70th anniversary of the Famine. MAUP depicts itself as one of Ukraine's largest higher educational institutions, but has hosted such extremist luminaries as the US activist David Duke, who was teaching in Kyiv at the time of writing. Thus, although peripheral, the anti-Semitic trend in the writing of Ukrainian history cannot be omitted altogether. Among anti-Semitic writings, those on the Famine are probably the most notable in that they attempt to assemble a theory that Jews, as a group, were behind the Famine, which they used as an instrument to undermine and eliminate Ukrainians. Here we will cite several examples, most of which emanate from the former L'viv newspaper, *Za vil'nu Ukrainu*, one of the more outspoken nationalist sources of the 1990s, although there are other isolated articles that appeared elsewhere as well.

An article by Vasyl Mazorchuk on genocide in the black-earth regions is ostensibly about the motives behind the maltreatment of Ukrainians, but it also has a strong political component. He believes there was a serious danger that Ukrainian lands would be sold off to foreigners, leaving Ukrainians without a native land. He lists 13 decrees of the CC CPU and the Ukrainian government that determined the course of genocide. Often he misuses quotations to offer meanings that seem to have no basis in reality; for example, his interpretation of a comment of Ukraine's Minister of Agriculture, that the population growth would result in a surplus of 5 million people of working age to mean that these people had been singled out for destruction. As for the perpetrators of the Famine, Mazorchuk singles out people from Stalin's ruling circle, as well as President Franklin D. Roosevelt of the USA, a man who was a mason since 1911, adds the author. The US president failed to provide economic assistance to the starving. The concluding section of the article discusses the ways in which Ukrainians are being oppressed in their own country by "cosmopolitans" (a familiar euphemism for Jews used in the Stalin period) and foreigners. He maintains that the section indicating "nationality" was removed from Ukrainian passports in order to conceal the foreign takeover of key posts in the government and local administration of the country.[67]

Even more inflammatory in tone is an article by Pavlo Chemerys from September 1993, which overtly lays the blame for the 1932–33 Famine on Jews.

He concludes by stating that in 1932-33, Jews occupied 80-100% of the leading positions in the USSR and ruled the country "despotically." He cites the books of US Senator Jack Finney, which purport to show that Zionist billionaires made an agreement with the Soviet government to deport Ukrainians from their native land and populate it with Jews. Since the mass shootings, arrests, and deportations of Ukrainians to Siberia were proceeding too slowly, these same people advised the regime to organize a famine that killed 12 [!] million people. The Jewish claims to Ukraine, Chemerys continues, date back 1,000 years. Persecuted in Byzantium in the 8th century, they moved to Crimea. From 1917 this migration accelerated, and a special "joint agro" committee was established for the colonization of Crimea and Southern Ukraine headed by Lewis Marshall, Meier London, and Felix Warburg. He also maintains that after the Second World War, the Jewish Anti-Fascist Committee demanded from Stalin Southern Ukraine and Crimea for Jewish settlement. The political problems in Crimea at the time Chemerys wrote the article are also attributed to Jewish agitation.[68] Though it seems unnecessary to analyze or discount the comments in this far-fetched article, it is worth reiterating that in the southern regions of Ukraine, as already noted by other authors, Jews suffered from the Famine on a substantial scale.

Chemerys returned to this same theme three years later in an article that begins with quotations from the Tora, Talmud, and the fabricated Protocols of the Elders of Zion, in which plans for world domination are elaborated by "Judeo-Zionists." He outlines the onset of death and famine in many parts of the Soviet Union, and asks a rhetorical question: "Why did they take all the grain? Did enemies threaten us? No. On the contrary capitalism was going through the most severe crisis in its history." Bread requisitions turned into a war with the peasantry in the Soviet Union. The explanation, says the author, is simple. Having attained absolute power in the disguise of Bolshevism, the Judeo-Zionists started to implement their Tora-Talmudic program for the total destruction of alien people. In his postscript, Chemerys accuses Judeo-Zionists of organizing revolutions, two world wars, terror, and the Famine.[69] The same newspaper also cited extensively an article in the Canadian newspaper, the *Edmonton Sun*, in 1999 on the Famine as genocide, even though that article never suggested in any way that Jews were responsible for this event. Author Erik Margolis had also dwelled on the massive reprisals in the Baltic States, deportation of Germans, and persecution of Muslims in the USSR as well as the Famine, blaming the concealment of the latter on the predominance of left-wing public opinion in the wake of German aggression in Europe. Margolis, Chemery editorializes, "is himself a Jew... and Jewish authors themselves cannot deny the truth of history."[70]

What is this "truth of history" as defined by this former L'viv newspaper? It is that the Jews had penetrated the higher echelons of the Communist Party and the NKVD. For publishing such statements, says one of the editors in this same issue of the newspaper, they were categorized unambiguously as anti-Semitic and periodically harassed by complaints from below and calls to the office of the Prosecutor-General.[71] The same theme is also to be found in a quasi-academic article by a "Professor" Pavlo Skochii, who also presents the Famine as artificial and the article begins with a Preface, which declares that the aim of the genocide was to free the land of Ukraine for a future state, the New Jerusalem, for which world Jewry had amassed a sum of $139 million by 1929. Having made these comments, the remainder of the article is a straight-forward account of the Famine from the genocide-theory perspective, which leads to the suspicion that the Preface was written by another author—possibly Chemerys—that was simply tacked on to the account by Skochii.[72] Like the widely circulated newspaper *Sil's'ki visti* in 2004, which was suspended after a series of anti-Semitic articles, *Za vil'nu Ukrainu* was eventually closed down, ostensibly in part because of its degeneration into a nationalist and anti-Semitic pamphlet that pandered to the most extreme views. One could dismiss these views as peripheral to the analysis of the Famine but for the fact that they appear with some regularity, and works by authors propagating such views can still be found quite easily in major bookstores in cities such as Kyiv and Kharkiv. The quest to find culprits for the Famine has sometimes resulted in simplistic and deeply wounding accusations against the Jews, a small minority group in contemporary Ukraine, but one with a lengthy history.

James E. Mace

The US-born historian James E. Mace will always be identified with the study of the Famine in Ukraine, a subject that appeared as a chapter in his PhD thesis (later a 1983 book)[73] and, was the hallmark of his career that began as chairman of the US Commission on the Ukraine Famine in the period 1984–88. However, Mace is unique in that in addition to being influential in determining the prevailing discourse on the Famine in contemporary Ukraine, he is also a representative of both Western scholarship (some would argue of the Ukrainian Diaspora, too) and the Ukrainian media. Through the Famine Commission's conclusions, Mace was the first Western scholar to maintain that the Famine was an act of genocide perpetrated against the Ukrainians as a nation, a statement that was also supported by his PhD thesis/book with its focus on national self-assertion in Ukraine during the 1920s and early 1930s. According to his close friend and colleague Stanislav Kul'chyts'kyi, Mace was unable to get a permanent academic position in the United States because of his outspoken views on the Famine.[74] There is little evidence to support such a statement—indeed Mace acquired the prestigious position of Research Fellow at the Center for Russian and East European Studies at the University of Illinois once the Famine Commission completed its work—but it is clear that Mace had strong disagreements with a number of Western scholars working in the area of the first Soviet collectivization campaign who disputed his views and those of the Commission on a number of occasions.

Mace visited Ukraine in 1990 and moved there permanently in 1993. Though affiliated with a university, his most notable writings were those contributed to the editorial pages of the newspaper *Den'*, which appears in Ukrainian, Russian, and English. Mace was thus able to write in his native language and at the same time reach a Ukrainian audience through the translated version. His columns coincided with a period when historians and the general public in Ukraine were inquisitive to know more about the Famine. As Kul'chyts'kyi has noted, Mace's focus on the national question in the Famine added a new dimension to the topic. Gradually—and it is a factor that is difficult to measure precisely—historians in Ukraine came closer to the views propagated by Mace. This was a process that might have occurred without the latter's presence, but there is little doubt that his writings accelerated matters. Mace died prematurely in May 2004 at the age of 52, and at a time when the program to commemorate the Famine as a national tragedy in Ukraine was reaching a culmination point. His death was marked as a national tragedy and Mace was regarded as a figure irrevocably tied to Ukraine. His contributions to the discourse on the Famine are significant in two areas: first, his relentless emphasis on the national issues as the key factor; and second, his recourse on several occasions to emotional aspects linked to national memory. It appears that this latter issue had the widest appeal, and it is a notable feature of his later writings, in which he would regularly cite his past experiences with Famine victims, as well as those of his protracted disputes with Western scholars who opposed his point of view. Let us recount a few examples of these writings as illustrative of Mace's contribution to the debate on the Famine.

In May 2002, Mace commented that as the 70th anniversary of the Famine approached, "presumably tenured professors" from the United States were once again engaged in a discussion with comments that it never occurred or no one had wanted it to occur, without looking at the evidence available. Such comments, he added bitterly, were even appearing in prestigious journals of

Slavic studies.[75] Later in this same year Mace recounted that in 1981, the Ukrainian Research Institute at Harvard University approached him to take up study of the topic of the Ukrainian Famine. Later he became the director of the US Commission, but the "silence was deafening." The first assault on his views came in 1985 from the British-born economist Stephen Wheatcroft, who informed Mace that his "sums were off." However, writes Mace, the real sin he had committed was to connect the destruction of the Ukrainian peasants with that of the nation as a whole. In so doing, according to Wheatcroft, he had debased the field of Soviet studies. Mace makes an appeal to history, to be the judge, and declares that the history of Ukraine will be manufactured in that country as part of the creation of the state. He then reverts back to his tormentors. Though numerous eyewitnesses had appeared to give testimony about the Famine some twenty years earlier, now the American historian Mark Tauger was declaring that such testimony was not reliable, even when there were thousands of such witnesses. Why were Mace's views so unacceptable in his homeland? His belief is that studies of the USSR were under the control of people who once condemned totalitarianism but now seem linked to the notion of the "great friendship of Soviet peoples."[76]

Mace denounced Western scholarship for viewing the Soviet period as a single history rather than one of individual nations. In turn, he praised then President Leonid Kuchma for declaring that Ukraine must inform the world of the truth of the events of 1933. It is correct, Mace stated, to link the Famine with the general period of repressions. When Stalin dispatched Kaganovich to the North Caucasus, he [Stalin] made it clear that the difficulties lay in the Ukrainian-speaking regions. In December 1932, Molotov, who had been sent to Ukraine, blamed the failure to collect sufficient grain on Ukrainian nationalism. Tauger, on the other hand, places the blame on a bad harvest "that no one who lived through it seems to have remembered."[77] According to Mace, the Famine must be explained in terms of the totalitarian paradigm—another theme later taken up by his mentor Kul'chyts'kyi—as a consequence of the "zoological anti-peasant hatred of Lenin and Trotsky" and Stalin's continuation of the same tradition. This was a war with Ukraine, he continues in a leap in logic. To an interviewer's question as to why Stalin remained popular to the extent that people mourned on the day he died, Mace responds that the mourning was ritualistic and that the cult of Stalin continues to exist in the contemporary era. Turning to Ukrainian society, Mace refers to it as "post-genocidal," indicating that the survivors of that period remain too afraid to divulge their memories. However, says Mace, memories are the critical factor in order for Ukrainian society to recover from its brutal past.[78]

One suggestion offered by Mace was for residents of Ukraine to light a candle in their windows on a national day of commemoration of the Famine. This idea, which was eventually taken up by many (including President Yushchenko), is perhaps the most apposite example of this historian's focus on the emotional side of the Famine and its memory. One writer considered that the proposal should contribute toward the national idea of the unity of the Ukrainian people, a people that should be living an existence merited by a large European nation with a rich culture.[79] At one point Mace declared that the Famine was a tragedy that had long "weighed like a stone on my heart." As an editor of oral histories in his capacity as director of the US Commission, he had shared the suffering of those who were victims of the tragedy. Though it might be regarded as unusual for an historian to become so emotionally involved in the issues he studies, it was impossible for him to respond otherwise, just as people could not study the Holocaust without being moved to the stage at which one's spirit becomes "half-Jewish." Perhaps, continues Mace with regard to his residence in Ukraine "this is why I now live here and spend so much of my energy trying to understand what was done to this people and what scars from it this country still bears." Again, the reference to a post-genocidal society is offered: Ukraine is a country that still carries "the psychological and physical scars of genocide." Such a dilemma, and the failure of residents to extricate themselves from it, is the only way to explain the disgraceful things that appear in the press, Mace writes. Sometimes he wonders whether the country "will ever be whole."[80]

In an interview on the Maidan website, Mace was asked two questions: "How did the study of famine change your world view? Do you think the famine belongs only to the past, to just [sic!] history?" He responded to the first question by recalling how like many people of his generation (he was born in 1952) he used to have left-wing political views, but he had recognized how slogans advocating social justice could lead to horrors similar to those generated by a Fascist system. His reply to the second question is worth quoting in full:

I think that these 2 questions should be answered together. The very phrase "just history" leads to a mistake. Every person, every community, every nation, mankind as a whole is the result of its own personal history. But what happened in Ukraine in 1933 and in the 30s overall caused a fundamental breakdown in the normal course of development of a European nation. In this sense we can refer to Ukraine as a post-genocidal society in which there is no agreement as to the basic national values, a problem which does not exist in most European countries.[81]

Mace is probably not on solid ground in offering analogies with other European nations. First of all one would have to accept his view that Ukraine was actually a nation in 1933, which makes the assumption that the processes of the 1920s had reached a critical point and distinguished Ukraine from the Soviet Union. Second, one could make a similar argument about Germany after the First World War or during the interwar years, for example. Third, though the losses in Ukraine in the 1930s were catastrophic, the same argument could be made about Belarus, a Slavic republic that arguably never recovered from the elimination of its cultural and national leadership in the 1930s. However, the key point is that Mace was offering a new interpretation of Ukraine's recent history, with the Famine as the pivotal event, and tragedy and suffering as the hallmarks of Ukraine's Soviet experience, an experience in which there were two clearly delineated sides namely the Soviet government (and Communist Party) in Moscow, and the national leadership as reflected by figures such as Skrypnyk, and by the Ukrainian peasantry as a whole. The role of the CPU, the ostensible leadership of Ukraine at this time in Kharkiv, is somewhat unclear from this analysis. The interpretation offered by Mace might well have been developed further but for his untimely death. However, it was taken up by two different generations of Ukrainian historians led by Kul'chyts'kyi, who had also pioneered some of the early attempts to have the Famine recognized as a national tragedy and one that merited not only deeper study, but as the pivotal event in the creation of the Ukrainian state.

Kul'chyts'kyi's Analysis, 2005

In 2005, Kul'chyts'kyi once again returned to the issue of the Famine with a six-part series in the newspaper *Den'*, which refined his earlier works and offered a new perspective on why Stalin killed Ukrainians. The title makes it evident that he had rejected some of his earlier views on the economic foundations of the Famine, but the articles tried to cover the whole background to the Famine as the author perceives it. Throughout the paper, which runs to more than 55 pages of text, Kul'chyts'kyi is anxious to portray himself as one steeped in the Soviet period, who had to dispense with past views in order to reach his current understanding. At the same time, he rather ungraciously dismisses those who did not live through the Soviet experience as being unable to reach the same level of understanding. Throughout the articles, he makes reference to Mace, his junior by a generation, and it is evident that his discussions with the transplanted American caused him to revise his views, adding new elements that he felt were critical to the overall picture. That said, it should be remarked from the outset that Kul'chyts'kyi's new analysis is disappointing in its failure to answer the question that he poses in the title. By the end of the narrative, the reader emerges with a picture scarcely clearer than that with which he began. Let us look at each of the six parts in turn.

Part one begins with a rather unusual plea to historians, namely that they "must" reach the legal and political conclusion "that the Holodomor was an act of genocide." They must take on such a task, in Kul'chyts'kyi's opinion, because politicians failed, in that the Third Committee of the UN General Assembly did not make it explicit that the Soviet regime exterminated Ukrainians. Its conclusion was founded on the testimony of survivors rather than documents. Earlier some progress had been made in this regard after the World Congress of Free Ukrainians prompted the convening in 1989 of an international commission to investigate the causes of mass famine in Ukraine. Led by Professor Jacob Sundberg, the commission concluded that the causes were collectivization and the concomitant elimination of the *kulak* sector, as well as the government's intention to eliminate "traditional Ukrainian nationalism." It declared the Famine to be an act of genocide. However, the question of the perpetrators of this genocide had been distorted, writes Kul'chyts'kyi, by activists such as Levko Lukyanenko, chairman of an association of Holodomor researchers, who unjustifiably expanded the Kremlin to the city of Moscow in his general denunciation of "Muscovites." Kul'chyts'kyi implicitly links such comments to attempts by individuals to further their careers, observing that the difficult past, rather than uniting a nation, has served to divide it. Citing Mace's phrase about a "post-genocidal society" in Ukraine, he maintains that people of his generation have yet to comprehend that the civilization in which they lived most of their lives was constructed on the bones of the previous generation.[82]

In Part 2, Kul'chyts'kyi notes that leaders of the outside world were made aware of the tragedy in Ukraine but for various reasons they chose to keep silent. Among the main culprits in this regard were the Italian dictator, Benito Mussolini, and US President Franklin D. Roosevelt. Some observers confuse the situation in 1932 and that in 1933, the author continues. In the former, there was no genocidal famine. Some 144,000 people died from hunger in that year, but the government tried to assist the hungry by supplying additional grain. In 1933, however, the situation was very different, and the government tried to conceal the Famine. In the West, there were some channels of information. One was through the US newspaper for Ukrainians, *Svoboda*.

Another was through the journalistic endeavors of Malcolm Muggeridge, who published the findings of his unsanctioned trip through Eastern Ukraine in the *Manchester Guardian*. This same newspaper also carried an article by a former aide to Lloyd George, the Prime Minister of Britain during the First World War, Gareth Jones. These reports were offset by the editorials of the notorious Walter Duranty, the *New York Times* correspondent in Moscow. In particular, an article penned by Duranty and published on 31 March 1933 denied explicitly that there were any hunger problems in "Russia" (Duranty never used the term Ukraine). Only some fifty years later did the US Famine Commission led by James Mace and Leonid Herets provide new insights, which they attained by "developing methods that made it possible to ensure the objectivity" of the testimonies provided by witnesses—irritatingly, the author never says what these methods were.[83]

Part 3 begins with another apparent non-sequitur: Kul'chyts'kyi states that Soviet historians began to recognize Soviet stereotypes and reject them, "which enabled them to elicit the true cause-and-effect relationships in the problem of the Holodomor." But were Soviet stereotypes the only problem in studying the Famine? He describes how he found himself on an anti-Famine commission established by the Communist Party of Ukraine in the fall of 1986, but sent a report demanding that the tragedy be recognized officially. It is necessary today, he continues, to cease playing on emotions and deal with facts that can be supported. In this respect, the national aspect needs to be highlighted. The first figure of note to pay attention to the national issues in Ukraine, he adds, was the writer Yurii Shcherbak. In July 1988, the Writers' Union of Ukraine gave Volodymyr Manyak the task of preparing a commemorative book containing the testimonies of Famine survivors, though the initiative for this project came from Maniak himself. Maniak, with the backing of the Writers' Union, sought the support of the Institute of History, and the two agencies joined forces to produce a large book of memories entitled *Famine 1933: the People's Memorial Book*, under the editorship of Maniak and his wife Lidiya Kovalenko. A second book was commissioned with the approval of the then Ukrainian Party leader (1989–90), Volodmyr Ivashko, *Famine of 1932-1933 in Ukraine: through the eyes of Historians and the Language of Documents*, published in September 1990 by Politvydav Ukrainy for the Institute of Party History of the CC CPU. A third volume of note appeared in March 1991 under Kul'chyts'kyi's authorship, and was entitled *Tsina velykoho perelomu*, though the author laments his failure to take into account the national question.[84]

In Part 4, he recounts how he and two younger colleagues published the book *Stalinism in Ukraine*, which he feels probably had a limited impact on people of his generation. In general, the impact of the Famine on Ukrainian society is dependent on the actions and propaganda of the state, he feels. A good beginning was made following the August 1991 declaration of independence by the Ukrainian Parliament, when "sovereign communists" led by Leonid Kravchuk tried to persuade voters that they had made the correct decision by using information about the horrors of the Holodomor. However, in the ensuing fifteen years, the Ukrainian leaders have not proved willing to support the republication of the three volumes of testimony gathered by the Mace Commission. The question of Russia is also dealt with in this section and Kul'chyts'kyi commendably offers both a warning against stereotyping of Russian perspectives and an explanation of how the official commemoration of World War II as a Russian legacy has led Russian officials to throw a cloak over Stalin's crimes. This section also includes comments on Conquest and Mace, again including the statement that Mace was unable to find employment in the United States. Kul'chyts'kyi relates also how a revisionist school in the West, including Wheatcroft, R. W. Davies, and Lynne Viola, has rejected the Famine as genocide theory, even though it was upheld at an important international conference in Vicenza, Italy, in October 2003, which was attended by Ukrainian and Russian historians, as well as Italians.[85]

The fifth and sixth parts of the lengthy series are by far the least satisfactory. Part 5 opens positively when Kul'chyts'kyi states that he cannot restrict his analysis to the socio-economic and national dimensions of the genocide, but must also encompass the ideological dimension. He then offers a lengthy and largely superfluous analysis of the Russian Revolution and its aftermath in a quest to emphasize the responsibility of Lenin for its consequences (a task already undertaken on several occasions by Western historians such as Conquest). Collectivization, he continues, was impossible without repressions, but why did Stalin choose the most repressive of measures, namely terror by famine? The reader is hard pressed to discern how this statement links with Kul'chyts'kyi's main thesis. However, Part 6 fails to elucidate this question and instead offers a protracted narrative on the familiar ground of collectivization and its consequences, repeating the citation of Stalin's 11 August 1932 letter to Kaganovich about agents of Pilsudski working in Ukraine. The goal of Stalin's terror, he concludes, "was to educate people by murdering them." His two orders were to halt the Skrypnyk measures to move Ukraine away from Russia, and second, to save those peasants who could still take part in the sowing campaign. He has not included everything he might have said, the author ends, but "what has been said will suffice to refute the superficial arguments of opponents of the idea of the Holodomor as an act of genocide."[86]

One suspects that these opponents will hardly have been overawed by the conclusions and analysis contained in this article.

Kul'chyts'kyi's lack of clarity, nevertheless, is an apt reflection of the position of both the Ukrainian government and Ukrainian society on the issue of the Famine and its role as a key event in the modern state. One can draw three main conclusions. First, the Famine of 1932–33 has not yet attained the sort of status in Ukraine that is warranted by the scale of the event and the suffering incurred. Its political implications are evident. Recognition of the Famine as an act of genocide has already alienated some Russians, and the Russian government has declined to accept any responsibility for what occurred under the Soviet leadership. Ukrainians of Communist or pro-Soviet orientation are unwilling to accept the designation of the Famine as genocide because of the highly negative coloration it applies to the history of Ukraine under Soviet rule. The divergence of views on 20th century Ukrainian history is aptly illustrated by the Kharkiv Museum of History, which in the summer of 2003 held an exhibit of the Famine on the first floor, highly critical of Soviet policies, and another on the second floor highlighting the "liberation" of the city by the Red Army and the restoration of Soviet rule after the removal of the occupying Germans. The broad differences in perspective were illustrated by the electoral distinctions manifested in Ukraine at the time of the 2004 presidential election, when during the re-voting of the second round, eastern regions continued to support the candidacy of Viktor Yanukovich, who advocated among other things closer ties to Russia and the elevation of Russian as the second language of Ukraine.

Second, there remain wide gaps between the perception of the Famine among the Ukrainian Diaspora, non-Diaspora Western scholars, and popular opinion in various parts of Ukraine. Ironically it is in Western Ukraine, an area untouched by the Famine, as it was not under Soviet rule until the outset of the Second World War, that the Famine-Genocide concept is most readily accepted because in Western Ukraine national discourse laced with a distinctly anti-Russian hue has a long history—a factor discussed at some length in Kul'chyts'kyi's article. Though Diaspora views on the Famine are more widely accepted in Ukraine today, they are far from representing a consensus. In the West, one can say that the two sides are as far apart as ever, i.e., the schools of thought represented by US or British academics (such as Mark Tauger or Stephen Wheatcroft) on one hand; and Diaspora scholars (such as Roman Serbyn and George Liber) and non-Diaspora scholars formerly known for their anti-Soviet views (such as Robert Conquest) on the other. James Mace's quest to unite Ukrainian views and perspectives on the Famine has had an impact, but it has not been an unqualified success, as the apparent disinterested voting in the Ukrainian Parliament on this issue reflects. Third, various aspects of the Famine have been well covered by Ukrainian academics, including eyewitness accounts and collections of documents that are now appearing at the regional level. However, the metamorphosis from academic text to school curriculum has been both slow and hesitant, as exemplified by the appearance of new national textbooks on Ukrainian history. The 70th anniversary may thus have been a landmark, but one can posit that only with the 75th anniversary in 2008 will some of these issues and debates be resolved, and only after heated discussions.

Notes

1   Stanislav Kul'chyts'kyi, "Skeletons in the Closet in the Light of Perestroika," *Den'; The Day Weekly Digest*, 4 December 2001; [http://www.day.kiev.ua/268404/].

2   Mark Tol'ts, "Skol'ko zhe nas togda bylo?" *Ogonyok*, No. 51 (December 1987): 10–11.

3   Stanislav Kul'chyts'kyi, "Pam'yat' pro trydtsyat' tretii," *Istoriya Ukrainy*, No. 24 (June 1998): 4.

4   Stanislav Kul'chyts'kyi, "Do otsinky stanovyshcha v sil's'komu hospodarstvi URSS u 1931–1938 rr." *Ukrains'kyi istorychnyi zhurnal*, No. 3 (March 1988): 16.

5   Ibid.

6   Ibid., p. 17.

7   Ibid., p. 22.

8   Ibid., pp. 24–25.

9   Dr. Yurii Shcherbak, a medical doctor and writer, was a founder and former chairman of the Ukrainian ecological association Green World, as well as the Green Party of Ukraine. He has served as Ukraine's ambassador to Israel, the United States, and Canada.

10 V. Savel'ev, "V poiske istiny: k voprosy o prichinakh goloda 1932–1933 godov na Ukrainy," *Pravda Ukrainy*, 8 July 1989, p. 2.

11 See, for example, Yar Slavutych, "Holodomor buv splanovanyi," *Za vil'nu Ukrainu*, 3 November 1990, p. 2. Slavutych, a professor emeritus at the University of Alberta, is a famine survivor.

12 Grigoriy Koinash, "Etot strashnyi 32-i," *L'vovs'kaya pravda*, 15 May 1990, p. 3.

13 Viktor Polozhin, "Fil'm 'Holod-33' u roboti," *Literaturna Ukraina*, 21 March 1991, p. 6.

14 Yelena Pozdnyakova, "Narodnyi fil'm: Snimayut ukrainskiye kinematografisty o golode 1933 goda," *Pravda Ukrainy*, 13 June 1991, p. 3.

15 Volodymyr Tatarenko, "A koshty peredaty zhertvam...," *Literaturna Ukraina*, 20 June 1991, p. 2.

16 Commission on the Ukraine Famine, *Report to Congress: Investigation of the Ukraine Famine 1932-1933* (Washington, D.C.: Government Printing Office, 1988), p. vii.

17 Stanislav Kul'chyts'kyi, "Vitchyznyana istoriya u shkolakh i VNZ Ukrainy: ostannye desyatyrichchya," in *Istoriya Ukrainy*, No. 15 (2003): 3. See also Stanislav Kul'chyts'kyi,

"Nerozv'yazani problemy vykladannya istorii u serednii shkoli," in *Istoriya Ukrainy*, No. 11 (1998): 1-2.

18 Orest Subtelny, *Ukraine: A History*, 3rd edition (Toronto: University of Toronto Press, 2000), p. 415.

19 Cited in Serhiy Makhun, et al, "History as Taught in Schools: time to decide," *Den'; The Day Weekly Digest*, 14 October 2003; [http://www.day.kiev.ua/261121/].

20 Stanislav Kul'chyts'kyi, "Mizh dvoma viinamy (1921-1941 rr.)," *Ukrains'kyi istorychnyi zhurnal*, No. 9 (September 1991): 3-17.

21 Stanislav Kul'chyts'kyi, "Mizh dvoma viinamy (1921-1941 rr.)," p. 6.

22 Stanislav Kul'chyts'kyi, "Mizh dvoma viinamy (1921-1941 rr.)," p. 7.

23 Yurii Shapoval, "Stalinizm i Ukraina," *Ukrains'kyi istorychnyi zhurnal*, No. 8 (August 1991): 32.

24 Vitol'd Kyrylyuk, "Chas hromadyty kaminnya: rozmova s holovoyu Ukrains'koi asotsiatsii "Holod-33" Lidiyeyu Kovalenko-Manyak," *Literaturna Ukraina*, 6 August 1992, p. 2.

25 Ivan Drach, "Henotsyd Ukrainy—vyklyk XX stolittya," *Literaturna Ukraina*, 3 September 1992, p. 3.

26 Ivan Drach, "Henotsyd Ukrainy—vyklyk XX stolittya," p. 1.

27 V. Kyrylyuk, "I vdaryat' dzvony pam'yati," *Literaturna Ukraina*, 25 March 1993, p. 1.

28 Vasyl Mazorchuk, "Henotsyd na Chornozemakh," *Osvita*, No. 21-22, (1993): 10-12.

29 Ivan Drach, "Chy pokaets'ya Rosiya?" in Taras Hunczak, ed. *Tysyacha rokiv Ukrains'-koi suspil'no-politychnoi dumky,"* Vol. 9 (1989-2001) (Kyiv: Dnipro, 2001), pp. 282, 284.

30 Vasyl Marochko, "Holodomor v Ukraini: prychyny i naslidky (1932-1933)," *Osvita*, No. 21-22, (1993): pp. 3-9.

31 Ibid.

32 Dmytro Brylins'kyi, "Ya perezhyv Holod," *Samostiina Ukraina*, No. 25, (June 1992): 3.

33 Oleksii Kuz'menko, "Na Holod pishly svidomo," *Osvita*, No. 21-22, (1993): 12.

34 Yaryna Mytsyk, "Holod u Vyshnopoli," *Osvita*, 10 September 1993, pp. 14-15.

35 Oles' Berdnyk, "Na rynkakh u Kyevi likari provodyly lektsii," *Za vil'nu Ukrainu*, 2 October 1993, p. 3.

36 Ivan Rudenko, "Trahediya Kozats'koho," *Za vil'nu Ukrainy*, 23 October 1993, p. 4.

37 Kateryna Marchenko, "Mama proty 'chervonoi' valky," *Ukraina moloda*, 26 June 2003, p. 11.

38 Tamara Ruchko, "A bratyk plakav, prosyv isty..." *Ukrains'ke slovo*," 24-30 July 2003, p. 13.

39 Stanislav Kul'chyts'kyi, "Pam'yat' pro trydtsat' tretii," *Istoriya Ukrainy*, No. 24 (June 1998): 4.

40 Ibid.

41 Mykhailo Hoyan, "Na rodyuchii zemli pomyraly khliboroby," *Ukraina moloda*, 8 September 1998, p. 12.

42 Dana Romanets', "Pochatkom 1937-ho roku v Ukraini stav 1933-i," *Ukraina moloda*, 1 December 2000, p. 5.

43 Yaroslava Muzychenko, "Z choho pochynalasya 'Rodina'?" *Ukraina moloda*, 17 May 2002, p. 5.

44 Yaroslava Muzychenko, "Holod proty voli," *Ukraina moloda*, 22 November 2002, p. 4.

45 M. Savchenko, "70-richchya holodomoru v Ukraini: metodychni porady do provedennya zakhodiv pam'yati zhertv holodomoru 1932-1933 rokiv v Ukraini," *Istoriya Ukrainy*, No. 3 (January 2003): 17-19.

46 Robert Conquest, *Harvest of Sorrow: Soviet Collectivization and the Terror-Famine* (New York: Oxford University Press, 1986). Conquest (b. 1916) is a British born academic and not of Ukrainian ancestry. As such he might more logically be included in group b) below. However, his work belongs more properly in the first group, as it was commissioned by a Ukrainian institute and specifically for the anniversary of the Famine of 1932-33.

47 The chairman of the commission and (as noted in Chapter 1) one of the initiators of the campaign was Dr. Lubomyr Y. Luciuk, a political geographer and professor at the Royal Military College of Canada.

48 On Duranty, see, for example, Sally J. Taylor, *Stalin's Apologist: Walter Duranty, the New York Times' Man in Moscow* (New York: Oxford University Press, 1990).

49 Though the distinction between academics of Ukrainian and non-Ukrainian ancestry is somewhat arbitrary I have opted to use it for convenience. In general, it is fair to say that there are several academics of non-Ukrainian ancestry who do not regard the Famine as genocide; whereas it is extremely rare to find an academic whose ancestry is Ukrainian of the same opinion. Conquest, perhaps the closest to the perspective of the genocide school, does not make such a specific attribution in his book *Harvest of Sorrow*.

50 See, for example, Mark B. Tauger, "The 1932 Harvest and the Soviet Famine of 1932–1933," *Slavic Review*, Vol. 50, No. 1 (Spring 1991): 70-89, and Tauger's attack on James E. Mace and Taras Kuzio: Mark B. Tauger, "What Caused Famine in Ukraine? A Polemical Response," *RFE/RL Poland, Belarus and Ukraine Report*, 25 June 2002; [http://www.rferl.org/reports/pbureport/2002/06/25-250602.asp].

51 Terry Martin, *The Affirmative Action Empire: Nations and Nationalism in the Soviet Union* (Ithaca, New York: Cornell University Press, 2001), p. 305.

52 Martin, who is preparing a book on the Ukrainian Famine, has since amended his views somewhat in the light of new archival evidence, noting that the nationalities factor in fact played a major role from 1932 in Stalin's thinking and policies. He cites a letter from Kaganovich to Stalin about the disruption of grain requisitions by "agents of counter-revolutionary Ukrainian organizations and Petlyurites" who were working alongside Pilsudski and other "agents of world imperialism." Terry Martin, "The Great Famine in Ukraine: New Documentation on the Thought Process of Stalin," paper presented at Harvard Ukrainian Research Institute, October 2003. Dr. Martin provided the author with a copy of this paper. Incidentally, Martin's revised view brings him closer to a scholar who can be associated with the Ukrainian Diaspora in the United States, George Liber. See George O. Liber, *Soviet Nationality Policy, Urban Growth, and Identity Change in the Ukrainian SSR 1923-1934* (Cambridge: Cambridge University Press, 1992), pp. 165-166.

53 Stanislav Kul'chyts'kyi, "Velykyi holod," *Istoriya v shkolakh Ukrainy*, No. 3 (2003): 51-52.

54 Ibid., p. 52.

55 Ibid.

56 Stanislav Kul'chyts'kyi, "Kryza kolhospnoho ladu," *Ukrains'kyi istorychnyi zhurnal*, No. 5 (May 2003): 5-25, and especially page 11.

57 Yurii Shapoval, "The Famine of 1932-33 in Ukraine: What do we know about it today?" Paper presented at the Ukrainian Youth Centre in Edmonton, Canada, 16 November 2003.

58 V. M. Danylenko and M. M. Kuz'menko, "Naukovo-pedahohichna intelihentsiya v roky holodu," *Ukrains'kyi istorychnyi zhurnal*, No. 5 (May 2003): 145-155.

59 Vasyl Marochko, "Holodomor v Ukraini: prychyny i naslidky (1932-1933)," *Osvita*, No. 21 (1993): 3-9.

60 Yakov Konigsman, "Golodomor 1933 goda i upadok yevreiskogo zemledeliya," *Evreiskiye vesti*, No. 17-18 (September 1993): 4.

61 Ibid.

62 Etia Shatnaya, "Pod rodnym nebom," *Evreiskiye vesti*, No. 21-22 (November 1993): 15.

63 Iosif Shaikin, "Na yuge Ukrainy," *Evreiskiye vesti*, No. 1-2 (January 1994): 6.

64 Vasyl Marochko, "Holod u natsional'nykh rayonakh Ukrainy," *Evreiskiye vesti*, No. 15-16 (August 1996): 1-2.

65 See, for example, the article by my PhD student at the University of Alberta: Per Anders Rudling, "Organized Anti-Semitism in Contemporary Ukraine: Structure, Influence, and Ideology," *Canadian Slavonic Papers*, Vol. 48, No. 1-2 (March-June 2006): 81-118.

66 V. M. Chyrkov, ed., *Holodomor 1932-33 rokiv yak velychezna trahediya ukrains'koho narodu* (Kyiv: MAUP, 2003).

67 Vasyl Mazorchuk, "Henotsyd na Chornozemakh," *Osvita*, No. 22, (1993) 10-14.

68 Pavlo Chemerys, "Nasha plata 'nayvnym'...," *Za vil'nu Ukrainu*, 11 September 1993, p. 3.

69 Pavlo Chemerys, "Operatsiya Holod," *Za vil'nu Ukrainu*, 28 September 1996, p. 2.

70 Erik Margolis, "Zhaduyuchy nevidomyi holokost Ukrainy," *Za vil'nu Ukrainu*, 6 February 1999, p. 2.

71 Ibid.

72 Pavlo Skochii, "Nadislannyi tsar-holod," *Za vil'nu Ukrainu*, 9 April 1998, p. 2.

73 James E. Mace, *Communism and the Dilemmas of National Liberation: National Communism in Soviet Ukraine, 1918-1933* (Cambridge, Mass: distributed by Harvard University for the Harvard Ukrainian Research Institute and the Ukrainian Academy of Arts and Sciences in the U. S., 1983).

74 Stanislav Kul'chyts'kyi, "Why did Stalin exterminate the Ukrainians?" *The Day Digest*, No. 37 (22 November 2005). As noted above, Taras Kuzio has made the same assertion.

75 James Mace, "Denying the undeniable," *Den'; The Day Weekly Digest*, 28 May 2002; [http://www.day.kiev.ua/259000/].

76 James Mace, "Dealing with 1933," *Den'; The Day Weekly Digest*, 12 November 2002; [http://www.day.kiev.ua/259745/].

77 James Mace, "Truth and Fact," *Den'; The Day Weekly Digest*, 26 November 2002, [http://day.kiev.ua/259821/].

78 Ruslana Pisots'ka, "Inodi treba vse zhadaty, shchob vyduzhaty," *Ukraina moloda*, 4 March 2003, p. 5.

79 Tetyana Nykytyuk, "A candle lit in memory and hope," *Den'; The Day Weekly Digest*, 25 March 2003, [http://day.kiev.ua/260363/].

80 James Mace, "Facing past suffering," *Den'; The Day Weekly Digest*, 28 November 2000; [http://www.day.kiev.ua/266745/].

81 "Internet-konferentsiya Dzheymsa Meysa," [http://www.maidan.org.ua], 11 February 2003.

82 Stanislav Kul'chyts'kyi, "Why did Stalin exterminate the Ukrainians?" *Den'; The Day Weekly Digest*, Number 33, 25 October 2005; [http://www.day.kiev.ua/151228/].

83 Stanislav Kul'chyts'kyi, "Why did Stalin exterminate the Ukrainians? Comprehending the Holodomor," *Den'; The Day Weekly Digest*, Number 34, 1 November 2005; [http://www.day.kiev.ua/151682/].

84 Stanislav Kul'chyts'kyi, "Why did Stalin exterminate the Ukrainians: Comprehending the Holodomor. The position of Soviet historians," *Den'; The Day Weekly Digest*, 8 November 2005; [http://www.day.kiev.ua/152116/].

85 Stanislav Kul'chyts'kyi, "Why did Stalin exterminate the Ukrainians: Comprehending the Holodomor. The position of Soviet historians," *Den; The Day Weekly Digest*, 22 November 2005; [http://www.day.kiev.ua/153028/].

86 Stanislav Kul'chyts'kyi, "Why did Stalin exterminate the Ukrainians? Socioeconomic and national dimensions of the Famine," *Den'; The Day Weekly Digest*, 6 December 2005; [http://www.day.kiev.ua/153901/].

CHAPTER 3

THE OUN, 1929–43

Introduction

This chapter analyzes discourse and writings on the Organization of Ukrainian Nationalists (OUN), founded in 1929 in the territories of Ukraine that were included in Poland as a result of the Paris Peace treaties that followed the First World War. The OUN offered an extreme nationalist perspective somewhat similar to parties in various East European states in the interwar period, though it is compared most frequently with Mussolini's version of Fascism in Italy. Through the writings of Dmytro Dontsov, a mentor rather than a member, the theory it embraced is known as "integral nationalism." Though forced into an illegal existence, the OUN became popular in the ethnically Ukrainian territories of Galicia, particularly in the 1930s. In 1940, and following the 1938 assassination of its original leader Yevhen Konovalets', the OUN split into two bitterly opposed factions: an older group led by Andrii Mel'nyk and a more militant youthful faction under Stepan Bandera. After the war ended, further factions appeared in the emigration. The OUN represented a particularly contentious issue in the Soviet period because of its alleged collaboration with the Germans, as well as its association with the military organization of the Ukrainian Insurgent Army (UPA) after 1943. In the Soviet period, the OUN's members were regarded as traitors to the motherland, who preferred to side with the enemy during the greatest crisis in Soviet history. Most OUN publications appeared either in underground form or in the Diaspora, where the World War II generation constituted a highly politicized group in their new homelands in Europe, North America, and Australia.

Why is the OUN important in the development of a national history of Ukraine? It is precisely because it constituted the closest approximation to a national army on one hand, and through its consistent advocacy of an independent Ukraine on the other. For exactly this same reason, the group was always anathema to the Soviet authorities, and referred to by the derogatory, all-encompassing names of "Banderites" or "Ukrainian bourgeois nationalists." Soviet propaganda never made much effort to distinguish between the various factions of the OUN and generally linked the OUN and the UPA to-gether as one organization, even when describing periods of history prior to the formation of UPA. Entire generations grew up in the central and eastern parts of Ukraine believing that OUN-UPA was a treacherous organization that collaborated with the enemy throughout the course of the war, and then con-tinued to resist Soviet rule long afterward with the assistance of US and Brit-ish intelligence. On the other hand, generations deriving from the World War II group of émigrés that had moved to western countries were raised to believe that the OUN represented the interests of a substantial group of Ukrainians—perhaps even a majority in Western Ukraine—who boldly resisted not one, but two occupation forces in their homeland: Nazi Germany and totalitarian USSR under an equally malevolent dictator, Stalin.

In the next three chapters we will trace the history of the OUN and the UPA through Soviet and post-Soviet writings and examine the changing per-spectives, and how the government of Ukraine under Viktor Yushchenko sought to elevate the OUN-UPA to the rank of official war veterans and he-roes of the Second World War. Perhaps more than any other aspect of recent history, the subject of OUN-UPA continues to divide residents of Ukraine. On the occasion of the commemoration of the 60th anniversary of the Second World War, Red Army and UPA veterans were witnessed fighting in the streets of Kyiv. In addition to the confrontation with Soviet forces and the question of OUN-UPA's relationship with the occupation forces, which is dealt with in detail below, there are also two very thorny issues: the attitude of the OUN in its early phases to the Jewish population of Ukraine; and the mass slaughter by the OUN-UPA of the Polish population—the former ruling group—of Volhynia in 1943. As with the Famine, it is too early to state that a consensus has been reached on any of these subjects, but it is possible to dis-cern a radical change of perspective, particularly during the start of the sec-ond decade of Ukraine's independence. Though the opening of the Ukrainian archives has added appreciably to the picture of the OUN-UPA since the late 1980s, most of the articles that appear in newspapers and journals could be termed propagandistic, even those written by quite distinguished scholars. It is as though even highly educated Ukrainian historians or political scientists approach the subject from a certain viewpoint, which would be understand-able given the fact that virtually every family in Ukraine lost relatives in the war, while many had relatives sent to the Gulag (where OUN-UPA members made up a large proportion of the camp population, particularly the politi-cized sectors).

Writings of the Late Glasnost Period

To provide some examples of the flavor of late Soviet writings on OUN-UPA, one can turn to the main party newspaper in Western Ukraine, *L'vovs'kaya pravda*. In early 1988, the Communist perspective still held sway in the media and readers were still being regaled with horror stories about the crimes of Ukrainian nationalists. A fairly typical example was the story of a hero of the secret police, Fedor Ulanov, to whom a monument was erected in his native village of Ryhove, in the Turkivs'kyi district of the L'viv region on 14 February 1988. Ulanov was in charge of an MGB unit given the task of capturing alive a "Banderite" leader with the pseudonym of Roman, an operation that began on 16 February 1945. According to the story, four soldiers, together with Ulanov, reached the cottage where Roman was rumored to be hiding. However, only an old woman was found there, and recklessly the MGB allowed her outside her cottage, at which point the soldiers found themselves surrounded by insurgents, clearly forewarned by the old lady. One MGB soldier got trapped in the house covering the retreat of his comrades, and took his own life with his last bullet after killing an insurgent. Ulanov was left alone inside the cottage to face the insurgents. The latter set the cottage ablaze, and Ulanov emerged from the flames, shooting at them with a machine gun. However, he was captured and tortured with needles under his fingernails. He stoically resisted his tormentors, the article continues, and kept silent even though his body was eventually hacked to pieces. His last words—one wonders who recorded them!—were "God damn you animals! Long live Communism!"[1]

The articles often take on a highly moral tone, particularly when making reference to alleged war criminals now living abroad. Thus one related how the village assembly in Radekhiv district had called for the extradition of an OUN member, Ivan Stetsiv, a resident of Canada. This episode began when Ivanna Semenyuk from Ohlyadiv visited her father in Canada, to which he had emigrated in the 1930s. From her father she heard about the presence of Stetsiv, a name that was well-known to her from stories circulating in her native village. Stetsiv, the article noted, was born in 1916 and became a member of the OUN, fighting against Soviet forces as a member of an unspecified German formation. The writer accuses him of war crimes causing the deaths of peaceful citizens, women, and children. In August 1987 in Radekhiv there was an open trial of a man called R. Didukh, reportedly a collaborator of Stetsiv. In this hearing Didukh revealed that he had joined the OUN in 1941 and was recruited by Stetsiv. The latter ordered the execution of Ohlyadiv "activists" and allegedly tortured two young girls and killed a young male. He also, according to this account, burned an entire family in its home and massacred 21 Polish families in Kuty and was a "willing tool" of the German police. Following the trial Didukh was sentenced to death and the assembled throng appealed to the Canadian government to extradite Stetsiv.[2] The tale, gruesome though it may have been, was a fairly typical affair. Whether or not Stetsiv committed the crimes of which he was accused, the key issue for the authorities was to ensure that the villagers believed in such crimes and his and other nationalists' responsibility for them.

It was considered important for the Soviet leadership to discredit the OUN and the UPA in every way possible to try to limit their influence among the population of Western Ukraine. This goal was the main theme of a book by Klym Dmytruk, which attempted to expose the history and the class roots of "Ukrainian bourgeois nationalism" and its connections with "international imperialism." The two reviewers who discussed the volume in the pages of L'vovskaya pravda support Dmytruk's contention that Ukrainian nationalism is "the enemy of the Ukrainian people" and "a servant of German Fascism." Dmytruk also chronicles the Soviet struggle against OUN-UPA, including the creation of 292 "destruction battalions" with a total strength of 24,000.[3] In a similar vein, the newspaper Pravda Ukrainy ran a series of articles under the general title of "Banderovshchina" in the fall of 1989, a period when the media was becoming more open and the stereotypical perspective of the OUN-UPA became a topic for discussion. The early articles sought to counter "nationalist" claims that the UPA was a national liberation movement that represented the interests of the population of Western Ukraine. It states that workers, peasants, and intellectuals of that region gave Soviet troops an enthusiastic welcome when they crossed the Soviet border in September 1939, and under the guidance of the Communist Party, the working people eagerly started to rebuild the economy. But from the first days of "liberation" they met ferocious resistance from the leaders of the UPA and the OUN underground. This assertion barely takes into account historical accuracy. In fact, the UPA had not even been formed by 1939, and the OUN went into an underground existence on the Soviet side of the border and began to negotiate with the German military regime on the western side of the former Polish state.[4]

This same series provided an outline of the Communist perspective. The OUN, it noted, was founded by Konovalets', Mel'nyk, and Yaryi, who "personally" took part in shootings of workers, particularly a rebellious faction in the "Arsenal." Once Hitler came to power in Germany, the OUN became his "paid agents." The OUN members entered Ukraine as part of the Nachtigal unit, which killed 5,000 civilians. The UPA presented a more difficult subject since the insurgents without doubt opposed the Germans for some time. The Communist discourse counters this apparent contradiction in its narrative by noting an alleged agreement between the Germans and the nationalists that led to the latter changing its tactics. The link between the OUN leadership and the Germans, the article declares, was kept secret from rank-and-file members. Further, the article selectively uses documents to highlight atrocities of OUN-UPA in Western Ukraine, including over 3,000 assaults on Soviet activists, as well as attacks on innocent victims such as women and children. All these actions, the authors declare, were orchestrated by the Germans who to the very last days of the war used nationalist groups behind the lines as saboteurs. However, they also acknowledge that many OUN members were simple and honest people who were duped by the leaders, and that is why toward the end of the war the Soviet authorities offered an amnesty to all OUN personnel who surrendered willingly. Before the end of the year 1945, state the authors, about 38,000 insurgents gave themselves up.[5]

A lengthy article of October 1989 counters "nationalist" claims that the UPA was a national liberation movement that represented the interests of the population of Western Ukraine. It familiarizes readers with accounts of the postwar trials of "Banderites" and the information uncovered on these occasions about the barbaric methods used by OUN-UPA, including the torturing of prisoners. Of particular concern to the author was coverage of the trial of the assassins of the Soviet agent and writer, Yaroslav Halan: Ilarii Lukashevych and Mykhailo Stakhur, who conducted this murder on the instructions of the regional OUN leader, Roman Shchepans'kyi (known as Bui-Tur) who was apprehended four years later. After a failed first attempt, the assassins killed Halan with an axe. Lukashevych and Stakhur were executed after a trial in L'viv in 1951. Shchepans'kyi began to speak in Communist language at his trial in 1953, declaring that the OUN was an organization of fanatics and under its influence he committed numerous crimes against the Ukrainian people, the Soviet authorities, and his motherland. He said that he recognized the enormity of the deed—destroying a talented Ukrainian writer—but he had organized the murder on the orders of his higher authorities in the OUN leadership.[6] The way that Shchepans'kyi confesses to his crimes suggests some lengthy sessions in the hands of the NKVD. Indeed, the Soviet secret police excelled in such tactics, and public confessions were favored during the later years of Stalin's leadership. In print, however, the confessions and admissions of guilt seem formalistic.

Ukrainian Communist newspapers published a number of letters from readers in the late 1980s that expressed concern with the gradual and partial rehabilitation of OUN-UPA, as well as about the denunciations of Stalinist crimes that became more accentuated in the Gorbachev period. A letter to one newspaper from Mykhailo Hryshchenko of Cherkasy pointed out that in an earlier issue, materials had been published about the horrors of Stalinism, "which was all well and good." But, he wanted to know, why was there nothing about the atrocities of Banderites in the western regions against their fellow Ukrainians? He sought information about the reburial of the victims of the UPA in the Rivne region, and the testimony of eyewitnesses about these "terrible crimes."[7] Two authors of a summer-1991 article lamented the fact that a Congress of the Brotherhood of UPA soldiers had taken place in April, and defended Fascist ideology while denying Communist accusations that the movement had collaborated with Fascists. It outlined the OUN ideology, which it equated with racism, and declared that the "OUN struggles for the domination over the Ukrainian people and for the expansion of Lebensraum." The authors cite Ukrainian claims to ethnically linked regions of Czechoslovakia, Poland, Belarus, the Bryansk, Kursk, and Voronezh regions of Russia, as well as the Kuban'. They describe OUN members as immoral, and operating according to the maxim "the cause justifies the means." The OUN, the article avows, advocated a totalitarian regime based on the Fuehrer (Leader) principle, and they reproduced a list of OUN tenets.[8]

Sometimes, articles denouncing the OUN could be found in more scholarly form, particularly in the late 1980s when the topic increasingly came up for debate. Soviet writers always stressed the link between the OUN and the Germans, particularly in the 1930s. One author writes that in the interwar period, Ukrainian nationalists, using subsidies and other forms of aid from Berlin and Rome, turned to terrorist methods of struggle against "progressive forces." Nationalist theoreticians at the same time outlined the general compatibility of Fascism and Ukrainian nationalism. Even in the 1930s, he continues, there is no doubt that the Hitlerites regarded the OUN as political partners, including in terrorist acts such as the assassination of the Polish Minister of the Interior, Bronislaw Pieracki, in 1934. The attack of the Germans on Poland had led to discussion about the possibility of creating a West Ukrainian puppet state. However, the Germans were accused of betraying the Ukrainians on this issue.[9] Another author believes that even more moderate Ukrainian political groups operating under Polish rule in the 1930s were evolving in the direction of Fascism, particularly after the adoption of the Polish Constitution in 1935. He points to the OUN alliance with Germany in the 1930s, the objective of which was to win Ukrainian independence. The value of the nationalists to the Germans increased after the fall of Poland, and the

Hitler regime had sponsored the creation of the Ukrainian Legion with two units: *Nachtigal* and *Roland* by May 1941, and the former entered L'viv in the wake of the German army.[10] As the Soviet regime declined and finally dissolved, Ukrainian historians were thus faced with the task of dealing with the thorny topic of OUN-UPA, and how this history should be rewritten. How could one explain the history of an organization that had collaborated with the Hitler regime, even if that link was forged with the sole purpose of creating an independent Ukrainian state? In the world at large the search for pro-Nazi war criminals was continuing apace, and time had not dispelled the gruesome image of the Hitler period. The task was a formidable one, particularly after the lengthy years of Soviet propaganda about OUN-UPA, which led residents of Ukraine to adopt polarized views of the organization. In Western Ukraine, particularly the Galician provinces, the OUN-UPA was resurrected as an organization that embodied patriotism and an independent Ukraine, whereas in the rest of the country it was still regarded as collaborationist and bloodthirsty, and comprised of traitors to the motherland.

OUN under Polish Rule

Initially, a number of articles attempted to humanize the OUN by focusing on the lives of individual members. In doing so, the emphasis was often on the cruelties of the Polish regime and the creation of nationalist martyrs. Young and politicized Ukrainian intellectuals, it is postulated, really had little choice about adherence to the OUN, as other organizations, such as the Ukrainian National Democratic Union (UNDO), had failed the Ukrainian cause through close cooperation with the Polish regime. National heroes and heroines were created at the rank-and-file level, as well as at the level of leadership through figures like Konovalets', Mel'nyk, and Bandera. The writings are obliged to deal with the issue of murder and terrorism directed against Polish officials, and attempt to convey the impression that support for the OUN was widespread in the Ukrainian ethnic regions of interwar Poland, and that a mass movement was taking shape. In general, the Ukrainian communities are portrayed as politically active and highly religious—many of the activists came from families headed by Greek Catholic (Uniate) priests. One critic notes the importance of the philosopher Dmytro Dontsov and his influential pamphlet *Natsionalizm*, which became a sort of guideline for OUN activists, even though Dontsov himself was never formally a member of the organization. Through Dontsov, politically active Ukrainians came to the belief that the

Ukrainian nation was the highest value, to which all other values had to be subordinated, and the ethnically homogeneous group had to seek to establish the future nation by any means. The "national will" found its expression through a charismatic leader figure, and a national elite that was encompassed in a single party. This same critic claims that the strategic objective of Ukrainian nationalism, as outlined at the first OUN Congress in Vienna in 1929, was the establishment of a Ukrainian nation in all ethnically Ukrainian territories. He cites Petro Mirchuk that "only the complete removal of all occupants from Ukrainian lands will create the possibility for an expansive development of the Ukrainian nation" and believes that the model for integral Ukrainian nationalism was that of Fascist Italy. To carry out this mission, OUN members swore to a decalogue, vowing to destroy Ukraine's enemies, and to establish a Ukrainian state for Ukrainians, or to die in the attempt to do so.[11]

One of the martyrs described in the nationalist vision of history in the early years of independence was Ol'ha Basarab, born Ol'ha Levyts'ka, in 1889 near Rohatyn. Her father was a priest and a nationalist. She was educated at the local gymnasium and later at the University of Vienna and became active in several Ukrainian organizations: the Union of Ukrainian Women, the Red Cross, and the Sich Society, an organization which also included Dontsov. In 1914, Ol'ha married Dmytro Basarab, an officer in the Hungarian army, who was killed in 1915 at the front. In November 1918 when the West Ukrainian Republic was created, Ol'ha Basarab went to Vienna and disseminated propaganda among demobilized Ukrainian soldiers of the former Austrian army, with the goal of building up the units of the Ukrainian Galician Army, now engaged in a conflict with the Poles. After the failure of the republic, Basarab worked for the émigré government of Ye. Petrushevych, but was gradually drawn into the orbit of the Ukrainian Military Organization (UVO) led by Yevhen Konovalets'. While she was working in L'viv, on 9 February 1924, the Polish police arrested her by accident when they were searching for a Communist. During their search of the premises, the police discovered materials about UVO and demanded to know the origin of the documents. Ol'ha was reportedly subjected to cruel torture for the next three days, suffering beatings and broken fingers, and she was unable to survive such treatment for long. Finally she scratched the following on the wall of her prison cell with her fingernails: "Dying a martyr, take revenge!" The article exemplifies the genre of OUN martyrdom, with a young heroine suffering at the hands of her cruel oppressors, in this case the Polish authorities. Though Basarab became an important figure in the eyes of émigré organizations, for many years her name was forbidden in Ukraine. The article describes how the torturer of Basarab,

Kaidan, became so haunted by her image that he fled to Western Poland. A local priest passed this information to UVO members, who then organized and carried out the murder of Kaidan, in revenge for his treatment of Basarab.[12]

In the early 1990s, there were numerous accounts about the activities of young OUN members in the 1920s and 1930s, which gradually created a picture of the organization in its early days that countered the prevailing former Soviet perspective. One newspaper interviewed Petro Duzhyi, a member of the OUN leadership (Provid). Duzhyi recounted that he had joined the OUN as a 16-year-old in 1932, after being encouraged by his friend Zelenyi, who was two years his senior. He became acquainted with the OUN ideology through the journal *Rozbudova natsii*, which was published in Prague from 1928 and outlawed in Poland and Romania. The UVO organ *Surma* as well as *Rozbudova natsii* stopped circulation in 1934 after the Polish crackdown on the OUN. In Galicia, OUN supporters could read the monthly *Yunak*, as well as numerous leaflets, brochures, and books by Dmytro Dontsov. When young people joined the OUN, Duzhyi recalled, they had to observe the forty-four rules in the life of a Ukrainian nationalist, compiled by Z. Kossak, as well as the "Prayer of the Ukrainian Nationalist" by Mashchak.[13] In similar vein is an interview with Marta Kravtsiv-Barabash, daughter of the OUN Provid member, Mykhailo Kravtsiv. She grew up in Stryi and attended OUN youth organizations where participants read works by Dontsov. In 1937-38 she worked as a liaison person between Oleksa Hasyn and Yaroslav Stets'ko on the one hand, and the regional leaders Lev and Dariya Rebet on the other. She studied in Vienna and had a passport so that she was free to cross the border regularly. After the war she immigrated to Canada. Her father was prominent in the OUN, and fought for the Western Ukrainian People's Republic, as well as the Ukrainian National Rada founded in 1918. Her father believed that "socialists" had destroyed Ukraine. In 1934, she was arrested and sent to the Polish concentration camp at Bereza Kartuska. In 1939 she moved to the German-occupied part of Poland, returning to Ukraine in 1941 where she joined the short-lived Stets'ko government in L'viv (discussed below). Arrested on 15 September 1941, she was incarcerated at Auschwitz camp until December 1944.[14]

Another article concerned Oleh Kandyba Ol'zhych, a prominent OUN member and son of a famous poet, Oleksandr Oles'. Born in 1907, Ol'zhych attended the department of archeology at Prague University, where he received a doctoral degree. In 1929 he joined the OUN, and was on personal terms with Konovalets'. In 1938-39 he took part in the unsuccessful campaign to secure the independence of Transcarpathian Ukraine, but was taken prisoner by the Hungarians. At the start of the German–Soviet war in the summer of 1941, Ol'zhych directed the OUN underground in Kyiv and avoided arrest (the article neglects to state that he was a member of the OUN faction that followed Andrii Mel'nyk). He was arrested by the retreating Germans in L'viv in May 1944 and died in the concentration camp at Sachsenhausen.[15] The portrayal of Ol'zhych was provided under the title of "the unknown warrior." Other OUN heroes were better known, including two of the most famous figures from the 1930s, Vasyl' Bilas and Dmytro Danylyshyn, who fulfilled the OUN mission of terrorism by murdering a Polish postmaster after a bungled attempt to rob the post office at Horodok to obtain funds for the organization. The attack took place on 30 December 1932, and after its failure, Bilas and Danylyshyn fled to the village of Veryn. According to one account, Polish police disseminated a rumor that they had robbed the local Ukrainian cooperative, in order to solicit help for the apprehension of the two activists. As a result they were detained by Veryn peasants who handed them to the Polish police. At the ensuing trial they were sentenced to death. The author of the article is at pains to emphasize that the resort to such terrorist acts was simply a response to the harsh policies of the Polish authorities. His theme is that although heroes may suffer a physical death, they remain alive in people's memory. Thus the graves of Bilas and Danylyshyn at the Yaniv cemetery in L'viv have been a site for pilgrimage for some time.[16]

A more elaborate account of the same episode is provided by nationalist scribe Roman Pastukh. He writes that the two young men had been "raised in the Ukrainian nationalist spirit" and enrolled in the OUN to avenge Polish oppression of the Ukrainian population. He states that the action took place on 30 November 1932 (rather than 30 December as cited in the earlier article). The action did not go as planned and resulted in a skirmish, in which there were dead on both sides. Bilas and Danylyshyn attempted to flee to Drohobych but were caught after the ruse by the Polish police. In Pastukh's account, the peasants were informed of the blunder they had made by Danylyshyn, who declared that "We are members of the Ukrainian military organization. If you continue to behave this way, you will never see a free Ukraine." The peasants then fell on their knees as if before icons, the account continues. Bilas and Danylyshyn were executed in the Bryhidky prison in L'viv on 23 December 1932. Pastukh observes the ways in which the two heroes have been immortalized in popular memory, and their exploit has been the subject of songs, reflected in a number of scholarly publications, and their portraits hung in the reading rooms of the Prosvita society.[17] The link between "martyrs" like Basarab, Bilas, and Danylyshyn and the modern Ukrainian state is cited frequently by supporters of the nationalist cause. The sixteenth volume of the *Litopys UPA* series, for example, dates the start of Ukrainian resistance to the Poles to the action in Horodok,[18] and publicist Myron Kuropas links Bilas and Danylyshyn to later martyrs such as Vasyl' Stus (as well as Stepan Bandera), as key factors in the ultimate success of Ukrainian independence.[19] The outsider is left to ponder how the death of an innocent postmaster could serve as an act of martyrdom and courage in the Ukrainian cause. Yet the key point is that the creation of martyrs is an integral part of mythmaking.

Some of the more general accounts of the creation and evolution of the OUN are replete with hyperbole. Historian Viktor Koval' declares that following the defeat of the attempt to create an independent Ukrainian state in 1917-20, the "single force" that carried out the will of the Ukrainian people was the OUN underground, which struggled against Polish domination throughout the interwar period. The programmatic goal of the OUN, he writes, was the creation of a Ukrainian independent sovereign state. Because of its military operations against the Polish government, and its organization of mass protests among the Ukrainian community, OUN members constituted a majority of the inmates of the Bereza Kartuska camp.[20] The same sort of reasoning is employed by Stepan Mudryk-Mechnyk, who writes that after the loss of statehood in 1920, Ukrainian resistance did not end and activists organized the UVO, which destroyed Polish settlements in "Ukraine," deprived Poles of money confiscated from Ukrainians, and punished functionaries of the Polish authorities. In January–February 1929, the First Congress of the OUN was held, and the new organization was created from UVO and a number of Ukrainian youth organizations. The OUN, the author writes without corroboration, "represented the majority of Ukrainians" but representatives of other legal parties refused to accept it. The OUN spread its conspiratorial network and directed the struggle against the Polish government. For example, in response to a Polish ban on the sale of land to Ukrainian peasants, the OUN constructed grave mounds with the inscription "Ukrainian land belongs to the Ukrainian peasants!" In addition to the assassination of Pieracki, the Soviet trade attaché in L'viv was also killed to protest the deaths of millions of Ukrainian peasants in the Famine of 1932-33.[21]

Two serious attempts to come to terms with the impact of the OUN on Ukrainian life were offered in 1999 and 2000 by Mykhailo Koval' and Stanislav Kul'chyts'kyi. The former writes that the national liberation struggle of 1918-21 failed to bring about a permanent Ukrainian independent state, and therefore other means to accomplish that goal were sought. The OUN, established in 1929, took on this same task and united the "national-liberation forces" of Galicia in response to anti-Ukrainian policies introduced by the Polish government. He also perceives the formation of the OUN as an instrument to prevent the expansion of the Stalin regime into Western Ukraine, though such an assertion seems to take advantage of the benefit of hindsight. The OUN operated during a period in which totalitarianism dominated the political landscape, not only in Ukraine, but in most of Europe. The OUN was a product of the epoch in the same way as Bolshevism or German National Socialism, Koval' writes, with equivalents in many of the nations of Europe. In the struggle for Ukrainian statehood and independence, the OUN from the outset relied on radical methods, such as propaganda and terror, to accomplish its goals. The extreme radicalism of this revolutionary organization was expressed in its program, which envisaged a state ruled by the nation, expressed in a leader figure. In its policies of a charismatic leader, economic power merged with the political authority of the nation, and its Russophobia, the OUN adopted several policies that had much in common with German National Socialism.[22] This argument is not new, and was propagated by well-known Diaspora historians such as Ivan Lysyak-Rudnyts'kyi in the 1970s, i.e., that the anti-democratic movements appeared to be the main catalysts for change, and that if change were to come to Ukrainian lands, then it was likely to occur through Germany rather than any other power. Thus the title of this section of Koval's book is how the OUN and the Third Reich took advantage of each other, in fulfilling their political goals.

Kul'chyts'kyi writes less frequently about the OUN than he does on the Famine, but he gives a succinct account of the history of UVO, placing the evolution of Ukrainian nationalism in a pan-European context and observing the erosion of democratic ideologies and their gradual replacement with extreme nationalism or Communism by the late 1920s. Ukrainian nationalists rejected the liberal slogans offered by writers and philosophers such as Mykhailo Drahomaniv and Mykhailo Hrushevs'kyi because ostensibly these policies had failed to provide an independent Ukrainian state. Instead, they adopted the ideas of Mikhnovs'kyi—"Ukraine for Ukrainians!" or Dontsov's more moderate slogan of "Ukrainians for Ukraine!" The Nationalist movement, in his view, was set in motion by the formation of the Legion of Sich Sharpshooters within the army of the Ukrainian National Republic (UNR). The Legion was disbanded in Prague in 1920, and simultaneously its leaders announced the creation of the Ukrainian Military Organization (UVO). He describes the activities of UVO as terrorist and directed against figures of authority within interwar Poland. In 1921, for example, he cites an attempt on the life of Jozef Pilsudski and the L'viv governor, Kazimierz Grabowski, both of which resulted in failure. UVO also practiced sabotage, expropriations of money, and the destruction of farms owned by Polish settlers. The peak of UVO's activities occurred in 1922 when its servicemen destroyed 38 Polish farms and burned 2,300 items of Polish property, but it is difficult to distinguish its actions from those of the Communists, who conducted similar tactics. The UVO suffered a major setback when the Entente Council of Ambassadors gave Galicia to Poland, and a split occurred in the movement, with one faction advocating a united Ukraine and a second backing an independent Western Ukrainian state. The former perspective prevailed.[23]

Most writers concur that the UVO was one of the principal foundation stones for the creation of OUN, which—Kost' Bondarenko maintains—"was a classical, radical rightist terrorist organization," ideologically close to Fascism of the Italian type, which was believed to be the "avant-garde European ideology" of that time. He warns that Fascism should not be confused with German National Socialism and says that the OUN did not espouse racist principles. Several OUN leaders were married to Jewish women. However, it was commonly believed in Soviet times that the OUN was financed by Germany, and indeed Konovalets' had made use of money from a fund set up during the Weimar Republic to support stateless nations. But by the late 1920s, the Germans preferred to finance the former Hetmanate leader Pavlo Skoropads'kyi, and once Hitler came to power, support for the OUN ended. The new donors were Lithuania, Japan, Italy, and the Ukrainian Diaspora in the United States. Bondarenko gives a lengthy account of the best-known event in the interwar history of the OUN, namely the 1934 assassination of the Polish Interior Minister, General Bronislaw Pieracki. He comments on the cooperation between Nazi Germany and Poland in apprehending the culprits: Germany extradited the terrorist Mykola Lebed' to Poland, for example. Other nationalist activists were arrested and later sent to a concentration camp. However, the trials that ensued in Warsaw and L'viv turned into a forum for the OUN, which gained them huge popularity in Galicia and transformed them into the most respected political force. In prisons and camps, nationalists and Communists combined to organize actions against the authorities.[24] Bondarenko's account is for a general readership, offering one of the most sympathetic accounts to that date (2002) of the development and program of the OUN, but it is lacking in detail. One recalls, for example, Kul'chyts'kyi's earlier remark about the difference between those who adhered to the ideas of Mikhnovs'kyi and those who preferred the writings of Dontsov as guidance for their actions, a distinction that is ignored by Bondarenko.

A recent scholarly account, which primarily focuses on the rival Polish-Ukrainian aspirations during the Second World War, also provides a portrayal of the early years of the OUN as well as the opposing Ukrainian perspective. I. I. Il'yushyn writes that by the end of the 1930s the two major influences on Ukrainians had been formed, but two entirely different ideological-political groupings, the UNDO-UNR (followers of Symon Petlyura) and the OUN. The former included activists and supporters of UNDO (which he describes as "the most authoritative" legal force in Ukrainian national democracy in Western Ukraine in the interwar period) and activists of the Ukrainian National Republic State Center in exile, which was the only legitimate carrier of Ukrainian statehood after the collapse of the liberation efforts of 1917-20. Il'yushyn's use of words like "legal" and "legitimate" imply from the outset that the OUN was something contrived and subversive. He continues with an account of the main figures in the UNR camp. They included leader Vasyl' Mudryi, president of the UNR Andrii Livyts'kyi, the Minister of Foreign Affairs, Professor Roman Smal'-Stots'kyi, and the War Minister, Volodymyr Sals'kyi.

The ex-government camp anticipated an armed conflict between the democratic western countries and the Bolshevik regime of the USSR, which they believed would end in the defeat of the latter—the so-called Prometheist conception. The leading role in that program belonged to Poland, which would form a federation with a newly created Ukrainian state. Hence the Union disseminated the view that Ukrainians should cooperate with the Poles rather than oppose them, and questions about the future status of ethnic Ukrainian territories like eastern Galicia, Volhynia, Bukovyna, and Transcarpathia would be decided by the diplomatic route and discussions with the relevant powers, i.e., Poland, Romania, and Czechoslovakia. In contrast, the OUN perspective was formed under the leadership of Andrii Mel'nyk, following the death of Konovalets' in May 1938. The OUN activists, writes Il'yushyn, had a negative attitude toward any form of cooperation with the "occupiers of Ukrainian lands" and their supporters, among which were considered first and foremost the members of the UNR government. They were oriented toward Germany rather than Poland, and saw Poland and the USSR as their chief enemies. The coming conflict, it was hoped, would achieve the OUN's only goal, an independent sovereign state that would include all Ukrainian lands "without exception."[25] In contrast to Bondarenko's account, Il'yushyn suggests that the OUN was indeed an extremist organization.

Konovalets'

One of the most important tasks of those propagating new analyses of the OUN and its incorporation into the mainstream of Ukrainian history is the examination of individual leaders, their lives, and policies. Konovalets' is one of the most important early leaders of the Ukrainian nationalist cause. At the end of 1938, an editorial in *Literaturna Ukraina* states, Yevhen Konovalets' tragically lost his life at the age of only 47. He was a colonel in the army of the Ukrainian National Republic, a military leader and politician, commander of the UVO, and Chairman of the Provid of Ukrainian Nationalists.[26] However, from the nationalist perspective, his name had been "tarred" by both Bolshevik propagandists and well-known Communist professors. Therefore, Ihor Hulyk, writing in the late Soviet period, sets himself the task of informing the public about Konovalets' and his relevance to the modern Ukrainian state. The article is a straightforward attempt "to set the record straight." Hulyk notes that Konovalets' was born on 14 June 1891 in the village of Zashkiv (L'viv region). His father was a teacher and supporter of the Ukrainian idea. After finishing the gymnasium, Konovalets' entered the Faculty of Law at L'viv University, and during this period he participated in Prosvita, Ukrainian cooperatives, and the Ukrainian Students' Union. One of the major influences on his ideological outlook was Dontsov. Prior to the First World War, Konovalets' organized the Sich Sharpshooters. In 1915, fighting on the Austrian side, he was taken prisoner by Russian forces, but he subsequently took part in the formation of the Ukrainian National Republic in Kyiv, and also organized a Galician branch of the Sharpshooters.[27]

Hulyk's message is explicitly political and he draws a direct line between Konovalets' public career and the situation in Ukraine today. The struggle for the nation is a lengthy one and "cannot be carried out with kid gloves." If Konovalets' outlook is projected to the present day, declares the author, then its relevance is self-evident. The Galician youngsters' resistance to the Bolsheviks played a direct role in the issuance of the Fourth Universal in January 1918 by which Ukraine declared its full independence from Russia. When Skoropads'kyi came to power (at the behest of the German occupation regime), Konovalets' proposed an alliance by which the Sharpshooters would support his regime if it confirmed the idea of a sovereign and independent Ukraine. On the other hand, he (Konovalets') refused to assist the West Ukrainian Republic in its conflict with the Poles and did not participate in its alliance with the White Russian general, Anton Denikin. In 1920, Konovalets' created the UVO, which provided both military training for young Ukrainians as well as "political enlightenment." When Galicia was attached to Poland in 1923, UVO abandoned its enlightenment ideology and four years later, in the wake of the assassination of Symon Petlyura, Konovalets' was able to unite the disjointed nationalist organizations with the first OUN Congress in 1929. In the 1930s, the author writes, Konovalets' lived a precarious existence in Switzerland where he was monitored by Polish police and was the subject of assassination attempts by the Soviet secret police, the NKVD. On 23 May 1938, the NKVD finally succeeded, by arranging a meeting with Konovalets' at the Café Atlanta in Rotterdam, Holland, and passing on to him a package that exploded. The OUN Provid declared that Moscow had recognized that Konovalets' represented Ukraine, and Ukraine is Konovalets'. "History confirmed the truth of these words," writes Hulyk, and "Konovalets' is coming back to us."[28]

The same story, with a few modifications, is provided by Volodymyr Yavors'kyi. In 1915, he states, after his capture by the Russian army, Konovalets' spent two years at a Russian POW camp near Tsaritsyn (later Stalingrad, today Volgograd). After the February Revolution broke out in Russia he was freed to travel to Kyiv, where he met with M. Mikhnovs'kyi, and the two Ukrainian leaders began to organize the Ukrainian armed forces, the Sharpshooters' Legion. He imposed strict discipline on his troops and on 18 January 1918, his unit crushed a rebellion at the Kyiv arsenal. He agreed to work for Hetman Skoropads'kyi but only on the condition that the latter would support the Ukrainian cause. Whereas Skoropads'kyi turned to the Russian White Guardists for support, Konovalets' switched his allegiance to the UNR leaders, Petlyura and Volodymyr Vynnychenko. The collapse of the UNR government, the Directory, led Konovalets' to ponder the causes of the defeat, and he reached the conclusion that it had resulted from an underestimation of the Ukrainian national idea, weak discipline in the armed forces, and the "socialist utopianism" of many of the Directory leaders. In the future, writes Yavors'kyi, Konovalets' decided that the struggle for liberation must be based on quite different principles: strength and the nation. Under his leadership the OUN became very active, both in Poland and the Ukrainian SSR, in responding to the Pacification in Poland, and Soviet repressions in Ukraine. As for the death of the OUN leader, Yavors'kyi writes that in Rotterdam he was supposed to meet an OUN delegate from Eastern Ukraine called Valyukh, who turned out to be an agent of the NKVD. By 1992, it became known that the figure who organized the murder was P. A. Sudoplatov.[29]

Much of the mystery surrounding Konovalets', an upright military figure, has centered on his untimely death and subsequent martyrdom. Thus there are a number of articles that focus on his murder. We will cite two examples here. In 1992, the all-Ukrainian association "Derzhavna Samostiinist' Ukrainy" sent a request to the Prosecutor-General of Ukraine to initiate a criminal case against Pavel Anatol'evich Sudoplatov, a retired general lieutenant in the KGB, born in 1907 and currently residing in Moscow. The pretext of this appeal, writes Mykola Oleksyuk, was a letter from Sudoplatov to the 23rd Congress of the CC CPSU, in which he clearly and unambiguously stated that on 23 March 1938 in Rotterdam, fulfilling the orders of the Central Committee, he personally eliminated Yevhen Konovalets' using a bomb. This author goes further, however, and accuses Sudoplatov also of murdering the Ukrainian Communist writer Yaroslav Halan in 1949.[30] A later article comments that in 1937 the NKVD succeeded in planting an agent inside the OUN, a man called Lebed'. According to Sudoplatov, who was behind the murder of Konovalets', Lebed' was an officer in the Austrian army who served in the war alongside Konovalets'. Reportedly, Lebed' introduced Konovalets' to a man called Valyukh (Sudoplatov), claiming that the latter was a secret member of the OUN. The attack, according to this article, was planned meticulously. In addition to an explosive device, Sudoplatov was equipped with a gun and a large sum of money. He met Konovalets' in the "Atlanta" restaurant and they arranged a second meeting a few hours later. Valyukh gave Konovalets' a box of chocolates as a small gift (which later exploded). After the meeting, Sudoplatov left for Paris and subsequently Barcelona. Konovalets' was buried on 23 May in a funeral attended by Ukrainian general Kurmanovych, several nationalists, and a Lithuanian consul.[31]

The significance of these lengthy descriptions is in the link between the past and the present. Sudoplatov, who died in September 1996, is better known for his role in the assassination of L. D. Trotsky in 1940, and for his role in the Soviet atomic project. In some ways he appears the archetypal evil Soviet agent. In this instance he is revealed belatedly to have been the man behind the assassination of one of Ukraine's new heroes, a man bedeviled in his lifetime by adverse depictions of his career, but now perceived as a genuine hero of Ukraine who elevated nationalism and military discipline as the main watchwords in order to attain his future goal. Sudoplatov, on the other hand, despite his mixed Ukrainian–Russian parentage and Ukrainian birth, represents the truculence of both the Soviet Union and Russia: devious, cunning, and treacherous. Strangely there is a scarcity of discourse about Konovalets' chosen successor, Andrii Mel'nyk, probably because of the fractious split in the OUN two years later that divided it into two wings: that under Mel'nyk and that under the younger, more dynamic, and more extremist Stepan Bandera. Bandera, on the other hand, is the subject of polemics both for and against him, and in the pantheon of national heroes, it is Bandera—at least in terms of discussion in the newspapers and journals surveyed—who takes his place alongside Konovalets' prior to the UPA leader Roman Shuk-hevych on the national stage. This statement is not to say that Mel'nyk was a less important or even more diplomatic and sensible leader than the head-strong Bandera; it rather suggests that he was less charismatic and unlikely to encourage fanaticism and self-sacrifice on the part of his followers. For this reason, rather than any objective choice, the next figure for focus in this dis-cussion of late- and post-Soviet discourse is Bandera.

Stepan Bandera

There are few more controversial figures in contemporary Ukraine than Stepan Bandera. A national hero to some and a war criminal to others, he is venerated as a hero in many parts of Western Ukraine, with statues, museums, and even one of the more prominent streets of L'viv named after him. Clearly, he is a substantial figure in the recent past of Ukraine and one that had a con-tinuing and lasting impact in the Diaspora after the Second World War. It is probably impossible at the present time in Ukraine to obtain an objective and dispassionate assessment of Bandera because he evokes such strong emotions even fifty years after his death. However, what is evident is his gradual but almost relentless transformation into a national hero, as the Ukrainian public is confronted with a volte-face and the erstwhile traitor becomes a figure for admiration and veneration. Though the main events in Bandera's life are clearly delineated, there is also a lack of detail, especially during the war years and his long incarceration in Germany. His links to the Germans throughout his career are also a subject for debate. Further, unlike Dontsov, Bandera was no philosopher, left no memoirs of note, nor did he provide any lasting trea-tises regarding his political outlook. According to one source, "rank-and-file fighters never saw Bandera or Mel'nyk." The commanders lived relatively well, whereas the troops endured hardships living in the forest.[32] We examine here discourse on various aspects of Bandera's life in approximate chronological or-der, starting with the hostile portrayals of the late Soviet period and ending with the positive accounts of the early 21st century when writers were attempting to consolidate the position of Bandera as a Ukrainian national hero.

An early and very negative account of Bandera's political career was pro-vided on the pages of *Pravda Ukrainy* in late 1990 by V. Dovgan'. It begins with Bandera's appointment as head of the regional executive of the OUN in Western Ukraine in 1932. From that point, Dovgan' argues, this particular branch became increasingly terror-oriented in its activity. The victims of the OUN included not only Poles, but also those Ukrainians who overtly disagreed with OUN tactics. One example provided is that of M. Bilets'kyi, a peasant activist brutally murdered by the OUN. Another victim was a professor of philology at L'viv Ukrainian Gymnasium, Babii, who refused to allow political agitation on the school premises. A student called Bachyns'kyi, who was interested in joining the OUN, was killed on suspicion that he was a provocateur. The 1936 trial of Bandera, the author points out, revealed that Bandera had personally ordered the murders of Babii and Bachyns'kyi. After the murders of the Soviet consulate worker A. Mailov in L'viv, and the assassination of Interior Minister Pieracki in 1933–34, Bandera was arrested and trials took place in Warsaw in 1935 and L'viv in 1936. Dovgan' writes that Bandera never received the death sentence, as some sources claim, but only life imprisonment. It is suggested that he received a relatively light sentence because of an agreement between Nazi Germany and Poland in 1934—no evidence is given for such a statement. The author also maintains that Bandera fled from Polish confinement during the relocation of prisoners in September 1939. Other sources state that he was released by the Germans.[33] This article is concerned in particular in emphasizing the close links between the latter and Bandera.

His main thesis is the close collaboration between Richard Yarii, a man with long-term contacts with the Abwehr, and Bandera, and that the two worked together to bring down the leadership of the Provid. The implication is that the Germans were behind the 1940 split in the OUN leadership, but soon began to be concerned that the mutual assassinations of key members in the two wings of the OUN might prove detrimental to German war aims. Dovgan' is also at some pains to demonstrate that the OUN did not reflect the mood of the population of Western Ukraine, i.e., that it was an alien force in the region. He cites an OUN directive calling local activists to arrange a cordial welcome for the German "liberators" in Ukrainian villages. Leaflets were reportedly handed to Red Army soldiers that read: "At the front, surrender, and say that you are Ukrainians who wish to fight against Moscow under the leadership of the OUN-B." The article also refers to German-OUN appeals to the civilian population to cross the border into Eastern Ukraine to spread panic and sow disbelief in the fighting capacity of the Red Army, and guide them in carrying out anti-Moscow resistance. An entire propaganda apparatus was to be set up, including radios, loud-speakers, and radio stations, as well as the dissemination of leaflets, orders, and appeals. Such tactics, the author writes, are exactly the same as those applied by Rukh members and Bandera supporters "today." In this way, the OUN-B is depicted as a primary agent of a hostile occupation force fighting against the interests of the majority of Ukrainians. Likewise, Dovgan' argues that although Bandera was taken into captivity in Germany, from the Fall of 1941, he was treated well and continued to cooperate with the Germans. He writes that SS leader Heinrich Himmler personally released Bandera so that he could conduct anti-Soviet activities in Ukraine![34]

By 1992, writers in the media were trying to "correct" such harsh interpretations of Bandera. Ol'ha Ivanova, for example, responds to a reader from Kyiv who did not understand "how can one glorify someone [Bandera] who killed people?" The author calls on her readers to become nationally conscious, to cast off all past propaganda mixed with lies that had been fed to residents of Ukraine since kindergarten. Instead one should "look into the face of history with honest and unbiased eyes." One should not turn away from obvious facts known to the world for years, but which Ukrainians still question. In order to familiarize readers with such facts she provides an "ABC of Ukrainian History," which declares that Bandera was arrested in 1936 for fighting for the independence of Ukraine and given a death sentence by the Polish authorities (the fact that he may have been responsible for the murders of two officials is not mentioned by the author). She also cites Bandera's arrest in July 1941 for his part in the proclamation of Ukrainian independence in L'viv on 30 June 1941 (discussed below). In her opinion, Bandera refused to work with the Germans against the Bolsheviks. Rather, the OUN leadership under Bandera was prominent in resistance against the occupiers, and the OUN was the only genuine opposition force, even in Eastern Ukraine. There she maintains, the Young Guard, which in past writings has usually been associated with the Communist Party, was in fact a creation of the OUN. Any part of this version of history that does not comply with Ivanova's version is dismissed as an invention of enemy propaganda that might be Polish, Communist, or Jewish.[35]

Several articles focus on the background and personality of Bandera. Roman Pastukh has tried to reconstruct the Bandera family history, noting that his grandfather Mykhailo, who was a church deacon, lived in Stryi with his wife Yefrosynya. They had two sons and two daughters. The oldest son was Andrii, the father of Stepan. Andrii studied theology in L'viv University and was ordained as a priest in 1906. His house was something of a magnet for the cultural elite, and was the locale for lively discussions on social and political life in Galicia, with regular visits from people like Pavlo Hlozdins'kyi, founder of the Ukrainian cooperative movement, Yaroslav Veselovs'kyi, a member of parliament, and the well-known sculptor Havrylko. When the Habsburg Empire disintegrated at the end of the First World War, the author points out, the Ukrainian Galician army emerged, and Andrii became a chaplain in one of the units, returning to Galicia only after this army was defeated in the field. He continued to serve as a priest in the village Uhryniv until 1933, but by then life had become difficult because the Polish police regularly searched the house because of son Stepan's affiliation with the OUN. During the first Soviet occupation of Western Ukraine, in May 1941, Andrii and his sisters Oksana and Mariya were arrested, and Andrii was executed in July 1941. The two sisters were deported to Siberia.[36] The story continues with the return of Stepan's own sisters from Siberian exile in the independence period. They reportedly settled in the village Kozakivtsi, near Bolekhiv, in the Ivano-Frankivs'k region. The Stryi branch of the Congress of Ukrainian Nationalists appealed to the Stryi city council, which found an apartment for the two elderly women, and the local furniture factory provided for free the furnishings for the apartment.[37] The Bandera legend in Western Ukraine could be maintained through the presence of his family members.

Another biography of Bandera's father Andrii appeared in 1999 in the popular youth newspaper *Ukraina moloda*. It is reportedly based on materials from the Polish police contained in the regional archives of Ivano-Frankivs'k, as well as NKVD materials made available in Kyiv. In addition to the material contained in the earlier account, it also notes that in November 1928, Andrii was arrested for conducting a mass for slain soldiers of the Ukrainian Galician Army. According to the police report, he was attempting to sow hatred of the Poles and the Polish government, and had argued that Galicia was an inseparable part of Ukraine, and sooner or later would gain independence. The criminal case also contained several leaflets, which according to the testimony of the witnesses, were disseminated by Stepan Bandera. Four days later, both Andrii and Stepan (who had also been arrested) were released for lack of evidence (November 1928). Andrii was arrested by the Soviet authorities who made use of the criminal case conducted in Poland. In this way a direct link is implied between the two occupation authorities, although these countries had remained bitterly hostile between their two wars of 1920 and 1939. Andrii was arrested again on 23 May 1941, together with his daughters Marta and Oksana in the village Trostyanets' in Dolyna district on charges of hiding the OUN member Stefanyshyn. Andrii never hid his close ties with his son and while in prison boldly enunciated his support for the OUN: "I am a Ukrainian nationalist according to my world view, but I am not a chauvinist. I believe the only true state for Ukrainians is a united, independent, Ukraine." As noted above, the tribunal in Kyiv Military District on 8 July 1941 imposed a death sentence on him.[38] The article has demonstrated the direct link between the elder Bandera and the modern Ukrainian state.

Would-be biographers have tended to provide a rather wishful characterization of the OUN leader. One writes that he lived a Spartan life and one of constant struggle for his family. "He was a good man and father, and deeply religious with a strong and forceful character. This is why the Communists killed him."[39] Yaroslav Kitura follows suit, observing that Bandera was raised in a patriotic Ukrainian family and joined the Ukrainian youth organizations Plast and Sokil while attending the Ukrainian gymnasium in Stryi. When he was in the fourth grade, writes Kitura, he joined the UVO and became a formal member of the association when he was a university student in 1928. A year later, the OUN was created, and the 20-year-old Bandera became a member. From 1931 he was head of the propaganda section of the regional OUN executive branch. In 1932–33 he was the deputy leader of the regional branch. In the 1930s, the young nationalist carried out several "revolutionary acts" against representatives of the Polish and Soviet governments. Kitura points out that the Soviet official, Mailov, who was assassinated in 1933, was an agent of Stalin's intelligentsia. After the murder of minister Pieracki in 1934, Bandera was sentenced to life imprisonment, but he was freed at the beginning of the war and moved to Krakow. This biographical account is notable for several omissions, most notably the split in the OUN in 1940 and its division into the two wings following Mel'nyk and Bandera. This account would imply to an uninformed reader that Bandera was the natural successor to Konovalets'. This same author maintains that Bandera was arrested by the Germans in 1941 because he refused to cooperate with them, and that he was assassinated in Munich by the Soviet agent Stashyns'kyi in 1959.[40]

Concerning Bandera's political thought, another account declared that the OUN-B was different from other political parties. It did not represent the interests of a certain faction of the population, but struggled for the liberation of an independent and united Ukraine. The Ukrainian people would have an opportunity to live well only after it was freed from the tyranny of "Russian Bolshevik imperialism" and had become the sole master in its own state. Bandera, according to this account, never anticipated that Ukraine would be isolated politically. However, it would enter alliances only when such agreements were made by sovereign nations, as equal partners, to achieve common goals with

no privileges for one group of people at the expense of another. The principle
of sovereignty would not be broken if such alliances were concluded voluntarily "by non-imperialist peoples." Bandera, in Kitura's view, contended that the
major objective for Ukrainians should be the restoration of an independent,
united Ukraine through the dismemberment of the Russian empire and the
destruction of Bolshevism. The author concludes in the same fashion, taking
on Bandera's mantle and stressing the importance of the Bandera heritage for
modern Ukraine. "The struggle for Ukrainian sovereignty continues. It will
end only after the Russian Empire is completely dissolved, regardless of what
name or ideology conceals its real aims."[41] In other words, just as Bandera can
be equated with today's Ukraine, so also can Stalin's USSR be equated with
the then Russian Federation under President Boris Yeltsin. In this way, Bandera becomes a modern hero rather than a figure of the past.

In addition to the reinterpretation of Bandera and his relatives in the popular press, other means of resurrecting him as a natural hero have also been
deployed. These have included monuments and even a movie. The latter was
evidently initiated by the Ukrainian Congress of America, and directed by
Oles' Yanchuk under the title: "Assassination: the autumn murder in Munich." The role of Bandera was played by L'viv actor Yaroslav Muka. In an
interview, the actor claimed that the major objective of the film was to fill a
gap in history, that of Bandera who hitherto had never been depicted on
screen. In "Assassination," Bandera is depicted as a simple man who stands
by his beliefs, rather than the "devil incarnate" described in Soviet-era publications. Muka points out that the idea was also to commemorate people who
fought for their ideals, for the state, and who frequently sacrificed their lives
in a seemingly hopeless struggle, when it seemed impossible to beat the [So-
viet] machine. However, they had also fought for the victory that was finally
attained by independence in 1991. It was also important to trace the lives of
Ukrainian heroes who eventually resurfaced in Canada and the United States,
having fled from Stalin's forces. Muka prepared for the role by sifting through
photographs collected in American archives and private collections. He tried
to depict Bandera as a real, living person. However, he emphasizes, the movie
was not only about Bandera because there were other important characters,
too.[42] By 2002 there were several official monuments to Bandera, including
one in the village of Dublyany on the premises of the L'viv State Agrarian
University, at which Bandera was enrolled as a student.[43]

Writings on other OUN Leaders

Though the figure of Bandera has monopolized discourse on nationalist thinkers, other leaders have also been the subject of media focus. In the past, two obvious targets for Soviet vitriol were Yaroslav Stets'ko, Bandera's subordinate, and Stets'ko's wife Yaroslava, who later became a well-known politician in Ukraine.[44] Yaroslava Stets'ko provided an interview to *Za vil'nu Ukrainu* in 1994 that represented the OUN as the voice of the Ukrainian nation. She stressed its spiritual values, high morality, honesty, heroism, and the bravery of its members. It was linked directly with the people: "they relied on the people and on their own strength." When OUN members appeared in the villages, it signified that there would be order and an end to thievery. What were the nationalists struggling for six decades later in an independent Ukraine? "To fill the Ukrainian state with Ukrainian content, and make it a truly national state."[45] The same link between past and present is made in the memorial about the late Yaroslav Stets'ko by his former secretary, the then deputy of the Supreme Soviet Roman Zvarych, who became Justice Minister in the first year of the Yushchenko presidency (he lost his position in the governmental upheaval of September 2005 but was recalled to office in August 2006). Stets'ko, he recalls, was an extremely optimistic person who never lost faith, even in the darkest times, that Ukraine would soon become independent. Such optimism derived from his belief "in the invincibility of the human thirst for freedom." To Stets'ko the Soviet Union was always called the Russian or Moscow Empire because a real union can only be based on free will. The nationalist leader emerges from this biographical account as a prophet of the Ukrainian people who anticipated independence as early as 1986, the time of the dramatic nuclear disaster at Chernobyl (Chornobyl) in Northern Ukraine. Once when Zvarych informed Stets'ko that Ukraine was experiencing bad weather, the latter replied that the inclement weather was the fault of Muscovites who had cut down Ukrainian forests, which generally dispersed the clouds, bringing fair weather.[46]

In 1991, historian Vasyl' Marochkin visited the United States, ostensibly to offer a series of lectures on Ivan Mazepa. However, the article he wrote upon his return spends far more time on his encounters with his host, Mykola Lebed', a controversial figure within the OUN for his alleged role within the security service. Marochkin presents Lebed' as an outstanding leader of the Ukrainian liberation movement and the prime organizer of a number of successful terrorist attacks, including those that accounted for the deaths of Pieracki and Mailov. These actions are depicted as justifiable and laudable deeds.

In the next section of the article, Marochkin sets himself the task of debunk-
ing the notion that Lebed' was the head of the SB. Rather, he asserts, after the
arrest of Bandera, Lebed' became the head of the OUN-B. Moreover, the
emergence subsequently of the Ukrainian Insurgent Army (UPA) was a result
of the labors and organizational work of Lebed'. He maintains that the security service was not as bad as the image conveyed in Communist writings,
which depict it eliminating enemies and unreliable Ukrainians with impunity.
Its main task was to protect the leaders of the OUN-B. Though Lebed' has
been accused in a number of sources of carrying out war crimes, Marochkin
dismisses the notion and perceives his actions as revenge against an outside
and alien impostor who has broken into one's home at night and killed one's
wife and children. He wonders how one could be blamed for committing a
violent act under such circumstances.[47]

More details about Lebed' (or Lebid') emerged from an interview he gave
to the newspaper *Za vil'nu Ukrainu* in 1992, a year after Ukraine's independence. He recalled that he had joined a circle of nationalists at L'viv gymnasium in 1927, which formed the basis of the future Union of Nationalist
Youth. After the OUN was created in 1929, he was instructed to organize an
OUN cell in the gymnasium and other places. In turn, the group denounced
traditional Polish national holidays, such as the birthday of Jozef Pilsudski.
One Polish professor had spoken disrespectfully about the Ukrainian trident
symbol and "had to be taught a lesson." When a Polish eagle was hung in the
classroom, the young Ukrainians painted it with ink and broke its wing. The
eagle had to be removed. Lebed' maintains that Ukrainian national identity
was crafted in part as a response to the Polish Pacification of the early 1930s.
Although three policemen had been killed, he recalls, he felt that such retribution was inadequate because the real guilty parties were those giving the orders. Therefore the OUN regional executive decided to assassinate a member
of the government, and eventually Pieracki was selected. The goal of the attack was to "tell the world" about the Ukrainian national movement. Shortly
after the assassination Lebed' was arrested in Germany and escorted to Poland. An open trial took place a year later, and he served his term in the
harshest of prisons, attaining his release only after German troops entered
Warsaw in 1939. Once released from prison, the younger members of the
OUN gathered in Krakow. Lebed' makes it plain that they were dissatisfied
with the leadership of Mel'nyk. Also, "we knew Ukraine was waiting for us,"
and therefore the younger nationalists resolved to get military training in
Germany, fearing that some day the Germans would round them up and im-
prison them all.[48] The account seems far-fetched in that in the years prior to

1941, it would appear from most accounts that cooperation with the Germans was anticipated to be of mutual benefit.

The biographical accounts of Bandera, Lebed', and Stets'ko, perhaps the best known leaders of the OUN-B, all serve a purpose: to nullify the impressions provided in Soviet accounts of nationalist cut-throats in the pay of the Germans, who were about to invade the USSR in the summer of 1941. A laudatory biography of Bandera was published in L'viv in 2001 by a professional writer from Ternopil', Halyna Hordasevych,[49] who was a member of the Democratic Party of Ukraine and also of the Popular Movement for Perestroika (Rukh). Its appearance was the culmination of an outpouring of literature, both scholarly and popular, on OUN-UPA in Western Ukraine in the independence years, some of which initially appeared in the West and mainly in English; and some that represented new scholarship on the OUN and its leaders. Bandera at least is a mythical figure in his native region, though not yet in his native land as a whole. The difficulty with such a figure is his distance from the events that took place in his name for most of his career. His legend was really made during his youth as a terrorist in Western Ukraine, and for his stance as the most implacable of nationalists after the death of Konovalets' in 1938. Thereafter, he remained in German-occupied territory during the most traumatic events in Ukraine, the invasion, the immediate aftermath (that saw the German refusal to countenance an independent Ukrainian state), and the UPA's emergence and conflict with Soviet and Polish forces (for the most part) in the late war and post-war years. Bandera's murder in Munich in 1959 by a West-Ukrainian-born Soviet agent Bohdan Stashyns'kyi (who was also responsible for the murder of his associate Lev Rebet in 1957) has added to the myth and the emergence of a modern-day hero.

The Nazi–Soviet Pact and its Aftermath

The period of 1939–41 is a critical one in Ukrainian history and for the OUN-B. It begins with the Nazi–Soviet Pact of August 1939, an event that led to the reunification of Ukrainian lands inside a single republic, similar to the borders of the contemporary state.[50] This event has been the subject of an acclaimed book by the Polish–American historian Jan Gross, which provides an accurate perspective of the mixed blessings of Soviet rule for the local population.[51] From the Soviet perspective, the Pact with Hitler was a strategic necessity that led directly to the "liberation" of territories that had long yearned for reunion with their ethnic counterparts in Soviet Ukraine and Soviet Belorussia. Some of these writings can be illustrated by examples from the late Gorbachev period, a time when the Baltic States had already renounced the Nazi-Soviet Pact as an illegal treaty that had led to the annexation of these states by Stalin's Soviet Union through the use of military threats and the presence of the Soviet army. As a result, Soviet writings took on a more defensive aspect as it became necessary to justify what was perceived as an imperialistic piece of land grabbing. The period is also an important one for the OUN, which continued its underground existence at a time when all legal Ukrainian political parties were dissolved. Even the Communist Party of Western Ukraine (KPZU) had minimal influence since it had been officially terminated, along with its mother organization, the Communist Party of Poland, by the Comintern on Stalin's orders in July 1938.

One of the earliest discussions of the Perestroika period to comment on the consequences of the Pact with Hitler appeared in October 1988 in a L'viv newspaper. The article, by S. Makarchuk, set out to explain how Western Ukraine became part of the USSR after the Soviet invasion of 17 September 1939. The historical context was that the Soviet leadership had extended "a helping hand" to fraternal Ukrainians and Belorussians living in Poland. The author decried Hitler's earlier annexation of Austria, as well as the dismantling of the state of Czechoslovakia after the Munich Treaty, and the failure of Soviet-British negotiations, thanks to the lack of interest on the British side, in August 1939. The Western powers acted insincerely in the hope that Hitler's forces could be turned against the Soviet Union. As a result the Soviet-German Pact was a "historical necessity" in order to win time and protect the Soviet Union in the event of an outbreak of war with Poland. However, Stalin's collaboration with Hitler in dismantling the Polish state, according to Makarchuk, was "politically incorrect" and "destroyed the dignity of the Polish nation." He cites Molotov's reference to Poland as "the ugly offspring" of the Versailles Treaty. The author maintains that the invasion did not ipso facto attach Western Ukraine and Western Belorussia to the USSR, it simply created the prerequisites for such an action. He states that the concept of a union of these lands with the Soviet territories was not new, and had even been advocated by native Communists in the 1920s and 1930s. In 1936, the KPZU had spoken out in favor of the autonomy of Western Ukraine and even its secession from the Polish state. Its strategic goal by this time was union (or reunion) of these territories with the Soviet Union. In 1939, the "age-old dreams" of the Ukrainian people were realized, and the concept was extremely popular with workers and peasants. Makarchuk admits that the elections to the People's Assembly in L'viv to decide the fate of the region were rigged, but he perceives no contradiction because the CC CPU was taking care of the people. The vote count was not distorted.[52]

A deputy of the L'viv city council, V. E. Honcharuk, addressed the "Act of Union" of Western Ukraine with Soviet Ukraine in a speech of early 1991. While condemning the crimes of the Soviet period, Honcharuk stressed that only under Soviet rule was it possible to unite the Ukrainian lands and Ukrainian people. He criticizes those politicians and historians who seek to diminish the significance of the October 1939 People's Assembly that issued the decree on unification. He believes that such views were prevailing because some politicians are prejudiced against any measures that were introduced by Communists. He maintains that the allegations of illegal actions, falsifications, and Red Army interference in these elections are unfounded. In the past, Ukrainian residents of Poland had generally boycotted Polish elections, and yet in 1939 about 92% of the electorate participated in the process. As for the apparent lack of democracy, Honcharuk observes, 340,000 people opted not to vote and a further 326,000 voted against the single list of candidates, which is an indication that dissent was possible. He acknowledges that at the time of writing, the Nazi–Soviet Pact was being assailed from various sides. Did this affect the unification of ethnic Ukrainian lands? He feels the answer is no because the decision to incorporate Western Ukraine was a reflection of the popular will.[53] It needs hardly to be said that the accounts of Makarchuk and Honcharuk soon receded into the background, as more analytical studies were offered from the perspective of an independent Ukraine. They represented the last attempts to offer a Soviet perspective of one of the more blatant examples of Stalin's empire-building.

In this same year of 1991, historian V. Kovalyuk examined the impact of the Ukrainian question on the making of the Nazi–Soviet Pact. He agrees with the émigré historian Basil Dmytryshyn that the Ukrainian question was one of Stalin's key considerations in pursuing an agreement with Germany. The Germans sought to use the Ukraine issue to destabilize Poland, thus using the OUN underground, but never contemplated seriously the formation of an independent Ukrainian state. The concept of an independent Ukraine could be used to prod the Soviet leadership into invading the eastern part of Poland, thus facilitating the downfall of the troublesome Polish regime. At the very outset of the war, Kovalyuk claims, Ukrainians openly expressed their anti-Polish sentiments. The Poles responded by arresting Ukrainian activists. When Ukrainians (and particularly those in the OUN) perpetrated violent attacks on the Poles, these were a direct response to Polish excesses: "Violence breeds violence." The Red Army, in Kovalyuk's account, had orders to avoid engagements with Polish forces provided there was no resistance to the invasion. Another order prohibited artillery and aerial bombardment of Polish centers. The Polish authorities took advantage of this mild approach to evacuate a large number of troops into Romania and Hungary. Kovalyuk addresses the question of the reception of Soviet troops in Western Ukraine, contrasting the views of Gross—who maintains that the welcome was quite warm—and Dmytryshyn, who asserts that there was little popular enthusiasm for them. Kovalyuk states that many people welcomed the Red Army, but members of intellectual and business elites, as well as OUN members, remained suspicious of the new rulers.[54]

The Pact receives short shrift from historian Yurii Shapoval. He notes that Communists "then and now" have claimed that the Pact permitted the postponement of the inevitable conflict between Hitler's forces and the Red Army for 20 months, but says that this is only part of the story. In fact, Stalin's regime had violated the very principles of Leninist diplomacy that opposed any secret treaties. How can one ignore the fact that the Pact led to the dissolution of the Polish state, he asks? Such an agreement was brazen aggression that had little to do with the liberation of Ukrainian and Belarusian territories, particularly when one takes into account the NKVD reprisals against the local population that occurred after 1939. He also cites evidence that a part of the Soviet population had difficulty comprehending the rapid volte-face in Soviet diplomacy. NKVD monitoring of the population uncovered the following comment:

We older people became accustomed to many things under the Soviets. We learned not to be surprised by anything. But the young people are not only shocked, they are also angry. In the demonstrations of friendship with the instigators of pogroms they see treason on the part of the party leadership. We teach young people to hate Fascism and yet Stalin stands alongside these people.

Shapoval stresses that the secret protocols that supplemented the Pact—specifying the division of Polish and Baltic territories between Germany and the Soviet Union—were unknown not only to the population, but also to many Politburo and Central Committee members. They were thus manifestations of Stalin's personal authority that did not reflect the mood of the people, who could not understand why it was necessary to form an alliance with the enemy. Shapoval discusses the disruptive impact of the Pact on Communist parties worldwide and the failure thereafter of the common front against Fascism. In fact many German Communists who had sought refuge in the USSR were handed over to the Gestapo.[55]

So should the date 17 September 1939, when the Red Army crossed the Soviet border, be celebrated as an important date in Ukrainian national history? Stanislav Kul'chyts'kyi calls for a thorough and accurate analysis of the various events. He looks in depth at the terms of the Pact, signed on 23 August in Moscow with a secret protocol that envisaged the division of "zones of mutual interests" between the two signatories. The second article of the secret protocol declared that most of the German–Soviet line demarking control was to run along the Narew, Vistula, and San rivers, with the larger part of Polish territory falling under Soviet control. Kul'chyts'kyi sees the Pact as the start of the Second World War (rather than 22 June 1941, the traditional Soviet starting point), and argues that Hitler hoped the Western democracies would simply swallow the occupation of Poland in the same way they had accepted—albeit grudgingly—the Anschluss of Austria and the incorporation of most of Czechoslovakia into Germany. On 3 September the German ambassador to the USSR, Count Schulenberg, requested that Molotov inform his German counterpart von Ribbentrop when Moscow intended to deploy troops to its section of Polish territory, as the Germans were concerned about a possible war with European powers. On 5 September Molotov had responded evasively without stating a precise date for the movement of the Red Army. On 17 September when Stalin gave the order to advance, the Soviet side depicted the event as a mission of liberation to protect vulnerable ethnic Ukrainians and Belarusians after the Polish state "had ceased to exist." Therefore a media campaign was launched that condemned the Polish authorities for their brutal treatment of the Ukrainian and Belarusian communities. Though there was in Kul'chyts'kyi's view some grounds for that comment, the issue had never come up publicly prior to 1939.[56]

German diplomats were disappointed with the publicly expressed Soviet perspective, particularly as Molotov admitted in his conversations with Schulenberg that the USSR hitherto had not expressed concern for national minorities in Poland. The new interpretation of the invasion forced the Soviet leadership to abandon plans to occupy Lublin and a portion of Warsaw provinces, as stipulated by the Pact. In a subsequent agreement of 27 September 1939 Stalin allowed Germany to occupy these territories in return for obtaining Lithuania. Hitler meanwhile was obliged to go along with Stalin's wishes at this point because he could not risk a two-front war. As is well known, neither the British nor the French declared war on the Soviet Union after the latter's invasion of Poland, and the Polish Government-in-Exile (which moved from Romania to France, and ultimately to London, England) was obliged to accept the situation, too. Kul'chyts'kyi acknowledges that initially the population of Eastern Poland welcomed the Soviet troops, and the Ukrainian SSR grew by almost 8 million people. Initially he perceives both benefits and drawbacks to Soviet rule from the Ukrainian perspective: standards of living rose and unemployment was virtually eradicated, and about 500,000 peasant families received land and property, while industrial goods began to arrive from Eastern Ukraine. On the other hand, repressions soon began against so-called unreliable elements. The Poles estimated that about 1 million ethnic Poles had been removed from their native lands but, Kul'chyts'kyi notes, the Soviet side remained unwilling to divulge such information. One should admit, he points out, that the Soviet authorities had played a crucial role in re-uniting Ukrainian territories, but on the other hand it is also possible to comprehend why local Ukrainians offered such a hearty welcome to Hitler's forces when they crossed the border on 22 June 1941.[57]

Kul'chyts'kyi also observes that some basic facts from this period have rarely entered the debate hitherto. On 31 July 1941, the USSR officially declared the Nazi-Soviet Pact to be invalid. In September 1941, the USSR joined the Atlantic Charter, rejecting the use of force to gain advantages in international relations. Thirdly, the conferences of the wartime leaders at Tehran (November-December 1943) and Crimea (February 1945) recognized Soviet control over formerly Polish territories, while the Poles were compensated by the return of western and southern regions that had been Germanized since medieval times. In conclusion, he believes that the analysis of the Pact requires a broad-minded approach. The historical circumstances of 1939 provided a rare opportunity to reunite Ukrainian territories and it was necessary to take advantage of this situation—Kul'chyts'kyi does not incidentally indicate why Stalin would have wanted to expand the territory of Ukraine specifically; particular given this same author's depiction of Stalin's hostile attitude to Ukrainians during the Famine of 1932-33. However, only at this juncture and under the corresponding circumstances was it possible to ensure international recognition of the new Ukrainian borders. Thus, had such borders only been changed in later years, as Soviet Ukraine underwent a metamorphosis into an independent state, the international community would not have supported such a notion. Therefore notwithstanding some of the negative connotations, 17 September is a great historical date for Ukrainians and should be celebrated accordingly.[58] The logic of Kul'chyts'kyi's argument is somewhat bewildering if one is to believe that violent annexation of territory rather than negotiated treaty was a means to ensure that most ethnic Ukrainian territories were to be included in what became the modern state. An argument could equally be made that according to the principles of the Paris peace treaties that followed the First World War, the independent Polish state had agreed to the autonomy of the large region inhabited by ethnic Ukrainians. Presumably what is behind his statement is an understandable reluctance to even broach the question of potential revisions of the borders of contemporary Ukraine. However, such a question—other than briefly over the future of Crimea in the early 1990s—has never entered public discussion.

The Nazi–Soviet Pact also changed the situation of the OUN, which faced a leadership crisis after the assassination of Konovalets'. Historian Mykhailo Koval' provides an entertaining outline of the evolution of the OUN, including the period of the German and Soviet occupation of Ukrainian lands in the period September 1939 to June 1941. Koval' notes that Stepan Bandera became one of the most important figures of the Western Ukrainian "national liberation movement." "The intense winds of history," i.e., the start of the Second World War, brought about a split in the OUN leadership. There had been serious differences regarding tactical strategy that manifested themselves at an early stage in the movement's history. He points out that at the OUN conference in February 1940, the older generation of members supported Andrii Mel'nyk, but the majority of the attendees—young people of the democratic persuasion (he does not define what he means by democratic)—backed Bandera as leader. In April 1941, the followers of Bandera convened for the Second Great Congress of the OUN in Krakow. At this meeting Mel'nyk was excluded from the organization, and the OUN formally split into two wings: the group following Mel'nyk (OUN-M) and that following Bandera (OUN-B). The split was caused in part by disagreements concerning their respective attitudes toward Germany. German preparations for an attack on the USSR were well known and thus played a role in the key question of the leadership of an anticipated future independent Ukrainian state. Should those leaders be the veterans of the organization or the leaders of the younger generation? Koval' seems in no doubt as to the correct answer to this question. The rift, which lasted for dozens of years, prevented the unification of all national liberation movements in Western Ukraine, thus enabling foreigners to take control of Ukrainian lands. However, the consequences of the division were not immediately apparent as OUN leaders wished to take advantage of an international situation that promised much for the emergence of an independent Ukraine.[59]

What Koval' deems as requiring an explanation is why the strategic conceptions of the OUN anticipated that an alliance with the German dictator would be of benefit or advantage to Ukraine. He cites OUN leader Myroslav Prokop,

who wrote in 1989 that in post-Versailles Europe only one revisionist force
had the capability to start a war that could alter the international situation by
force. Therefore the OUN oriented itself toward Germany and sought allies
among the members of the German government. Koval' also comments that
the strategic thinking of the OUN was based on the ideas of Dmytro Dontsov,
according to whose writings Ukraine would be liberated from the Bolsheviks
"in the shadow of the German war in the east." The Germans regarded both
factions of the OUN as reliable partners in the quest to transform Germany
into a great power. In turn, the Ukrainian leaders did not anticipate German
aggression against Ukraine during the coming military operations. From a
scientific perspective, Koval' reflects, that paradox is hard to explain. In retro-
spect, it is plain that the OUN leaders would have little impact on the thinking
of the Nazi leadership, but they seem to have been swayed by the old image of
the relatively tolerant German leadership under Kaiser Wilhelm II that had
seen German troops occupy Ukraine in the latter months of the First World
War. Such naivety, says Koval', betrayed a lack of political skill on behalf of
the OUN leadership. However, the OUN–Nazi link emulated similar contacts
by authoritarian governments of Central Europe during the 1930s. It should
not be described as collaboration, in part because most of the OUN functionaries were not Soviet citizens, and even Stalin and Molotov had entered into a
union with the Nazis—the logic of this deduction is somewhat hard to follow.[60]

The period 1939–41 in the Soviet-held territory was a relatively quiet one in
terms of overt activities of the OUN, the leaders of which for the most part
had moved to the German-occupied lands. However, the political situation for
the Ukrainian population in the Soviet zone soon began to deteriorate.
Shapoval notes that one of the consequences of the Nazi–Soviet Pact was the
deportation between the autumn of 1939 and autumn of 1940 of 312,000
families, or 1,173,170 people.[61] Most of these early victims were Poles. According to another writer, V. Kovalyuk, who is commemorating the 50th anniversary of a little-known event, the first OUN encounter with the NKVD
occurred on 27 February 1941, when seven young Ukrainians rose up against
"the regime of Red Terror" on the farmstead Kuleby, located at the juncture
of L'viv, Ternopil', and Ivano-Frankivs'k (then Stanyslaviv) oblasts. Two of the
rebels are described as "aliens" from Zbarazh Rayon. Kovalyuk portrays the
protests as part of a struggle that had lasted hundreds of years and which was
continuing, i.e., the desire for Ukraine to become a free country.[62] In the
summer of 1941, the NKVD massacred thousands of prisoners in West
Ukrainian jails before retreating eastward. One article focuses on the explora-

tion of the prison at Volodymyr-Volyns'k by the L'viv association Memorial. In 1941, the open prison gates confronted the new German occupants and civilians with the sight of hundreds of dead prisoners, but only twenty bodies could be identified. Likely, the author writes, these were not Poles since they had already been moved to the east or killed elsewhere. The skeletons all had a single bullet hole in the back of the head and the majority of victims were young men aged 20–30 years. "The memory," the title of the non-attributed article states, "shoots right through you."[63]

The "Akt" of 30 June 1941

Easily the most controversial episode to this point in the war from the perspective of the OUN was the declaration of independence by supporters of the Bandera faction which had entered L'viv with the *Nachtigal* unit, accompanying the German army into Ukraine. That the announcement was premature seems self-evident looking at the event from the perspective of 65 years. Equally controversial is the aftermath to the declaration, with the eventual arrest of the OUN leaders, including Bandera who did not enter Ukraine; and the rapid demise of the period of cooperation between the OUN-B and the German authorities. Among Ukrainians today, one finds a broad range of views on the significance of the *Akt* from those who regard it as one of the most important events in the history of Ukraine—the prelude to what occurred in 1991—to those who maintain that independence was announced without popular support and under the auspices of Hitler, hence a signal of the close links between the OUN-B and the German High Command, if not the Nazi regime itself. Here we will look more or less chronologically at a sampling of writings on this event and its consequences, based both on scholarly research and more popular writings in the Ukrainian media, in order to assess the importance of the *Akt* for the modern state, and its place in the minds of residents of Ukraine, as well as being a symbol of national aspirations for an independent state during the anticipated opening of Ukraine and defeat of the Soviet forces.

In an article published in May 1988, V. P. Troshchyns'kyi writes that just a few days after the attack on the Soviet Union, the Germans demonstrated definitively their negative attitude to the notion of creating even a fictional, puppet "Ukrainian state." Berlin regarded the announcement of an independent Ukraine in L'viv "under Fascist occupation" as inexpedient. However, the Ukrainian nationalists continued to perceive their future through the instrument of Germany. That is why the *Akt* included the statement that the Ukrainian state would be closely linked with National Socialist Greater Germany which, under the leadership of Hitler, "is creating a new order in Europe and the world." As to the immediate task, together with the independence declaration, the nationalists gave priority to the creation of a Ukrainian army, which would assist the German army and enter immediately into battle. When the *Akt* was announced, texts of the statement by acting premier Yaroslav Stets'ko were telegraphed to Hitler, Goering, Mussolini, Spanish dictator Franco, and other Fascist leaders. Troshchyns'kyi remarks that the telegram to Hitler referred to him as "our Fuehrer." He concludes that the declaration of an independent Ukraine on 30 June was a propaganda action carried out by the German leaders through their agents, "the Ukrainian bourgeois nationalists." However, it was never approved by Hitler. Despite such reticence, the collaboration continued, and according to some spokespersons among the nationalists, the lack of approval from the German leadership did not have great significance and the subsequent arrest of Stets'ko was nothing more than a temporary misunderstanding.[64]

On 30 June 1990, activists from the Ukrainian Rukh and the Ukrainian Republican Party organized a meeting in the market square of L'viv. To commemorate the declaration of 30 June 1941, the black and red flag of the OUN was hung on a house in front of the tribune. Author L. Chishkun took exception to what he termed the "nationalists' open-air history lesson" and accused them of falsifying history. He expressed surprise that one of the speakers at the meeting, Y. Nikols'kyi, should characterize the *Akt* restoring the Ukrainian state as an unknown page of Ukrainian history. In fact, he pointed out, the speakers took care to ignore "the treacherous essence" of the independent government of Stets'ko. In future writings, the "nationalists" omitted the third point of the *Akt*, i.e., the words pledging loyalty of the new government to the Third Reich, which is building a new order in Europe and the world, "and helps the Ukrainian people to liberate themselves from the Moscow occupation." One of the major Nationalist myths, continues Chishken, is that of OUN resistance to the Nazis. He doubts that an independent Ukrainian state could have been proclaimed without the prior knowledge of the Germans and he accuses leaders of *Nachtigal,* like the future UPA leader Roman Shukhevych, of murdering Polish scholars in L'viv. Such distortions of history, in the writer's view, had a clear political objective, namely to elicit Nationalist sentiment. He quotes one of the youth leaders among the Ukrainian nationalists as referring to a "struggle to the death with Moscow" and urging his compatriots not to get carried away with support for democracy or a parliamentary system.[65] The purpose of this article seems clear: to equate the OUN-B closely with Hitler's Germany, dispense with the notion that the Ukrainians only allied with the Germans in order to attain an independent Ukraine, and to undermine the emerging sentiment that the OUN-B represented interests that had come to fruition in modern Ukraine, now on the verge of independence. This was a fairly typical propagandistic piece of the late Soviet period. But how was the *Akt* portrayed in subsequent discourse?

One rejoinder appeared in mid-1992, a time when many of the more controversial issues of Ukraine's recent past were questioned. The author, R. Rakhmannyi, attempts to make sense of the Second World War through the prism of the "Ukrainian Question." In the author's view, the date of 30 June 1941 ranks as the most important in 20th-century Ukrainian history, because it was on this date that the Ukrainians unambiguously charted their future path in the struggle for liberation. He perceives the war as the struggle of Western democracies to re-establish state borders as they existed in 1935, and to restore the Versailles system, which had ignored the principle of self-determination. The Atlantic Charter, he observes, speaks only of the restoration of states destroyed by Germany, Italy, and Japan. To the cohort of these states, belongs the "aggressive state" of Poland and "destructive" Russia, signifying that all those people "melting away in the Russian pot" were supposed to do the same in the future as they had done after Versailles, thus forming a single Soviet people. In this way, the war was completely anti-popular and totally unnecessary. Implicitly Rakhmannyi appears to be arguing that the war might have been just if the Ukrainian question had not been ignored. The importance of 30 June 1941 is that it revealed the real strivings of the Ukrainian people and augured the creation of the armed resistance in the Ukrainian Insurgent Army.[66]

A more detailed account of the events behind the *Akt* is offered by Mykhailo Koval'. He writes that on the night of 29 June 1941, the OUN-B leadership took control of the city of L'viv in order to carry out the declaration of independence. Within seven hours after the German occupation of the city, the battalion *Nachtigal,* together with underground resistance fighters, fought with the retreating Soviet army, which departed from the city in panic and chaos. On 30 June, the OUN-B leadership met in secret, but with the knowledge of the German authorities, and declared Ukrainian independence in order to confront the Germans with a fait accompli. However, Koval' writes, such insubordination elicited a sharply negative reaction in Berlin. It became clear that Ukraine had a new and uncompromising enemy that would adopt an imperialistic policy toward it. This reaction led to a crisis in German-

OUN-B relations both in Berlin and with the occupation authorities. The message given to Bandera was that only the Fuehrer could lead the fight against Moscow, and Ukrainian allies were not needed. Therefore relations between the OUN-B and the Germans deteriorated and links between the two wings of the OUN also became more complex. The Mel'nyk wing was permitted to exist legally and collaborated openly with the occupation authorities, even though some rank-and-file OUN-M did carry out some acts of resistance against the new occupants. The OUN-B, on the other hand, suffered as a result of the *Akt*. Bandera and Stets'ko were arrested and sent to the Sachsenhausen concentration camp, and they were later joined by several hundred OUN members arrested in July. In consequence, the OUN-B ordered its units to go underground and added the Germans to its list of irrevocable enemies.[67]

Koval's namesake, Viktor Koval', provides a succinct account of this same event. On 30 June, Banderites entering L'viv ahead of the main German forces announced the L'viv *Akt* of the rebirth of the Ukrainian state and created a government. On 5 July, the members of this government were arrested by the Gestapo. On 15 September, before the capture of Kyiv, the Germans shot many OUN-B members, and Bandera and many of his supporters were taken to a concentration camp. On 25 November 1941, a German report was issued that warned of OUN-B preparations for an uprising in the Reichskommissariat Ukraine with the goal of establishing Ukrainian independence. It was therefore necessary to arrest all Banderite activists immediately and exterminate them in secret as thieves. Thus in December a new wave of executions began. The followers of Mel'nyk, on the other hand, operated freely on the territory of Galicia and in the Generalgouvernement, created on former Polish territories by the German administration.[68] This account elevates the OUN-B to the main resistance force among the Ukrainian activists, and the OUN-M as the collaborators. A former member of the *Nachtigal* battalion, taking issue with a hostile account of the OUN-B written by Wiktor Poliszczuk, writes that although Poliszczuk has tried to implicate OUN-B in collaborating with the Germans, the two battalions formed, *Nachtigal* and *Roland*, did not commit a single crime against either Communists or the Polish population of Western Ukraine.[69] Reviewer Stepan Zlupko, citing a book by V. Kosyk on Ukraine and Germany in the Second World War, likewise comments approvingly on the author's contention that the OUN-UPA was a more dangerous enemy of the Germans than the Soviet Partisans. This same author evidently cited the OUN-B Memorandum of 15 June 1941 that an alliance with Germany could be possible only if the interests of both sides were respected.[70] Both these sources offer a strongly slanted perspective of history.

A more academic analyst, Stanislav Kul'chyts'kyi, for his part observes in a 1999 article that the OUN tried to embellish the *Akt* by removing the words expressing allegiance to Nazi Germany, which opponents of the OUN subsequently used as evidence of collaboration. However, the OUN-B, in this writer's view, may have had little choice and it would be naïve to think that the *Akt* heralded anything other than a puppet state. Nationalists proclaimed the state, in other words, so that they could ascertain Germany's intentions, and the German response accordingly deprived them of any illusions. As for the long-term consequences of the *Akt*, it convinced the Western allies that the OUN was indeed a firm supporter of Hitler, and this belief was supported by the barrage of Soviet propaganda that followed. However, the Germans came to realize that the OUN (he does make any distinction between the two branches) was the enemy and began repressions.[71] A year later, the same author offered a more lengthy espousal of his views on the *Akt* in an article written for Ukrainian schoolteachers. In this article he states that between September 1939 and June 1941 relations between the Nazi officials and Ukrainian nationalists were practically problem-free. Since the OUN members were the enemies of the Poles, they were ipso facto the allies of the Germans. Although there was a formal ban on activities of non-German organizations on territories occupied by the Third Reich, the OUN leadership (Provid) in Krakow began to prepare the way for creation of future state structures in Ukraine. The OUN-B thus created the State Commission of the OUN, while the OUN-M established a Commission on State Planning. It was evident to both groups that a German–Soviet war would break out in the near future. The OUN believed that the Germans would support an independent Ukraine as it was in their strategic interest, and after the expected destruction of the USSR there would be a union of Germany and the enemies of Russia.[72]

Kul'chyts'kyi notes the similarities between the ideologies of German National Socialism and Ukrainian integral nationalism, and also the interest of the German special services in deploying the OUN forces on the territory of Ukraine. He adds that Ukrainians took part in preparatory work at instruction centers of the German Abwehr, as well as in specially created police schools and OUN organizations in Krakow. By the end of 1940, units of the Ukrainian auxiliary police had been created. Subsequently, in March–May 1941 two battalions—*Roland* and *Nachtigal*—were created in special detachments of the Abwehr. Clearly, Kul'chys'kyi believes, the Germans were exploiting the Ukrainian nationalist forces, but the latter were quite genuine in their desire for cooperation. He cites an NKVD document of 31 May 1941, stating that "the Mel'nyk faction openly supports links with the Gestapo." On 22 June

1941, the leader of the diversionary administration of the Abwehr, Captain E. Stolz, instructed Bandera and Mel'nyk to carry out provocative actions in the rear of the Soviet army. These actions were reportedly carried out by Bandera's forces in Galicia and Volyn, and by Mel'nyk's troops in Bukovyna. Soviet sources, writes Kul'chyts'kyi, interpreted this cooperation in only one way, that of actions against the true interests of the Ukrainian people. This perspective was heightened following the 2nd Great Assembly of the OUN in Krakow in April 1941, which elaborated the tactics of the OUN-B for the immediate future, with the primary goal of establishing Ukrainian independence. Both wings of the OUN sought that same goal, but as German archival materials demonstrate, Kul'chyts'kyi writes, OUN-M wanted to expand Ukrainian lands at the expense of Russia, and with German support, whereas the OUN-B wanted to use its own forces to create the independent state. To the West, such distinctions were unclear, and the Western democracies did not generally see beyond the obvious: that the OUN as a whole was standing behind the forces of Hitler. In Kul'chyts'kyi's opinion, the attitude of the West toward the nationalists did not change much even when the Cold War started; a statement that would not be accepted everywhere.[73]

Kul'chyts'kyi goes on to detail the specific events surrounding the *Akt*. On 30 June, Stets'ko, speaking on behalf of his absent leader Bandera, announced the Act of Independence, which was broadcast twice on a L'viv radio station, on the evening of 30 June and the early morning of 1 July. For several days afterward the Stets'ko government operated legally.[74] This time was used to prepare the administrative apparatus and to form a Ukrainian national-revolutionary army. On 3 July, the author reveals, Stets'ko declared that the Ukrainian state was part of a "new European order subordinate to the great Fuehrer of the German army and the German people." To this point evidently the reader should consider the OUN-B as close partners of the occupants. However, on 2 July the Gestapo in L'viv informed Berlin about the formation of a Ukrainian political government, as well as its organization of a militia and a magistrate's office. So, Kul'chyts'kyi asks: should we consider the *Akt* of 30 June 1941 one of the episodes marking state-creation activity of the Ukrainian people in the 20th century? Such a view is expressed quite often in certain literature, he adds. But the real goal was to force the hand of the Germans, who were not allies of the Ukrainian nationalists, but the conquerors of Soviet Russian territory. At the same time, Kul'chyts'kyi indicates that events happened with almost painful slowness—at least from the Ukrainian nationalist perspective. It took three weeks before Bandera refused to reject the declaration of independence, at which point he was sent to a concentration camp.

Only on 5 August was the order given by the German army commander in Ukraine to arrest Bandera's followers. At that time *Roland* and *Nachtigal* were disbanded. Yet the first mass arrests and executions of OUN-B members did not begin until mid-September, and the wholesale crackdown on them began only after 25 November, five months after the original declaration.[75]

Ukrainian writers continued to struggle with the events of this period, ostensibly in an attempt to reconcile a period of cooperation with the Germans and the short-lived *Akt*. The reflective and intelligent article published by Kost' Bondarenko under the title "The history we don't know or don't care to know" has been cited above. Bondarenko rationalizes that after Poland surrendered, the OUN faced a situation in which one harsh ruler was replaced by an even more ruthless one. The Ukrainian peasants had long recognized two clearly delineated enemies: the Polish and Soviet authorities, but the new situation brought just one enemy: the USSR. Hence it became necessary to use the assistance of Germany to defeat this oppressor. He describes the beginning of the split in the OUN and how the dissenting group formed under Bandera was unable to reach a compromise with the forces of Mel'nyk. Nevertheless, he observes, both OUN factions hoped for a military victory by the Germans, and each branch cooperated with different sections of the German authority: Mel'nyk had close links with the Gestapo and the Wehrmacht, whereas Bandera maintained contact and worked with the Abwehr. He provides perhaps the key point in this whole debate, namely that Hitler's state was far from monolithic and agencies could operate independently. Other historians have pointed out Hitler's policy of "divide and rule" among his minions. Ukrainians benefited from such disorder but ultimately suffered for it as well. Even prior to the formation of the two battalions, one of Mel'nyk's followers, Roman Sushko, formed a military unit called the *Bergsbauernhilfe*, which advanced as far as Stryi but had to leave the town in September 1939 as it had been designated as Soviet territory according to the Nazi–Soviet Pact.[76]

Bondarenko acknowledges that the *Nachtigal* and *Roland* units were accused by both Polish and Soviet historians of wartime atrocities after they entered Western Ukraine, including the execution of Polish officials and subsequently—in July 1941—taking part in *pogroms* against L'viv's Jewish population. He notes that none of these accusations has ever been convincingly proved and that those who took part in these campaigns have been consistent in their avowals of innocence. He states that the battalions were disbanded in 1942—which is quite different from the August 1941 date cited by Kul'-chyts'kyi. They were dispatched to Belarus, but most of the troops deserted and eventually found their way into the UPA. Concerning the *Akt*, he outlines the tactical differences between the two branches of the OUN at this time. The OUN-B's plan was to accompany the Germans through Ukraine and to declare independence as they moved from one town to another. The OUN-M, on the other hand, considered the *Akt* premature because the declaration of an independent Ukraine could only take place in Kyiv. Both plans proved to be pipedreams because the Germans did not take such programs seriously. After the arrest of the 29-year-old Stets'ko in early July, the occupier concealed as far as possible the events of 30 June. Such a decision ran counter to the plans of Hitler's associates such as Alfred Rosenberg, who considered that an independent Ukraine might supply some 4 million troops that could assist the German army in its push eastward. Bondarenko notes that the OUN-M leaders suffered dreadful fates and several were executed at Babyn Yar in February 1942. Like Bandera, Mel'nyk was eventually transferred to the Sachsenhausen camp.[77]

Finally, an account of the happenings of late June 1941 was provided in a scholarly account in Ukraine's main historical journal by I. I. Il'yushyn. He lists the main events: Stets'ko's proclamation of a Ukrainian state after a 23-year hiatus; the formation of a revolutionary army by Ivan Klymiv (Lehenda) on 1 July for the protection of the new state; and Stets'ko's 3 July decree about the creation of a Ukrainian state administration. Despite the apparent initial success of the new government, he notes, the attitude of Ukrainian groups was mixed and dramatically different. The Banderites offered unequivocal support, while the OUN-M was strongly opposed. The supporters of the Hetmanate of Skoropads'kyi were also hostile not to the creation of a state per se, but to the way that the OUN-B had tried to bring it about. Many Ukrainians of the older generation were of the opinion that a long-term administration could only be constructed with the aid of the Germans. Documents indicate that a considerable portion of Ukrainian society of Volhynia and Eastern Galicia regarded the *Akt* positively, but the same cannot be said of Central and Eastern Ukraine, where the basic mass of the population felt that independence could better be attained by a struggle with, not alongside, the Fascists. What was the attitude of the German leadership, Il'yushyn asks? The German reaction was extremely negative. The Nazi leadership did not consider the Ukrainian people suitable for independent statehood. That is why on 3 July members of the Ukrainian National Committee and leaders of the OUN-B were brought to Krakow to explain their actions to the Understate Secretary of the Generalgouvernement, Kundt. A week later, a directive was issued by Rosenberg in his capacity as Reich Minister for Occupied

Eastern Territories concerning the non-recognition of the Ukrainian government.[78]

According to Il'yushyn, however, the mass arrests occurred mainly among the OUN-B, as the OUN-M managed to get its representatives into key leadership posts in the organs of civil government in Kyiv, Kharkiv, Zhytomyr, and other towns and smaller settlements of Central and Eastern Ukraine. Following the German occupation of Kyiv, the OUN-M, together with local Ukrainians, created on 5 October 1941 a Ukrainian National Council led by Professor Mykola Velychkivs'kyi. However, Hitler never agreed with Slavic peoples holding significant positions, and the Council proved short-lived despite protests from the Ukrainian leaders.[79] This account provides some new insights into the thorny issue of the OUN and the *Akt* of 1941. Clearly its importance has been emphasized over those actions that were conducted in Ukraine's capital by the followers of Mel'nyk. It is the *Akt* that is becoming recognized in modern Ukraine as the forerunner of the declaration of independence of August 1991. Yet the episode represents no more than a small footnote in the horrific events of the German–Soviet war. The overwhelming impression from the overall discourse that has pervaded Ukraine since the late 1980s is of the naivety of the youthful nationalists who clearly misread German intentions regarding the establishment of the future state. Of unspoken significance is the fact that no Ukrainian state could in reality be announced from L'viv, which at best was the unofficial capital of Western Ukraine—and indeed only recognized as such by the Soviet creation of the People's Assembly in October 1939. However, the ramifications for the future do not represent the most discussed issue: that position belongs to the alleged collaboration with a regime that has been consigned to infamy, riddled with war criminals, and forever linked with the events of the Holocaust and its death camps scattered across Central and Eastern Europe. This same issue was to plague the Ukrainian Insurgent Army (UPA) as well.

Notes

1   Nikolai Romanchenko, "Plamya," *L'vovs'kaya pravda*, 16 February 1988, p. 3.

2   Myron Sluka, "Palacha k otvetu," *L'vovs'kaya pravda*, 12 March 1988, p. 3.

3   P. Maksimyuk and G. Slivka, "Ispytannym oruzhiyem pravdy," *L'vovs'kaya pravda*, 20 February 1988, p. 3.

4   V. Zarechnyi and O. Lastovets, "Banderovshchina," *Pravda Ukrainy*, 9 August 1989, pp. 3–4.

5   Ibid., *Pravda Ukrainy*, 9 August 1989, pp. 3–4; 10 August 1989, p. 4; 11 August 1989, p. 3; 17 August 1989, pp. 3–4; and 19 August 1989, p. 3.

6 A. Gorban', "Krovavyye sledy banderovtsev," *Pravda Ukrainy*, 11-12 October 1989, p. 3.

7 *Visti z Ukrainy*, No. 3 (January 1991): 1.

8 V. Maslovskii, V. Pomogayev, "OUN-UPA: Dokumenty svidetel'stvuyut'," *L'vovs'kaya pravda*, 11 June 1991, p. 2.

9 V. P. Troshchyns'kyi, "Proty vyhadok pro tak zvanyi 'antyfashysts'kyi rukh oporu' Ukrains'kykh natsionalistiv," *Ukrains'kyi istorychnyi zhurnal*, No. 5 (1988): 77-78.

10 S. Makarchuk, "OUN: Metamorfozy voennogo vremeni," *L'vovs'kaya pravda*, 27 November 1988, p. 3.

11 Wiktor Poliszczuk, *Legal and Political Assessment of the OUN and UPA* (Toronto, 1997), pp. 13-26. For a more objective account, see Alexander J. Motyl, *The Turn to the Right: the Ideological Origins and Development of Ukrainian Nationalism, 1919-1929* (Boulder, CO: East European Monographs, 1980), pp. 142-143.

12 Roman Holovyn, "Pomsta za smert' Ol'hy Basarab," *Za vil'nu Ukrainu*, 13 February 1999, p. 2.

13 Mariya Bazelyuk, "Zaplatoyu nam radist' borot'by," *Za vil'nu Ukrainu*, 11 February 1994, p. 2.

14 Mariya Bazelyuk, "Z rodu Kravtsivykh," *Za vil'nu Ukrainu*, 22 February 1994, p. 2.

15 Leonid Cherevatenko, "Heznanyi voyak," *Za vil'nu Ukrainu*, 10 June 1994, p. 2.

16 Roman Pastukh, "Za narod poklaly molodi zhyttya," *Za vil'nu Ukrainu*, 23 December 1995, p. 2.

17 Roman Pastukh, "Dva portrety narodnykh heroiv," *Za vil'nu Ukrainu*, 22 December 1998, p. 3.

18 Peter J. Potichnyj, ed. *Litopys UPA: Underground Journals from Beyond the Curzon Line: 1945-1947*, Vol. 16 (Toronto: Litopys UPA, 1987), p. 112.

19 Myron Kuropas, "Free at last! Free at last!" *The Ukrainian Weekly*, 8 December 1991, p. 7.

20 Viktor Koval', "Ukrains'ka Povstans'ka Armiya: Dovidka Instytutu istorii AN URSR dlya Komisii Verkhovnoi Rady Ukrainy z pytan' bezpeky vid 1 lypnya 1991 roku," *Ukraina i svit*, No. 35 (18-24 September 1996).

21 Stepan Mudryk-Mechnyk, "OUN—kermanych nashoi borot'by," *Za vil'nu Ukrainu*, 5 February 1998, p. 2.

22 Mykhailo Koval', *Ukraina v Druhii svitovii i Velykii Vitchyznyanii viinakh, 1939-1945 rr.* (Kyiv: Vydannyi Dim Al'ternatyvy, 1999), p. 144.

23 Stanislav Kul'chyts'kyi, "Za Ukrainu, za ii volyu," *Ukraina moloda*, 31 August 2000, p. 10.

24 Kost' Bondarenko, "Istoriya, yakoi ne znayemo, chy ne khochemo znaty?" *Dzerkalo tyzhnya*, No. 12, 29 March-5 April 2002 [http://www.zn.kiev.ua/ie/index/387/].

25 I. I. Il'yushyn, "Natsional'no-vyzvol'ni prahnennya ukrains'kykh ta pol's'kykh samostiinyts'kykh syl za chasiv Druhoi svitovoi viiny," *Ukrains'kyi istorychnyi zhurnal*, No. 1 (2003): 82-96.

26 "Yevhen Konovalets': do natsional'noho kalendarya," *Literaturna Ukraina*, 28 May 1992, p. 7.

27 Ihor Hulyk, "Yevhen Konovalets'—za Ukrainu i za ii idei," *Za vil'nu Ukrainu*, 14 June 1991, p. 2.

28 Ibid.

29 Volodymyr Yavors'kyi, "Vin ne vpadav u vidchai. Vin borovsya," *Za vil'nu Ukrainu*, 22 May 1993, pp. 1-2.

30 Mykola Oleksyuk, "Ubyvtsya Konoval'tsya vidomyi," *Za vil'nu Ukrainu*, 19 September 1992, p. 1.

31 Mykhailo Yatsura, "Vidlunnya zlochynu," *Za vil'nu Ukrainu*, 23 May 1998, p. 2.

32 N. Karpova, "Vybor," *Pravda Ukrainy*, 4 January 1990, p. 4.

33 V. Dovgan', "Kem byl Bandera: shtrikhi k politicheskomu portretu," *Pravda Ukrainy*, 13 December 1990, p. 3. In another article of this same period, S. Karnautska cites the proceedings of the interrogation of the Abwehr colonel, Erwin Stolz. Stolz states that in September 1939, after the defeat of the Polish army, the Germans released Stepan Bandera from prison and recruited him as an agent. S. Karnautska, "Portret bez retushi," *L'vovs'kaya pravda*, 8 May 1991, p. 2.

34 Ibid.

35 Ol'ha Ivanova, "Kto vin, Stepan Bandera?" *Samostiina Ukraina*, No. 15 (April 1992): 4.

36 Roman Pastukh, "Rodyna Stepana Bandery," *Za vil'nu Ukrainu*, 13, October 1994, p. 2; 14 October 1994, p. 2; 15 October 1994, p. 2; and 18 October 1994, p. 2.

37 Roman Pastukh, "Sestry Stepana Bandery pereizhdzhayut' do Stryya," *Za vil'nu Ukrainu*, 18 January 1995, p. 2.

38 Ivan Krainii, "Vo im'ya ottsya Andriya Bandery," *Ukraina moloda*, 28 October 1999, p. 10.

39 Omelyan Kushpeta, "Znav ioho osobysto," *Literaturna Ukraina*, 23 January 1992, p. 6.

40 Yaroslav Kitura, "Stepan Bandera—symvol svobody," *Za vil'nu Ukrainu*, 4 January 1996, p. 2.

41 Petro Duzhyi, "Borot'ba za derzhavu tryvaye," *Za vil'nu Ukrainu*, 1 January 1997, p. 2.

42 Nataliya Khramamova, "Rol' Bandery: bez pyshnykh vusiv ta ek'zal'tovanoho patriotyzmu," *Ukraina moloda*, 23 July 1996, p. 8.

43 Yuri Kril, "Stepan Bandera is back home," *Den'; The Day Weekly Digest*, 15 October 2002 [http://www.day.kiev.ua/259594/].

44 See, for example, the vitriolic article by Nikolai Shybyk, "Porkhavka," *Pravda Ukrainy*, 21 November 1989, p. 4.

45 Mariya Bazelyuk, "Khto vidvazhnyi, nekhai ide z namy," *Za vil'nu Ukrainu*, 28 January 1994, p. 2.

46 Ivan Krainii, "Nevidomyi Yaroslav Stets'ko," *Ukraina moloda*, 1 February 2002, p. 4.

47 Vasyl' Marochkin, "Trydtsyat' dniv z Mykoloyu Lebed'em," *Visti z Ukrainy*, No. 27 (June 1991): 3.

48 Mykola Lebed', "My znaly-nas chekae Ukraina," *Za vil'nu Ukrainu* (22 August 1992): 1–2.

49 Halyna Hordasevych, *Stepan Bandera: lyudyna i mif* (L'viv: Piramida, 2001).

50 Transcarpathia was incorporated in June 1945, by agreement with Czechoslovakia, and the Crimea was transferred from Russia to Ukraine as a "gift" in 1954 to mark the 300th anniversary of the Treaty of Pereyaslav. Otherwise the boundary changes that occurred in September 1939 basically were adhered to in the formation of the modern state.

51 Jan T. Gross, *Revolution from Abroad: the Soviet Conquest of Poland's Western Ukraine and Western Belorussia* (Princeton, NJ: Princeton University Press, 2002).

52 S. Makarchuk, "Volya naroda," *L'vovs'kaya pravda*, 26 October 1988, p. 2.

53 Cited in V. Bondarchuk, "Velichiye oktyabrs'kikh dnei," *L'vovs'kaya pravda*, 28 February 1991, p. 2.

54 V. Kovalyuk, "Zakhidna Ukraina na pochatku Druhoi svitovoi viiny," *Ukrains'kyi istorychnyi zhurnal*, No. 9 (September 1991): 36.

55 Yurii Shapoval, "Komunistychno-fashysts'kyi 'roman.' Podii 1939 roku ochyma komunistiv todi i teper," *Ukraina moloda*, 22 October 1999, p. 4.

56 Stanislav Kul'chyts'kyi, "I znovu pro 17 veresnya 1939 roku," *Istoriya Ukrainy*, No. 38 (October 2000): 9.

57 Ibid.

58 Ibid.

59 Koval', *Ukraina v Druhii svitovii i Velykyii Vitchyznyanii viinakh (1939-1945 rr.)* p. 146.

60 Ibid.

61 Yurii Shapoval, "Skazaty vsyu pravdu: do 50-richchya UPA," *Literaturna Ukraina*, 1 October 1992, p. 7.

62 Larysa Hupalo, "Vony polehly na Kulebakh," *Za vil'nu Ukrainu*, 7 March 1991, p. 4.

63 "Tsya pamyat' rozstrilyuye hrudy," *Za vil'nu Ukrainu*, 16 January 1999, p. 3.

64 V. P. Troshchyns'kyi, "Proty vyhadok pro tak zvany 'antyfashysts'kyi rukh oporu' Ukrains'kykh natsionalistiv," *Ukrains'kyi istorychnyi zhurnal*, No. 5 (May 1988): 79-80.

65 L. Chishkun, "Ploshchad' Rynok 10, 30 yunya 1941-90 gg." *L'vovs'kaya pravda*, 6 July 1990, p. 4.

66 R. Rakhmannyi, "Vyznachnyi Akt istorii," *Za vil'nu Ukrainu*, 30 June 1992, p. 2.

67 Koval', *Ukraina v Druhii svitovii i Velykii Vitchyznyanii viinakh*, p. 148.

68 Viktor Koval', "Ukrains'ka Povstans'ka Armiya: dovidka instytutu istorii AN URSR dlya Komisii Verkhovnoi Rady Ukrainy z pytan' bezpeky vid 1 lypnya 1991 roku," *Ukraina i svit*, No. 55 (18-24 September 1996).

69 Myroslav Kalba, "Hirka-pravda—zlochynnist' OUN-UPA," *Za vil'nu Ukrainu*, 25 June 1996, p. 2.

70 Stepan Zlupko, "Ukraina v svitli nimets'kykh dokumentiv," *Za vil'nu Ukrainu*, 28 June 1997, p. 2.

71 Stanislav Kul'chyts'kyi, "Kolaboratsionizm OUN-UPA: derzhavnoi zrady ne bulo," *Ukraina moloda*, 8 December 1999, p. 7.

72 S. Kul'chyts'kyi, "Akt 30 chervnya 1941 roku," *Istoriya Ukrainy*, No. 23-24 (June 2000): 6-9.

73 Ibid.

74 Of course the question of what was legal is surely up for debate. The city had been under Austrian rule until the outbreak of the First World War; Polish after the Treaty of Riga; Soviet from September 1939; and was now Ukrainian under German auspices!

75 Ibid.

76 Bondarenko, "Istoriya, kotoruyu ne znaem, ili ne khotim znat'," *Zerkalo Nedeli*, No. 12 (29 March-5 April 2002).

77 Ibid.

78 Il'yushyn, "Natsional'no-vyzvol'ni prahnennya ukrains'kykh ta pol's'kykh samostiinyts'kykh syl za chasiv Druhoi svitovoi viiny," pp. 88-89.

79 Ibid., p. 89.

CHAPTER 4

MAKING HEROES: THE EARLY DAYS OF OUN-UPA

Introduction

This chapter examines interpretations of the topic of OUN-UPA[1] as constituents in the process of constructing a national history in Ukraine, and in particular the changing interpretations of this organization in Ukraine. Several introductory premises need to be stated. First, as earlier, the goal is not to determine factual truth per se, but rather to analyze the prevailing narratives. Second, this chapter includes a sampling of newspapers of different political perspectives and readership published in the period from the late 1980s until the early 21st century, from different geographical regions of Ukraine, as well as journals, scholarly works, and contemporary textbooks. Third, no organization is monolithic or static, and OUN-UPA was no exception. Conceivably, also, it might have been possible to focus solely on the Organization of Ukrainian Nationalists (OUN), or one of its branches (Banderivtsi or Melnykivtsi), or even to look at the Ukrainian Insurgent Army without the antecedent of the OUN.[2] However, the tradition of Soviet historiography was to treat the organization as one entity, and historians and government leaders of contemporary Ukraine follow that same practice. Thus we will adhere to the acronym OUN-UPA, with the understanding that in so doing, there is a tendency to simplify the nature of this political and military formation.

The subject matter is as controversial today as it was shortly after the end of the Second World War. It is a topic that continues to divide Ukraine, as exemplified by a recent survey (examined in more detail below), which indicates a geographical split in attitudes toward OUN-UPA: the most favorable are people in the western regions and the least well disposed, those in the far east and south. My focus is on several key events that have elicited the most discussion in recent years, beginning with the formation of UPA. This chapter will ask several questions: in what ways has the interpretation of OUN-UPA changed since the late 1980s? To what extent has one form of propaganda— the Soviet—been replaced by another, which is very supportive of the insurgency of the OUN and the UPA and identifies it with the current independent

Ukrainian state? In what way has this modern "nationalist" narrative created heroes from the wartime OUN and the early UPA insurgency? Are there common themes in this "hero creation"? Have myths been created about UPA warfare itself? How has what was essentially an anti-Soviet operation directed against the triumphant and powerful Red Army been depicted in modern analyses and in what ways have these analyses changed since the late Perestroika period? How have the writings dealt with the difficult question of collaboration with the Germans? In turn, how have these same narratives dealt with Soviet wartime heroes and to what extent have these figures been removed from the pantheon of heroes suitable for independent Ukraine?

The Late Glasnost Period

Though the later years of the Gorbachev administration in the USSR witnessed a reassessment of Stalinism similar to that of the Khrushchev era, the insurgency of OUN-UPA in Western Ukraine over the years 1942–53 remained more or less a taboo subject. The insurgents were labeled "bourgeois nationalists," and described as the "worst enemies of the Ukrainian nation," traitors who fought against their own people and in collaboration with the German invaders. The portrayal was typified by the book of historian V. Cherednychenko, *Natsionalizm proty Natsii,* one of the basic Soviet texts of the 1970s.[3] The era of Glasnost brought only tentative amendments to this perspective. Even two decades later, P. Maksym'yuk and G. Slyvka, making reference to a 1988 book by the polemicist Klym Dmytruk—author of numerous derogatory works on OUN-UPA and the Ukrainian Catholic Church—agree that Ukrainian nationalism was "the enemy of the Ukrainian people, a servant of German Fascism." They approve of the way Dmytruk debunks the myths propagated by Ukrainian émigré historians about the OUN's quest for Ukrainian independence.[4] Also typical were demands for extradition of insurgents now living abroad for alleged war crimes. One such example was that of OUN member Ivan Stetsiv, a native of Canada, reportedly a member of the German-backed police, and responsible for the deaths of several local pro-Soviet activists, as well as 21 Polish families.[5] The usual practice was to inform a local village assembly of the atrocities carried out, after which the assembly demanded the extradition.

At the same time, Soviet writers and propagandists went to great lengths to discredit scholarship in the West, particularly articles and books that emanated from Ukrainian institutions. According to one author, the CIA began to establish centers specializing in Ukrainian subjects, such as the Prolog Research and Publishing Corporation in New York in 1952, and Smoloskyp in Baltimore. The American secret services also reportedly created the international Samizdat headquarters in Munich, Germany in 1977. In such an anti-Soviet climate, former "Nazi henchmen" were permitted easy entry into the United States and Canada "disguised as scientists and writers." This same author maintains that the Russian Institute at Columbia University, spearheaded by Philip Moseley, introduced a project for the study of the Ukrainian SSR in three parts, two of which—1917-20 by J. Reshetar and 1939-45 by J. Armstrong—were completed in 1952 and 1955 respectively. Concerning the OUN and the UPA, the contention is that scholars such as Professor G. Strobel of the University of Mainz tried to introduce the notion, "borrowed from anti-Soviet Ukrainology," that the UPA directed its operations against both the Germans and the Russians. He perceives the goal as the concealment of the connection of "OUN bands" with Fascist German occupation and the intelligence agencies of the Third Reich. In 1981, under the auspices of the American Association for the Advancement of Slavic Studies, the "falsifiers" organized a round-table on the topic of Ukrainians in the Second World War, featuring as speakers Armstrong, G. Kulchycky, and K. Farmer, who tried to demonstrate that the UPA was a popular movement in Ukraine. Such works are familiar to anyone who has studied the Soviet versions of Ukrainian history, but this one surprisingly appeared as late as 1987 from the leading publisher in Kyiv and at the behest of the Institute of History, Ukrainian Academy of Sciences.[6]

In 1989, *Pravda Ukrainy* published a series of articles on the Bandera movement, which investigated both the early years of the OUN and the UPA insurgency. Having condemned OUN's earlier leaders Evhen Konovalets' and Andrii Mel'nyk for "personally" shooting Kyiv workers in 1918, it accuses the Nationalists of the OUN of participating in *pogroms* in L'viv after the German invasion of the summer of 1941. The writers selectively employ documents to demonstrate atrocities of OUN-UPA in Western Ukraine, particularly innocent victims such as old women and children, under the close supervision of the German occupation forces. The authors also acknowledge that many OUN members were "simple, honest people" who had been "duped" by their leaders.[7] The ostensible purpose of such a remark is to explain to the readers why so many people in Western Ukraine appeared to sympathize with the insurgency in the later years of the war and early postwar years. The campaign against OUN-UPA also required emphasis on the cruelty of their deeds, particularly on individual examples extracted from the general conflict between the various forces. According to one account, the methods used by the insurgents exceeded those of the Germans in brutality. Before killing their victims, it was pointed out, they would poke out their eyes, cut off their noses and ears, torture them using electric currents, and bury them alive or throw them into wells.[8]

The effectiveness of Soviet propaganda about OUN-UPA is hard to measure. But as late as 1991, a date when the press was relatively open, there were still letters appearing in the press about "nationalist crimes." A typical example came from the Cherkasy region in the form of a letter to the weekly *Visti z Ukrainy*. Its author pointed out that issue 48 from 1990 had examined the horrors of the Stalin period, "which was all well and good." But, he wanted to know, why was there nothing about the atrocities of the Banderites against their fellow Ukrainians in Western Ukraine?[9] In his article published in July 1991, V. I. Maslovs'kyi writes that there was a deep political confrontation in Western Ukraine in 1944–52. On one side was the majority of population, the interests of which were protected by the Soviet state under the leadership of the Communist Party and Soviet organs. This sector fought for the final destruction of Nazism and now wished to overcome the political and psychological repercussions of the war. On the other side stood the Ukrainian nationalists and various sorts of German collaborators, organized in military formations and later in an underground army. They fought fiercely against the Soviet state and its people. The peak of this confrontation occurred in 1944–47. Today, the author writes, as new conceptions of many historical events are devised, political forces in Western Ukraine are changing the narrative. Destructive, ultra-radical forces disguised as democrats not only declare their heritage in the nationalist formations of the past, but also create new organizations for young people. They attempt to rehabilitate OUN-UPA, deny its collaboration with Nazi Germany, and either keep silent about the crimes of the Banderites or present them as inevitable sacrifices for freedom. They sing the praises of these same people as national heroes and erect monuments to the leaders of the OUN. Nationalist ideas appear on the pages of newspapers and all the so-called nationalists, as well as remnants of nationalist formations abroad, call the national movement of the 1940s "the national liberation struggle."[10]

Maslovs'kyi's article is an indicator of the limits to a revision of views by 1991. Clearly by the end of the Soviet period, the OUN-UPA was still widely treated as a treacherous and collaborative body that had committed war crimes in Ukraine. The very terms Banderite or OUNite were considered the worst of epithets outside Galicia and Volhynia, the former Polish territories of

Ukraine. Conversely, the memory of OUN-UPA in émigré Ukrainian circles was quite different: one of heroism against enemies that were far more powerful, as it fought a dual battle against the forces of Hitler's Third Reich, on one hand, and the Soviet Red Army and police forces on the other. Over the past decade what may be termed the heroic conception of OUN-UPA, prevalent among these western circles, and perpetuated by the selections of documents in series like *Litopys UPA*,[11] has gradually come to displace the one-sided and partisan Soviet perspective, though it has been a difficult evolution, not least for historians in contemporary Ukraine.

How the UPA was formed

The creation of the UPA has been dealt with in detail by the American political scientist, John A. Armstrong, who perceives its formation as a direct response to Soviet Partisan raids into Volhynia led by Sydir Kovpak, starting in the late summer of 1942. By the winter of this year, the Germans had begun a counterattack, accompanied by ruthless measures against Communist supporters and the local peasantry. By early 1943, Armstrong notes, the OUN-B decided on a full-scale insurgency, with two main bases in Volhynia. Close to the town of Rovno (Rivne), there were two main OUN groups: one under Kruk, backing the OUN-B, and close by, and working with it, another group under an OUN-M commander called "Khrin." Several other small groups operated in this area, and the concept of a single command emanated from Taras Bul'ba-Borovets', leader of the original UPA. By the spring of 1943, the situation became exacerbated with new Partisan raids from Kovpak, following orders from Moscow.[12] Armstrong notes that the negotiations between the OUN-B, OUN-M, and Borovets' were unsuccessful, and the former began to seize control of the resistance movement. The OUN-B commander, Dmytro Klyachkivs'kyi, expropriated the original name UPA, which was already well known to the local population. The key military leader from *Nachtigal*, Roman Shukhevych, also arrived in L'viv in the spring of 1943 and was appointed commander of the OUN-B insurgents. In July and August, to ensure its supremacy, the OUN-B had begun to attack units of the OUN-M and those following Borovets', with the latter fleeing to Warsaw. Armstrong believes that the suddenness of the defeat of these forces and the triumph of the OUN-B was a result of the former groups not wishing to fight their compatriots and cause the outbreak of a civil war. He also attributes the results to the stronger organization of the OUN-B. By the autumn of 1943, it basically occupied the rural regions of Volhynia and southwest Polissya.[13] Quite clearly then, the UPA emerged from an organization of the same name in the spring and summer of 1943, clearing the area not only of rival Ukrainian groups, but also—as noted below, though curiously not by Armstrong—of the local Polish population.

Yet the formation of the UPA, according to its participants and supporters, dates from October 1942. Historian Viktor Koval' outlined the official version of its formation in Ukrainian academic circles in 1996. Koval' maintains that in April 1942, the Bandera wing of the OUN organized the Second Conference of OUN Independent Statehood Supporters, at which it appraised the Soviet–German war as essentially a struggle of two imperialist powers based in Moscow and Berlin for dominion over Ukraine. At that time, the OUN believed that the Germans would win this war, and therefore adopted the policy of opposition to Hitler. Such a policy was predetermined in part by the Germans' refusal to countenance an independent state in L'viv in June 1941. A regional war would be fought, after which the OUN might extend its influence to the rest of Ukraine. The first two "hundreds" (cavalry units of 130–200 troops) were created in the Volyn' region in October 1942, reportedly to protect local residents from terrorist bands from the Polish underground—the Armia Krajowa (AK)—as well as Soviet partisans. The first *sustained* activities began in March and April 1943. Discipline was said to be exceptionally rigorous, with punishment administered by the security service (*Sluzhba bezpeky*) on behalf of both the OUN and the UPA. The UPA was divided into three territorial-operative groups: UPA-North, UPA-West, and UPA-South; and its first commander was Klyachkivs'kyi ("Klym Savur").[14]

Writing a few years earlier, V. P. Troshchyns'kyi suggests that if the UPA formed as a response to Germany's non-recognition of the "Akt" of 30 June 1941, then it would logically have been established in that same year. In fact, he declares, the first armed units were founded only in the spring of 1943, and they were created to fight the Bolsheviks rather than as a response to localized terror in Volyn' and Polissya. He believes that initial orders were given to Borovets', who ran the so-called Polis'ka Sich, to put together a nationalist army in the spring of 1943 and direct it against Soviet Partisans concentrated in the Polissyan forests. After November 1943, Borovets' was isolated as the Germans made a separate agreement with the OUN-B to incorporate his (Borovets') band into a new unit run by the OUN, under the general umbrella name of the Ukrainian Insurgent Army (UPA).[15] Another, more recent source (echoing Armstrong for the most part), explains that a negotiated agreement between Borovets' and the OUN-B was later violated by the latter, which disarmed units affiliated with both Borovets' and Mel'nyk, murdering some of the commanders of these units.[16] According to an overtly hostile source, the historian Wiktor Poliszczuk, the decisive event in the formation of the UPA was the German defeat at Stalingrad, after which the OUN-B recognized that Germany would eventually lose the war. In the hope that the Western allies would create a second front in the Balkans, the OUN-B thus resolved to establish its own force in an effort to control Western Ukraine.[17]

In his 1999 book, Mykhailo Koval' comments that the basis of the national armed formations of the OUN were the rebel formations established in the forests of Volhynia and Polissya by Borovets' and called UPA. Many officers who had been part of the Ukrainian battalions *Nachtigal* and *Roland*, which accompanied the German army into Western Ukraine in the summer of 1941, took part in its creation. Subsequently it attracted a large number of volunteers who were trained by the OUN, and in October 1942, a united rebel army under Klyachkivs'kyi (Klym Savur) was established along with the SB military intelligence unit. However, he maintains, the initial operations were on a limited scale, and the UPA leaders were careful to avoid German garrisons, dedicating most of their activities to the single cause of preventing a new "Bolshevik occupation." Local divisions and individuals did conduct spontaneous attacks on German forces. After the end of June 1943, when Germany removed the Waffen SS and police forces from Ukraine, the UPA activities began to expand.[18] The overall picture then suggests first of all that the main body of the OUN-B-UPA forces was formed in the spring of 1943, and that it was an anti-Soviet formation that occasionally resisted the Germans as well, but avoided a sustained conflict with the Wehrmacht, perhaps in the knowledge that the principal contest would inevitably be with the incoming Soviet forces.

There is similar controversy over the size of the insurgent army. The detailed 1991 article by Maslovs'kyi cites figures of 40,000 men in 1943–44 (from the *Encyclopedia of Ukraine* published in Paris in 1980) and 80,000 with 20,000 sympathizers in early 1944, and support from 100,000 in the OUN underground (from émigré UPA historian Petro Mirchuk). He adds that careful analysis leads to the conclusion that in early 1944 the UPA comprised about 90,000 fighters.[19] Writing in 1997, Kul'chyts'kyi cites German estimates from 1944 that the UPA numbered between 100,000 and 200,000, but notes that Soviet figures were lower at 90–100,000. Ukrainian nationalist sources, in turn, he observes, have mentioned a figure of 30,000 troops. The numbers are difficult to determine, in his view, because of UPA's peasant composition and the combination of armed resistance with daily life in the villages. However, according to NKVD documents from February 1944 to December 1945, the

Soviet organs had killed 103,000 insurgents, and captured 127,000, while 50,000 had surrendered voluntarily—a total of 230,000.[20] The same author, writing two years later, states that the UPA was formed from late 1942 and within a year had 40,000 members.[21] Thus there would logically have to have been a massive rise in numbers over the next two years to reach the figure of a quarter of a million men. Further, an army of such size would hardly constitute a partisan or guerrilla force, since it would be impossible to conceal such numbers of troops, even in the forests. What seems to be the case is that the population of entire villages has been included in the overall totals of OUN-UPA membership.

Personalities and Heroes

To reverse the Soviet perspective of the armed insurgency, nationalist historians have produced new narratives that describe the bold and heroic deeds of individual members of the UPA troops. This device has been employed consistently in the nationalist as well as the non-nationalist media of Ukraine in the independence period. The ostensible goal has been to add OUN-UPA members to a pantheon of local heroes that has appended to the list of Bohdan Khmelnyts'kyi, Ivan Mazepa, and Symon Petlyura, the names of Yevhen Konovalets', Roman Shukhevych, and Stepan Bandera, and a host of lesser figures, all of which are said to have had as their primary goal the attainment of an independent Ukrainian state.[22] Such articles date from the first months of Ukrainian independence. They include the story of Yaroslav Halashchuk, a former member of an UPA hundred who spent 44 years in hiding, after concealing himself in his sister's house in 1948, and avoiding the MGB by hiding in a closet.[23] Another "hero" was Petro Fedun, a native of the town of Brody, and former member of the Red Army who later fell into German captivity. In 1943 he joined the UPA, losing his brother, a fellow member in 1946, and witnessing the deportation of his parents to Siberia. Under the pseudonym Petro Poltava, Fedun became one of the main ideologues of the underground, counteracting the figure of the "new Soviet man" with the Ukrainian patriot, who knows and is proud of Ukraine's past, and for whom the highest principle is "the good of the nation."[24]

More common were tales of the heroism of UPA members, and conversely the crimes and general moral degeneracy of their Soviet opponents. An article about the UPA fighter Petro Saranchuk, for example, notes that the first drunken people he ever met were "Soviets." Saranchuk was earmarked for forced labor in Germany, but escaped from the train and joined the UPA in the forest, even though he was only 14 years of age. The young conscript organized teenagers from neighboring villages, and convinced them to steal weapons from the Germans. Later, while imprisoned in the Gulag—having been arrested by the NKVD in 1946—Saranchuk was reportedly among the organizers of a rebellion in the camp at Noril'sk.[25] The legendary UPA insurgent, Roman Riznyak-Makomats'kyi, together with a companion, disguised himself as a Soviet officer sometime in late 1945 or early 1946, and held up a staff car containing the head of the Drohobych MGB, Saburov. Saburov's life was spared in return for a box of secret documents. In 1948, however, Makomats'kyi was ambushed by the MGB and incarcerated. Allegedly his death sentence was commuted to life imprisonment at the behest of his former captive Saburov.[26] The Makomats'kyi story is somewhat unusual in that the MGB representative appears to have a human side. However, the stories vary, and occasionally one reads of UPA members who were not heroes and even vacillated in loyalty between UPA and the authorities, such as Luka Pavlyshyn, who initially had opposed the OUN policy of terrorism in interwar Poland, and was later accused of collaboration with the Soviet forces. Accused by nationalists of betraying the location of UPA leader Roman Shukhevych, Pavlyshyn was arrested by the Soviet authorities a week after Shukhevych's death and imprisoned in the Gulag.[27]

Dmytro Hrytsai joined the underground OUN in the early 1930s and was among those arrested for the assassination of Polish Deputy Defense Minister Bronislaw Pieracki. He spent two years in the concentration camp at Bereza Kartuska and "the Poles beat him cruelly." In 1939, when the German army invaded Poland, Hrytsai was arrested again by the Polish authorities, but he escaped when the Polish guards deserted their post. He was among those who proclaimed an independent Ukrainian state in L'viv on 30 June 1941. In 1943, the Germans arrested Hrytsai, but he was freed "miraculously" by the OUN, who managed to bribe a German prison guard, after which OUN troops, dressed as German guards, escorted him out of L'viv. He later became a well-known UPA general who was killed in December 1945.[28] Another victim of the Germans portrayed in narratives of the early years of Ukrainian independence was Andrii P'yasets'kyi, Minister of Forestry in the government of Stets'ko. He was born in 1909 in Velyki Mosty (L'viv region), and lost an older brother, who died in 1919 serving in the Ukrainian Galician Army. Andrii was a member of the scouting organization Plast, which was dissolved by the Polish authorities during the Pacification of Ukrainian regions. P'yasets'kyi graduated from the L'viv Polytechnical Institute and worked in an office that looked after forests on private estates. One of his "customers" was the Greek Catholic Church. In 1941 he was arrested by the NKVD and imprisoned not far from L'viv. On 30 June 1941, he was appointed Minister of Forestry in the newly proclaimed Ukrainian government and organized a research institute. He protested the Germans' cutting down of forests in the following year, after which the Yaniv forests were declared a scientific reserve. The article claims that P'yasets'kyi's initiatives irritated the Germans and thus they arrested him. He was executed together with 99 other hostages in retaliation for the murder of a German police officer.[29]

A fairly typical story is that of Ivan Klymiv-Lehenda, a native of the village Sol'tsi (Sokal' District, L'viv Oblast), who became an OUN member after entering the law faculty at L'viv University. During the Polish pacification campaign, Klymiv was arrested in his native village in September 1930 and "cruelly beaten" by police and gendarmes. In 1932 he was rearrested and given a six-month prison sentence. In 1933 he was sentenced again. In 1936, he began to train OUN members and took the name "Lehenda." Imprisoned following a trial of forty-two Ukrainian students in Luts'k in 1937, he was freed when the war broke out. He organized the evacuation of Ukrainians from Soviet to German-occupied Poland, and was a close collaborator of Stets'ko in the summer of 1941. The story continues to relate how he saved Jews and spread the OUN network into Eastern Ukraine. He was arrested by the Gestapo in December 1942 and killed shortly afterward.[30] In a subsequent article on the same subject, the same author adds to the biography of Lehenda, noting that in 1935 he spread the OUN's network into Volhynia, as a result of which he was arrested in Luts'k in 1937. During his work in Soviet-occupied Poland, he was responsible for the evacuation into German-held territory of businessmen, priests, lawyers, and writers, and he maintained close contacts with Metropolitan Andrii Sheptyts'kyi in Krakow. When the war broke out, he led mobile groups into Eastern Ukraine, managing to evade arrest for some time by establishing friendly relations with Slovak officers. As with several other nationalist heroes, the story is of a figure who initially seems to have been prepared to cooperate with the Germans (moving people into the German-occupied zone is clear evidence that the USSR was considered the hostile power), but eventually fell foul of them and suffered death as a result.

Volodymyr Shchyhel's'kyi (Burlaka) was another legendary UPA commander who led a "hundred" in the territories of the Zakerzonnya (Eastern Poland after the Second World War). He began his service in the Ukrainian police, and in June 1944, on the orders of the UPA, he and his police unit retreated to the Carpathian Mountains. His first combat operation took place

in the Stanyslaviv (Ivano-Frankivs'k) region, when his hundred defeated an
NKVD unit. In Zakerzonnya, his operations were directed against Poles. The
1947 agreement between the police forces of the USSR and Poland (Czechoslovakia was also a signatory) made UPA operations in Zakerzonnya impossible, particularly after those sympathetic to the insurgents were deported. Burlaka's unit was moving westward when it was ambushed by Czechoslovak
troops. Burlaka was captured in 1947 and extradited to Poland two years
later.[31] By contrast, Kharkiv native Andrii Matviyenko entered the UPA via
the Red Army, in which he was a lieutenant. In June 1944, a military tribunal
sentenced him to death for desertion. He was imprisoned in L'viv but together
with a number of inmates he managed to escape during a German air raid. His
desertion is portrayed in the nationalist press as a conscious rejection of Stalinism. He joined the UPA and married a woman from Galicia. During his
activities, the NKVD deported Matviyenko's wife and their small child to Siberia as punishment for their link to "an enemy of the people." Matviyenko
was in charge of an UPA security unit and took the name "Zir." His exploits
included the destruction of a large NKVD unit at the village of Yasinka in
1947. In 1949, he was surrounded by NKVD troops and took his own life.
The author comments that the Soviet authorities refused to rehabilitate Matviyenko, a state of affairs that the author hopes will be remedied by independent Ukraine.[32]

Occasionally there are attempts to reconcile the two visions of the war
years in Ukraine. Nina Romanyuk focuses specifically on Ukrainian women
in the OUN and UPA. She asks whether the Kharkiv nurse working for the
Red Army knows that while she carried out her daily work at the front,
somewhere far away in Volhynia friends of her age were dying in a different
war. They died in disgrace, cursed and forgotten for decades, but all the
same young, naïve, and committed to their Motherland, albeit a different
one. She asks whether that same Kharkiv nurse would be aware that young
Ukrainian girls took care of wounded men in the underground hospitals of
the UPA, risking their lives, daily and hourly, just like she did. The names of
these UPA nurses are not imprinted on memorials and traces of their graves
have long since been obliterated by tractors and bulldozers. Someone might
erect a cross to commemorate them, but it would be destroyed again and
again. Their photographs remained in the archives of the MGB, along with
laconic inscriptions like "sentenced" or "killed in the bunker." The author
then provides several biographical accounts of UPA women that she found
in the MGB archives. Included among them is that of Nadiya Borodyuk
(born 1921) who heard about the OUN from her brother in 1936, and be-

gan to read the Decalogue and underground literature though she did not participate formally in any organizations. She was very much affected by the NKVD massacres of prisoners in Western Ukraine prior to the Soviet retreat from the Germans. In March 1942 she came into contact with the OUN and was ordered to organize a women's network in the district. She left her autobiography in a bunker, with the last entry dated 19 January 1948. On 12 March 1949, the note was found in the bunker by the NKVD after its inhabitants had all been killed. Romanyuk also relates the stories of other women killed in postwar conflicts with the Soviet security forces, including one who collected linen for the insurgents, a typist of the local OUN branch in Hirka Polonka, Luts'k region, and the owner of a house who provided a bunker for the insurgents.[33]

A somewhat different vision is presented in the account of Luka Pavlyshyn's grandfather, who died in 1987. Pavlyshyn studied at the L'viv teachers' training seminary, became involved with the nationalist movement, and began to read the works of Dontsov. He did not fully accept the nationalist Decalogue, and advocated ideas more akin to democracy and humanism. Reportedly he also opposed the OUN's campaign of terrorism in interwar Poland. Nevertheless, Pavlyshyn did become a member of the OUN in 1937, and as a graduate of a Polish military school he was responsible for training peasants in the techniques of warfare. In 1939, he appeared in Krakow, where he made the acquaintance of a number of prominent figures, such as Roman Shukhevych (the future commander of the UPA) and Yaroslav Stets'ko. In 1941 he was among those OUN scouting missions dispatched into Eastern Ukraine and subsequently became a member of the UPA. The author offers a sympathetic account of the activities of his grandfather in 1944–47, but it is also evident that he is seeking to defend him from accusations (from OUN-B members) of collaboration with the Soviet authorities. The author maintains that his grandfather worked in the OUN underground and kept in contact with Shukhevych. He responds to reports that Pavlyshyn betrayed the UPA commander by stating that his grandfather and family were arrested one week after Shukhevych's death in 1950. He also describes how in the Gulag, Pavlyshyn organized a prisoners' rebellion. The author concludes by stating that

Some patriots died for the idea, others betrayed it to survive. My grandfather did what he could for Ukraine, but he was not a hero. He survived because he chose the middle ground, saying 'If we cannot be lions, let us be sly foxes.' The key point is that he did not betray anyone; rather he offered assistance to many people.[34]

In some reports, the hero figure is forced to serve two masters, and most often joined the UPA before being drafted into the Red Army. One case is that of Kostyantyn Oksenyuk, who was forced to join the UPA after an UPA representative arrived in his village and demanded that every family should send one representative to the insurgents. During his time in the UPA, Oksenyuk reportedly was engaged in fighting the Germans on eight different occasions. Meanwhile Soviet Partisans attacked the village of Huta Lisovs'ka and beheaded several villagers, demanding to know where "Banderites" were hiding. The same village was later destroyed by the Germans. In the spring of 1944 as the front moved to the west, Oksenyuk returned to his village and was drafted into the Red Army, serving in a punitive battalion before he returned home in 1946. He was arrested on suspicion of supplying food to the "Banderites" and was tortured by the NKVD. On one occasion near his village, Oksenyuk was obliged to bury slain insurgents in a common grave at Kolky cemetery. After the war he worked on a collective farm, but was never able to shake off the accusations of being linked to the insurgents, and was unable to acquire the status of a war invalid.[35] Likewise, Ivan Ivanych joined the UPA as an 18-year old to avoid being sent for forced labor in Germany. In October 1943 his unit was attacked by German forces and Ivanych made for his native village. Three months later he was mobilized into the Red Army. However, in 1947 he was arrested as a former insurgent, despite the fact that he held Soviet military decorations.[36]

Myths of UPA Warfare

Alongside the individual heroes, popular discourse in Western Ukraine on the independence period in Ukraine has centered on UPA warfare as a liberation struggle; of heroes fighting oppression; of selfless warriors prepared to give up their lives for the cause of an independent Ukraine. The prelude to this sort of writing is found in the chronicles of UPA warfare by Petro Mirchuk and Lew Shankowsky, published in the West, with many of the latter's works republished in the late Soviet period in the journal *Ratusha* in L'viv. One critic notes that Shankowsky's accounts should be categorized in the realms of fantasy because he describes UPA actions in locations far distant from the location of the insurgents—Odesa, Donbas, Kryvyi Rih, and others.[37] Further, though the totals suggested above indicate heavy UPA losses in the conflict with Soviet forces, many of these accounts present stories of heavy casualties for the Soviets and minimal ones for the insurgents. One describes, for example, an ambush of Soviet forces near Rushir, organized by Myroslav Symchych (Kryvonis), which reportedly trapped an NKVD unit and killed some 400 of its troops in the ensuing battle. The insurgents in question had formed a base in the forests near the village of Kosmach, which became known unofficially as Bandera's capital.[38]

Kryvonis was also the subject of a novel by Mykhailo Andrusyak, the description of which, in the newspaper *Ukraina moloda*, adds to the UPA legend. In his early life, it is reported, his main inspiration came from his history teacher, Volodymyr Pryhorods'ko:

Awakened by the wise, passionate word, my child's imagination hurled me into the depths of historical events. With the prince's regiments, I defended Rus' Ukraine against the rapacious aliens... But most of the time I was a Cossack. At 7 years old I was ready to die for Ukraine at any time.

In the novel, the hero joins the OUN at the age of 17, and takes part in stealing the printing press of a German office—already it seems the Germans were the enemy. In 1943, Symchych, our hero joins the UPA which is portrayed primarily as an anti-Bolshevik force that includes members of different national groups. The insurgents, writes Andrusyak, were moved by a knightly spirit "that helped them to fight an armed enemy, but urged them to treat humanely an enemy without weapons." Symchych, however, would show pity on an adversary if he revealed himself as a brave and skilled warrior. Ultimately, the UPA was destroyed because of the numerical superiority of the enemy and a massive network of informers.[39] The ingredients of the myths of the UPA warrior are thus all present: idealism, self-sacrifice, bravery, and valor, and the links between medieval heroes, Cossacks, and the insurgents are clearly delineated.

Another more lengthy but typical example is the portrayal of Vasyl' Sydir (Colonel Shelest), a UPA commander in Galicia. In April 1941, Sydir became a member of the OUN Provid (leadership body) after the Second Congress of the OUN-B and was given the assignment of creating professional UPA units in Volhynia. He was also founder of schools for UPA officers: two in Volhynia and one in the Carpathians. By 1946, the UPA had become a popular force in Western Ukraine according to this account because of Soviet repression using mass terror and abuse of the local population. The NKVD tried to change the popular mood by forming fake units of the UPA security service, the SB, which was made up of MGB agents and Soviet Partisans, and which robbed the population, raped the women, and executed civilians. The author, however, also obfuscates the issue by noting that he once disguised himself as an NKVD officer on a mission to a city. There are some other characteristic trends evident in this series of articles about Shelest: the UPA managed to subvert several NKVD agents, all "Jews who betrayed secrets for money." The author claims that secret documents reveal that by 1946, "Moscow" had losses of 15,500 dead and 47,000 wounded, including 62 colonels. This information was derived from a Colonel Dorofeyev and is allegedly secret and not to be found in any archives. The account closes with a graphic description of the death of Sydir-Shelest in combat with the NKVD in April 1949, one that the author had not personally witnessed![40] Myths, legends, and reality are all intertwined in the stories of UPA's heroism.

One account offers a retrospective conceptualization of Ukrainian history: "We were insignificant people, but we were aware that the cruel enemy Bolshevik was walking on our land, trampling down with his leather boots everything that was dear to us." The NKVD men, even in appearance, are portrayed as monsters. On one occasion cited by this author, the UPA member Taras was visiting the author's family, and—alerted by a treacherous neighbor—the NKVD raided the house. Taras escaped but the author's sister was taken in reprisal and the family never saw her again. Each Christmas the family would pray for the sister's return, for the protection of the Ukrainian people and the insurgents, and for all those struggling against "the hateful Communist regime."[41] Martyrs are commonplace in the narratives of UPA-NKVD warfare. They include the story of the UPA unit in the village Medvezhe, Drohobych region, in 1944, when NKVD troops surrounded the house of UPA members: the brothers Lyalyuk. The insurgents burned compromising literature and after a brief but intense battle, blew themselves up.[42] In Mykolaiv district of L'viv region, the local UPA hundred was led by Ivan Pankiv (Yavir), which reportedly destroyed an NKVD unit in 1945, killing 22 people. This unit, it was reported, would repeatedly raid Ukrainian villages, looting and raping the women. During the skirmish, two prisoners were taken, and one was crying "Kill me, I am Russian!" However, the UPA troops did not kill the prisoners. On 4 May 1950, the account continues, Yavir's bunker was destroyed by the NKVD, and the last bunker in this district fell on 22 July 1950.[43]

Occasionally, the narratives take on elements of stark realism, rendering the accounts very valuable in terms of ascertaining the precise nature of the conditions during the prolonged warfare. An interview with a former UPA insurgent, Mykhailo Zelenchuk, is a case in point. He starts with a description of a winter's sojourn in the bunker. For several months the insurgents did not venture outside, receiving information about world events from a radio. It was a difficult time, he recalls, but they were motivated by the notion of attaining an independent Ukraine. He comments on the hopes of the OUN in 1941 that the Germans would grant independence to Ukraine, Belarus, and the Baltic States. The arrests of Bandera and Stets'ko, as well as the executions of several hundred rank-and-file nationalists deprived them of any illusions. His statement that the UPA never carried out forced mobilization of the population and that every member was a volunteer is somewhat less convincing. He cites confrontations with Red Army soldiers who were rather reluctant to fight. UPA troops and Soviet soldiers would pass each other without firing. The Soviet authorities, however, developed quite a successful counterinsurgency through a developed network of agents and secret informers. The Soviet side also tried to discredit the reputations of leading insurgents, sowing discord and suspicion within UPA ranks. There were also public displays of violence, such as an insurgent with a rope around his neck being dragged by a horse until his neck was broken. As a result, many peasants agreed to cooperate with the authorities, but others continued to supply the insurgents with food and clothing. By early 1950, Zelenchuk continues, the informers' network was so extensive that the UPA could no longer eliminate individuals through acts of terror. His unit was often forced to resort to different methods to deal with traitors.[44] These methods became increasingly violent. As the account by Zelenchuk illustrates, the local population had by now been subdued and the position of the insurgents had become precarious. Thus the "realist" discourse tends to offer a more accurate account of events than what might be termed "image-building" or heroic narratives, intended to portray a united struggle against an implacable enemy. At times also the line between hostile and friendly elements in Ukrainian villages blurred and it was impossible to know whether one might be betrayed or for whom a particular individual was working. The situation reflected the gradual strengthening of Soviet power into the late 1940s and early 1950s, particularly after the consolidation of Stalin's control over Eastern Europe and the collectivization of individual peasant farms in Western Ukraine.

A second example of "realist" narratives is an overview of the book "Thousand Roads" by Mariya Savchyn, who took part in various underground activities, along with her husband Vasyl' "the Orlan"[45] Halas, deputy leader of the Zakerzonnya division of the OUN. Savchyn was born in the village of Zadvir'ya (L'viv region) and at the age of 14 she joined the youth faction of the OUN. She evaded death numerous times, leaping from trains, escaping through windows, and taking refuge in a bunker that was surrounded by

NKVD troops. Because she survived in miraculous fashion, she decided it was her duty to maintain the memory of the liberation struggle, especially its final phase. While providing a detailed description and some documentary activities of OUN actions,[46] she tried to depict the mood and the atmosphere of the struggle. She describes her companions in meticulous detail even though she often knew them only by their pseudonyms. Most attention is devoted to the final years of the campaign, when special troops and agents of the Soviet security forces were hunting down the remaining insurgents, who in turn by this time were often exhausted and in poor health. Orlan and Mariya Savchyn were finally captured in 1953 with the assistance of former insurgents. By this time, everyone but the commander Vasyl' Kuk had been captured and the authorities could claim a complete victory. As torture was useless with Orlan, he was taken to Zaporizhzhya and shown various examples of the "socialist paradise" such as a kindergarten, a local museum, and a factory. It evidently made little impact on him. Savchyn asks why the authorities were so afraid of a handful of insurgents, and concludes that the Soviet authorities wished to demonstrate to the population of Ukraine that resistance was futile. The insurgents believed, in contrast, that resistance, even if only moral, was still feasible.[47]

Actions in Eastern Ukraine

Part of these narratives focuses on the so-called "marching groups" that moved into Eastern Ukraine (which is defined as the territories that belonged to Soviet Ukraine at the time of the outbreak of war). Koval' notes that the marching groups operated as "servants" of the German army and the occupation authorities and thus had permission to travel beyond the borders of Western Ukraine. The groups' members thus often traveled with the German army and sometimes even wore the same uniforms. However, the initial camaraderie began to dissipate after October 1941, when the OUN-B was outlawed. Koval' cites German documents, which state that from the fall of 1941 to the fall of 1942, members of both wings of the OUN were able to strengthen their followings in East Ukrainian cities, and in contrast to their hostility in their native regions, they often worked together. They published pamphlets and were occupied with organizational work that proved a major headache for the Abwehr and SD. By 3 January 1942, Koval' reports, German intelligence revealed that the army was being attacked by supporters of the OUN on the orders of the OUN leadership. Resistance had spread "all the way down to Crimea." Throughout 1942, the German authorities continued to express anxiety at the actions of illegal OUN formations in cities such as Kyiv, Dnipropet-rovs'k, Kharkiv, Stalino (Donets'k), Mariupil', and Odesa. After November 1941, propaganda was disseminated widely by the Bandera group "east of the Dnipro." After this point, the occupiers began to shoot anyone proposing Ukrainian independence, without trial or other legalities.[48]

Perhaps a more fanciful account is that of Bohdan Chervak, who describes the activities of Petro Voinovs'kyi, commander of the Bukovynian "Kurin'" of the Ukrainian nationalists. Voinovs'kyi was a native of Chernivtsi (born in 1913) who joined the OUN and was eventually arrested by the Romanian au-thorities and forced to serve in the Romanian army. In 1940, the article con-tinues, when Romania was forced to cede Bukovyna to the Soviet Union, the OUN attempted to take power in the region. Once the Soviet authorities took control, the NKVD arrested Voinovs'kyi, but promptly released him. When the German–Soviet war broke out, Voinovs'kyi initiated the creation of the Bukovynian "Kurin'," which consisted of three fighting groups, composed of 3,000 men. The OUN leadership reportedly ordered the "Kurin'" to move to Kyiv, a transfer of personnel that could hardly have been plausible without German cooperation. The route selected for the journey—Vinnytsya, Berdy-chiv, Zhytomyr, and Bila Tserkva—suggests that the group went along the main route to the Ukrainian capital. It is also claimed that at each major cen-ter along the road, the Bukovynians left people behind to organize "Ukrainian national life." In Kyiv, the article continues, the Kurin' swore allegiance to the Ukrainian National Council, which was under the control of the OUN-M. Voinovs'kyi also made contact with the city's OUN-M leaders. It is alleged that the Bukovynians immediately went about restoring Ukrainian national life in the capital, with some moving to recruit volunteers in neighboring set-tlements and others forming a local police force and working in the city ad-ministration. By late 1941, Voinovs'kyi was obliged to flee to Galicia, but he was arrested there by the Gestapo.[49]

In 1992, one writer interviewed Evhen Stakhiv, the man responsible for the OUN organization in the Donbas region. Stakhiv dispelled the notion that the OUN underground existed only in Western Ukraine and claimed that it em-braced all of the Donbas-Kryvyi Rih Basin. By contrast, the Communist un-derground was negligible. However, Stakhiv acknowledges, the local popula-tion did not support the nationalist ideas of Dontsov, which it equated with Fascism. This attitude led the OUN to modify the doctrine—integral national-ism was abandoned, and the organization introduced calls for social justice, the equality of nations, and humanism. Much of the interview is devoted to Aleksandr Fadeyev's story the *Young Guard* (1951), in which the local organization resisting the Nazis in occupied Ukraine is betrayed by a man called Stakhovich (i.e. Stakhiv). Stakhiv's explanation is that Fadeyev likely wrote the novel based on existing Gestapo documents and denunciations. Leaflets that included his name were disseminated in the markets of towns such as Donets'k and Horlivka. Stakhiv questions the very existence of the "Young Guard" and claims that the only authentic figure in the novel is Lyubov' Shevtsova, who was a Red Army radio operator rather than an underground warrior. He questions the acts of sabotage conducted in the novel since only provocateurs or German collaborators would carry out such self-defeating operations. On the other hand, in his opinion, the Germans constantly persecuted nationalists. In Mariupil', in a single day, the Germans allegedly executed 20 members of the OUN.[50]

One month later, in the same newspaper, A. Nykytenko, director of the museum "Young Guard," offered a response to Stakhiv's version of events. Referring to Stakhiv's remarks, Nykytenko comments that not for the first time when speaking to the press, Stakhiv refers to himself as the prototype for Evhen Stakhovich from Fadeyev's novel. Nykytenko maintains that by this means he is trying to convince the public that the "Young Guard" could actually be a link in the chain of the nationalist underground in the Donbas region. By making such comments about the Young Guard, Stakhiv attempts to draw attention to himself and events in which he allegedly participated, according to Nykytenko. However, he continues, neither during a meeting with students at Donets'k University nor in the interview with the newspaper did Stakhiv provide any documents or facts to back up his claims. Where, he wonders, are the leaflets with inscriptions like "Death to Hitler!" and "Death to Stalin!"? If the underground really had such an extensive network, Nykytenko continues, then why are there no people left who can support the words of Stakhiv? He believes that the town of Krasnodar has been deliberately omitted from Stakhiv's narrative because there are Ukrainian patriots from the war years who are still living there, but who have no recollection of the organization cited by Stakhiv. Nykytenko is also adamant that the personality of Stakhiv could not have been the prototype for the character of Stakhovich in Fadeyev's book. Fadeyev maintained that there was a prototype for this character, but since his parents were still living at the time, the novelist altered the name to Stakhovich.[51]

Despite the dispute concerning the authenticity of Stakhiv's account, reports about the effectiveness of the scouting missions continued to appear in the media of the early 1990s. Volodymyr Mazur from Poltava thus recollected that in 1941, when Germany invaded the Soviet Union, his community received a visit from mobile groups of OUN-UPA (an error of fact since the UPA had not been formed at that time). They brought a gleam of hope and the notion of national liberation. At this time Mazur joined the OUN, and eventually moved through the ranks until he was in a position of leadership. The interviewer asks whether it was difficult for a 17-year-old nurtured in the tenets of Communism to undergo such a transformation. Mazur responds that his progress was assisted by the atmosphere at his home. His mother was very religious and his family could still remember the Ukrainian National Republic of 1918. Males from his family had fought with Petlyura. Thus his family rather than his school was the defining influence on his career choice.[52] How typical Mazur was as a resident of his city is not known. Two other authors discussed the situation of OUN networks in the Dnipropetrovs'k region. They comment that it was not unusual for people to begin the war in the ranks of the Red Army but end up in the UPA or vice-versa. An OUN underground reportedly existed in Dnipropetrovs'k from 1944. Its members tried to join the UPA in order to avoid relocation for forced labor in Germany. Usually, he writes, they moved in groups through the forests of Kyiv and Kyrovohrad regions, carrying literature, weapons, and food. Sometimes such groups were dispersed by the Germans or Soviet Partisans. Some Dnipropetrovs'k OUN members attained high positions in the UPA, including one member who became Shukhevych's bodyguard.[53]

A more detailed account of alleged extensive OUN underground networks in Dnipropetrovs'k, reportedly the OUN capital in Eastern Ukraine, came from a conversation with local historian Dmytro Kudelya, published in the summer of 1995. According to this account, OUN members appeared in the city as members of expeditionary groups that followed the German army deep into Soviet Ukraine. They were mainly followers of Bandera and engaged in propaganda that in the early period of the occupation was "not anti-German." However, relations with the Germans were deteriorating after the *Akt* of 30 June 1941 and the German reprisals that followed. From 1942, says Kudelya, the struggle against the occupiers became overt. Subsequently, the author compares the OUN and the Communist underground in the city, and claims that the latter did not exist outside the materials of Soviet propaganda organs. By contrast, the Nationalists had a well-developed network and had connections to many prominent citizens, including Mayor Panas Oliinychenko. Kudelya maintains that the OUN underground in Dnipropetrovs'k had 2,000 members, several of which were prominent in later years. In order to reach accurate conclusions about the state of the OUN in this city, the author reports that he and his colleagues compared the memoirs of Evhen Stakhiv with the detailed NKVD examinations, and drew conclusions only when they were completely convinced of the correctness of their interpretation.[54] They appear to have concluded that the network was considerable and owed allegiance to Bandera.

Writing three years later, Vakhtang Kipiani elucidates the situation in Mykolaiv region in Southern Ukraine in the years 1941-1943. He outlines his personal perspectives quite openly: whereas the OUN-M was pro-German in orientation, in his view the OUN-B relied on its own strength to combat both "the Bolsheviks" and the Germans. He reports that when the war broke out, both wings of the OUN organized expeditionary groups and sent them to the east to establish local governments and distribute propaganda. Group South, led by Zenon Matla and Tymish Semchyshyn, comprised around 10,000 members. In Mykolaiv, most of the OUN members derived from Bukovyna, and joined the local administration, the auxiliary police, and the editorial boards of newspapers. Following Germany's failure to acknowledge the government of Stets'ko and the arrest of OUN-B leaders, expeditionary groups North and East were destroyed. Meanwhile, the network in Mykolaiv came under attack in late 1941 and early 1942. Forty-five members were arrested, reportedly as a result of their betrayal by one Kokot, who held the chair in Ukrainian language at Mykolaiv Pedagogical Institute. The author avows that the available materials testify that the OUN had substantial support in Soviet Ukraine, and cites an organization called "For an independent Ukraine," which was active in the village Pisky in Mykolaiv region. He refers to a statement by an OUN political leader, Yaroslav Haivas, that residents of Kharkiv, Poltava, Dnipropetrovs'k, Mykolaiv, and Kherson sympathized with OUN slogans and principles and considered themselves as true members of the organization.[55] Such claims seem inflated.

A more academic and balanced account of the expeditionary groups appears in the 1999 textbook on Ukraine in the Second World War by Mykhailo Koval', cited above. He maintains that the OUN-B operated initially as the "servants" of the German army, with which its members traveled, and even wore the same uniforms when they entered the various cities. They provided assistance to the Gestapo, the police, and the organs of the occupation. However, after October 1941, the OUN-B began to carry out anti-German actions, which they expanded to areas of Ukraine beyond their native one. In 1941-42, both wings of the OUN—which he claims could work together in Eastern Ukraine—strengthened and intensified their work to recruit new followers. In addition to underground organizations, they issued flyers and caused the occupiers great anxiety. German intelligence and Special Forces were thus ordered to regard the OUN as an organization that was harming German interests in Ukraine (obviously, one can deduce from this statement that this was not the case hitherto). Gestapo documents point to anxiety among the Germans concerning the activities of illegal OUN units in various cities, including Kyiv, Dnipropetrovs'k, Kharkiv, and Stalino. On the other hand, Koval' indicates, prior to the German occupation, the OUN propaganda network was invisible. The Germans began to lose trust in the Ukrainian auxiliary police, which it believed had been infiltrated by the OUN. Henceforth, the occupiers began to shoot all proponents of Ukrainian independence, including, according to historians from the "Ukrainian Diaspora," 621 OUN members in Kyiv alone.[56]

How can one summarize these accounts in terms of new narratives? Clearly the Soviet version of events in the early war years—particularly of the early war years in Eastern Ukraine—has been discredited. The new interpretation undermines in particular the early activities of the Soviet Partisans or former Communist officials working with them or in the rear of the German army. What is more difficult to ascertain is the degree to which it has been supplanted by the Nationalist one with respect to the expeditionary groups and indeed OUN influence in Eastern Ukraine generally. A Ukrainian administration was established in Kyiv by the OUN-M, which tried to open, or reopen, Ukrainian universities, organized a Union of Writers, and convened a form of the Ukrainian Parliament. On the other hand, the figures released in the various newspaper accounts of the OUN networks in East Ukrainian cities seem unrealistic, if not outright fantasy. The accounts also corroborate the two clearly demarcated events of the early war years: OUN–German collaboration in the summer and early autumn of 1941, followed by a period of OUN–German hostility. The narratives hardly alter the fundamental issue: that without the first event, the second could not have occurred. The German occupation thus facilitated the expeditionary groups, whereas German anger and repression of the OUN served to distinguish them from the regular occupiers in the minds of the East Ukrainians.

UPA-German Relations

One of the most sensitive issues in the reinterpretation of UPA's role during the war is its relationship, and that of the OUN before it, with the Germans. In order to illustrate the change of direction, some examples of the earlier narrative need to be demonstrated. Writing in Ukraine's most authoritative historical journal, V. P. Troshchyns'kyi commented in 1988: "Despite all their efforts, nationalist historians have found no materials in foreign archives that testify to authentic battles of the UPA with Hitlerite military units. The reason is that there were no such battles."[57] Another writer notes that the relationship of the OUN-B with the Germans became complex after the latter had failed to recognize the Ukrainian government proclaimed in L'viv on 30 June 1941. However, the OUN-B, in his opinion, never fought the Germans. Later, grassroots UPA units periodically engaged German forces, but acted on their own initiative, without orders from above. He cites German sources to show that UPA representatives allegedly assured the German side from the outset that the UPA would not attack its forces. From 1944, moreover, the UPA became an overt ally of the Germans in the struggle against the advancing Red Army.[58] An interview with former insurgent Petro Hlyn, who received a 25-year prison sentence from a Soviet tribunal, also offers evidence that the UPA "massacred not only Poles, but their own fraternal Ukrainians"[59] (the Polish issue is discussed in Chapter 6).

Further support for the theory of a sustained alliance between the UPA and the German forces is derived from archival documents from both the Germans and the KGB. Between 1988 and 1991, this interpretation constituted the official Soviet line, but already it was coming under fire. One source cites an interview with Robert Rupp, a German who worked for the SD, and served as a conduit between the UPA and the Germans. After his arrest in Prague in April 1945, Rupp revealed that he had established contacts with the OUN in 1942 on the order of the SD chief Kleinert. The OUN promised to cease attacks on Germans (so evidently they were occurring), if the Germans agreed to Ukrainian autonomy under a German protectorate. Another German officer reportedly revealed other agreements between the Wehrmacht and the UPA (rather than the OUN), according to which the UPA would cease its assault on Germans, and the Germans would not prevent UPA's elimination of the Polish population in August 1944.[60] Yet another document cited in the pro-Soviet press was a secret directive of a General Brenner, Brigade Leader 22, from 12 February 1944, which mentioned German negotiations with UPA: the UPA pledged not to attack German units and to supply intelligence information. The general in turn ordered his subordinates not to attack the insurgents even if provoked.[61] By 1944, it should be recalled, the Soviet forces were advancing rapidly through the former Polish territories of Volhynia and Galicia, and thus there was some logic to focusing forces on a common enemy. However, if the Soviet version of events had become more moderate, the nationalist narrative developed into an analysis that at the least was far-fetched, and at times entered the realms of mythmaking.

Thus writer Volodymyr Kosyk, author of a book called *Natsional-sotsialists'ka Nimechchyna i Ukraina*, comments categorically that with the exception of a few individuals, mainly associated with the Ukrainian Central Committee in Krakow, "no Ukrainian organization collaborated with the Germans." Those who cooperated with the occupation authorities were either of German pedigree or "Volksdeutsche." Though Soviet historiography often wrote about the collaboration between the Nazis and the OUN, German documents testify that the OUN-B "struggled actively" against the Fascists. In the winter of 1942, the OUN-B began to organize armed units, and by April 1943 these units were turned against the Nazi forces in Polissya, Volyn', and Zhytomyr regions.[62] Omitted in this approach is the formation of Ukrainian battalions in German occupied territory, as well as the creation of the SS Division Halychyna in 1943, to say nothing of the extensive contacts of both wings of the OUN with German forces prior to the outbreak of the German–Soviet conflict. Similarly, another author argues that the UPA did not collaborate with the Germans in any way. In 1944, she notes, UPA commander Antonyuk-Sosenko was executed for negotiating with the Germans. She also denies that the UPA committed any atrocities, arguing that these were always carried out by NKVD agents disguised as insurgents.[63]

The prolific Stanislav Kul'chyts'kyi has written frequently on the most sensitive topics of the Stalin period, including the Famine-Holodomor and OUN-UPA. He provides an interesting example of how an historian has made the metamorphosis from writing Soviet-style polemics to one who has slowly but clearly adopted something closer to the nationalist narrative. In a 1997 article, he asks the question: was the UPA a force that was collaborating with the Germans? His answer is that the relationship between OUN-UPA and Nazi Germany was far too complex to be dismissed simply as collaborationist. Western Ukrainians, having suffered ruthless NKVD reprisals prior to the Soviet retreat from their territory, "were not appalled" by the arrival of the Germans. The OUN tried to use the Germans for their own ends, i.e., the establishment of an independent Ukrainian state. The failure of the Germans to satisfy OUN aspirations in the long term led to the creation of the UPA. Kul'chyst'kyi provides some examples of the UPA fighting the Germans, but notes that with the approach of Soviet Partisans and the Red Army, the nationalists began to perceive the Germans as the lesser evil. Local agreements were made with German army units, but the Germans considered the UPA unreliable and did not seek any long-term commitment. Nevertheless, the greatest danger for the Ukrainian people was National Socialism, and the Soviet Army was the only force that could defeat the Germans. Therefore by not fighting the Wehrmacht, the UPA was working against the interests of the Ukrainian people, even though the Red Army presence signified a return to totalitarianism.[64]

In an article written two years later, Kul'chyts'kyi elaborates his views. Noting that the OUN are "national heroes for some people and traitors for others," he explains the polarity of views by the fact that in the past, Ukraine was divided between different states that harnessed the Ukrainian population to their own national and ideological values, and used Ukrainians in their conflicts as "cannon fodder." The situation, he adds, became especially acute during the German–Soviet war, which history has largely supplanted by myth. If there was collaboration between the OUN and the Germans, it existed only within an unequal alliance. The OUN was in fact willing to agree to such an alliance because of the harsh Soviet policy in Western Ukraine. He acknowledges that there were some ideological similarities between the Ukrainian nationalism of the OUN and German National Socialism, but the OUN ideology, in his view, was devoid of any racist content. Kul'chyts'kyi then partially contradicts his earlier comments with the assertion that the OUN activists were not collaborators because the Nazi leadership did not want such an alliance, and the OUN aspired for an independent Ukrainian state. The UPA, in turn, was essentially anti-Soviet, rather than anti-German, because Stalin was the principal enemy and was winning the war.[65]

An attempt to find a middle ground between anti-OUN and anti-Soviet polemics was made by historian Mykhailo Koval', in his 1999 book on Ukraine during the Second World War. Koval' correctly separates links between the OUN and the Germans, and those of the UPA and the Germans. In the case of the former, he observes that the OUN SB was organized by and modeled on the German secret police. Almost all its leaders were graduates of the German military school in Zakopane, Poland, in 1939–40. The SB's objective was to sentence and punish members of Soviet Partisan forces, Communists, Soviet and collective farm activists, so-called "easterners," and other "enemies of the Ukrainian people." The OUN strategy changed after the German defeat at Stalingrad. The concept of developing a simultaneous two-front war against the two armies representing totalitarian states was simply unrealistic. Though Hitler's attitude to Ukraine was by now well-known, compared to the prospect of outright and total "Sovietization," with massive repressions of innocent people, even the harsh German occupation appeared to be the lesser of two evils.[66] Koval' thus clearly links the OUN to the Germans even in the middle years of the war, when leaders like Bandera and Stets'ko had been placed under arrest, and OUN-B members were systematically rounded up.

OUN-UPA contacts with the Germans, however, occurred somewhat later, starting in February 1944 and continuing until the summer of that year. According to documents of the German administration, as cited by Koval', the OUN-B wished to remain outside the Soviet–German conflict, but sought assistance from the German side. The eventual outcome was that the OUN-B would trade information about the presence of Red Army troops in return for weapons. Koval' comments that the "indisputable fact" of the OUN-B-UPA leadership conducting negotiations with the Germans was something about which Ukrainian historians in the Diaspora preferred to remain silent. Soviet historians, on the other hand, chose to emphasize it, since it depicted the OUN-UPA as collaborators. The Soviet authorities discovered evidence of the talks between the OUN-UPA and the German occupiers only in April 1945. The Ukrainian NKVD informed party secretary N. S. Khrushchev in a special memorandum it had obtained after removing the Germans from the city of L'viv. However, and conversely, the documents discovered also revealed that the Germans had questioned OUN-B leaders as to why its earlier actions had been directed against the German occupying forces. Though after April 1944 they agreed to unite against a common enemy, such amity had not always been the case. Thus the relationship was essentially a tactical one, and opportunistic in character. And in terms of resolving the "Ukrainian question" the results of the cooperation were minimal.[67]

The tactical issues of the later war years need to be measured alongside the more overt collaboration with the Germans in the prewar and early years of the war, at which point the German Reich was the obvious agent for change. Nevertheless the OUN espoused extreme policies similar to those of European dictatorships, not least those of Fascist Italy and National Socialist Germany. Again, a key question is whether OUN-B ideology changed during the course of the war as its adherents claim, or whether it was moderated to appeal to residents of other parts of Ukraine, or for that matter to the Western allies, which—the Ukrainian nationalists reasoned—would sooner or later become embroiled in a new war with Stalin's USSR. That all these events occurred within the broader context of the most brutal war between Germany and the USSR should never be forgotten. But nor should it be overlooked that, as Timothy Snyder has pointed out, the war brought to the fore, through a combination of circumstances, "led by immature and angry men,"[68] the most fanatical wing of the most extreme faction of Ukrainian nationalism, one that in a democratic setting could not have hoped to win the support of the majority of the population. That it collaborated with Hitler's regime in order to win

independence for Ukraine seems quite clear; but whether the anticipated independent state would have satisfied the aspirations of most residents of a
free Ukraine is another issue.

The Death of Soviet Heroes

YAROSLAV HALAN

Yaroslav Halan (1902–1949) was a Socialist Realist, writer, and play-
wright, born in Galicia, who served as a propagandist for the Soviet regime,
particularly against the Ukrainian Catholic (Uniate) Church and nationalist
underground, both of which he accused of collaboration with the German
occupiers. He attended the Nuremberg Trials and published numerous books
and pamphlets, some of which were translated into English.[69] He also wrote at
times under the pseudonym Volodymyr Rosovych. He was assassinated by
Ilarii Lukashevych, son of a Catholic priest, and Mykhailo Stakhur, a member
of the OUN. The two assassins were discovered almost two years later and
sentenced to death.[70] As with several assassinations of Soviet hero-figures (and
for that matter nationalist heroes who suffered the same fate), there is considerable conjecture as to who might have done the killing. According to Ukrainian nationalist sources, Stalin and the KGB may have been responsible for the
murder of a writer who was a former member of the Communist Party of
Western Ukraine (dissolved in the late 1930s, with many of its leaders murdered on Stalin's orders); opposed to the anti-Semitic campaigns in the Soviet
Union toward the end of Stalin's life; and who maintained close friendships
with Poles and others. The discourse on Halan occurs quite frequently in the
Soviet and post-Soviet media without ever resolving satisfactorily the circumstances behind his death or even his outlook and loyalties. A few examples
will suffice to illustrate the debate around Halan.

In 1990, the official Ukrainian Communist Party newspaper issued an article in response to a Ukrainian radio broadcast that Halan had been murdered
by the KGB in October 1949. It observed that the "nationalist" version of his
death made several arguments. First, two to three weeks prior to his death,
Halan was expelled from his newspaper and forced to hand over his gun to
the authorities. Second, the advocates of the KGB murder theory spent some
time going over original materials in order to demonstrate that Halan was
killed on the orders of Kaganovich and Stalin. However, the Communist author claims, the real motive for the assassination was Halan's stand against

the nationalists.[71] The debate continued in the pages of *Literaturna Ukraina*, in which author Stefaniya Andrusiv asked whether Halan was a writer whose talent was warped by Communist ideology, or a militant nobody, elevated to the heights of world literature through collaboration with the enemies of his people, servitude, reports, provocations, and insinuations. Her essay, she remarks, poses more questions than it provides answers. She was unable to find any new materials on Halan's death in the archives of the secret services, most likely because they do not exist. Instead, her article is based on Soviet publications, as well as the book on Halan published in Toronto in 1992 by P. Tereshchuk; thus a classic case of material available in the West to the Ukrainian community being transferred back to Ukraine as evidence of a widespread polemical debate on a former Soviet Ukrainian hero. Andrusiv makes her position plain at the outset with her remark that Halan was the Pavlik Morozov of Ukrainian literature, whose image was crafted by the NKVD-KGB for others to follow.[72]

Andrusiv provides a detailed account of the life of Halan, who was born into a Muscophile family in the Peremyszl region. During the First World War, the Austrian government imprisoned Halan's father for his pro-Russian activities, and the family was sent to Rostov-on-Don, where Yaroslav attended a gymnasium. Later he studied at the University of Vienna and the University of Krakow, from which he either graduated (the Soviet version) or failed to graduate (Tereshchuk's account). In 1924 he joined the Communist Party of Western Ukraine, later moving to the parent organization, the Communist Party of Poland. At that time he worked for the Communist magazines *Vikna* and *Novi shlyakhy*. The author points out that several foreign sources have maintained that Halan was a double agent who worked for both the Polish and Soviet intelligence services. Another author, writing in the mid-1950s, had also declared that Halan was a Polish agent and provocateur who actively recruited agents for the Polish service. However, Halan tried to establish himself as an opinionated journalist who worked against leaders of the national-liberation movement in Galicia. During the Second World War, Halan worked at the Saratov radio station, and after 1942 he joined the editorial board of the newspaper *Sovetskaya Ukraina*. Subsequently, he worked for the Kharkiv radio station, the newspaper *Radyans'ka Ukraina*, as well as several Polish organs. The author notes that Halan's rationale was that "The last 30 years have taught us that love for Moscow is love for Ukraine, that to hate Moscow is tantamount to hating Ukraine." Despite being a Greek Catholic and being married to one (his wife was a victim of the Stalin Purges), he was one of the most active proponents of the liquidation of that church, and it was Halan's pamphlets, such as "With cross or knife?" and "What is the Union?" that paved the way for the dissolution of the Uniate Church and the establishment of the Russian Orthodox Church in Western Ukraine.[73]

Andrusiv remarks that Halan was original in attacking the Pope while issuing the usual smear campaign against traditional enemies. His failing was that he did not recognize that the Communist system could destroy its own advocates. There was a need for a ritual victim in order to introduce Soviet terror into Western Ukraine, and it was relatively easy for the authorities to blame Halan's murder on the Banderites. By the late 1940s, some of Halan's writings were not being accepted in Moscow and Kyiv. His book *The Faces* was banned, reportedly because it exaggerated the impression of the strength of OUN-B forces. Before his death, his dog had been killed and the guards removed from around his house. Andrusiv cites a letter from the KGB in Moscow to its West Ukrainian counterpart concerning how to react to Halan's death. The letter was written prior to the assassination. Two years later, the two alleged killers of Halan, Stakhur and Lukashevych, were arrested, tried, and executed. The author states that there are three possible versions of Halan's murder. The first version, appearing in Soviet publications and popular abroad, is that he was killed on the orders of the nationalist underground by Stakhur and Lukashevych. A second version is that Lukashevych believed he was acting on behalf of the nationalist underground, but that Stakhur had been compromised by the NKVD and belonged to a fictitious unit of the OUN created by the NKVD. Andrusiv cites the existence of special "Banderite" schools in Russia, which instructed Western Ukrainian youths. The third version is of Soviet responsibility, and the author compares the axe assault on Halan to that on Trotsky. Militarily educated Banderites would likely have shot him. Resolution of the question of who killed the Ukrainian writer, the author believes, will likely come from those born after August 1991 and will be taught in Ukrainian schools.[74]

Evidence of the Soviet disillusionment with—and possible implication in—the murder of Halan, is provided in an article by Mykola Oleksyuk, an historian at the State Musical Institute. Initially, Oleksyuk had a conversation with the notorious Pavel Sudoplatov, the ex-KGB general linked to the assassination of Trotsky, as well as Evhen Konovalets'. In an earlier article, Oleksyuk had not managed to prove Soviet complicity in Halan's death. In a series of articles published in 1993, he turns to the testimony of OUN member Petro Duzhyi. Duzhyi recalls that during his interrogation by the secret police, Tymofii Strokach, deputy chairman of the Ukrainian NKVD, asked whether Roman Shukhevych knew Halan personally and then added: "We will try Halan. Halan is a traitor." Duzhyi's response was: "Why is Halan a traitor when he writes exactly what the Soviets want?" Strokach reportedly responded that Halan had lied to them, by suggesting that if the authorities arrested Metropolitan Slipyi and other leading Greek Catholic bishops, then the rest of the priests would be cowed. In reality, it had incited a general revolt. It is a strange story, which suggests that Strokach would share information with a leading OUN member during an interrogation. To support his theory, Oleksyuk also cites the assassination of the Mukachiv bishop, Teodor, by agents of Strokach and Sudoplatov. Teodor's carriage was run over by a Soviet tank, and although Teodor was not killed instantly, he died later in hospital. The suggestion is that he was poisoned there by a nurse posted by the MGB.[75]

These articles demonstrate the difficulty sometimes encountered in uncovering the details of the assassination of a prominent figure, in this case of one intricately linked with the various parties in the protracted struggle between Ukrainian insurgents and the Soviet regime. Halan, however, was clearly despised at the time of his death by both sides. Three years later, Oleksyuk returned to the same theme. By this time, he seems to have reconciled himself to the likelihood that Stakhiv and Lukashevych operated on the instructions of the district OUN leader, Roman Shchepans'kyi. In the first half of the newer article, he tries to present Halan's murder as an MGB/NKVD provocation and hints strongly—albeit without much evidence—that Shchepans'kyi (pseudonym Bui-Tur) was an NKVD agent. However, in the latter part of the article, which is reliant on testimony from various OUN members, he acknowledges that Stakhiv could have been functioning on the orders of the OUN. He concludes by stating that however one interprets this tragedy of the past, the cause of all the suffering of Ukrainians was Stalin's regime, which was resented by all. It nurtured freedom fighters, among whom were some prepared to carry out murder.[76] Such a conclusion appears to be offered to account for the relative ruthlessness of OUN actions, and there is no question that the removal of Halan is an example of how far ideological enemies were prepared to go. There were very few Soviet heroes who survived the test of time. Sooner or later most were discredited, imprisoned, demoted, or eliminated. On the other hand, the pro-Moscow version of events was simply unacceptable to the OUN.

NIKOLAI KUZNETSOV

A more authentic Soviet hero was Nikolai Ivanovich Kuznetsov (1911-1944), a Soviet intelligence agent and Partisan who operated in Ukraine during the war years, and who led various operations against German officials in Rivne and L'viv. A native of Yekaterinburg region, Kuznetsov moved to Moscow and joined the NKVD in 1938. After the German occupation of Ukraine, he fought in a guerrilla group in Central and Western Ukraine called "Victors," led by Dmitrii N. Medvedev. On 9 March 1944, he was killed during a skirmish with Ukrainian insurgents near L'viv, and subsequently he was awarded the title of Hero of the Soviet Union posthumously.[77] A fairly typical Soviet account of the career of Kuznetsov comments that he was a civilian with an outstanding knowledge of German and a good athlete. This article cites his official biography, which notes that he was parachuted into the Medvedev [Partisan] unit on 25 August 1942 under the pseudonym Nikolai Vasil'yevich Grachev. The article's author believes that he was responsible for procuring intelligence information about German plans for the offensive the following summer at the Kursk Salient. The later section of the article discusses Kuznetsov's time in L'viv during which he had no contact with the Partisans. He and his group arrived there on 18 January 1944, and little is known about Kuznetsov over the following month. German documents report that he organized the assassination of the Vice-Governor of Galicia, Bauer, as well as several German generals.[78] For years, tourists visiting Western Ukraine during the Soviet era were taken to the "Hill of Glory" and other locations in L'viv known to have been frequented by Kuznetsov. The Sverdlovsk film studio also produced a movie about Kuznetsov's exploits called "Strong in Spirit." But like Halan, Kuznetsov did not fit easily into the modern era of independent Ukraine and before long his exploits came under close scrutiny.

Writing in 1992, Bohdan Dem'yanchuk observes that in the recent past the general attitude toward Kuznetsov has been that of veneration for a legendary hero. However, some organizations began to question his status in the pantheon of heroes, and even alleged that he was a provocateur, who was responsible for the deaths of dozens of Ukrainian patriots through German reprisals against his actions. As a result, youths from the militant nationalist organization UNSO[79] had thrown Molotov cocktails at Kuznetsov's memorial and the Kuznetsov museum in L'viv had been closed. Dem'yanchuk relies on the memoirs of D. Medvedev, the commander of Kuznetsov's Partisan detachment. Here, Medvedev recalls that Kuznetsov dropped a wallet that had been taken from one of Bandera's emissaries and added to it a fake directive calling for a struggle against the Germans, following the attempted assassination of General Dargel (deputy of Reichskommissar Erich Koch) in September 1943. In response, the Germans executed 38 Ukrainian hostages, all of whom were Ukrainian nationalists. In summing up this event, Dem'yanchuk recommends that readers focus on the memoirs of Vlas Samchuk, who in 1943 was a journalist and editor of the newspaper *Volyn'*. According to Samchuk, shortly after the assassination of the head of finances in Koch's office, Zehl (the attempt had been on the life of Dargel), there were rumors that the murder had been carried out by someone in the uniform of a German officer, but who was in fact a Partisan or a Ukrainian nationalist. Some Ukrainians even welcomed the action. However, Samchuk believes that the assassination was a provocation directed by Moscow. Altogether, about 500 people lost their lives in reprisals for this murder. Dem'yanchuk concludes by asking whether this memoir-literature is enough to incriminate Kuznetsov for the deaths of Ukrainian citizens.[80]

The following year, Roman Pastukh explored the circumstances around the death of Kuznetsov. According to the Soviet version, Kuznetsov died in February 1944 in Brody region during a battle with Ukrainian nationalists. The author discovered witnesses to his death among UPA fighters of the Chornohora (Karpii) unit. According to one of these witnesses, Myron Pavlyuk, the unit was quartered in the village of Boratyn, near Brody. It was learned that two German officers had been detained and were confined at the house of Holubovych. Pavlyuk and a companion arrived at the house to discover the two Germans guarded by two UPA men. Chornohora arrived, at that point dressed in Gestapo uniform and followed by guards, and demanded that the two Germans surrender their weapons. Evidently he greeted one of the Germans as Herr Siebert, which was one of Kuznetsov's pseudonyms. "Siebert" gave up his pistol, but his fellow officer exploded a hand grenade. In the confusion that followed, Siebert jumped out of the window, but was killed by machine gun fire. Pavlyuk did not discover what happened to the bodies. Pastukh, however, puts together the following narrative: in 1944 Kuznetsov was fleeing L'viv and entered the hut to keep warm, and was apprehended by Chornohora's unit. Therefore the remains of a body found in Boratyn and later identified by a Soviet anthropologist indeed belonged to Kuznetsov. However, documents about the discovery were never made public. Pastukh thinks that the files might contain materials about the Medvedev brigade, including details of countless deaths of hostages killed by the Germans in reprisal. Possibly also, there would be cases of the NKVD committing crimes while dressed as UPA fighters.[81]

The same theme is pursued by Petro Yakovchuk, who claims that the body buried in L'viv, and to whom a memorial is erected, does not belong to Nikolai Kuznetsov. Rather it is the body of a German officer. His story relates that Kuznetsov was a terrorist of the Medvedev Partisan brigade who specialized in attacks on prominent functionaries of the German administration. Yakovchuk maintains that such attacks were deliberate provocations in order to turn the Germans against OUN-UPA. In September 1943, Kuznetsov killed Zehl, and the Germans retaliated by arresting 38 nationalists. They took this action after discovering the wallet of an OUN member that had been deliberately dropped by Kuznetsov to divert blame to the nationalists. Subsequently, Kuznetsov threw a hand grenade at General Paul Dargel, and 300 hostages were executed. Following another attack—this time on Deputy Gauleiter Knust—the Germans shot 300 inmates of Rivne prison. In L'viv, Kuznetsov attempted the assassination of deputy governor Bauer, while crying "Glory to Ukraine!" He then tried to flee from L'viv but was abandoned by his Partisan detachment, which was being pressured by UPA forces. Kuznetsov was then apprehended by the nationalists and executed. In the 1950s, Yakovchuk writes, the Soviet authorities organized a search for Kuznetsov, but the body that was found—the author offers no corroboration—was that of a German officer.[82] Once again, then, the claim is that the Partisan hero had a mission to eliminate members of OUN-UPA through assassinating German officials and leaving behind evidence that incriminated the nationalists. In this way, a Soviet war hero is depicted as being both duplicitous and working against the interests of Ukraine.

NIKOLAI VATUTIN

Nikolai Fedorovich Vatutin (1901–1944) had a spectacular military career. He was born near Kursk into a peasant family, and joined the Red Army in 1920. The following year he was accepted as a member of the Communist Party. He attended military schools and academies in Kyiv and Moscow, and subsequently served as the deputy commander and commander of the headquarters of the Kyiv Military District. From 1940 he was head of the Operative Group and the Deputy Chairman of the General Headquarters of the Red Army. After the outbreak of the German–Soviet war, he was chairman of the headquarters of the North-Western Front, and the deputy chairman of the General Headquarters. From 1942 he commanded the armies in the Voronezh region, the Southwestern region (at the time of the Battle of Stalingrad) and the First Ukrainian Front (Kursk Salient). Armies led by Vatutin took part in the liberation of various cities, including Belgorod, Kharkiv, and Kyiv, and his armies had forced their way across the Dnipro River. On 29 February 1944, he was wounded during an ambush of his cortege by UPA forces and died on 15 April from gangrene. A statue of Vatutin was erected in Kyiv. His case is an interesting one because of the juxtaposition of two heroic narratives during the war: that of the Soviets and that of the Ukrainian nationalists. The hero of the war was regarded as an enemy of Ukrainians according to the nationalist version of events that slowly took shape after Ukraine became independent. But how did the nationalist version depict Vatutin and the events surrounding his death?

Writing in 1997, Bohdan Fik illustrates what he perceives as the general's crimes against Ukrainian youth born from 1924 to 1926. He points out that they were mobilized to fight against the Germans, and although they were ill equipped and poorly trained, they were flung forward against the German machine guns. Fik writes that according to official statistics, only 3% of people born in these years survived. Vatutin, who was in charge of the campaign to liberate the city of Kyiv, dispatched 250,000 Ukrainian young men who had been mobilized in Chernihiv, Cherkasy, Poltava, and Kyiv regions to certain deaths in the cold waters of the Dnipro River. Some Moscow newspapers reported in the 1980s that those who could not swim were shot so that they did not instinctively drown others when crossing the river at Kyiv. As a result of such measures, the UPA sentenced Vatutin to death for crimes against the Ukrainian people. He ponders why the statue of Vatutin in Kyiv bears an inscription in Ukrainian, whereas the other Soviet heroes all have inscriptions in Russian, and posits that the reason may have been that he was killed by nationalist Ukrainians.[83] In a related article, Panteleimon Vasylevs'kyi agrees with the reason behind the assassination of Vatutin and describes the attack in more detail. Vatutin's cortege was attacked near the village of Mylyatyn on the border of Rivne and Zhytomyr *oblasts*. Vatutin was hit in the legs and evacuated from the skirmish area, but it was some time before medical assistance could reach him. Members of his cortege removed his left leg but could not stop infection from spreading. Fifteen soldiers of the Red Army reportedly died in the ambush, along with three insurgents. In 1947, the sculptor Vuchetich made the monument to Vatutin, with the inscription "To General Vatutin from the Ukrainian people." Several days later someone had added the words "three bullets." The MGB arrested two students from Nizhyn whose fathers had drowned at Kyiv.[84]

Vasylevs'kyi continues with this theme later in the same year with a list of enemy generals and other targets assassinated by the UPA. He states that all were prepared in advance because the UPA had been informed of the movements of the targets by the OUN-UPA security force. In addition to Vatutin, they include SA general Viktor Lutze, SS General Funk, NKVD boss of the Ternopil' region, General Morozov, NKVD General, D. Fedorov, and General Karol ["Walther"] Swierczewski, the Polish Deputy Minister of Defense.[85] The source does not elucidate why such assassinations conducted by the UPA differed significantly from those carried out by Communists such as Kuznetsov. In both cases they led to German reprisals against the local population. However, when Communists murdered Germans they are accused of doing so to provoke a German response. Why would UPA murders not produce the same consequences one wonders? Bondarenko believes that after the defeat of Ukrainian SS Division Halychyna near Brody (see Chapter 5), servicemen from the Division joined the UPA forces near the Brody River. At that time the UPA was considering the question of whether to negotiate a neutrality agreement with Soviet troops. Such an arrangement had already been made with an underground attachment of the Partisan forces of Sydir Kovpak. However, in early 1944 in the Rivne region, UPA paratroopers fired on the car carrying Vatutin and mortally wounded the general. Soviet forces then began a ruthless cleansing operation against the UPA, during which the civilian population was brutalized. Those who helped UPA members with food and shelter were proclaimed accomplices and sent to Siberia with their families. Those who refused to assist in this way were killed by the UPA.[86]

The lengthy efforts to resurrect OUN-UPA and provide accounts of the heroism of its members has as its natural counterpart, attempts to "deheroize" existing Soviet heroes, who were linked in some way to events in those regions of Ukraine in which OUN-UPA were fighting or hiding. It is difficult to discern how successful these writings were in their mission. Most of the sources cited come from the radical L'viv newspaper, *Za vil'nu Ukrainu* rather than the mainstream press, though *Literaturna Ukraina* was also part of this campaign. The Soviet authorities had behind them years of propaganda and lengthy volumes about the glorious campaigns of the "Great Patriotic War." What was different here was that in the past, the Ukrainian participation in that war, and Ukrainian sacrifices, had been melded into the official version of history. Kyiv, after all was a "city of glory." The nationalist narrative, on the other hand, was dissecting accounts of the Soviet drive to the West to demonstrate that Ukrainians were deliberately sacrificed by generals such as Vatutin. Because of this needless loss of lives, it was necessary for the

UPA (or the OUN) to exact revenge by eliminating the man who had given the order for the crossing of the Dnipro. It need hardly be added that the accounts simplify what occurred and that the drowned soldiers were not exclusively of Ukrainian origin. On the other hand, perhaps slowly but without doubt, the Soviet version of events has come under closer scrutiny. In turn, the "nationalist" version is becoming more plausible, particularly when the reader of such accounts can have in mind events such as the 1932–33 Famine. What stands in the way of a complete vindication of OUN-UPA, aside from the long-term effects of Soviet propaganda on a large section of the Ukrainian population, are the events of the latter years of the war and early postwar years, which we will turn to in Chapter 5.

Summary

The efforts to reinterpret the events of the Second World War in order to create heroes out of "villains" and to reexamine former heroes accordingly are incomplete. Many of the versions of the past are unclear and subjected frequently to new interpretations. Moreover, the war years are the most difficult in terms of historical memory because new narratives often coincide and clash with the results of new archival research. To date, despite a plethora of articles that seek to reshape the image of the OUN and the UPA, the impact of Soviet propaganda has still not been entirely eradicated. It remains problematic to convince a reading public that of the two major warring powers, Hitler's Germany and the Soviet Union, the Ukrainian nationalists opted for the former as the lesser of two evils. Whether or not such a perception—that the USSR under Stalin constituted a worse threat to Ukraine than the German occupiers—may be accurate or not, such judgment has not received widespread acceptance outside Ukraine and in many areas within it. Since the Red Army was bearing the brunt of the war against Hitler's troops, a complete reassessment of the Soviet campaign seems unlikely. The Western allies could only express gratitude to the USSR, despite the obduracy of Stalin at summit meetings in Tehran and Yalta, and his suspicion of Allied motives throughout the war. Some Ukrainian sources suggest that lives were wasted by Stalin, or that Ukrainian soldiers were sent on missions in which death was unavoidable. There is also the issue of overall Ukrainian "losses" under the Stalin regime, in which historians, journalists, and writers take into account events such as the Famine of 1932–33, the Purges, deportations, as well as the prolonged conflict with various Soviet forces both during the war and afterward.

The casualties when tallied render Stalin's regime a worse enemy to Ukrainians than the Germans, and thus a temporary alliance with Germany could be justified on these grounds. Nevertheless, outside the confines of their own environment, the advocates of such a perception of the Stalin years have not found widespread support and, in some cases, have provoked hostile responses.

Likewise the campaign to make heroes out of the adherents of the OUN-B or the UPA can be considered thus far no more than a partial success. In the case of the OUN-B there are far too many road blocks, which can be listed as follows: an ideology that was authoritarian and even extreme by the standards of Central or Eastern Europe in the interwar period; the period of collaboration with the Germans that applies to both wings of the OUN up to the summer or fall of 1941; the question of the OUN-B's attitude toward the Jewish population of Ukraine, as well as the overtly anti-Semitic nature of some of the propaganda issued by the Ukrainian Central Committee in Krakow;[87] and the nature of the campaign to unite the UPA, involving the enforced cooperation and partial elimination of rival groups, particularly the followers of Bul'ba-Borovets'. In the latter part of the war, there is also no question that the OUN-B and the UPA made a conscious decision to—at the least—adhere temporarily to the side of the retreating Germans in what was a logical maneuver to consolidate and replenish their forces prior to the arrival of Stalin's armies. The relationship between the German occupiers and the nationalists was ambivalent. Possibly one could say that both sides tried to exploit the other for their own benefit. If so, the ploy was unsuccessful, in both cases. The Germans regarded the OUN-B as an unreliable ally that was dangerously ambitious. The OUN-B likely thought that the Germans reneged on earlier promises to permit the establishment of an independent Ukraine. The problem for historians or indeed those trying to create a national history is that a portion of the wartime narrative must make sense of this relationship and perceive that there were times of cooperation and times of animosity. It is akin to an alliance with one devil in order to avoid another devil. However, the supporters of the OUN-B and the UPA have yet to produce a really convincing wartime narrative that takes all the fluctuations of the period into account and includes both the good and the bad. One can write history in a different way, but only in the form of propaganda.

Notes

1 The acronym refers to the Organization of Ukrainian Nationalists and the Ukrainian Insurgent Army.

2 Peter J. Potichnyj, a professor emeritus of political science at McMaster University in Canada, notes that UPA is often portrayed as the military arm of the OUN. As a result, he maintains, the OUN's collaboration with the German forces prior to June 1941 is often applied to UPA as well, and despite what he perceives as UPA's very definite anti-German direction. Peter J. Potichnyj, "The Ukrainian Insurgent Army (UPA) and the German Authorities," in Hans-Joachim Torke and John-Paul Himka, ed. *German-Ukrainian Relations in Historical Perspective* (Edmonton: Canadian Institute of Ukrainian Studies Press, 1994), p. 168.

3 V. Cherednychenko, *Natsionalizm proty natsii* (Kyiv: Vydavnytstvo politychnoi literatury Ukrainy, 1970).

4 P. Maksym'yuk and G. Slyvka, "Ispytannym oruzhiyem pravdy," *L'vovs'kaya pravda*, 20 February 1988, p. 3.

5 Myron Sluka, "Palacha k otvetu," *L'vovs'kaya pravda*, 12 March 1988, p. 3.

6 Nikolai N. Varvatsev, *Ukrainian History in the Distorting Mirror of Sovietology* (Kyiv: Naukova dumka, 1987), pp. 22, 36, 43, and 126-127.

7 V. Zarechnyi and O. Lastovets, "Banderovshchina," *Pravda Ukrainy* (9 August 1989), pp. 3-4; (10 August 1989), p. 4; (17 August 1989), pp. 3-4; and (19 August 1989), p. 3.

8 A. Gorban', "Krovavyye sledy banderovtsev," *Pravda Ukrainy*, 11 October 1989, p. 3.

9 *Visti z Ukrainy*, No. 3 (January 1991), p. 1.

10 V. I. Maslovs'kyi, "Shchto na 'oltari svobody'? Dekil'la utochen' viiny 'na dva fronty,' yaku vela UPA, ta skil'koma nevynnymy zhertvamy oplachuvas' tsey propahdandyts'kyi myf," *Komunist Ukrainy*, No. 7 (July 1991), pp. 67-68.

11 *Litopys UPA*, edited by Peter J. Potichnyj and Yevhen Shtendera, has published over 50 volumes of UPA memoirs. The collection has been criticized, however, for offering a one-sided selection of documents in order to portray the insurgents in a favorable light. According to one account, UPA did not generally maintain a detailed record of its activities. Also the surrounded guerrillas destroyed documents rather than allowing the enemy access to them. Many of the documents captured are today held in the archives of the former KGB and inaccessible to scholars. *Litopys UPA* thus represents a small fraction of the collection, mainly documents from the archives of the Ukrainian Supreme Liberation Council and the UPA central command. See Yurii Kyrychuk, "Heroichnyi litopys," *Za vil'nu Ukrainu*, 11 July 1996, p. 2. The accusation that the selection of documents was in any way partial was denied strongly by Professor Potichnyj at a symposium on "Ukraine in World War II," held at the University of Alberta on 29 November 2006.

12 Armstrong, *Ukrainian Nationalism*, pp. 146-152.

13 Ibid., pp. 153-156.

14 Viktor Koval', "Ukrains'ka Povstans'ka Armiya: Dovidka Instytutu istorii AN URSR dlya Komisii Verkhovnoi Rady Ukrainy z pytan' bezpeky vid 1 lypnya 1991 roku," *Ukraina i Svit*, No. 35 (18-24 September 1996), pp. 9-10.

15 V. P. Troshchyns'kyi, "Proty vyhadok pro tak zvany 'antyfashysts'kyi rukh oporu' ukrains'kykh natsionalistiv," *Ukrains'kyi istorychnyi zhurnal*, No. 5 (1988): 83-84.

16 Kost' Bondarenko, "Istoriya, kotoruyu ne znaem, ili ne khotim znat'," *Zerkalo nedeli*, No. 12 (29 March-5 April 2002).

17 Wiktor Poliszczuk, *Legal and Political Assessment of the OUN and UPA* (Toronto, 1997), p. 32.

18 M. V. Koval', *Ukraina v Druhii svitovii i Velykii vitchyznyanii viinakh (1939-1945 rr.)* (Kyiv: Vydavnychyi dim Al'ternatyvy, 1999), pp. 152-153.

19 Maslovs'kyi, "Shcho na 'altari sbobody'?" pp. 67-73.

20 Stanislav Kul'chyts'kyi, "Trahediya pysana samoyu istoriyeyu," *Za vil'nu Ukrainu*, 14 October 1997, p. 2.

21 Stanislav Kul'chyts'kyi, "Ukrainski natsionalisty v chervono-korychneviy Yevropi (do 70-richchya stvorennya OUN," *Istoriya Ukrainy*, No. 5 (February 1999) 6-7.

22 See, for example, P. Maslii, "V UPA buly heroi," *Visti z Ukrainy*, No. 42 (October 1991), p. 4.

23 Ivan Krainii, "Sorok chotyry roky strakhu," *Ukraina moloda*, 21 January 1992, p. 7.

24 Ihor Hulyk, "Petro Poltava i ioho kontseptsiya ukrains'koho derzhavnosti," *Za vil'nu Ukrainu*, 18 July 1992, p. 2.

25 Ol'ha Ivanova, "Kotyhoroshko povstans'koho lisu," *Samostiina Ukraina*, No. 38 (October 1992): 3.

26 Roman Pastukh, "Enkavedysts'kyi heneral u rukakh u nashykh povstantsiv," *Za vil'nu Ukrainu*, 19 July 1997, p. 2.

27 Bohdan Zalyps'kyi, "Zberehty sebe, shchob vykhovuvaty nove pokolonia," *Za vil'nu Ukrainu*, 7 April 2000, pp. 6-7.

28 Roman Pastukh, "Dmytro Hrytsai-heneral UPA," *Za vil'nu Ukrainu*," 20 March 1991, p. 2.

29 Myroslav Horoshko and Volodymyr Dudok, "Lystar ukrains'koho lisu," *Za vil'nu Ukrainu*, 8 September 1992, p. 3; and 10 September 1992, p. 3.

30 Ivan Vashkiv, "I stav vin Lehendoyu," *Za vil'nu Ukrainu*, 31 October 1991, p. 2.

31 Les' Solomonchuk, "Povernennya Burlaka," *Za vil'nu Ukrainu*," 24 September 1999, p. 5.

32 Myron Sluka, "Kharkivs'kyi 'bandiora'," *Za vil'nu Ukrainu*, 30 January 1999, p. 2.

33 Nina Romanyuk, "Vony ishly do lyubovi i myloserdya, a pomyraly zradnykamy i vorohamy," *Ukraina moloda*, 19 May 1995, p. 7.

34 Bohdan Zalyps'kyi, "Zberehty sebe, shchob vykhovuvaty nove pokolonia," *Za vil'nu Ukrainu*, 7 April 2000, pp. 6-7.

35 Ivan Romanyk, "Banderivs'kyi chervonoarmiets," *Ukraina moloda*, 12 September 2001, p. 13.

36 Nina Romanyuk, "Khoroshyi u vas cholovik. Ot choho vin u tii UPA buv?" *Ukraina moloda*, 12 October 2002, p. 4.

37 Maslovs'kyi, "Shcho na 'altari sbobody'?" p. 72.

38 Panteleimon Vasylevs'kyi, "Bii za 'banderivs'ku stolytsu," *Za vil'nu Ukrainu*, 13 January 1995, p. 2.

39 Mykola Vasyl'chuk, "Pobratani z hromom: nova knyha Mykhaila Andrusyaka pro UPA," *Ukraina moloda*, 30 January 2002, p. 6.

40 Bohdan Mak, "Polkovnyk Shelest," *Za vil'nu Ukrainu,* 27 April 1996, p. 2; 30 April 1996, p. 2; 4 May 1996, p. 2; 7 May 1996, p. 2; 14 May 1996, p. 2.

41 Fedir Solovei, "Sumni svyata buly v sorok shostomu rotsi," *Za vil'nu Ukrainu*, 19 January 1991, p. 4.

42 Ostap Moroz, "Na terenakh Drohobychchyny," *Za vil'nu Ukrainu*, 24 November 1992, p. 2.

43 Ivan Vorobel', "Ostannii bunker," *Za vil'nu Ukrainu*, 17 October 1996, pp. 2-3.

44 Ivan Krainii, "Ostanni z pidzemnoho bunkera," *Ukraina moloda*, 15 November 2002, p. 5.

45 "Orlan" translates literally as white-tailed eagle.

46 Based on this review, the book makes no distinction between activities linked to the OUN and those associated with UPA.

47 Mariya Lytvyn, "Povstanskymy stezhkamy," *Literaturna Ukraina*, 18 September 2003, p. 1.

48 Koval', *Ukraina v Druhii svitovii i Velykii vitchyznyanii viinakh*, pp. 149-151.

49 Bohdan Chervak, "Lehendarnyi Sotnyk," *Ukrains'ke slovo*, No. 37 (September 2003): 1, 3.

50 Evhen Stakhiv, "I v Krasnodoni diyalo natsionalistychne pidpillya," *Ukraina moloda*, 21 August 1992, p. 6.

51 Editorial, "Istoriya i mif," *Ukraina moloda*, 25 September 1992, p. 3.

52 Mariya Bazelyuk, "Nevyanuche istoriya OUN," *Za vil'nu Ukrainu*, 13 October 1992, p. 2.

53 P. Khobot, L. Kudelia, "Dnepropetrovskiye Banderovtsy," *Za vil'nu Ukrainu*, 20 October 1994, p. 2.

54 Serhii Dovhal', "Dnipropetrovs'k-stolytsa banderivtsiv na skhodi Ukrainy," *Ukraina moloda*, 2 June 1995, p. 10.

55 Vakhtang Kipiani, "Ukrains'ki natsionalisty na Mykolaivshchyni. Roky 1941-1943," *Ukraina moloda*, 16 April 1998, p. 6.

56 Koval', *Ukraina v Druhii svitovii i Velykii vitchyznyanii viinakh (1939-1945)*, pp. 149-151.

57 Troshchnys'kyi, "Proty vyhadok pro tak zvanyi 'antifashysts'kyi rukh oporu' ukrains'kykh natsionalistiv," p. 82.

58 S. Makarchuk, "OUN: Metamorfozy voennoho vremeni," *L'vovs'kaya pravda*, 27 November 1988, p. 3.

59 N. Karpova, "Vybor," *Pravda Ukrainy*, 4 January 1990, p. 4.

60 B. Gusev, "Kak ono bulo," *L'vovs'kaya pravda*, 30 June 1990, p. 3.

61 S. Karnautska, "Portret bez retushi," *L'vovs'kaya pravda*, 8 May 1991, p. 2.

62 Volodymyr Kosyk, "Svoboda dast' nam shans," *Literaturna Ukraina*, 23 January 1992, pp. 3, 8.

63 Ol'ha Ivanova, "Khto vin, Stepan Bandera?" *Samostiina Ukraina*, 15 April 1992, p. 4.

64 Stanislav Kul'chyts'kyi, "Trahediya pysana samoyu istoriyeyu," *Za vil'nu Ukrainu*, 14 October 1997, p. 2.

65 Stanislav Kul'chyts'kyi, "Kolaboratsionizm OUN-UPA: derzhavnoi zrady ne bulo," *Ukraina moloda*, 8 December 1999, p. 7.

66 Koval', *Ukraina v Druhii svitovii i Velykii vitchyznyanii viinakh*, pp. 153-154.

67 Ibid. pp. 155-156.

68 Timothy Snyder, "The Causes of Ukrainian-Polish Ethnic Cleansing," *Past and Present*, Vol. 179, No. 1 (2003): 208.

69 For example, Yaroslav Halan, *Lest People Forget: Pamphlets, Articles, and Reports* (Kyiv: Dnipro, 1986).

70 "Turning the Pages Back," (editorial), *The Ukrainian Weekly*, [http://www.ukrweekly.com/Archive/2001/420112.shtml].

71 N. Karpova, "Vtoroye ubiystvo: po povody odnoy al'ternativnoi versii," *Pravda Ukrainy*, 15 March 1990, p. 4.

72 Stefaniya Andrusiv, "Khto vin, obdurena zhertva chy svidomyi kat? Pro Yaroslava Halana i Halanivs'kyi typ lyudyny," *Literaturna Ukraina*, 3 September 1992, p. 7.

73 Ibid. On the dissolution of the Ukrainian Catholic Church, the most authoritative source is Bohdan R. Bociurkiw, *The Ukrainian Greek Catholic Church and the Soviet State (1939-1950)* (Edmonton: Canadian Institute of Ukrainian Studies Press, 1996).

74 Ibid.

75 Mykola Oleksyuk, "Rozmova z ubyvtseyu," *Za vil'nu Ukrainu*, 6 March 1993, p. 2; 20 March 1993, p. 2; and 30 March 1993, pp. 2-3.

76 Mykola Oleksyuk, "Zlovisnyi symvol." *Za vil'nu Ukrainu*, 2 August 1996, p. 2; and 5 August 1996, p. 2.

77 [http://www.psychcentral.com/psypsych/Nikolai_Ivanovich_Kuznetsov].

78 P. Grigoruk, "V otryade znali tol'ko Gracheva," *L'vovs'kaya pravda*, 27 July 1991, p. 4.

79 UNSO refers to the Ukrainian Self-Defense Organization, the paramilitary wing of the Ukrainian National Assembly, one of the most radical extremist political parties to emerge in post-1991 Ukraine. It perceives as its "divine destiny" an empire modeled on that of Kievan Rus'. See, for example, Taras Kuzio, "Loyal Nationalism in Postcommunist States," *RFE/RL Newsline*, Vol. 7, No. 122 (30 June 2003).

80 Bohdan Dem'yanchuk, "Heroi z tinnyu provokatora," *Ukraina moloda*, 17 April 1992, p. 12.

81 Roman Pastukh, "Zahynu pokynutyi napryzvolyashche svoimy," *Za vil'nu Ukrainu*, 6 May 1993, p. 2. The intriguing question of why the UPA commander was dressed in Gestapo uniform is not addressed.

82 Petro Yakovchuk, "Pam'yatnyk fashystu," *Za vil'nu Ukrainu*, 4-10 July 1993, p. 3.

83 Bohdan Fik, "Heneralu Vatutinu vid ukrains'koho narodu," *Za vil'nu Ukrainu*, 18 February 1997, p. 2. The same theme is also covered by Tetyana Kharchenko, "Mizh povstantsyamy i chervonymy partyzanamy nemaye niyakoho antahonizmy," *Ukraina moloda*, 20 July 2003, p. 5.

84 Panteleimon Vasylevs'kyi, "Heneralu Vatutinu vid ukrains'koho narodu," *Za vil'nu Ukrainu*, 9 May 1997, p. 2.

85 Panteleimon Vasylevs'kyi, "Tsili-vorozhi heneraly," *Za vil'nu Ukrainu*, 14 October 1997, p. 2.

86 Bondarenko, "Istoriya, kotoruyu ne znaem, ili ne khotim znat'," *Zerkalo nedeli*, No. 12 (29 March-5 April 2002).

87 See, for an extreme example, B. F. Sabrin, ed. *Alliance for Murder: the Nazi-Ukrainian Nationalist Partnership in Genocide* (New York: Sarpedon, 1991).

CHAPTER 5

UPA'S CONFLICT WITH THE RED ARMY AND SOVIET SECURITY FORCES

Introduction

This chapter takes the discussion and debates about the Ukrainian insurgence one step further, into the later war years, with focus on two major issues: first, it analyzes discussions of UPA's conflict with the Soviet security forces and the Red Army; and second, it looks at writings on the alleged change of outlook and "democratization" of the OUN in 1943–44. It also examines the creation of the SS Division Halychyna, and its place in the narrative about wartime nationalist formations, and to what extent the Division occupies a place today in the nationalist pantheon. In the background were the epic events of the Second World War: the German defeat at Stalingrad and the Battle of the Kursk Salient in July 1943, followed by the lengthy and costly German retreat from the Soviet Union. Under these circumstances, the question for the nationalist forces was no longer the degree to which it was feasible to collaborate with the occupiers, but how to prepare for a potential new Soviet takeover. Ideologically, perhaps, the situation was more straightforward as the Soviet Union had always been the principal foe. In the changed conditions, the conflict became more extreme, particularly after Soviet forces arrived in Western Ukraine where there had been bitter fighting between Ukrainians and Poles (the subject of the next chapter), with the presence of a hostile population. Under the new conditions, the OUN-B, in particular underwent a partial metamorphosis to a more moderate and "democratic" ideology and the chapter addresses the continuing debate as to the extent to which this conversion was a genuine phenomenon or a matter of convenience.

The Long Struggle: Soviet Security Forces versus UPA

The most documented and discussed aspect of Ukraine during World War II is the conflict that occurred in the later part of the war between the Ukrainian Insurgent Army and the Soviet security forces of the NKVD.[1] The NKVD was not the only unit involved, many other forces were deployed against the guerrillas, including members of the *Komsomol*. Throughout the postwar years, the conflict was narrated in Soviet writings as one of patriots fighting against ruthless and treacherous bandits, who were tarred with the phrase "Ukrainian-German nationalists," evidently coined by Nikita Khrushchev, the Ukrainian party boss in the late 1930s who was again sent into the region in 1944. It is also possible that it derives from Soviet propaganda organs. It signified that in official eyes the UPA was a close partner of the retreating Germans and fought on their behalf. However, this view was already being questioned prior to the end of the Soviet period. Thus in 1991, a people's deputy from the Rivne region, Mykola Porovs'kyi, was reminding the public that the 30,000 people reportedly killed by the UPA—mainly party members sent to Western Ukraine—was the lamentable outcome of a fratricidal struggle initiated by Stalin and his cronies. He noted the crimes committed against the Ukrainian population by the NKVD and demanded the equal treatment of criminals irrespective of what parties or organizations they represented.[2]

Perhaps the most important article to appear on the subject in the Soviet period was that of V. I. Maslovs'kyi in the journal *Komunist Ukrainy*. Its appearance in this source indicated that the question was being discussed at the highest levels of the party hierarchy in Ukraine, with an eye to revising the official perspective. Maslovs'kyi remarked that the complexity of the acute political confrontation in the western areas of Ukraine needed to be reflected truthfully by social scientists and historians. Hitherto, discussion had been dominated by clichés and stereotypes. In the Brezhnev years, it had been a taboo subject, and the authorities limited inquiry by restricting or prohibiting access to special archival holdings. However, most people could now acknowledge the archaic methods by which the past was formerly studied; it had led to deformations or even outright falsifications in interpretation. The reason was that the authorities in the area of research and ideology did not like the truth about these dramatic events. By the late 1970s and early 1980s, the political struggles in Western Ukraine came under review, but there was still a marked reluctance to expose the social and political roots of the confrontations: their brutality and scale. It was now time in Maslovs'kyi's view to begin the discussion. The Communist Party in the spring of 1943 had tried to avoid bloodshed. It published and disseminated slogans that guaranteed amnesty to UPA members and supporters if they would cease fighting. This leniency, however, was only one side of the story. Stalin and NKVD chief, L. P. Beria, undermined this humanistic decision and there simultaneously occurred illegal and inhuman actions. Thus Stalin and Beria essentially ignored the official decision to end the conflict in the western areas and escalated the violence. For the first time in an official narrative, it was suggested that anti-Soviet treachery was not the root cause of the violence in this region.[3]

According to Maslovs'kyi, after the liberation of Western Ukraine from German occupation, it was possible to avoid large-scale conflict with OUN-UPA since the armed underground and armed formations of the nationalists had begun to disintegrate politically, organizationally, and psychologically. At that time, over 13,000 UPA soldiers had given themselves up to Soviet organs. From February 1944 to 1 June 1945, the Ministry of Internal Affairs, the NKGB, and the people's "destruction battalions"[4] had eliminated 9,619 UPA troops, 24,888 had been arrested, and 40,395 had surrendered voluntarily. These figures constituted some 74,902 men out of a total membership of 90,000. Thus by mid-1945, major formations of the UPA barely existed. Its remnants were forced to go underground and change their tactics. At this stage they were "brutalized and doomed." However, by the end of this same year, these remnants had managed to fill the enormous gaps in their ranks. These reinforcements arrived in the shape of the OUN underground and those who wished to avoid being drafted into the Soviet army. As a result the armed nationalist underground returned to its original strength. Maslovs'kyi asks: how could this have happened? The main answer, he finds, lies in the massive reprisals against the local Ukrainian population initiated by Stalin and Beria. The first wave began immediately once the area had been cleared of the Germans and continued until the spring of 1945. Even in the autumn of 1944, reprisals had begun against the families of German collaborators and OUN-UPA members. Illegally repressed, with no resort to trial and adequate investigations, tens of thousands of people (including the elderly and children) were dispatched to remote areas of the country. Such punishment befell not only prisoners, but even those who had surrendered voluntarily to Soviet organs. Such measures aroused a wave of indignation and immediately increased the number of people in the armed underground. This factor was the most significant reason why 300,000 people came through the ranks of the OUN-UPA in the postwar years, writes Maslovs'kyi.[5]

Having revealed such astonishing figures, Maslovs'kyi then tries to convince his readers that the pro-Soviet section of the population nonetheless constituted a majority. He writes that from the time of the liberation of Western Ukraine from the Germans, i.e., from February 1944 until the autumn of 1945, the Soviet army mobilized over 750,000 working class people from these regions, which was 95–98% of those subject to recruitment. All reportedly fought bravely against the enemy, and half were decorated with orders and medals, including twenty-three that won the award "Hero of the Soviet Union". In 1945, he continues, the *Komsomol* organizations encompassed 65,000 young Western Ukrainians, and in May of this year, the village Soviets employed 300,000 activists. By the end of the year there were 33,165 Communists in this region. By May 1945, 57,000 troops operated in destruction battalions, and organizations of women and the intelligentsia were growing. By the end of the 1940s, there were reportedly around 500,000 Soviet and *Komsomol* activists in Western Ukraine, and "it is an inviolable fact" that most inhabitants of the region had been consolidated to fight in the battle against the nationalist "bandits."[6] The figures seem inflated, but they only add credence to the perception of Western Ukraine as a mass battleground in the 1940s, especially at a time when the front had long moved forward, and well after the end of the "Great Patriotic War" following the April 1945 Battle of Berlin. Nevertheless, the Maslovs'kyi article marked a turning point because it ended the one-sided depiction of events and opened the way for further discussion of issues that had long divided residents of Ukraine. One now had a portrayal of more than one million combatants operating in a small agricultural region, flanked on the western side by the Carpathian Mountains, and with village after village divided in their allegiance, but no doubt more inclined toward native sons than to outsiders sent by the Soviet regime. There followed from the nationalists a sustained campaign to denigrate the Soviet forces.

An article reprinted from the *Litopys UPA* series noted that numerous NKVD garrisons began to appear in Western Ukraine from January 1946. The NKVD would drive local residents out of their houses. These garrisons were moved frequently from one location to another so that their members could not strike up an acquaintance with local residents. With their arrival, an "extraordinary state" was established in which people required a permit to travel from one village to another. Those caught at night would be arrested or shot outright. The main theme in this article, however, is that of the rape of women and young girls and sometimes even elderly women by NKVD men. To the incidence of rape is linked the transmission of venereal disease, which was allegedly brought to the West Ukrainian village by "the Bolsheviks," since none existed hitherto. In every village that had an NKVD garrison, there were said to be 10–20 women with venereal disease. The article maintains that its dissemination was a deliberate plot on the part of the NKVD to infect local Ukrainians. On 22 June 1946, UPA insurgents detained an NKVD soldier with venereal disease and under interrogation he confessed that his task was to infect girls held in prisons. The NKVD is also charged with desecrating the bodies of insurgents. In the village of Oleshiv (Stanislav region), the NKVD men tied the body of a dead insurgent to the tail of a horse and dragged it through the streets. Dead bodies were also reportedly left along the roadside with inscriptions on them, while in Sambir cigarettes were inserted into the mouths of dead insurgents and used for target practice.[7] The Soviet security forces are thus characterized as despicable and brutal in their actions against the local population.

The image was developed further in a series of articles by Ivan Bilas, which appeared in the reputable weekly of the Ukrainian Writers' Union, *Literaturna Ukraina*. Bilas begins his account with the story of the most treacherous method used by the Soviet authorities to fight Ukrainian nationalists, namely the creation and deployment of special units that masqueraded as UPA members and as the security services of the OUN. The goal was to compromise the nationalists by killing civilians in the name of the UPA, as well as to eliminate the leaders of both the OUN and UPA. The beginnings of such an operation reportedly began with the dissolution of Kovpak's Partisan Brigade and its division into mobile units on 20 September 1944. The goal of these units was to combat UPA insurgents, while the staff and property of the Kovpak brigade were transferred to the NKVD. In 1944–45, most NKVD attacks on so-called bandits and rebels took place in Volyn, Rivne, and Ternopil' *oblasts*. Bilas cites a commander of a special NKVD unit in the Rivne region called Boris Pavlovich Koryakov (b. 1921, Gorky region), and wounded during the encirclement of Kyiv in September 1941. Under his leadership, the NKVD conducted some 200 operations in the Rivne region. Sometimes they posed as UPA insurgents to gain access into villages, and in this way they could inflict large numbers of casualties among the rebels. The victims of such operations, Bilas notes, were predominantly civilians, and sometimes the scope of the terror inflicted was so extreme that even the NKVD began to complain—this was the case in the spring of 1949. The chief culprits were "special units" of the MGB, created to "root out remnants of the nationalist underground." Allegedly these units led to tensions between the Ministry of Internal Affairs and the Ministry of State Security because the former was in control of criminal activities, and the special units were committing robberies and murders. It was thus difficult to distinguish who was a mere criminal and who was acting on the orders of the MGB.[8]

Similarly, on 9 June 1949, the Minister of Internal Affairs of the Ukrainian SSR, Tymofii Strokach, sent a report to his all-Union counterpart in Moscow, S. N. Kruglov, in which he complained that there had been several occasions when persons posing as MGB agents carried out robberies in Western

Ukraine. The MGB had provided them with weapons but refused to clamp down on their ties to the criminal world. Consequently, these employees pretended to be OUN bandits and robbed and plundered the civilian population.[9] Bilas clearly has perused the archives in depth in his coverage of the role of NKVD-MGB punitive and military units that operated in Western Ukraine as the Soviet fronts moved westward. In a subsequent article, he notes that there were a total of 26,304 troops of military police forces already in action by the spring of 1944, of which the largest numbers were in Rivne, L'viv, and Volyn *oblasts*. Two infantry brigades were about to be transferred to the region from the Caucasus, and a tank battalion with 22 tanks was also to be deployed. Later a further 7,700 troops were dispatched from Russia, and this large contingent would be increased each year to fight UPA insurgents until 1953. In general, these intruders, according to Bilas's account, behaved barbarically. His examples, taken from the autumn of 1944, portray drunken state officials and troops carrying out rape and murder, executing the elderly, beating priests, and setting fire to property. In one case, in the village of Kryven'ke, Ternopil' *oblast*, 60 NKVD troops under the command of a Major Polyans'kyi burned 45 households, 20 of which belonged to families of sons currently serving in the Red Army at the front. Several senior officials of the NKGB and NKVD were present during this mission, but did nothing to stop the provocative actions of Polyans'kyi.[10]

Bilas points out that Western Ukraine, from the perspective of the authorities, was a hostile war zone. He provides stark statistics to illustrate this contention (taken from 1 January 1946, seven months after the end of the Second World War in Europe), citing the completion of almost 40,000 security missions, the deaths of 103,313 "bandits," the arrest of almost 16,000 active insurgents, and the voluntary surrender of a further 50,058. In the second quarter of 1946 there were reportedly instances when Soviet soldiers fell under the influence of OUN-UPA and began to slander the *kolkhoz* system and demonstrate an unwillingness to fight the "Ukrainian–German nationalists." One soldier, born in Gorky *oblast*, evidently commented to his comrades: "I am tired of this duty. Why did they bring us to Western Ukraine? We are fighting Banderites but they have done no harm to us." Crime rates among these troops began to soar, and, as a result of the lenient attitude of some officers, a number of unit commanders had become morally decayed. Together with subordinates, they embarked on drinking sprees and often took part in committing crimes. Torture and abuse, says Bilas, became common in some units, usually involving drinking vodka or moonshine, and then abusing and raping women (including both pregnant women, minors, and the elderly), and frequently posing as OUN bandits. On 23 October 1945, Soviet troops broke into a local branch of the L'viv Historical Museum and stole 18 artworks. Some of the items were discovered after an official inquiry, but others were destroyed or used to decorate local clubs. Another such action occurred at the L'viv archives, involving Soviet cadets training to be military cooks who stole 128 valuable documents of Russian and Polish princes. However, the precise link between this event and those involving actions against Ukrainian insurgents is difficult to discern from Bilas's text. Yet many MVD and MGB commanders operating in such capacity are cited as committing robberies, often furnishing their apartments with the takings.[11] Alongside the rape and pillage there occurred the systematic deportations of large numbers of Western Ukrainians, which reached a peak of 15,597 persons in 1945, and in the period 1944–49 totaled 50,453 families and 143,141 residents. During the deportations, the mortality rates were very high, and many died from hunger and cold. At the special settlement, the regime was harsh and there was a high death rate. On 17 December 1948, Bilas notes, Strokach sent a letter to Kruglov, in which he suggested that as a result of the situation in the western regions of Ukraine, the return of those who had completed their terms in exile was "inexpedient." On 6 April 1950, the USSR Council of Ministers issued a secret directive that revoked the original sentences and stipulated that there were no term limits on the period in exile.[12]

Bilas's account is a very detailed one that offers a picture of the Soviet security forces as depraved and vindictive, while citing numerous examples of individual atrocities that he found in the Ukrainian Central Archives. It was published during the first year of independence in Ukraine's main literary weekly, arguably the most authoritative newspaper in Ukraine (at least at that time). His articles describe a repressive regime clamping down on the "national liberation movement of the Ukrainian people," but he seems to adopt a viewpoint that is based on a non-sequitur, namely that if the authorities are repressive, then the movement of the repressed is necessarily democratic and imbued with ideas of freedom and humanity. The question of disguise is also an important one, but raises the question of whether such a ruse could not be adopted by the other side, i.e., UPA insurgents posing as members of the security forces. It is also cited in the publication of an abridged version of the report that Koshars'kyi, the military prosecutor of Ukraine, sent to Nikita Khrushchev in February 1949, concerning the activities of MGB special task forces disguised as UPA combatants. This document enables the editors of the newspaper in which it appeared to brand all accusations against the UPA of crimes against humanity as deliberate falsifications of history. They adopt the perspective that all the crimes were perpetrated by the MGB to discredit UPA. Undoubtedly some were, but the statement is too sweeping. The editors cite from the report the detention and torture of individuals in Western Ukraine, many of which had no links to the Ukrainian underground. In general, the examples replicate those in the accounts offered by Bilas.[13] An article written three years later continues this same theme. It was evidently provoked by a publication in the newspaper *Vil'na Ukraina*, in which an author wrote that an UPA unit had killed twenty-two civilians in the village Novosilky. It was based on the testimony of an H. Boshyk, who had witnessed the events in which his family died. The 1995 author, Bohdan Pasichnyk, refers to the *Vil'na Ukraina* article as a deliberate attempt to create a rift in OUN ranks. He maintains that it is a creation of Bolshevik propaganda, a fabrication that does not contain a single accurate sentence. He rejects the testimony of Boshyk, who was only 12 years of age at the time, remarking that international law would only consider the testimony of those over 16 years. How does the author know, asks Pasichnyk, that these were not NKVD men in disguise? He adds several examples of NKVD atrocities, and then comments that Boshyk himself belonged to a pro-Soviet family, and that two of his uncles had positions in Soviet destruction battalions.[14]

Several articles focus on the early days of the UPA–Soviet conflict and the goals of the opposing sides. Viktor Koval' writes that by the start of 1944, the forces of the UPA had expanded substantially, but so had those of the Soviet Partisans. Following a raid by Partisan leader Sydir Kovpak into the Carpathian Mountains, the number of direct clashes between his unit and the UPA began to increase. In this author's opinion, the Red Partisans appeared to aid the Germans against the insurgents. One assumes that such aid was indirect. An anti-Communist underground, Koval' adds, was organized on the territory of Western Ukraine at the time of the defeat of the Germans and the arrival of Soviet power in the region. The UPA could not logically fight against the forces of the Soviet Union. However, the OUN Provid took the view that at the end of the war the empire would be weakened, or else Stalin would be obliged to fight a war with the West. Thus under these circumstances the UPA could lead the entire Ukrainian people for the attainment of independence.[15] Koval's namesake, Mykhailo Koval', notes that the UPA was carrying out the orders of the central leadership of the OUN-B and the decisions of the Third Extraordinary Congress of the OUN (August 1943) (discussed below), which prepared the way for armed clashes with Soviet Partisans and the Red Army. The UPA's achievements, he maintains, were remarkable and elicited as much concern from the Soviet authorities as the major conflicts on the war front. Its methods included poisoning soldiers garrisoned in villages and killing others while they slept (Belashivka, Rivne region, 9 January 1944).[16] In these conditions, Khrushchev and his associates demanded ruthless treatment, including the hanging of captured prisoners rather than shooting, in order to intimidate the population. In fact, stresses one author, hardly any prisoners were taken as the NKVD simply killed all the insurgents that fell into its hands.[17]

M. V. Koval' states that the local population received the Soviet Army calmly and without enthusiasm, with most people staying in their homes and dealing coldly with soldiers and officers when they were forced to come into contact with them. In conversations recounted by Koval' from local residents, many were afraid of hunger and famine if the collective farm system were to be introduced. However, although the Soviet regime assumed control, there was a competing power structure in all areas in which the OUN operated underground. Thus the rival network operated in apartments and lodgings, in forests, at regional, local and national levels. Even in those areas in which the Soviet authorities had a monopoly of power, there was "an invisible" OUN presence under the control of the OUN security service (SB). Practically on a daily basis for the following decade there were reports of the murders of party or Soviet government functionaries, as well teachers, doctors, and industrial leaders who arrived from the eastern regions; attacks on the lodgings of security and internal police officials; and acts of arson against collective farms, agricultural buildings, silos, and barns. Official figures cited by Koval' note that there were about 14,500 terrorist acts carried out by the OUN in towns and villages, as a result of which more than 30,000 people were killed, including over 4,000 Soviet officials. Why did such a conflict occur? Koval' believes that failure was guaranteed and the costs for the people would inevitably be high. However, the Bandera leadership was hoping for a Third World War and an Anglo-American victory. After 1943, the OUN reoriented itself from Germany to the United States, as the dominant world power. It faced a vindictive Khrushchev, who recommended the sort of "dirty tricks" vis-à-vis the local population as described above.[18]

What occurred afterward, according to M. V. Koval's account, was a decade-long "secret war." The NKVD and MVD acted as if they were above party rules, took on the roles of both judge and executioner, and turned the entire territory of Western Ukraine into an alienated zone. He cites the notes made by Strokach, indicating that cities and villages were covered by a vast network of agents from state security that included more than 13,000 secret informers by 1945, and 22,000 employees of security and internal affairs directed into this area. The MGB went from one workplace and residence to another, arresting suspicious characters and deporting some 200,000 insurgents. By 1945, the authorities had introduced an internal passport system, and entire villages were denounced as being "bandit" communities. This conflict appeared more natural in the light of the developing Cold War between the United States and the Soviet Union. Having followed the general inclination to highlight the deviousness of Soviet methods, Koval' then makes a telling admission: there are signs that in its turn the OUN SB also used its own methods to divert Soviet agents. On 29 November 1944, a large group of "Banderites" dressed in NKVD uniforms and surrounded the village of Bilyi Kamin', located between Zolochiv and Oles'ko (L'viv *oblast*) and shot 18 fighters from a counter-insurgency battalion that had gathered around a silo to deposit grain. This same author reports other similar attacks that offer a wider perspective of this vicious encounter.[19] Stanislav Kul'chyts'kyi has also made the same point, namely that the UPA (in this case) did not hesitate to use terror to control the local population and Soviet citizens who were sent to work in Western Ukraine.[20] In other words, although Soviet methods were arguably barbaric and ruthless, no quarter was offered on either side, as both agencies were seeking control—whether short or long term—over the territory formerly controlled by Poland prior to September 1939. The key question is whether the population was caught in the middle of two warring factions and obliged to choose one or the other side or whether it was a unified population, led by the forces of OUN-UPA in a quest for independence, which is the prevailing line of the more sympathetic narratives that began to appear in 1992.

In 2002, Ivan Krainii conducted an interview with the former UPA insurgent Mykhailo Zelenchuk, which offered a different perspective of the Soviet–UPA conflict. In Zelenchuk's recollection, Red Army soldiers (as opposed to state security and internal troops) were reluctant to fight. Often, UPA troops and Red Army men would pass each other without firing. He concurs, however, with the reports of the vast network of agents and secret informers in Western Ukraine and offers examples, similar to those cited, of operations to discredit leading insurgents, as well as public displays of violence by the Soviet occupiers. Many peasants, he states, gave in or agreed to cooperate with the Soviet regime, but others continued to supply food and clothing to the insurgents. However, by early 1950 the informer network was so extensive that the UPA could no longer counter it solely with acts of terror. His own unit was forced to use different methods. In one village, for example, they discovered that the local priest was informing for the MGB. They confronted the priest and offered him a choice: immediate execution or confession in front of the villagers. He chose confession and betrayed the location of the radio with which he kept in touch with the MGB. Several days afterward the MGB arrested the priest for loss of the radio and he received a 10-year prison sentence. Zelenchuk also maintains that the MGB used forms of biological warfare during the conflict, including supplying clothing to the insurgents that was infected with typhoid lice. In his underground bunker, all the insurgents became ill through such schemes, though none died.[21] The difficulty in assessing the nature of the Soviet–UPA conflict, inevitably, is the partisan nature of reports on both sides. Post-independence narratives have largely succeeded in depicting the Soviet forces as ruthless and cruel, and the stories of rape and theft have analogies in the way Red Army troops behaved when they occupied Eastern Europe in the spring of 1945. What remains debatable is the local response and to what degree it reflected the sentiments of the local population. Further, it is the vast scale of the conflict that becomes apparent from these discussions, particularly from figures on losses and casualties on both sides.

Turning to the accounts by Viktor Koval' (1996) and M. V. Koval' (1999), we find a variety of figures that at first glance appear inflated. Viktor Koval' cites historians' estimates that in the period of 1944–45, the number of UPA troops reached a maximum of 150,000. The UPA "lost" 56,600 dead and had 108,500 wounded. A further 48,300 "Banderites" emerged from the forest after Soviet promises of an amnesty. He remarks that the Soviet side tends to overestimate the losses of its opponents and underestimate those of its own troops—the same clearly might be said of any participant in a major conflict. He relies instead on the figures provided by the UPA command, which reported that in 1946 there were 1,945 clashes in which the UPA sustained losses of 5,186 men and Soviet forces 15,645. In 1947, the respective figures were 342 and 1,406. The UPA reportedly attained such a one-sided result despite the fact that in Galicia alone in 1944, the Red Army contingent amounted to 200,000 troops, in addition to over 300,000 punitive detachments formed from Partisan units.[22] M. V. Koval' has added the following information culled from the recently opened Central Archive of the Defense Ministry of the Russian Federation under the signature of Strokach: in the 21 months after February 1944, there were 26,685 armed operations against OUN-UPA. The "rebels," in turn, carried out 6,128 operations. Up to that date, 98,846 insurgents had been killed, 104,990 had been arrested, and 48,800 had deserted from the Red Army. On the Soviet side, 9,621 people had been killed, 1,343 wounded, and 2,456 had disappeared.[23] In one document it was reported that during eight months of fighting, 12,500 people had been killed, 146,000 arrested, and 66,000 rebels from UPA formations and underground sections of the OUN had surrendered. As the UPA losses began to rise, Koval' adds, between 1945 and 1948 about 50,000 insurgents escaped to the West, while those that remained were reorganized into smaller formations. Some foreign reports are cited, which suggest that the UPA controlled formally or informally more than ten *oblasts* with a combined territory of 150,000 square kilometers, and a population of 15 million people.[24] Perhaps this is a case of hyperbole, but these authors make a strong case for a mass movement and a full-scale military confrontation taking place within the confines first of the Second World War and later of the Cold War.

OUN-UPA in the GULAG

Gulag literature pertaining to members of OUN-UPA is a developing industry. Such figures already had a place—albeit a far from predominant one—in the writings of Solzhenitsyn. Narratives that have appeared since the late Soviet period have begun to undermine the existing image of the Gulag camps. While they are still represented as slave labor camps in which political prisoners were hapless victims deprived of their rights, a new image emerges of camps in which Ukrainian prisoners were the organizers of resistance within the vast camp system, and were in many respects treated differently from the other inmates. In other words, the time when Ukrainians were present in the camps in large numbers has been linked to the resistance in Western Ukraine and was to some extent a continuation of the struggle against Soviet power and for Ukrainian independence. The Gulag experience also represents an essential part of the life story of "heroes," or of insurgents removed from the battlefield in such large numbers that even in exile they constituted—or were perceived to constitute—a threat to the authorities. In terms of the construction of a national history, the story is important because it permits an uninterrupted narrative. Hitherto, many accounts of resistance in Western Ukraine after the war ended in 1950, and others in 1953. The death of Roman Shukhevych in a skirmish near L'viv in 1950 might be seen as the traditional conclusion to the epic struggle between freedom fighters and a repressive authority. However, through tales from the Gulag and the camp life, the long gap between the 1950s and the period of independence (or Perestroika, as the starting point for a revival of Ukrainian national consciousness) can be bridged. To do so, the Ukrainian experience in the camps needs to be singled out and made distinct from the general Soviet experience, a difficult task given the plethora of ethnic groups in the system, and the problems of offering any form of organized resistance.

The question of deportations was dealt with in some depth in the late Soviet period by M. Buhai. According to his account the decision to deport families of UPA insurgents to the eastern regions of the Soviet Union was taken by the NKVD in March 1944. By the end of 1945, 967,085 families were living in special settlements, with a total of 2.3 million deportees from across the USSR. This movement of people occurred at the same time as the forced relocation of ethnic minorities displaced by the war, among whom Czechs, Slovaks, Poles, and Ukrainians figured prominently (discussed below). NKVD troikas and special councils of the MVD-MGB supervised the process. Once forced collectivization began in Western Ukraine—it began in earnest in 1948—kulaks and former members of the Polish army led by General Anders were also added to the mix. With the death of Stalin in March 1953, the regime's attitude to the "special settlers" relaxed somewhat, and a USSR Council of Ministers' decree of 5 July 1954 lifted some of the restrictions, demanding that party organs reintensify their efforts to reeducate deportees and promote their integration into "active political and social life." However, such measures did not apply to the Nationalist insurgents, their accomplices, family members, and kulaks. Thus by the mid-1950s, 135,762 OUN members and their families remained in special settlements. On 15 May 1956 another government decree rescinded the restrictions on nationalist insurgents, and they began to return to their places of origin. However, the numbers were relatively small. By March 1957, the author notes, 20,043 members of the OUN, together with 22,497 accomplices, 1,666 German collaborators, 5,713 people who served in German military formations, and 6,416 people sentenced for anti-Soviet activity returned to Ukraine.[25] The period of the most intense activity of nationalist inmates appears to have been in the 1950s, and particularly in the uncertain time between the death of Stalin and the issuing of the new laws as the Khrushchev administration began to distance itself from its predecessor.

A fairly typical example of late-Soviet period accounts is that of Oles' Lernatovych, a native of Brody region who served in the Polish army and was taken prisoner. He comments that the German POW camps compared favorably with the Gulag. He was accused of belonging to the SS Division Halychyna (see below), and offers a recollection of brutal beatings and arduous work in the gold mines. He weighed less than 22 kilograms when he was in the camp.[26] A resident of a camp in Irkutsk, Mykhailo Lutsyk, was the subject of an article by Roman Pastukh in early 1991, who offers a stirring story of Lutsyk's early career working for the OUN cause. In 1943, it is reported, Lutsyk led an UPA unit that freed 500 POWs from a German labor camp. In the following year he was betrayed by a former POW and arrested by the NKVD in Transcarpathia. In the camp he met a Ukrainian inmate who informed him that the camp guards had massacred inmates after they started a brawl, and only one person survived under a pile of corpses. To protect inmates from a similar fate, Lutsyk decided to organize an underground cell for Ukrainian nationalists, which was called the Ukrainian Liberation Organization (UVO) and founded in July 1945. In the cell, every member knew no more than four of his comrades. When prisoners were transferred to other camps, members of UPA were added to the list in order to organize new cells. In his next camp Lutsyk organized an "academy" and taught history, philosophy, and law so that inmates could defend themselves at interrogations. They learned to make weapons, and reportedly could raise six to seven divisions in the camps. Yet the secrecy level was so high that the NKVD could not penetrate the movement. This organization, it is stated, lasted until the summer of 1953, when strikes began in the Gulag and many prisoners died. In 1957, Lutsyk was rearrested and accused of membership in the UVO, insurgency, and terrorism, and received a sentence of fifteen years, which he served in full before being placed in a psychiatric hospital for a further five years.[27]

The story of Lutsyk contains most of the ingredients of legend: heroic activities, followed by arrest, but continued resistance in the camp, and long-term persecution by the authorities. In the early years of independence, the literary weekly published the memoirs of Bohdan Pavliv, a native of L'viv region, which provide a much more detailed depiction of the role of insurgents in the Soviet camp system. Pavliv had joined the OUN at the age of 17 and took the alias "Zenko." His responsibilities included gathering information about events in the L'viv countryside and informing his superiors about measures taken by the authorities. In 1950, he entered the Department of English Language at L'viv University, but he was arrested in April 1951. His elderly parents were sent to Siberia and he was placed in a labor camp. After his release he worked at construction jobs in Irkutsk and Kyiv. In his later years he joined the Ukrainian Republican Party and he was officially rehabilitated in 1991. Recalling the early illusions of the insurgent movement, Pavliv recounts that by the end of 1946, it had become clear to all that there would be no Third World War, and that the OUN could not count on any allies in the struggle against the "Russian-Bolshevik Empire." Therefore the OUN leadership began to train a younger generation to lead a legal existence while at the same time carrying out clandestine work. In the postwar years in Western Ukraine, Lutsyk recalls, the NKVD took special measures to disrupt any contacts between the local population and the underground. The group with which he was in contact was eventually exposed, and encircled by the NKVD in the spring of 1950. Those arrested were tortured and one revealed Lutsyk's name. He was convicted under Articles 58-1 and 58-11 of the Soviet Criminal Code: treason and membership in the OUN. His sentence was 25 years in the camps and five years in exile.[28]

Having arrived at the Kamyshlag camp in Kemerovo *oblast* of Siberia, Lutsyk noted that he realized that its purpose was to use prisoners for work in the nearby coal mines. The authorities had evidently sent active young inmates there, most of whom were Ukrainian, with convoys arriving from all over Western Ukraine. Formerly, the inmates had been composed of intelligentsia and peasants, who felt they had been sent there by mistake and were inclined to behave passively. As in other camps, the administration used regular criminals to subdue the political prisoners. The criminals occupied the best positions and enjoyed privileges, whereas politicals were generally fearful and hungry. However, in 1949-53 the situation changed dramatically. Young people from the UPA arrived in the camps, but by this time they also had some experience of Soviet schools and knew some of the methods that would be employed in the camps. The camp administrators soon recognized that it was no longer possible to browbeat prisoners and that there was always a possibility that their weapons might end up in prisoners' hands. Conditions were as harsh as in the past: a 12-hour working day; searches in the morning and evening; hard labor; camp food consisting of sardines and porridge, 450 grams of bread, 9 grams of sugar, and 2 grams of oil; sleeping at night with lights on; the receipt of one letter per year; and no visitors. The insurgents, says Lutsyk, kept together to survive the cruelty of the criminals. Unfortunately, he adds, political prisoners from the Caucasus were not "on our side" and the Chechens and Ingushi were particularly hostile. The Baltic groups were neutral and the Belarusians sympathetic, but essentially the Ukrainians were alone. Skirmishes and full-scale conflicts occurred with the criminals, usually with the camp authorities taking the latter's side. As a result, many insurgents received extended sentences.[29]

In 1953, as Stalin approached his death, Ukrainian coal miners from the camps were the main organizers of a strike that put forward both economic and political demands. The strike began in Vorkuta on 3 March, and Lutsyk remembers how the authorities tried to prevent other prisoners from contact with the OUN. The situation, however, was unclear. Fellow Ukrainians had informed the strikers of Stalin's illness and they also had information from the radio. The camp appeared to be under the control of professional criminals. On the morning of Stalin's death, the camp leaders singled out 100 men, provided them with dry rations and marched them into the tundra. They began to sing insurgent songs, believing that they were about to be executed, but after an hour of wandering they were escorted back to the camp. NKVD officers confronted the prisoners, but ultimately they were afraid of the influence that the Bandera men would have on other prisoners and moved them to a power plant construction site by the Vorkuta River. Reportedly this was a site deployed as a center for the most troublesome inmates from other camps, too. After Stalin died and Beria was arrested, the author recalls, they felt sure they would be released, and together with other groups—including Russians, Germans, and inmates from the Caucasus and Central Asia—a delegation was sent to the camp administration with a demand to release all political prisoners. This demand was refused. The OUN group formed a committee led by "Sasha" Babinchuk, which elaborated a plan for easing work conditions until the prisoners were released. This included not locking the barracks, removing inmates' numbers, permitting correspondence with relatives on a monthly basis, and allowing visitors. Other mines, lacking the same discipline, entered into direct conflict with their guards and 60 were killed and hundreds injured as a result. When the amnesty was issued, it was offered only to those convicted of minor non-political crimes and to German POWs.[30]

According to Lutsyk, the critical issue at this time was to maintain a grip on events that were happening all-too quickly. A promising sign was the increasing criticism of Stalin. However, he considered the most advantageous development to be the rise of nationalism in the Third World. It reinforced his belief that the foundations of "our Ukrainian nationalism" were becoming a global phenomenon, and that the national-liberation ideology was not reactionary but held true for all oppressed nations. It is somewhat unclear whether the reference to the "Third World" is applied to less-developed countries as is sometimes implied by this term. It may refer rather to nations besides the Super Powers. By this time (after the 20th Party Congress of the CC CPSU in 1956), discipline in the camps had loosened considerably, and it was possible to dress in civilian clothing, grow one's hair, and visit the city twice a week, as well as subscribe to newspapers and magazines. Lutsyk's sentence was shortened by 15 years, and for good behavior, one day of a sentence would be counted as three. After a meeting with a camp committee—it comprised 10-12 men in civilian clothes—Lutsyk was released on 7 July. "My joy was unspeakable, but Ukraine was still occupied." The release was a result, he says, partly of "our own efforts." A difficult life lay ahead, but they were ready to continue the great ideals and goals of their struggle.[31] Again, the image presented is that of a protracted engagement that transcended the period of documented conflict between nationalist insurgents and the Soviet regime, with incarcerated prisoners keeping their cause alive while in captivity and claiming to represent the interests of Ukraine the nation rather than that of the relatively small area of the uprising.

Other accounts of camp life for insurgents have surfaced periodically. In the mid-1990s a former inmate recounted his experience in the Spask camp, some thirty miles south of Karaganda in Kazakhstan. He maintains that it was a death camp like Auschwitz, in which people were killed by hard labor. He was sent there in 1949, together with 10,000 political prisoners. The camp was run by a Major Vorobyev, and each prisoner had an ID number attached to his clothing and hat. Adjacent to the camp was a women's gulag, in which Ukrainian nationalist women were singled out for violent abuse. He reports that they would be sent into a camp for common criminals for a night and raped. "The guards laughed: 'Let the fellows have some fun with these Bande-rites. They wanted an independent Ukraine'."[32] More recently an interview was held with Mykola Symchych, an insurgent who spent a total of thirty-two years in Soviet camps and prisons. His unit was encircled by MGB troops on a cold winter night and he was taken prisoner in an unconscious state after the house in which he was staying was set on fire. He was placed in Ivano-Frankivs'k prison where MGB officers tried to persuade him to defect. Following his refusal he received a 25-year sentence in the Gulag. He maintains that in 1953, the Bandera prisoners rose up against the criminals; and for his participation in this clash, Symchych received an additional ten years to his sentence. He was transferred to Kolyma to extract lime, which brought on lung disease. His group refused to work there and received a further five years each. Later he served time in Perm region where he encountered many of the so-called 60ers. He portrays these dissidents as successors to the UPA, people who enabled the world to learn about the Ukrainian liberation movement. The author refutes the possible impression that the UPA looked down on the 60ers as Soviet people rather than sincere nationalists. Rather the dissidents were the carriers of the national message into a new generation.[33]

SS Division Halychyna

While the quest for recognition of UPA insurgents as Second World War veterans continues to elicit disputes in Ukraine, the position of the former members of the SS Division Halychyna is considerably more difficult. Formed in 1943 through negotiations between the Germans and the Ukrainian Central

Committee in Krakow, its members were cited in Soviet propaganda as the worst form of traitors: not only had they joined directly with the German army, they had linked-up with the SS, an organization guilty of some of the most heinous crimes against humanity. Several authors have offered English-language monographs on the topic and offered a variety of conclusions for the reader as to whether the Division was simply an effort to form a national army that would be directed solely against the incoming Red Army; or whether it represented a more sinister form of collaboration.[34] The Division's official title was the 14th Waffen-Grenadier Division of the SS, Halychyna No. 1, and it later became the 1st Ukrainian Division of the Ukrainian National Army. It was formed as the Germans belatedly tried to solicit the help of Soviet nationalities after the failure at the Battle of Stalingrad. Its organizer was the governor of Galicia, Otto von Waechter, who worked closely with the chairman of the Ukrainian Central Committee, Volodymyr Kubiiovych. Though many thousands volunteered to join the Division, its final contingent was around 18,000 troops, with three regiments of infantry, one of artillery, and one of training reserves. The title "Halychyna" (Galicia) was used either because the Germans wished to avoid direct use of the more inflammatory "Ukrainian" or to ensure tighter German control. Attached to the German 13th Army Corps, the Division was encircled by Soviet forces near Brody in the summer of 1944 and routed. It was later reformed and transferred to Slovakia, and in March 1945, the Germans declared the formation of a Ukrainian National Army under General Pavlo Shandruk to which the Division was attached. With the defeat of Germany and the loss of the war in Europe, a large portion of Division troops surrendered to the British. The POWs spent almost two years in Italy and were eventually permitted to enter the UK. Subsequently, many immigrated to North America.[35]

In the Soviet period, nothing of a positive nature appeared in official propaganda about the Division. Even at the end of the Soviet period, reports were uniformly hostile. One writer, for example, expressed fury at the erection of a monument to casualties of the Division in the village Yaseniv, Brody region, L'viv *oblast*. The author maintains that the Germans used the Division as a terrorist instrument against those who were defying German rule, and provides an excerpt from a chronicle of the Division's activities that tells of driving Poles in the region of the city of Ternopil' into a church and massacring them. The author writes that the archives objectively tell the story of a special commando unit from the Division that killed 1,500 civilians in L'viv, shooting Soviet POWs in Zolochiv, and of its members burning the settlement of Oles'ko, causing the deaths of 300 inhabitants. Its members are even accused of rounding up people for slave labor work in Germany. All the commanding positions in the Division, this same article reports, were held by Germans, and SS chief Heinrich Himmler had expressly forbidden the use of the term "Ukraine" and its derivatives when creating the unit.[36]

Ostensibly, the *raison d'être* of the Division was to create a national army that would be used to defend native territory against the Soviets. Its members have been identified by historians with the Mel'nyk branch of the OUN, which was prepared to cooperate with the German occupiers long after the Bandera wing turned hostile.[37] Its members have not been found guilty of war crimes. Indeed the Deschenes Commission in Canada, investigating such assertions in 1985, found no evidence to suggest that Division members had taken part in atrocities, guarded camps, etc. However, whatever its motives, by choosing to fight on the German side to attain its objectives, the Division would always be treacherous in Soviet eyes, and far from reputable in the eyes of neutrals. Many Ukrainians today appear divided in their assessments of the motives behind the creation of the Division and whether they were justified. In mid-June 1992, *Literaturna Ukraina* offered an interview with a former participant, Ivan Oleksyn, then president of the Ukrainian Fraternal Association in the United States and a man who was well-known for providing aid to the victims of the 1986 disaster at Chornobyl. The interviewer cited earlier comments from the newspaper *Visti z Ukrainy* (Kyiv) from 1979–80, which had referred to Oleksyn as an "SS-ite" and "Nazi stool pigeon." He then adds the following by way of an introduction: "Today most of our people know what the UPA fought for. But an understanding of what led Ukrainians into regular military formations needs to be developed." Oleksyn responds by saying that when the war began in Galicia, some people developed the idea of creating the UPA and others the Division. The political organizations of Bandera and Mel'nyk backed the insurgent army in order to mount a struggle against both enemies. Others considered that forces were too deficient to fight on two fronts, and no assistance to the Ukrainians was forthcoming from other states. So it was resolved to form a division with the German army—there was no alternative, he states, to a civil conflict.[38]

As the interview continues, Oleksyn is asked what the "SS" denotes in SS Division Halychyna. He responds that it did not have this name, but was the First Ukrainian Division of the Ukrainian National Army (in fact, it took that name only in 1945) and Ukrainian troops did not have the SS insignia on their uniforms. Its goal, in contrast to those depicted in Communist propaganda, was the struggle for Ukraine, to free it from the "Bolshevik yoke." Each member considered himself an inheritor of the mantle of the Sich Sharpshooters of the First World War, and had no wish to assist the Germans. As for the UPA, Oleksyn says that "we supported it" and many Division members eventually found their way into its ranks. Toward the end of the war, they found themselves in Austria, close to the border with Yugoslavia. But no one believed it was really the end of the war. Everyone "was convinced" that the United States would refuse to countenance the Soviet takeover of Central and Eastern Europe. After the 1945 Yalta summit, however, people recognized that a new situation had arisen. Many troops had died at Brody, because after the first engagement the Germans had retreated, leaving the Division to face the Soviet army. Many had subsequently been interned at the large camp in Rimini, Italy. Concerning his own and his associates' attitude to Hitler, Oleksyn responds that they believed he could not win the war. If matters had developed differently, then the Division might have turned arms against the Germans, except the latter had convinced the Ukrainians that they supported the idea of the liberation of Ukraine. Later, "when we realized that Hitler had other plans," many members went into the UPA and led the battle on two fronts.[39] The interview stretches the bounds of credibility at times. One wonders how in the summer of 1943 it was possible to believe that Hitler and the Germans supported the concept of Ukrainian independence. By this time both leaders of the OUN were confined in Sachsenhausen, the abortive declaration of independence in June 1941 was becoming a distant memory, and the concept of new collaboration was clearly induced by the changing circumstances of the war, i.e., with the Germans retreating and the Red Army advancing rapidly.

Another article by Vasyl' (Wasyl) Veryha in the same newspaper continues the theme, stating that the insurgency of the "sharpshooters division 'Halychyna'" in the summer of 1943, when all of Ukraine was occupied by the Germans and "Red Moscow imperialism," should be interpreted as a continuation of the struggle of the Ukrainian people for independent state life. Ukrainian youth, especially those in the Western territories, had been educated in the traditions and legends of the Liberation War of 1918-21. In 1941, when war broke out, "all Ukrainian people" sympathized with the Germans. Hundreds of thousands of Ukrainians in the Soviet army crossed the border to the German side, believing that the time had come for Ukrainian independence. However, by the end of 1941, it was revealed that an independent and sovereign Ukrainian state was not in the plans of the Germans. Ukraine had been transferred into an exploited colony, under the guise of the Reichskommissariat Ukraine run from the town of Rivne. On 2 February 1943, following the German defeat at Stalingrad, Ukrainians again faced the question "What is to be done?" In the following month, the German administration of Galicia took into account the fact that Ukrainians were prepared to take up arms in the struggle with Bolshevism and turned to the Ukrainian Central Committee under Kubiiovych. The proposition was to create a Ukrainian armed formation, one division in size. While it is true, writes Veryha, that the Germans made the proposal for their own political ends, leading Ukrainian circles accepted it for their own ideological reasons. A partisan struggle could not continue without a regular army, and Ukrainian leaders—especially veterans of the struggle of 1918–20—maintained that Germany could either conclude a peace preserving some of its occupied regions or else it would collapse, leaving behind a chaotic situation in Eastern Europe. How would Ukrainians respond?[40]

Veryha's response, in defense of the Division, is as follows. In the first scenario, the Division would stand as a Ukrainian people's army to restore and strengthen the independent state, similar to the way the Sich Sharpshooters operated after the First World War. In the second case, it was evident that Ukrainians required an armed formation in order to protect people and property from the Germans before the possible chaos of a revolution. A request was made to the Germans that the Division would only be used on the Eastern Front against the Bolsheviks, and never against the Western allies. It was clear, he writes, that the Division was not part of the structure of a German New Europe, but operated only in the interests of the Ukrainian people. Ukrainian military leaders had approved contacts with the Western allies. The Division was met with hostility by the Soviet Partisans under Kovpak, and by the Polish Government-in-Exile. However, Ukrainian young people supported it because it was Ukrainian, not because it was part of the SS. Again the question arose: Why the title SS? Veryha's response is that the Division was given this name "against the will of Ukrainians." But it was only a formal title and had no links with Nazi ideology or implications of subordination to the Nazi party. Officially, its title was the Waffen Grenadier Division of the SS rather than the SS Grenadier Division as was traditional for German organs. Its soldiers did not have the right to wear the SS emblem and bore the gold and blue color of Ukraine.[41] Thus runs Veryha's essentially defensive justification for the existence of the Division.

Yurii Pryhornyts'kyi took up the same cause some six months later. Until recently, he comments, we knew very little about the Division. The equation with the Germans was enough to frighten some people, eliciting feelings of righteous anger. But "sooner or later reality will become more ambivalent." The Division was never part of the German army, but the question remains whether Ukrainians took up the arms of an alien occupier that wished to enslave their country. That question can be answered in the negative based on materials published in the West, he concludes. He cites a 1990 brochure published in Toronto and New York, which comments that locals could recall vividly the Soviet occupiers' brutal massacre of prisoners before they retreated in the wake of the German invasion in the summer of 1941. They recognized the ruinous nature of Russian Communism and the harm it could inflict on Ukraine. They also realized that German rule had brought few benefits, but did not want to miss an opportunity to create a strong, modern, and well-trained Ukrainian military unit within the German armed forces that could constitute the core of a future Ukrainian army. The author cites, with reference to the book by Wolf-Dietrich Heike,[42] that the training also brought benefits for the UPA, which used division soldiers as military instructors. Various commissions subsequently investigated the Division for potential war crimes, but none were uncovered. They included the Porter Commission of 1947 in the UK, which resolved that in spirit Ukrainians were "anti-Fascists." In Toronto, a Congress of the Brotherhood of the former First Ukrainian Division of the Ukrainian National Army assembled, and its chairman noted that it was celebrating the 40th anniversary of its formation. While aware that there are people in Ukraine who are hostile to the Division veterans, writes Pryhornyts'kyi, a majority would understand the quiet, restrained celebration of the anniversary.[43]

    Other narratives have been more forthright. In one article, the author insists that the Division was not a collaboration force but fought for Ukrainian independence. Unlike German SS units, the Division did not commit crimes. Bolshevik propaganda, to the contrary, represents nothing more than the fabrications of a hostile power trying to discredit any force that challenged its authority. Why did they join the Germans? This author replies that they had no choice. The clash of two imperial powers demanded armed resistance, and "UPA could not take everyone." Therefore an opportunity was taken to train cadres. The Division received the blessing of the respected Metropolitan Andrii Sheptyts'kyi and the author tells of one Division soldier who saved thirty peasants from German reprisals.[44] Another author demands that the SS Division must be rehabilitated. It was a combat unit, its SS affiliation was a formality, and it did not carry out war crimes. Many people joined for patriotic reasons.[45] Not everyone agreed with this assessment. In Kyiv in 1993, there was a campaign to ban celebrations of the 50th anniversary of the 1st Ukrainian Division of the Ukrainian National Army.[46] One author deliberately distinguished this army from the earlier one that had "compromised itself" as a tool in the hands of the Germans. The later formation, in his view, was more worthy of Ukrainian national aspirations. As for the SS Division, it had been organized by the "collaborationist" Ukrainian Central Committee in Krakow. German attempts to recruit members, in this author's view, fell flat and young people had to be drafted by force. There was a high rate of desertion and a lack of commitment to serve under the German banner. This comment hardly explains why there were so many volunteers, however, so the author adds that a majority of recruits *did* believe that they were fighting for the national interests of Ukraine.[47]

What should these young people have done? In the opinion of this same author, the only true example of patriotism would have been to join the UPA and fight both the Bolsheviks and the Germans. In this context he denounces both the members of the Ukrainian Central Committee and the members of the OUN-M, which collaborated with the Germans, and allegedly provided impetus for Soviet propaganda and the unfortunate phrase "Ukrainian–German nationalists." The diverse examples of collaboration by the OUN-B are conveniently omitted from this onslaught, and the author quotes some insurgents who criticized the formation of the Division. However, he opines, it is now time for reconciliation between the remaining former SS men and the Ukrainians who advanced from the east but failed to bring democracy, statehood, and well-being.[48] One might describe the attitude of this author as one of reluctant acceptance of people who went astray. It is a far cry from other authors who insist that the heroism of Division fighters be recognized. Ihor Fedyk, for example, gives a full account of the battle of Brody, a time when morale of Division members was high because they were about to defend their motherland from a Bolshevik onslaught (no doubt including Ukrainians who also thought they were freeing their motherland!). For the first hours of its deployment at the front, the Division was subject to constant air strikes. On 13 July 1944, the Red Army began its offensive. Between 15 and 18 July, despite heroic resistance, the Division was encircled, together with the 13th German army corps, in the area of several villages. In each village the conflict continued, and many of the soldiers who fell into Soviet captivity were executed. About 7,000 Division soldiers died, and almost 3,000 of those who could not break out of encirclement joined the UPA. A further 3,000 did break out and retreated with the Germans, forming the 2nd Ukrainian Division on Austrian territory. Fifty years ago, writes Fedyk, Ukrainian soldiers died fighting for the freedom of Ukraine and their sacrifice was not wasted. "The echo of their valor, enshrined in our memory for 50 years" can now be heard in an independent Ukraine.[49]

In like fashion, another author retorts that patriotism is not measured by the kind of uniform a soldier is wearing. The volunteers for the Division, he argues, joined their military unit under German auspices because they were conscious of the need to fight for Ukraine. He is resentful at the way the UPA is being constantly glorified at the expense of the soldiers of the Division. Politicians and professors who seem to have allergies toward the German army, he claims, should remember that it was in German-sponsored units that the careers of Generals Myron Tarnavs'kyi and Roman Shukhevych began. Yet the UPA evaluates the Division negatively and derides its commemoration of its martyrs. It should be kept in mind, this author believes, that the battle of Brody cost 7,000 lives, but it saved the lives of thousands of Ukrainians who managed to flee to the West. It compares favorably with the millions of losses caused by the actions of UPA, including members of families that were deported to Siberia. In the 1940s, older and more experienced people had doubts about the creation of UPA, regarding this as tantamount to national suicide. Time has shown that they were accurate.[50] This angry diatribe, which takes the form of a review of a book by American professor Taras Hunczak about the SS Division, thus takes matters a step further. Hunczak is requesting not recognition of Division members, alongside UPA, as genuine Ukrainian heroes, but rather the replacement of the UPA with the Division as more deserving recipients of such an accolade. These comments are echoed in an anonymous article that appeared in August 1993, which explains the difficulties in organizing Ukrainian military formations in the General Government territory of Galicia. The key figure was Volodymyr Kubiiovych, head of the Ukrainian Central Committee. When approached by Governor Waechter, Kubiiovych claims that the Ukrainian side issued a list of demands: that the Division must be used only against the Bolsheviks; that officers must be Ukrainian; that the name and insignia should be Ukrainian; the Division had to be subordinate to the German army; and it must constitute the first step toward the creation of a Ukrainian national army. However, the Germans broke this agreement and subordinated it to the SS. Though members were hostile to Nazi ideology, they faced the option of slave labor in Germany if they did not join.[51]

Another author describes Kubiiovych as a Ukrainian patriot who was conscious of German goals and willing to promote the Ukrainian agenda. He was also aware of the expansion of the UPA insurgency in Volhynia and therefore at first was cautious about accepting Waechter's proposal to form the Ukrainian Division. He preferred to retain some control over the formation, according to this version, and therefore made the set of demands that the Germans largely ignored. The Germans needed the support of the Ukrainian Central Committee in order to recruit members. In this account, there is no question that the initiative came from the Germans and it was likely that they would have attempted the Division's formation even without Ukrainian assistance.[52] However, more recently there have been further attempts to shed more light on the Division and to explain the motives of its creators with more clarity and sympathy. One such article is authored by Ivan Haivanovych, who decries the lack of objectivity in contemporary Ukraine, which has acknowledged its inheritance from the 1918 Ukrainian National Republic, and showed some understanding toward OUN-UPA. The Division, however, is mistakenly accused of collaboration. He argues for proper historical context, stating that the key question is why Galicians volunteered *en masse* to join it. He maintains that by 18 June 1943 there were 84,000 volunteers. In his view this response was a reaction to the repressive policies of the Soviet regime, including mass deportations and the NKVD murders of 1941. Nazi propaganda had some appeal for the population but there was disappointment over the German failure to recognize an independent Ukraine on 30 June 1941. So why did Ukrainians continue to turn to the Germans? The answer is that after the battle of Stalingrad, joining up with the Germans was the lesser evil. The article contains an interview with a former Division recruit, Roman Debryts'kyi, from 1993, in which the interviewee states that the only alternative was forced labor in Germany (an argument discussed earlier). Debryts'kyi describes the war as a tragic period when Ukrainians had to fight each other. He and his comrades fought with the weapons of the SS, but they remained patriots.[53]

Ivan Krainii maintains that most allegations about the Division's war crimes derive from Polish memoir-literature. He finds these sources unconvincing and demands an unemotional examination of the Division's legacy. He believes that its soldiers should be rehabilitated, as was the case in the Baltic countries, where four similar divisions were organized by the Waffen SS. In the Soviet period, as a result of official propaganda, the public perceived the SS men as traitors and collaborators. Only in 1990 did some émigré memoirs about the Division arrive in Ukraine. The most ominous problem is that of the two letters "SS." However, he writes, the Division belonged to the Waffen SS and was intended to be a battle unit, and members of the Ukrainian Central Committee had insisted that it be a Ukrainian formation. Krainii interviewed a former member, Volodymyr Malkosh, who reveals that he joined the Division because of his strong anti-Soviet sentiments and nationalism. He had two roads open to him—UPA or the Division. He chose the latter because he felt it would be the basis of the future Ukrainian national army. He was fearful that "warlike neighbors" would lay claim to Ukraine's territory. After he joined up, there was a period of training and Ukrainian language instruction. After the Division's defeat at Brody, he remained in the area of Soviet occupation. He entered L'viv Polytechnic University in 1946, but was arrested when the authorities noticed a tattoo characteristic of the Waffen SS on his arm. He was then sent to the Gulag for fifteen years.[54] Krainii's account differs from the others in the issue of choice. Whereas fellow authors suggest that the alternative to joining the Division was forced labor in Germany, he maintains that the choice was between the SS unit and the UPA. Other authors have declared that joining the Division enhanced opportunities for ending up in the ranks of the insurgents. Evident here is a political division rather than diverse options for the average nationalist whose long-term goal was an independent Ukrainian state. In other words, those who joined the Division were influenced by political leaders with very different views from those of the chief determinants of how Western Ukrainians acted i.e., the OUN-B.

The latter statement is corroborated by Kost' Bondarenko, who explains the formation of the SS Division as follows. It was organized to take part in military operations rather than punitive actions, and the Ukrainian Central Committee was responsible for the recruitment of its servicemen. Whereas the Bandera faction of the OUN resented the idea of its creation, the OUN-M regarded it as a good opportunity for the future national army to gain skills and experience. Its top commanders were German, while the troops wore German uniforms with a blue and yellow insignia and the Halychyna lion in their buttonholes. The troops took an oath of allegiance to Ukraine, which later saved the Division's soldiers and officers from retribution—they were found not guilty of war crimes after the war. In 1944 it was almost completely destroyed, and its remnants were transferred to the south of Poland, and subsequently to Slovakia and Yugoslavia where it was merged with the 34th SD Battalion (the "Volyn' Legion") in the spring of 1945. By April 1945 it had surrendered to the Western allies and its troops were not subject to repatriation because in Allied eyes they had remained Polish subjects. Bondarenko maintains that when the German leaders made the decision to create the Division, they were of the opinion that residents of Galicia and Ukrainians were representatives of different nations. They felt that the former were close to the Aryans, and this myth was the basis on which the Division was formed. This author asserts that Hitler was well aware of the Division—some reports suggest that he was ignorant of its existence—and even used to discuss it during his dinner conversations. Its origins dated from 1941, when the Germans announced the goal of establishing an SS Division Sumy from Ukrainian POWs, with further efforts in 1944 in the Carpathians.[55] Presumably, however, if the Germans intended to establish a division from Ukrainian POWs, then the Aryan issue might have been a secondary factor.

At the time of writing, no consensus had been reached in Ukraine on the question of the SS Division Halychyna. It remains the most controversial of all the national formations of the interwar and war years, not least because members of the OUN and UPA insist that the recruits had an alternative. The Division was undoubtedly part of the German war effort, whether or not members joined with other motives. The SS appellation would already have had dark connotations among the population. It seems fair to say that the situation for the young recruits was extremely problematic with none of the possible options offering any prospect of an easy existence. Before long, a new option—joining the Soviet Army—would also be a possibility. On the other hand, the severe criticism emanating from some members of UPA also seems unjustified, in that the insurgents were also prepared eventually to reach a new *modus vivendi* with the retreating Germans as they awaited the advancing Red Army. However, it could be argued that the UPA did not operate as a military formation on the German side and always maintained its independence. Thus the SS Division represented more of a last hope of cooperation with the Germans on the part of the UCC and OUN-M, both organs that had favored collaboration and continued to work with the Germans even after the nature of the occupation regime had become evident. Undoubtedly, life under the Polish General-Government was much more tolerable and easygoing than in the Reichskommissariat Ukraine. The question, though, is whether such relative moderation could justify the establishment of a Ukrainian military formation on the German side and on the Germans' initiative, particularly at such a late stage of the war when it appeared to most observers that a German defeat was simply a question of time. It represented poor judgment and naivety on the part of Kubiiovych and others, and after more than sixty years, the motives of the UCC in particular seem just as inexplicable as they did at the time. No doubt the debates will continue.

The Moderation of the OUN Program

At its Third Congress in August 1943, the OUN moderated its official program, and according to its defenders, adopted a more tolerant and liberal outlook, divesting itself of some of the more unpleasant facets of what has been termed "integral nationalism." Following this meeting, a new all-Ukrainian assembly was formed, entitled the Ukrainian Supreme Liberation Council (UHVR) in July 1944, made up predominantly of members of the OUN-B, with a General Secretariat that was led by the military leader of the UPA, Roman Shukhevych. The new organization came after the establishment of a similar organization by the OUN-M, which had also recognized that policies of extreme nationalism were unlikely to win followers on a national basis in an independent Ukraine. The motives behind this change of policy are open to debate and they form the basis for the discussions that are to be found in narratives in Ukraine from the late Gorbachev period onward. The change of direction forms part of another history, that of the OUN in exile and the protracted and fractious disputes that have occurred among its members living in North America, Western Europe, and elsewhere. According to Myroslav Yurkevych, "The OUN factions have had a decisive impact on the Ukrainian émigré community. The community's identity and public image have been shaped largely by the nationalist commitment to Ukraine's liberation."[56] In turn, with the transfer of these discussions to an independent Ukraine after 1991, along with the physical presence of the OUN in Ukraine, the outlook of the nationalists—and the unbending hard-line integral nationalism that was retained by Bandera in exile—has become part of a wide-ranging discussion and many of the disputes in the Diaspora have been transferred to Ukraine (and sometimes back again).

The Communist view, even in the latter years of the Soviet state, was that the change of policy was a matter of expediency. Maslovs'kyi, in his authoritative article in *Komunist Ukrainy*, writes that the social doctrine of the OUN was purely "bourgeois." Only at its Third Extraordinary Congress did the nationalists make their program worker-friendly, but this occurred precisely because the Red Army was approaching the Dnipro River and was about to begin the liberation of Western Ukraine.[57] The nationalists themselves argue that the decision was more rational and based on careful rethinking of priorities. Petro Duzhyi, for example, writes that Ukrainian nationalists always proclaim the primacy of the idea over matter. Unlike pragmatists and adherents of realpolitik, they never lose faith. Enemies may beat them physically but the national idea remains intact. The Nazis and the Communists cultivated the principle of a supreme leader, and worshipped their Hitlers, Lenins, and Stalins, as well as lower-level leaders, but the Ukrainian nationalists, having recognized the negative repercussions of a leadership cult, categorically relinquished the *fuehrerprinzip* and at the Third Congress substituted a three-man leadership for the single leader, with all three leaders carrying the same weight. Duzhyi appeals for the democratization of society and says that the

OUN should not simply try to replace the CPSU in Ukraine, with its tradition of authoritarianism.[58] Likewise, Viktor Koval' notes that the Third Congress raised the question "What is UPA fighting for?" It concluded that the UPA was opposed to Russian Bolshevism and German occupation, and supported the reconstruction of the USSR without landowners, capitalists, and Bolshevik commissars. In this program, he writes, alongside the appeal for a democratic reconstruction of society, for the first time in the history of the peoples of the Soviet Union all the principles of the protection of people's rights were formed. The decision of the Congress was in solidarity with all those political moods prevailing in Ukraine after the resurrection of independence.[59] There could hardly be a clearer claim for the prevalence of the 1943 edition of the OUN in contemporary Ukraine.

Other writers are less convinced by the change of direction. M. V. Koval' comments that the Third Congress of the OUN decided that OUN-UPA would now fight against Nazi Germany, the collapse of which appeared imminent, as well as against a new Bolshevik occupation. However, the real course upon which the Congress embarked was one of truce with Germany, and the coordination of the armed struggle against Soviet forces. At the same time, losses suffered by the Germans on the Eastern Front had failed to change the outlook of the Mel'nyk wing of the OUN, and Mel'nyk, Kubiiovych and Kost' Pankivs'kyi supported a political line of loyalty to the German occupiers. He also cites as an example of this collaboration the initiative to establish the SS Division Halychyna. With the same goal of opposing the Soviet Union, the OUN attempted the political maneuver in the summer of 1944 of forming the Supreme Liberation Council, in which other nationalist movements from Western Ukraine were represented.[60] Kul'chyts'kyi has described the ideological change as remarkable. In August 1943, the OUN-B began to recognize the rights of minorities, and revoked the unlimited powers of the head of the SB, Mykola Lebed', and set up a leading council under the chairmanship of Shukhevych. In July 1944 the Supreme Liberation Council was formed, which controlled the UPA. However, he continues, this attempt at democratization eventually failed, leading to more ideologically motivated divisions among the leadership of the OUN-B.[61] Il'yushyn maintains that the Red Army had remained "the sole enemy" of the Ukrainian insurgents and that during the occupation of the Germans, the OUN-B leaders tried to restrict anti-German actions of the UPA. Similarly, during the period of retreat from Ukraine, some German officers and intelligence leaders began to regard the UPA as a tactical ally, and following a meeting of 19 April 1944, they decided to hold talks with the OUN to see if the UPA would halt its acts of sabotage. The formation of the UHVR, in Il'yushyn's view, did not denote a profound change of direction, and he cites the view of Taras Borovets' that the Banderites' attempt to consolidate all Ukrainian groups under one platform was a "falsification" similar to the aborted declaration of independence in June 1941.[62]

Finally, mention should be made of the convocation of a conference of peoples "suffering under the Soviet yoke" in Rivne region in November 1943, which allegedly led to the subsequent formation of the Anti-Bolshevik bloc of nations, established in the West and headed by OUN-B leader Yaroslav Stets'ko, and later by his wife and parliamentary deputy in Ukraine, Yaroslava Stets'ko. A laudatory account of this conference appeared in the newspaper *Den'*, which described it as a highly significant endeavor because for the first time the concept of uniting peoples in opposition to the Soviet Union was expressed. It noted that the highly secretive assembly was led by OUN member Rostyslav Voloshyn, and included UPA's first commander Dmytro Klyachkivs'kyi (Klym Savur), as well as Shukhevych. Among those represented were Ukrainians, Georgians, Azeris, Tatars, Ossetians, Poles, Czechs, Belarusians, Russians, Jews, Kazakhs, and Circassians, all with one thing in common: a hatred for the Stalin and Hitler regimes.[63] The conference is part of the nationalist conception of Ukrainian history and linked closely to the broadening of the OUN-B appeal and change of political direction.

Evolution of the OUN

The history of the OUN in the postwar period merits a separate discussion and is too complex to be fully incorporated within this study. At the end of the Second World War, the emigrant OUN-B used the name: the Foreign Sections of the OUN (Zakordonni Chastyny OUN or ZCh OUN). In February 1954 after a prolonged internal dispute between the so-called "orthodox" followers of Bandera and the revisionists, a breakaway group formed from the ZCh OUN, based on a joint leadership (Lev Rebet from the Bandera faction and Mykola Lebed' as the head of the Ukrainian Supreme Liberation Council) and called "*dviikari*" (OUN-Z). The split derived from attitudes toward the 1943 Congress, moderating the views of the OUN-B. Bandera's faction became known as the revolutionaries or OUN-R. In 1957 and 1959, KGB agents assassinated Rebet and Bandera respectively. Mel'nyk, whose faction also used the name "*solidarysty*" (OUN-S), was left untouched. H. V. Kas'yanov writes that all three wings of the OUN began to develop in different directions after the war. The OUN-B reverted to ideological dogmatism after expelling the revisionists; the *dviikari* adopted democratic nationalism without abandoning some ideological declarations; and the OUN-M, which published its newspaper *Ukrains'ke slovo* in Paris, revived after a period of stagnation and was to subsequently become active in Kyiv. In 1992, the Congress of Ukrainian Nationalists (KUN) was created in Kyiv by the OUN-R/OUN-B in Ukraine on the initiative of Roman Zvarych (Ukrainian Minister of Justice in the Yushchenko administration) and Slava Stets'ko, the widow of Yaroslav Stets'ko.[64] Some of the contentiousness and disputes that had been manifest in the Diaspora were soon transferred to Ukraine. A leader of the Ukrainian Republican Party noted in late 1992 that KUN wished to retain for itself the exclusive representation of what was termed "Ukrainian nationalism" while regarding those proto-nationalist organizations not sharing OUN-B ideology as "democrats-traitors." This author refuted this conception by referring to the important role played in the creation of an independent Ukrainian state by his own party, the Rukh, and the Association of Ukrainian Youth. In a subsequent article he also remarked that nationalism was not confined to noisy rhetoric but involved with concrete activities for the well-being of the people.[65]

The transferal of the headquarters of the OUN-B to Kyiv did not prove to be a decisive event, which is indicative of the marginal impact of the Bandera group on Ukrainian politics and Ukrainian political thought. After Stets'ko died in 2002, the leadership of the OUN-B/OUN-R devolved to Andrii Haidamakha in Brussels, and thus once again it became a Diaspora organization. The KUN and OUN-B/OUN-R split and went their different ways. The intolerance of the OUN-B has been its undoing, as well as its evident reluctance to cooperate with other organizations that are at least similar in spirit, such as the Rukh and the Ukrainian Republican Party. Ironically, the OUN-M, which arguably has been less effective in the Diaspora, has been better organized in Ukraine. According to Taras Kuzio, the Olzhych Foundation, affiliated with the OUN-M, published throughout the 1990s the popular monthly journal *Rozbudova derzhavy*, a revival of the magazine of the same name published by the (united) OUN in the 1930s. The OUN-M newspaper, *Ukrains'ke slovo*, transferred its headquarters from Paris to Kyiv after Ukraine became independent, and has taken an active part in some of the key debates on the war years, and in general has been a far more effective organ than its Bandera counterpart, *Shlyakh peremohy*.[66] The key issue here is the failure of the OUN-B-OUN-Z to propagate its version of the past as the key inheritance of the modern state. In this respect it has clearly failed, and its influence within Ukraine does not match its effectiveness outside its native land. One source puts the matter succinctly:

Every generation has its struggle and its heroes. Every generation has its victories and its defeats. Our victories occurred on 16 July 1990, 24 August, and 1 December 1991. They are forever engrained in the annals of Ukrainian history, and they cannot be sacrificed for the sake of any idea or organization, however "real" and "sincere" they may be, because they belong to the whole people and the whole nation.[67]

To what extent the perspective of the OUN and the UPA as the main representatives of the Ukrainian liberation movement has pervaded political thought in Ukraine is debatable. Certainly it is in a more favorable position than the SS Division Halychyna, which has as yet failed to find a positive place in the historical narrative, largely because there appeared to be alternatives to fighting in a German formation, and perhaps also because of its almost immediate destruction in the conflict that followed. The key question is whether nationalists could overnight be transformed into democrats, and largely because of the forthcoming defeat of their would-be patrons (at least at the outset of the war), the German army and occupation regime. It has proved hard to separate the change in political outlook from the transformation of the military situation. However, there is another issue to be considered. Arguably the largest stumbling block to a changed perception of the OUN and its military counterpart, the UPA are the events of the summer of 1943 in Volyn', namely the conflict with the Polish population, a topic that has elicited quite frenzied debates and the intervention of political leaders such as Viktor Yushchenko. It is to these issues that we will now turn.

Notes

1   The NKVD (Narodnyi komissariat vnutrennikh del: the People's Commissariat of Internal Affairs) was created on 10 July 1934 on the basis of the former OGPU (Unified Main Political Administration) and originated with the formation of the CHEKA (the Committee to Combat Counter-Revolution and Sabotage) by Lenin in December 1917. From February–July 1941 it was divided into two independent organizations, the NKVD and the NKGB USSR, but with the outbreak of war it again became a single commissariat under L. P. Beria until April 1943 when the two were once again divided. In March 1946 it was renamed the Ministry of Internal Affairs (MVD) of the USSR, and on 5 March 1953 a single, more powerful MVD USSR was created through the merging of the MVD and MGB (Ministry of State Security). The NKGB was renamed the Ministry of State Security (MGB) in March 1946. During the period under review it was led by V. N. Merkulov (1943–46) and V. A. Abakumov (1946–51).

2   Mykola Porovs'kyi, "Konvoi korovu z soboyu ne veze..." *Visti z Ukrainy*, No. 27 (1991): 1.

3 V. I. Maslovs'kyi, "Shcho na 'oltari svobody'? Dekil'ka utochen' shchodo viiny 'na dva fronty,' yaku vela UPA, ta skil'koma nevynnymy zhertvamy oplachuvavs' tsei propahandysts'kyi mif," *Komunist Ukrainy*, No. 7 (July 1991): 70-71.

4 These were local forces coerced into fighting against the insurgents.

5 Maslovs'kyi, "Shcho na 'oltari svobody'?" p. 72.

6 Ibid., pp. 72-73.

7 "Terror enkavedysts'kykh harnizoniv," *Samostiina Ukraina*, No. 85 (September 1992): 3.

8 Ivan Bilas, "Protystoyannya: aktsii represyvnoho aparatu totalitarnoho rezhymu proty natsional'no-vyzvol'noho rukhu ukrains'koho narodu," *Literaturna Ukraina*, 22 October 1992, p. 7.

9 Ibid.

10 Ivan Bilas, "Protystoyannya: aktsii represyvnoho aparatu totalitarnoho rezhymu proty natsional'no-vyzvol'noho rukhu ukrains'koho narodu," *Literaturna Ukraina*, 29 October 1992, p. 7.

11 Ibid.

12 Ibid.

13 "Emhebisty u formi UPA," *Samostiina Ukraina*, No. 45 (1992): 3.

14 Bohdan Pasichnyk, "Provokatsiya vyvirenym metodom," *Za vil'nu Ukrainu*, 4 May 1995, p. 2.

15 Viktor Koval', "Ukrains'ka povstans'ka armiya: dovidka Instytutu istorii AN URSR dlya Komisii Verkhovnoi Rady Ukrainy z pytan' bezpeky vid 1 lypnya 1991 roku," *Ukraina i svit*, No. 35 (18-24 September 1996): 9-10.

16 M. V. Koval', *Ukraina v Druhii svitovii i Velykii Vitchyznyanii viinakh (1939-1945 rr.)* (Kyiv: Vydavnychyi dim Al'ternatyvy, 1999), pp. 304-305.

17 Yaroslav Lyal'ko, "Vony povernuly nam muzhnist' i natsional'nu hidnist'," *Za vil'nu Ukrainu*, 12 September 1996, p. 2.

18 Koval', *Ukraina v Druhii svitovii i Velykii Vitchyznyanii viinakh*, pp. 304-308.

19 Ibid., p. 310.

20 Stanislav Kul'chyts'kyi, "Ukrains'ki natsionalisty v chervono-korychnevii Yevropi (do 70-richchya stvorennya OUN," *Istoriya Ukrainy*, No. 5 (February 1999): 6-7.

21 Ivan Krainii, "Ostanni z pidzemnoho bunkera," *Ukraina moloda*, 15 November 2002, p. 5.

22 Koval', "Ukrains'ka Povstans'ka Armiya," *Ukraina i svit*, No. 36 (25 September-1 October 1996): 10.

23 It is highly unusual to have a higher figure of dead than wounded in a military conflict, which casts suspicion on the authenticity of these figures.

24 Koval', *Ukraina v Druhii svitovii i Velykii Vitchyznyanii viinakh*, p. 305.

25 M. Buhai, "Deportatsii naselennya z Ukrainy," *Ukrains'kyi istorychnyi zhurnal*, No. 11 (1990): 21-25.

26 Oles' Lernatovych, "Svityt' zoreyu nadiya," *Za vil'nu Ukrainu*, 24 January 1991, p. 4.

27 Roman Pastukh, "Orhanizator hulahivs'koho pidpillya," *Za vil'nu Ukrainu*, 15 June 1991, p. 2.

28 Bohdan Pavliv, "I perevernem zaharbnyts'kyi svit: spomyn chlena OUN," *Literaturna Ukraina*, 15 October 1992, p. 7.

29 Ibid.

30 Ibid.

31 Ibid.

32 Yaroslav Demchyna, "Dolyna smerti," *Za vil'nu Ukrainu*, 16 February 1995, p. 2.

33 Tetyana Kharchenko, "Mizh povstantsiamy i chervonymy partyzanamy nemaye niyakoho antahonizmu," *Ukraina moloda*, 20 July 2003, p. 5.

34 See, for example, Wolf-Dietrich Heike, *The Ukrainian Division "Galicia," 1943–45: a Memoir* (Toronto: The Shevchenko Scientific Society, 1988); Taras Hunczak, *On the Horns of a Dilemma: the Story of the Ukrainian Division Halychyna* (Lanham, MD: University Press of America, 2000); Michael O. Logusz, *Galicia Division: the Waffen SS 14th Grenadier Division 1943–1945* (Atglen, PA: Schiffer Publishing, 2000); and the very unsympathetic Sol Littman, *Pure Soldiers or Bloodthirsty Murderers? The Ukrainian 14th Waffen-SS Galicia Division* (Toronto: Black Rose Books, 2003).

35 [http://encyclopediaofukraine.com/display.asp?linkpath=pages\G\A\GaliciaDivision.htm].

36 K. Doroshenko, "Pamyatnik fashistskim prikhvostnyam," *Pravda Ukrainy*, 25 May 1991, p. 3.

37 See, for example, John-Paul Himka, "A Central European Diaspora under the Shadow of World War II: The Galician Ukrainians in North America," *Austrian History Yearbook*, 37 (2006): 19.

38 Yurii Pryhornyts'kyi, "Ivan Oleksyn: Use zhyttya borovsya za Ukrainu. Dyviziya 'Halychyna'. Yak tse bulo," *Literaturna Ukraina*, 18 June 1992, p. 3.

39 Ibid.

40 Vasyl Veryha, "Im prysvichuvala velyka ideya.... Dyviziya 'Halychyna', yak tse bulo," *Literaturna Ukraina*, 25 June 1992, p. 3.

41 Ibid.

42 Heike, *The Ukrainian Division 'Galicia'*.

43 Yuri Pryhornyts'kyi, "Shcho ikh velo u dyviziyu?" *Literaturna Ukraina*, 14 January 1993, p. 6.

44 Oksana Snovydovych-Mazyar, "To chy byly vony kolaborantamy?" *Za vil'nu Ukrainu*, 8 June 1993, p. 2.

45 Yaroslav Yakymovych, "Z zhertovnym styahom ikh zvytyah," *Za vil'nu Ukrainu*, 21 August 1993, p. 4.

46 Strictly speaking, this was the 50th anniversary not of the 1st Ukrainian Division of the UNA, but of the SS Division *Halychyna*, in its original form.

47 Danylo Kulnyak, "Esesivs'ka chy 'Persha ukrains'ka?" Z pryvodu odnoho yuvileyu," *Ukraina moloda*, 3 September 1993, p. 10.

48 Ibid.

49 Ihor Fedyk, "Vystoyaly; prorvalysya!" *Za vil'nu Ukrainu*, 14 July 1994, p. 2.

50 Vasyl Sirs'kyi, "Knyha, yaka vymahaye dyskusii," *Za vil'nu Ukrainu*, 29 July 1994, p. 2.

51 "Ishly u bii za svoyu peremohu," *Za vil'nu Ukrainu*, 7 August 1993, p. 4.

52 Mykhailo Yatsura, "Professor Kubiiovych i Dyviziya 'Halychyna'," *Za vil'nu Ukrainu*, 30 September 1995, pp. 1–2.

53 Ivan Haivanovych, "Ne nazyvaite 'SS'!" *Ukraina moloda*, 30 January 2001, p. 4.

54 Ivan Krainii, "Za shcho voyuvala dyviziya 'Halychyna'?" *Ukraina moloda*, 7 February 2001, p. 10.

55 Kost' Bondarenko, "Istoriya, kotoruyu ne znaem ili ne khotim znat'?" *Zerkalo nedeli*, 29 March–5 April 2002.

56 M. Yurkevych, "Organization of Ukrainian Nationalists," *Encyclopedia of Ukraine*, online edition; [http://www.encyclopediaofukraine.com/display.asp?AddButton=pages\O\R\Organizationof UkrainianNationalists.htm].

57 Maslovs'kyi, "Shcho na 'oltari svobody'?" p. 68.
58 Petro Duzhyi, "Vede nas v bii bortsiv polehlykh slava," *Za vil'nu Ukrainu*, 4 February 1993, p. 2.
59 Koval', "Ukrains'ka povtsans'ka armiya," *Ukraina i svit*, 18–24 September 1996.
60 Koval', *Ukraina v Druhii svitovii i Velykii Vitchyznyanii viinakh*, p. 155.
61 Kul'chyts'kyi, "Ukrainski natsionalisty v chervono-korychnevii Yevropi," pp. 6–7.
62 I. I. Il'yushyn, "Natsional'no-vyzvol'ni prahnennya ukrains'kykh ta pol's'kykh samosti-inyts'kykh syl za chasiv Druhoi svitovoi viiny," *Ukrains'kyi istorychnyi zhurnal*, No. 1 (2003): 94–95.
63 Serhii Stepanyshyn, "Nationalist Internationalism: The Conference of the Captive Nations of Eastern Europe and Asia was held sixty years ago," *The Day Digest*, 9 December 2003 [http://www.day.kiev.ua/261419/].
64 H. V. Kasyanov, "Ideolohiya OUN: istoryko-retrospektyvnyi analiz," *Ukrains'kyi istorychnyi zhurnal*, No. 2 (February 2004): 30; and information provided to the author by Dr. Taras Kuzio in a letter of 19 August 2006.
65 Ivan Demyanyuk, "Natsionalizm: shlyakh do derzhavnosti chy do ruiiny," *Samostiina Ukraina*, No. 46 (12 December 1992): 3; No. 47 (19 December 1992): 3; and No. 48 (26 December 1992): 3.
66 Taras Kuzio, letter to the author, 19 August 2006.
67 Borys Hayevs'kyi, Fedir Kyrylyuk, and Mykola Obushnyi, "Pravda i domysly navkolo "naukovo natsionalizmu," *Osvita*, 22 June 1994, p. 8.

CHAPTER 6

THE UKRAINIAN-POLISH CONFLICT

Introduction

Of all the volatile issues emanating from Ukraine's participation in the Second World War, perhaps the most debated has been UPA's conflict with the Poles, which has been described by Yale historian Timothy Snyder as one of the earliest examples of ethnic cleansing in the 20th century. A landmark of sorts was reached in 2003, the 60th anniversary of the attempted elimination of the Polish population in Volhynia region, when scholars, writers, and journalists on both sides of the border discussed the matter openly, albeit without reaching any firm conclusions. On the level of government politicians, the then opposition leader, Viktor Yushchenko, made some conciliatory remarks to the Poles concerning responsibility for past events. The Ukrainian response at the grassroots level, from those generally sympathetic to the UPA at least, was that there were similar atrocities on both sides, as evidenced by the enforced deportations of populations from both sides of the border and the deliberate targeting of Ukrainian civilians in Operation Vistula. This chapter will offer some tentative conclusions both on the state of the debate and the authenticity of the views being expressed in various narratives, and assess the degree to which they have assisted our understanding of these very complex events. The discussion differs from the previous ones that have been analyzed in that it has taken on an international hue, with Ukrainians, for the most part, defending the actions of the insurgents against criticism from outsiders. However, while Soviet propaganda prevailed, the Polish question left the UPA vulnerable to attacks from the official media as well.

Because of the controversial nature of these events it is logical to reflect first, and in more detail than in the earlier summary (see Chapter 1), on the existing English versions of the events that are based on careful archival research. Snyder has noted that in 1939, the Polish population constituted about 16% of the overall population of Volhynia (Volyn and Rivne *oblasts*), and by 1943 it had decreased to about 8%. He maintains that the UPA mounted a campaign to identify the Volhynian Poles and the Polish government with the occupation regimes of the Soviet Union and Nazi Germany. He believes that the fury of the actions against the Polish population was the reason for the Polish retaliation against Ukrainians—reflected, for example, in Operation Vistula. They then provided the UPA with an excuse for introducing what Snyder calls "ethnic cleansing" in the territories of Halychyna to the south. However, Poles there were more numerous and better able to defend themselves.[1] In a related article, Snyder delves into the topic in more detail. In his view, the brutal operations of the Germans against Volhynian Jews provided training for many of the future UPA members for the 1943 actions against Poles. Ukrainians became familiar with violent death on a mass scale, and those who took part in German operations as auxiliary forces subsequently became the main recruits for the creation of the UPA in Volhynia by the OUN-B. The decision to take the latter action was taken following the German defeat at Stalingrad, when in April 1943 OUN SD leader Mykola Lebed' proposed to eliminate the entire Polish population in the area of the UPA forces. Poles were also under intense pressure from Soviet Partisans. Snyder describes members of the OUN-B security forces as extremists and fanatics, with an implacable hatred of people they considered to be enemies of the nation. Thus the Ukrainian political scene in Volhynia came under the domination of "immature and angry men" led by the 33-year-old Lebed' and practically the entire Ukrainian youth entered the ranks of the UPA (in part, the OUN-B achieved full membership by threatening to kill all those who remained in the service of the Germans). By removing the Poles, they could prevent any possibility of a return to Polish rule in this territory of northwestern Ukraine, and up to 60,000 Poles, mainly civilians, fell victim to this orgy of violence.[2]

The Soviet Perspective

Though Soviet propaganda rarely focused specifically on OUN-UPA actions against the Polish minority, it was replete with attempts to discredit the insurgents and their cruelty toward the local populations. However, one of the main vehicles for such denigration, the newspaper *Pravda Ukrainy*, began a discussion in early 1990, following the publication of an article that tried to understand the motivation of UPA fighters. One interviewee had explained that the UPA fought for an independent Ukraine; that it fought against both the Russians and the Germans. True, it had massacred Poles, but this was a response to the shooting of "our people" across the Buh River.[3] This article elicited numerous responses from readers, some of which described the attacks on Poles, albeit without much focus on the nature and meaning of the assault. Many readers scoffed at the notion of using the archives to discover what had occurred. One stated that any mentally sane Volhynian could testify that the UPA were murderers "condemned with the eternal stamp of Cain" and that they had seen what happened with their own eyes. A former member of the OUN, who later left the organization and "recanted," commented that 1943 was a climatic year. In the spring, the OUN had put together a group and ordered people to carry axes. The writer was left behind, but next day he learned that the axes had been used to carry out a "bloody massacre" in neighboring villages that did not spare even children. Villages were burned down, wells stuffed with dead bodies, and horses, cattle, and other livestock were driven away. The news disillusioned the writer who then broke with the nationalists and went into hiding. Another eyewitness maintains that the "bandits" were cowardly because they refused to fight the Soviet Partisans. Rather they practiced their bravery and chivalry on the defenseless population.[4]

Maslovs'kyi focuses on the Polish massacres in passing when examining the issue of "victims of OUN-UPA." He writes that statistics on the number of victims either do not exist or are imprecise. Current writing (in 1991) placed the number of victims somewhere between 30,000 and 1.5 million. He cites the Association of Victims of Ukrainian Nationalists that was created in Wroclaw in the fall of 1990, which addressed an open letter to members of the Polish Sejm and senators. This letter declared that Ukrainian nationalists had killed some 500,000 Poles, Ukrainians, and Jews. The Association requested an unambiguous statement from the Polish parliament and the government that would clearly and precisely attribute the crimes committed by the Ukrainian nationalists as genocide, and denounce them as Fascist criminal organizations, particularly the OUN, the UPA, the battalions *Nachtigal* and *Roland*, the SS Division, and the Ukrainian police. The letter declared that all crimes could not be written off as in the past, and it referred to a law that demanded that such criminals be prosecuted. Maslovs'kyi expresses his disappointment with the way that these issues were being dealt with in Ukraine by certain officials and journalists. He refers to the newspaper *Robitnycha hazeta*, which announced on 3 December 1988 that Ukrainian nationalists had accounted for the deaths of some 30,000 Soviet citizens. In February 1990, the Ukrainian KGB also announced in the media that over 30,000 civilians, as well as some 25,000 soldiers, NKVD personnel, and border guards had died at the hands of the Banderites. How can this be, asks the author, when in L'viv region alone (excluding Drohobych district), between July 1944 and May 1946, the nationalists killed 5,088 Soviet citizens, including 44 teachers, 218 village *soviet* heads and their deputies, 406 members of destruction battalions, and 3,105 peasants? In his view, the figure of 30,000 does not reflect the scale of the massacres carried out by the Banderites. He cites his own figures that in 1944–52, OUN-UPA accounted for the deaths of over 80,000 citizens, and that the wartime toll is likely to be twice as high. Data are lacking and "even today" it is difficult to access special archives.[5]

In July 1991, an article by S. Dluskiy focused on the tragedy of the Polish village of Hanachevka, which had been founded by Franciscan monks and had a pre-Second World War population of about 3,000 people. The author notes that in the spring and fall of 1940 (following the Soviet annexation of Eastern Poland), about 260 inhabitants were deported to Kazakhstan and Siberia, but several potential deportees managed to hide among their Ukrainian neighbors in nearby villages. Hanachevka is depicted as a Polish island amid a Ukrainian Greek Catholic population. Peace prevailed and there were high rates of intermarriage. Hostilities began, however, during the German occupation. In July 1941, Dluskiy writes, the OUN members carried out the first excesses, burning houses and stealing cattle. With these acts came OUN propaganda, with leaflets distributed demanding that the Polish peasants leave their homes and move to the territory of the General Government, otherwise they would be killed. By the fall of 1941 the attacks had become more frequent. Polish peasants sought protection from the Polish Committee in L'viv and managed to establish contact with the Polish Home Army. The latter could not provide weapons but sent members to organize self-defense units. Weapons were purchased from Hungarian soldiers, and training was conducted secretly in the forests. The German police discovered these units and arrested about a dozen residents. In early 1943, the OUN killed 12 and wounded 20 people, and 8 insurgents were killed in response. On 22 January 1944, Soviet Partisans arrived in the Polish village and reportedly helped the Poles establish defensive units. But several days later, on 2 February, the OUN conducted a massive attack, and the German police declined to intervene. One hundred people died and 80 houses were burned down. Atrocities were perpetrated on the victims. Polish peasants from neighboring villages arrived to evacuate the wounded and bury the dead. The village population was reduced to 1,500 inhabitants, but two subsequent attacks from "UPA" reduced the total to 400. Before long the village was completely eradicated.[6]

Articles such as the one cited above by Dluskiy clearly had the intention of countering efforts to revisit OUN-UPA in order to revise the impressions created by the long period of Soviet propaganda, when its members had been depicted as criminals and traitors. This is also the purpose of the article entitled "The Well of Death" that appeared in two issues of *Pravda Ukrainy* in the summer of 1991. The well in question was constructed by Wladislaw Labudinski, a resident of the village Dyadkovichi in Rivne *oblast*. The village was subjected to an attack by members of the UPA security service, headed by a V. Slobodyuk. The victims in this case were reportedly Poles, fleeing Soviet POWs, members of the *Komsomol*, militiamen, Jews, Czechs, and Soviet sympathizers. As the UPA was under instructions to save bullets, the victims were choked with ropes, writes the author. The second part of the article focuses on the motives behind the massacres. On 1 January 1945, a group of UPA soldiers was executed in Rivne, consisting of the following names: S. K. Trofimchuk, A. Zaichikov, V. S. Lohvynovych, A. S. Kyrylyuk, A. V. Hrytsyuk, V. Podolets', N. T. Slobodyuk, and V. A. Slobodyuk. The author comments that in the early 1990s the Nationalist press presented these people as martyrs for the cause of attaining an independent Ukraine. The author challenges this viewpoint by illustrating the reported crimes of each soldier in detail. One of the UPA members, V. Slobodyuk, described during his interrogation the murders of Poles in Dyadkovichi perpetrated by Security Unit 4 of the UPA District 10. Many of the UPA members did not initially belong to the security service, but had been recruited by V. Slobodyuk, who had arrived from Germany in 1942. The article provides no details of what he might have been doing in Germany. Early in August 1943, all members of the security service were called to Dyadkovichi where they were instructed by district head "Makar" to kill all enemies of the UPA, burning their homes and expropriating their property. They were also to shoot all Soviet POWs that had fled from German camps, and to ensure that local peasants offered regular supplies of food to the UPA, with reprisals against saboteurs. Failure to comply with the above orders was punishable by death. Most of the victims ended up in Labudinski's well, according to this article.[7]

To the Soviet perspective can be added the writings of Wiktor Poliszczuk, whose work is an indictment of the OUN and UPA, and who stresses that, in the spring of 1943, Mykola Lebed', the head of the OUN-B Provid, along with Shukhevych, carried out the proclamation of the First Congress of the OUN by massacring the Polish civilian population of Volhynia. Up to that time, the deaths of Poles at the hands of Ukrainians had been somewhat random and a result of personal animosities. He notes that in this period, the OUN-B demanded of the Ukrainian police still in the service of the Germans that they flee to the forests taking their weapons with them. Former members of the

Schutzmannschaften Battalion 201 arrived in Volhynia from Belarus, having completed the brutal pacification of Belarusian villages on behalf of the Germans. These men, he adds, in a similar vein to Snyder's account, had experience with the elimination of the Jewish population and were now to make up the foundation of the military forces of the OUN-B, along with the Security Service run by Lebed'. Most of the latter forces were made up of Ukrainians from Halychyna. Using the basis of the First OUN Congress and the Second OUN Conference, it was Lebed' who provided the instruction to the troops to undertake the systematic extermination of the Polish population of Volhynia. The deaths ran into the tens of thousands, he writes. Members of the Mel'nyk wing of the OUN, where present, were coerced into the same activity. The picture portrayed is one of ruthless ethnic cleansing led by the nationalist security units that had received training at the German political school in Zakopane in 1939–40.[8] Poliszczuk makes little attempt to explain the reasons behind the atrocities and his monograph, though detailed, takes the form of a polemic. Thus his book can be added to the Soviet perspective from which it differs little in terms of the one-sidedness of the outline. Nevertheless, all those dealing with the OUN-UPA as warriors for an independent Ukraine (particularly those who allege that the two organizations had taken on a more moderate and democratic complexion by 1943), have to come to terms with the events of Volhynia, which appear to contradict such an assessment.

Perspectives from Independent Ukraine

Ukrainian narratives about the Polish conflict in independent Ukraine are understandably defensive in tone, often denying outright OUN-UPA responsibility for the Volhynia massacres. An early example is an article by Nina Romanyuk and Yurii Mykolayenko, which explores the history of the Ukrainian–Polish conflict during the Second World War. The authors point out that they have made use of materials from the SBU archives in the Volyn region, including the interrogation of Mykhailo Stepanyak, head of the international section of the OUN in 1942–44. Stepanyak took part in several talks with the Polish Government-in-Exile based in London. The first session took place in L'viv in 1942, before UPA units appeared in Volhynia, and was organized by a Greek Catholic priest, Kladochnii. The questions considered included the status of Ukraine, Belarus, and the Baltic States vis-à-vis postwar Poland, and the problem of the Ukrainian–Polish alliance. Reportedly, the Polish representatives agreed with many of the Ukrainian demands. However, the two sides were unable to reach an agreement on the future status of Western Ukraine, which the Poles insisted was a "mixed" territory, the future of which had to be resolved through a postwar settlement. They promised to recognize Ukraine and to provide financial assistance to the OUN, but insisted that the nationalists disassociate themselves from the Greek Catholic Church. These negotiations proved unfruitful and shortly afterward the Polish delegates were arrested by the Germans—some suspect that the priest Kladochnii betrayed them. The authors write that on 28 May 1943, Polish armed formations, supported by Polish Partisans, burned down the village Tel'chi in Manevtsi district, destroying 20 houses and killing 27 Ukrainians. They comment that this attack renders the Polish side the primary culprit that forced Ukrainian retaliation. However, it is unlikely that the arson was the first act of violence. Again the two sides entered negotiations, but could reach no consensus on the issues of Galicia. As for the massacres that followed, Stepanyak, who was present during the negotiations, denied that the violence was perpetrated by the OUN and the UPA.[9]

Another author describes a conference organized by right-wing Polish radicals and dedicated to problems of the Ukrainian–Polish relationship. Evidently some participants at the conference had claimed that in Volhynia, Ukrainian nationalists killed 500,000 Poles. The author angrily rejects such figures. Any researcher, well-versed in the events of the period, he writes, will tell you that such figures do not correspond to reality. There were victims on both sides, and no winners and losers. Such a confrontation profited only those who wished to sow seeds of enmity between Ukrainians and Poles. He is also irate with the Polish classification of OUN-UPA as a Fascist organization comparable to the Croatian Ustashi or Khmer Rouge in Cambodia, while considering the Home Army soldiers as heroes. Revealingly, he also notes that "no serious Polish politicians" were in attendance.[10] In like fashion, a Polish author criticizes the attack by Polish nationalists on OUN-UPA and accuses the chauvinistic press of ignoring the real causes of the Volhynian tragedy, which he presents as a civil war situation rather than an act of genocide (or ethnic cleansing) carried out by UPA North. Jan Hasten writes that the roots of the Ukrainian insurgency are to be sought in the repressive policies of Pilsudski and his successors, who attempted to colonize Polish Eastern Galicia. He makes reference to the Pacification, the destruction of churches, and the closure of Ukrainian schools. UPA, Hasten maintains, emerged from Ukrainian policemen who left the Germans' service on the orders of the OUN-B. The UPA–Home Army clash is depicted as an act of self-defense by UPA, which was trying to protect Ukrainian villages from Polish raids. The Home Army, he alleges, killed 1,500 Ukrainians after it crossed the Buh on its retreat from Volhynia. The UPA then sought out the perpetrators and executed them and their sons.[11] In other words, there was no independent initiative on the Ukrainian side to carry out ethnic cleansing of Polish villages. All the actions were a result of lack of trust on both sides. The article, however, fails to discuss why most of the victims were not under arms, but innocent civilians.

The more sober analysis of M. V. Koval' points out that one of the main UPA targets was the Armia Krajowa and its partisan formations, which were under the control of the Polish government in London. The OUN wanted a complete and enforced resettlement of Poles from Western Ukraine, starting in Volhynia, then Halychyna, and lastly all the territory west of the Curzon Line, which had become the new western border of Soviet Ukraine in 1939. The situation was also influenced by the anarchy that prevailed in this territory. The OUN took advantage of this chaos in its struggle to "de-polonize" the borderlands and to eliminate any potential basis for Polish identity to be used in a future plebiscite on the status of the region. He writes that more than 40,000 Poles were killed as a result of these mutual acts of terrorism, including women, children, and elderly people, but a similar number of Ukrainians had also fallen victim to this conflict. He cites authors who provide combined figures of 60–80,000 people. The bloodshed benefited only the third party, namely the German Fascists. He quotes Reichskommisar Erich Koch as stating openly that "I would like the Pole to kill the Ukrainian and the Ukrainian the Pole as soon as they meet up. And if they also kill the Jews while they are at it, then that is exactly what we need."[12] Kul'chyts'kyi also observes that the OUN-B and the AK continued to regard each other as adversaries, and that their confrontation was instigated deliberately by the German occupiers; and that it had led to bloody massacres of the Ukrainian population in the Kholm region in 1942–45, and of the Poles in Volhynia in 1943–44. Polish scholars collected evidence of 34,647 killings, with 12,491 victims identified, but the actual casualties appear to have been much greater. The Germans used provocative tactics to incite clashes between the OUN and AK such as deploying punitive forces against the Ukrainian population that were dressed in Polish uniforms. Similar tactics, Kul'chyts'kyi writes, were later adopted by the AK, the Soviet security forces, and the OUN-B.[13]

A defense of the Ukrainian position on the Volhynia massacres was offered by the prominent L'viv-based historian Yaroslav Isayevich. He starts from the premise that in July 2003 (he is writing in February 2003), Ukraine and Poland were to honor the memory of those who died in the Ukrainian–Polish conflict in Volhynia. Politicians and historians of the two states were making every effort that the relations between the two people remain friendly and harmonious, attempting to comprehend not only their own arguments, but also the motives of those who held opposing views. One should begin, he continues, by stating that Ukrainians and Poles belong to those peoples who suffered most from the Hitlerites and "Bolshevik" terror in the Second World War. Ukraine remained, as before, neither the subject nor object of history. Various powers were competing for control of its lands: Bolshevik Russia (masked under the guise of the pseudo-internationalist USSR), Nazi Germany and its allies (Hungary and Romania are cited), and Poland. During the war, armed formations arose that allotted themselves the task of fighting with the enemies of an independent Ukraine. Although at this time and during the next decade that concept lacked the support of the majority of Ukrainians, the notion of independence arose as a final result of the future evolution of Ukraine. Under these circumstances there were good reasons for Poles and Ukrainians to unite, writes Isayevich, but there was no authentic cooperation between the two sides, and a bloody conflict between them erupted on the territory of Western Ukraine, which included not only confrontations between Polish and Ukrainian armed formations, but also treacherous and extremist actions against peaceful civilians.[14]

Among the causes of the tension between Ukrainians and Poles were social and national friction based on land ownership and the prewar policies of the Polish state, as well as the German–Soviet Non-Aggression Pact. The Poles were ruling areas in which they made up only a minority of the population. Ukrainians, writes Isayevich, were not opposed to Poles per se; only insofar as Polish policies were hostile to the idea of an independent Ukraine. The majority of Ukrainian leaders did not know that the future perspective of Bolshevik Russian hegemony (Isayevich appears wedded to the phrase "Bolshevik Russia") denoted a necessity to treat Poland as a strategic partner. In Polish and Ukrainian publications there are diverse views as to where, when, and how the deaths began of the peaceful population living on the Polish–Ukrainian border. Ukrainian writings, Isayevich observes, disseminate the opinion that the conflict originated with the killing of Ukrainian underground troops and public activists that were considered to be German collaborators in Zamoishyn by the Polish underground forces. In Polish publications, on the contrary, one finds the view that the main events occurred later. The initial stages in any case were a time of sporadic deaths, and an important document revealing the escalation of the conflict is the report from a representative of the Polish émigré government in Volhynia. He declares that these isolated murders were directed against Poles who were employed in the German service as administrators of property, forests, and road services. This document, Isayevich maintains, is important in view of the increasing belief in Polish society, that almost exclusively, the main collaborators with the occupiers were the Ukrainians, who often joined with the Germans in fighting the Poles. In reality there were unprincipled collaborators on both sides.[15]

Isayevich then arrives at the heart of his main argument. The characteristic direction of Polish publications commemorating the Second World War, he says, is to exaggerate the number of deaths on the Polish side, and to release versions that are based entirely on fantasy about exceptionally sadistic acts on the part of Ukrainians. Even in 1940, a book called "Lwow" was issued by Jerzy Janicki, in which one could read that Metropolitan Sheptyts'kyi blessed the wooden saw that Ukrainians used to cut up living Poles. However, such accounts do not correspond with reality. Propaganda directed toward fueling Polish–Ukrainian hostility was opposed resolutely by Polish intellectuals grouped around the Paris monthly journal, *Kultura*. Polish and Ukrainian oppositionists often banded together, particularly the members of the *Solidarnosc* movement and members of the Ukrainian Helsinki Union. After the restoration of an independent Ukraine, Isayevich notes, both neighboring states simultaneously tried to improve relations. If contemporary Poland is interested in an independent Ukraine, then it responds to Polish interests as well as to the approval in Ukraine of the traditional independence movement. But regrettably, in Isayevich's view, there are well-organized and active groups that try by all means to destroy this movement. In Ukraine, happily, there are no Ukrainian organizations and press organs that specialize in anti-Polish propaganda. However, information about the positive aspects of Polish–Ukrainian relations is still insufficient. Ukrainians still know very little about those Polish political and cultural activists who work fruitfully to create a climate of trust and cooperation in both societies.[16] Writing in this way Isayevich focuses on sentiment rather than historical facts, and the discussion of Volhynia takes second place to his analysis of benevolent or malevolent attitudes in contemporary Ukraine and Poland. As such it is a disappointing way to end an article that began in promising fashion, and ultimately he does not really address the main issues of the Volhynia tragedy.

In 2000, the Polish scholars Wladyslaw and Ewa Siemaszko published a major study on the Volhynia massacres that purported to provide the most convincing proof to date of OUN-UPA responsibility.[17] The book attracted a lot of attention in Ukraine, and in 2003 a leading Ukrainian historian, I. I. Il'yushyn, offered a critique. Il'yushyn set himself three tasks: first, to investigate the source base of this work and to establish if the facts cited therein really occurred; second, to question a conception of history based exclusively on Polish testimonies; and third, to introduce this book to a Ukrainian audience. He notes that the Siemaszkos wrote their monograph on the basis of some 1,500 personal testimonies and memoirs of witnesses dispersed throughout private collections and state archives in Poland. He questions how such testimonies could be impartial, adding that while Polish historians in general have praised the book, there is still a debate in that country whether it is appropriate to include, in an objective scholarly analysis of OUN-UPA, the testimonies of those Polish citizens who witnessed the events but could also find themselves among the victims of the Ukrainian insurgents. Similar reservations are advanced regarding memoirs written after the war. However, Il'yushyn does not reject personal testimonies completely. What is important, in his view, is how to check the information for accuracy, as well as to establish the circumstances in which a particular crime was committed. He considers that in order to carry out such an assignment, historians need to use supplementary sources and "be impartial." The Siemaszkos, in his view, were guilty in this regard. W. Siemaszko was a member of the Polish Home Army in Volhynia at the height of the conflict and therefore not a credible witness. The study also deploys only three OUN-UPA documents and makes no use at all of Soviet and German materials. Il'yushyn tries to demonstrate how dangerous it is to synthesize historical narrative based only on one sort of testimony with an illustration of a typical case when there were two completely different versions of the same event. The case in question is the Siemaszkos' example of the murder of nine Poles by Ukrainian nationalists on 15 September 1939 in Kovel' district, cited in the AK archives. The same event is found in the Ukrainian NKVD archives, where it is described as being carried out by members of the Communist Party of Western Ukraine.[18]

Il'yushyn posits, without delving into details, that Polish historians probably inflate the number of Polish victims. He continues his review by focusing on the Siemaszko's interpretation of Polish–Ukrainian relations prior to the outbreak of the Second World War, stating that the ethnic antagonism was a characteristic feature of the prewar years, and was not something that became accentuated immediately before the military conflict. He assigns responsibility to the Polish government's policies of assimilation, which were directed toward Ukrainians. Il'yushyn does concur that the campaign of ethnic cleansing began on the initiative of OUN-UPA and—implicitly at least—he rejects the claim of some Ukrainian writers that the attacks began in response to AK terror. The Home Army formations, according to both the Siemaszkos and Il'yushyn, appeared in Volhynia only after the OUN campaign had already claimed two-thirds of its victims. So what drove the Ukrainian insurgents to carry out atrocities against the Poles? He argues that the reason was the infiltration of the local administration by the Poles and comes close to endorsing some of the murders as being based on political motives. Certainly it is difficult to discern how Il'yushyn defines guilt and innocence in such a situation. He goes on to write that the tragedy of the situation as it developed in Volhynia, lay in the fact that what was ostensibly a "well-motivated" operation from the perspective of Ukrainian national interests, quickly escalated and took on an extraordinarily gruesome character. As it was conducted in a very cruel manner by armed peasants, and encompassed "apparently innocent people," including women, children, and the elderly, then the actions constitute a crime. Ultimately, the Poles of Volhynia were paying the price for the prewar policies of the Polish government as well as for their own attitudes to such policies. However, Il'yushyn then introduces a new argument: the UPA also decided to eliminate the Polish population because of the collaboration of Polish civilians with Soviet Partisans. He also disputes the Siemaszkos' contention that the massacres took place in collusion with the German occupiers as the latter would hardly have approved of the deaths of Polish officials. The two Polish authors, in his view, downplay the fact that the Germans used the UPA campaigns to recruit more policemen for operations against the Ukrainian insurgents.[19] Il'yushyn's article can be construed as a valiant attempt to use a book review to come up with a synthesis of the main problems of analyzing the Volhynia massacres and to try to reach a reasonable conclusion. It falls short of this goal, ultimately, because of its failure to distinguish between actions against officials (which, to some extent, he condones) and actions against innocent civilians.

The Transfer of Populations between Poland and Ukraine

The forced exchange of populations between Ukraine and Poland after the war, which followed a decree issued on 9 September 1944, has been the subject of numerous writings and narratives in Ukraine. The operation, carried out at the behest of the Soviet authorities, occurred with brutality, and Polish forces reportedly took the opportunity to inflict abuse on the Ukrainians that were uprooted from their homes. This event has been perceived as a Polish response to the Volhynia massacres, but in Ukrainian narratives it is more often treated in isolation, as an example of Polish persecution of Ukrainians that dates back to the period of interwar rule. As early as February 1990, when the CC CPU adopted a resolution about the need for a thorough study and objective evaluation of the history of the Ukrainian Communist Party, among the events singled out for a new evaluation was Operation Vistula (the final phase of the transfer of Ukrainians from Poland to Ukraine that began in 1944). Notably absent from the list of events to be perused were the Famine of 1932–33 and the history of OUN-UPA.[20] Thus the population exchange has long rankled Ukrainians even at the highest levels of the Communist Party. The Operation rivals the Volhynia massacres as a key point of contention between the Ukrainian and Polish governments, and represents another of the critical issues of the past that has the potential to sow bad feeling among scholars, writers, teachers, and others in the neighboring countries. On the other hand, it returns us to the theme of Ukrainians as victims in a major event of the 20th century as opposed to being perpetrators or alleged collaborators with a stronger force, as is the case with the German occupation regime. In turn, Poles being removed from Ukraine may also be perceived as victims, although sources suggest that their treatment was less severe. In examining the current narratives on this question, it is logical to begin with more detailed academic accounts, and then survey some of the popular narratives that are being disseminated more widely.

One of the most detailed of the academic articles to appear in Ukraine to date about the population transfers appeared in the main historical journal under the authorship of S. A. Makarchuk, though his focus is limited to the resettlement of Poles from Western Ukraine. Nevertheless, as an introductory article, it does illuminate some basic details of the mutual evacuations— particularly the relationship of this massive undertaking to wartime operations, and describes the expectations of the Poles for the restoration of the pre-September 1939 borders between their country and the Soviet Union/ Ukraine. He states that at first glance the theme has been thoroughly researched and certain facts are well-known. The decision on mutual resettlement took place in fulfillment of the agreement between the government of the Soviet Union and the Polish Committee of National Liberation, signed in Lublin on 9 September 1944. The agreement was signed by N. S. Khrushchev on behalf of the USSR and Edward Osubka-Morawski for the Poles. It stipulated that the mutual resettlement had to be carried out in a very brief period of time, namely from 15 October 1944 to 1 February 1945. The resettlement officially was stipulated as "voluntary." The Agreement specified that settlers who were moved into their countries of birth should receive the sum of R5,000 or the equivalent in Polish *zloty*. Each evacuee would be permitted to take food, agricultural equipment, up to two tons of property and up to

R1,000, and peasants could also take along their livestock. In theory they were also to be offered compensation for the loss of their residential and farm buildings. In the Polish-inhabited regions of Ukraine a register was made of the Polish population that had to be evacuated, as well as a list of those who had "volunteered" to move. It included, by 1 September 1944: 41,800 Poles in Volyn *oblast*; about 50,000 in Rivne *oblast*; and 162,229 in L'viv region, of which 84,680 (24,180 families) were residents of the city of L'viv. Registration continued in 1945 and added Ternopil' *oblast*, where over 76,000 families were listed and received documents for evacuation—a total of 226,952 people.[21]

Makarchuk states that the most serious problem encountered in removing the Poles was the time factor. By the end of 1944 it was already clear that the completion of the resettlement by 1 February 1945 was impossible. By the start of the New Year, the removals were just beginning. Therefore the deadline was extended to 1 May 1945. When this deadline was also deemed unrealistic, Khrushchev turned to Osubka-Morawski, the designated Prime Minister of the Provisional Government of Poland, with a proposal to change the date to 15 January 1946, and the agreement was officially fulfilled only in July 1946. Makarchuk cites figures from several sources—Jerzy Kochanowski on the Polish side; Serhii Tkachov and Volodymyr Serhiichuk on the Ukrainian—to provide a total of between 787,524 and 789,982 Poles evacuated from Western Ukraine to Poland in 1944–46, with the largest numbers moved from Ternopil' (233,617) and L'viv (218,711). Though the vast majority of these residents were ethnic Poles, researchers also concur that their numbers included more than 30,000 Jews. For the purposes of this study, the key issues are the political expectations of the Polish authorities for the future of the territory of Western Ukraine, and the attitudes of the Soviet government and Ukrainian activists. Makarchuk remarks that the Poles of this region were heavily influenced by broadcasts from the London government, which led them to believe that after the defeat of the Axis powers, the Polish state would be restored according to its pre-September 1939 borders. In response, the Polish underground movement in L'viv planned to establish its authority once the Germans retreated and before the arrival of the Red Army. Therefore one week before Soviet troops entered L'viv on 27 July 1944, the AK occupied major buildings and schools, and raised the Polish flag on them. On the building of L'viv Polytechnic, there was even a Union Jack flag hanging. However, the Soviet military leaders sent AK members to the Polish People's Army and arrested its leading activists. Many AK units remained in L'viv in the Polish underground, which remained in place more than a year after the reestablishment of Soviet power.[22]

The situation did not become clearer for some time, Makarchuk explains. Representatives of the London government continued to feed the rumors that Poland would regain Western Ukraine so that Polish officials had a negative attitude toward the enforced evacuation of Polish citizens. Many residents had lived in the region for generations and considered it their native land so there was also a powerful psychological tie. Poles daubed slogans such as "Long live Poland!" and "Death to the Bolsheviks!" on buildings, and in January 1945 hundreds were arrested. With each day Poles became more pessimistic about their situation. Archives contain information and memoirs of those arrested during the evacuation, with accounts that in the summer of 1945 they were not permitted to collect the harvest grown in their fields and were forced to travel to Poland without adequate food supplies for the journey. Overall, however, the conditions for the population moving to Poland were better than for Ukrainians coming in the opposite direction. The latter were subjected to bandit attacks, theft and murder.[23] Whereas the Poles of Western Ukraine were hoping for the return of Polish rule, and tried to mount a preemptive *fait accompli,* the situation in the regions across the Polish border was even more complex. The issue was exacerbated by the presence of the forces of the UPA, and the Soviet and Polish governments were in agreement that the insurgents needed to be eliminated during the operation to remove the Ukrainian inhabitants. As a result, what culminated in the April–July 1947 Operation Vistula (Akcja Wisla) continues to elicit anger and bitterness in Ukrainian narratives, especially because of the lack of discrimination between the militant insurgents and peaceful villagers who were attacked and assaulted without reason, and faced an arduous journey to their assigned homes on the Ukrainian side of the border. Until 1947, the Polish–Ukrainian conflict continued in the border regions and in that year, the police forces of Poland, the USSR, and Czechoslovakia combined to subdue UPA insurgents and force them into the underground. Ukrainian accounts focus heavily on Polish misdeeds and atrocities against the Ukrainian population. Essentially, these accounts are linked, implicitly or explicitly, to the Volhynia massacres, either in the form of Polish retribution against OUN-UPA, or in the guise of re-dating the conflict so that the actions taken against the Ukrainian population preceded the OUN-UPA attacks on Poles. We will cite a few typical examples here.

An account in the militantly nationalist newspaper *Za vil'nu Ukrainu* from 1994 interviews Omelya Lyshchyshyna, a former resident of the village Tysovo near Przemysl. The UPA bases were located nearby. In August 1945 a Polish army unit entered the village, armed with machine guns and some field guns. They carried out registration of the villagers for deportation to "Stalin's paradise." The UPA discovered these plans and attacked the Polish garrison on 1 September. Over 250 houses were burned during a battle that lasted throughout the night. In the morning UPA troops and the villagers began retreating to the forest. The Poles loaded up five trucks with the dead and wounded, while the UPA retreated to its bases. Lyshchyshyna's family hid in the forest but was discovered by three Polish soldiers at 10am. The family was beaten, after which the Poles decided to shoot them and take their goods. They were saved by a Polish major who supplied them with travel documents to the town where the assembly point was located.[24] Another article examines the tragedy of the Ukrainians in the region of the San River. The author describes the events as a deliberate act of genocide against them. In one village, called Sahryn, the Ukrainians created a self-defense group made up of fifty men to protect themselves from random Polish assaults. On 10 March 1944, Polish bands attacked the group and began to massacre the villagers. A chilling account follows of Polish vigilantes killing old people, women, and children. One girl was reportedly pierced with a hay fork, and some 600 Ukrainians were killed altogether. The author concludes by emphasizing the significance of informing the international public about the tragedy of Ukrainians in Poland in the postwar years. He emphasizes that they died not at the hands of the Fascists, but at the behest of Polish citizens who decided to build a national state in the most bloodthirsty way feasible: by eliminating those who were not ethnic Poles.[25]

In 1999, the same newspaper featured a lengthy article by Oleksandra Potichna about the Polish destruction of the Ukrainian village Pavlokoma in the spring of 1945. The village is located on the San River and there were a number of Polish settlements nearby. The author states that the antagonism between Ukrainians and Poles in this area went back to the end of the First World War, when a local Polish aristocrat was forced to distribute his estates among peasants of neighboring villages. Most of this land went to Polish farmers. During the war, writes Potichna, organized Polish military units assassinated leaders of the Ukrainian community in Pavlokoma. On 14 October, Poles killed the director of the Ukrainian school, Mykola Levyts'kyi. In 1943–44, they accounted for the deaths of several other prominent community members. Potichna, like the previous writers, again brings up the concept of genocide to explain such actions. After the retreat of the Germans, Polish bands, supported by the organs of authority, could carry out the genocide of entire communities, and such was the fate of Pavlokoma in March 1945. Once the Germans had retreated, Poles took command of community life in the village. They began encroaching on the rights of Ukrainians, who were, for example, forbidden to bury their dead at a newly constructed cemetery. Polish vigilantes began to harass Ukrainians for any manifestations of nationalist sentiment, which might include keeping portraits of Hetman Bohdan Khmelnytsky or the national bard Taras Shevchenko. These attacks spread from the neighboring Polish villages into the isolated Ukrainian settlement. As long as the Soviet garrison was stationed at Pavlokoma, the Polish bands refrained from making an all-out attack. At one point in early 1945, Potichna writes, a military unit composed of sixty men in Soviet uniforms, who had evidently arrived to replace the previous garrison, arrested a number of Polish residents. The Poles disseminated a rumor that these military troops were in reality disguised members of the UPA, who had executed the arrested Poles in the nearby forests. The mothers of the victims arrived in Pavlokoma a few days later, demanding that the Ukrainian priest hand over the bodies of the dead Poles. The Ukrainians had no knowledge of the location of the corpses.[26]

Following this incident, Potichna continues, the Poles formed bands from the villages of Syliongowa, Bartkowka, Silnykja, Bacjoz, and others, and attacked Pavlokoma. Some Ukrainians managed to hide, but others were murdered. The narrative makes it evident that the victims were well-known to the attackers. One woman managed to remain alive, along with her grandson, by bribing the band members. A month later, in March 1945, the bands returned and drove the Ukrainians into the church while beating them in the process. Once inside the church, they divided the victims: pregnant women and children under four were left inside, while others were taken to the cemetery, shot, and dumped in a pit. The priest was included among the victims. Potichna, the author, managed to hide in the stable under the hay. Her four sons who were hiding at their grandmother's house were caught and killed at the cemetery. The Poles threatened to burn the stable and so they were forced to reveal their hiding place. The Poles buried the dead and then cleaned blood from the church. She cites several individual Poles as notorious for their cruelty and concludes by stating that the survivors of this massacre were deported to Western Poland, and from there Potichna immigrated to Canada in 1950.[27] The story is significant in that it contains the basic ingredients of all narratives in this conflict: historical roots for the hatred usually dating back to the interwar period when Ukrainians fell under Polish rule; wanton and senseless killing of innocent people with an unusual degree of cruelty; and accusations of genocide—the more rational explanation of "ethnic cleansing" only appears in later narratives. There is very little difference incidentally between Polish descriptions of the Volhynia massacres, and Ukrainian accounts of maltreatment at the hands of the Poles as the war came to an end. The third element in the prewar equation—the Jewish population that made up a large portion, if not a majority, in many of the towns and cities in interwar Poland—was no longer present in large numbers having fallen victim to the wartime occupation regime.

The situation that developed by 1947 has been analyzed by two Ukrainian historians, who manage to provide a broader context for these events. V. Danylenko and V. Baran point out that in this year the CC CPU made the decision to introduce destruction battalions of up to 35,000 people to deal with the nationalist insurgents. At the beginning of 1947, this conflict came under the exclusive competence of the security organs, and almost 2,000 battalions were placed under the command of the Ukrainian MGB. This restructuring occurred while the UPA operated in the border regions—Lemkivshchyna, Nadysannya, and Kholmshchyna. The governments of the Soviet Union and Poland carried out the policy of resettlement by force and it resulted in numerous deaths. On the territory of Poland, almost 126,000 Ukrainian families were included on the register, and 122,500 (482,109 people) were actually removed or 96.8% of the designated population. They were deported to different parts of Ukraine, with a majority—322,868—dispatched to the western regions. At the time of this resettlement, in several areas of Polish territory, including Liskiv, Peremyszl, Yaroslav, Lyubachiv, Tomashiv, and Hrubeshiv districts, formations of the Polish Home Army operated actively against the UPA. As a result of its attacks, over 4,600 Ukrainians were killed, over 2,200 families suffered, and several hundred villages were burned, write the authors, adding that the suffering also encompassed the Polish population. The period April–July 1947 marked the concluding stage of the mutual deportations, which was given the name "Vistula." During these three months there occurred the removal of Ukrainians and members of mixed Ukrainian–Polish families from the lands of south-eastern Poland. They were resettled in the western and northern regions of Poland because the motivation behind this operation was to destroy the UPA groups. The authors cite I. Bilas that the chief goal of the Polish side was the "liquidation" of the Ukrainian minority and the assimilation of the migrants into Polish society. About 140,600 people were resettled in this action. Simultaneously, the Poles were moved out of the western regions of Ukraine, including the vast majority of the 797,907 people (256,428 families) who were listed on the official register on 1 October 1945.[28]

During these tumultuous upheavals, Danylenko and Baran point out, the Stalin regime also carried out a mass deportation of Ukrainians from Western Ukraine. Tens of thousands of "OUNites" were included in a special resettlement, and 75% of those removed were women and children. The Ministry of Internal Affairs of the Ukrainian SSR established its operational headquarters in L'viv, and the largest number of people were deported from L'viv, Drohobych, and Ternopil' *oblasts*, with their property transferred to the state organs. Altogether, the authors report, 26,300 families with 77,791 people were moved out of the western regions. The militia also blockaded an extended region in which the armed underground operated. Both the NKVD and MVD of Ukraine created several joint-operation groups for the elimination of the OUN Central Provid and regional leaders. Four divisions of the MVD were directed against the insurgents in 1948-49 under the leadership of Ukrainian Minister for State Security, M. Koval'chuk. During these operations, which reportedly ended with the death of UPA leader Shukhevych in the spring of 1950, some 171,500 members of the OUN were deported in special operations, with repressive measures taken against their family members. Those resettled ended up in various regions of Siberia and autonomous republics of Russia, as well as Kazakhstan.[29] The two authors offer a more polished and academic account of the events surrounding the mass exchange of populations, and they do not lean particularly to the view that crimes were carried out by one side over the other. Rather they suggest that the most severe measures were conducted by the Soviet authorities, with Ukrainians and Poles essentially in the role of victims. Another more recent account adopts this same viewpoint, namely that the repercussions of the fratricidal war between Poles and Ukrainians was of benefit only to the Russians and the Germans. This account suggests that some Ukrainians actually solicited Soviet help for relocation from Poland because of a constant fear of Polish attacks, and that Ukrainian life in this corner of Poland, despite a long 500-year history, had already entered a stage of marked decline, with destroyed churches and dilapidated cemeteries. It cites one source that there were up to 12,000 Ukrainian victims in Eastern Poland during this period, and up to 90,000 Polish victims in the Ukrainian–Polish conflict overall.[30]

The Debates on the 60th Anniversary of the Volhynia Massacres

On the 60th anniversary of the events in Volhynia, there was an extended exchange of opinions between various sectors in Poland and Ukraine, at both the official and unofficial levels. Our priority is with those letters and articles that appeared in Ukraine and would have been familiar to a large proportion of the Ukrainian public. Both sides sought some form of redress, though those making the most demands were naturally Poles—the victims in this instance—while Ukrainians offered defensive explanations or alternative versions of events. What is clear is that from the Ukrainian perspective, and particularly those who supported the notion of recognition of the UPA, the anniversary had the potential to do a lot of damage. Above any other event in the history of the UPA (and of the OUN-B, which provided the instruction to carry out the ethnic cleansing), Volhynia in 1943–44 is the most damaging in its impact on the reputation of the insurgents. From the Ukrainian perspective, to generalize somewhat, the accusations have been narrow and one-sided. Furthermore they tend to neglect the early problems in the Polish–Ukrainian relationship when the Poles were clearly in the ascendancy and failed to fulfill their mandate to give autonomy to the region of Eastern Galicia, treating it instead as a virtual colony and conducting a brutal Pacification policy and transplanting Polish farmers to occupy lands in ethnically Ukrainian regions. The Poles, in their turn, fail to comprehend the unwillingness of the Ukrainian side to acknowledge guilt in wholesale massacres for which there is no lack of evidence and which undoubtedly had the overall goal of cleansing an entire region of Poles. Such an admission, in the Polish view, would help to ameliorate relations with a friendly neighbor, and it is often pointed out that Polish democrats, writers, scholars, and others overtly supported the independence of Ukraine and have maintained close and regular ties with their Ukrainian counterparts. In short, Volhynia is something of a stumbling block to what would otherwise be a complete friendship. This is largely because of the obdurate and illogical stance of those who support a different perspective of OUN-UPA as freedom fighters, quasi-democrats, and heroes who sought only the long-term goal of an independent Ukraine.

These dilemmas were outlined succinctly in an article by UK-based scholar Katarina Wolczuk in 2002, on the eve of the anniversary. She writes that at the level of society, the Volhynia issue still has the potential to cause friction between the two neighbors and that the preparations for the commemoration had the potential to exacerbate matters. In her outline, she comments that the military wing of the OUN—the UPA—carried out acts of ethnic cleansing that led to the deaths of 60–100,000 Poles in the period from March 1943 until early 1944. The goal was to ensure a Ukrainian "takeover" of both Volhynia and Eastern Galicia by bringing about the complete removal of the Polish population. She maintains that the shocking impact of the massacres was worsened by the fact that the UPA had the overt assistance of peasants from nearby Ukrainian villages. The Poles subsequently conducted retaliatory actions that caused the deaths of between 15,000 and 30,000 Ukrainians. The Polish head of National Security, Marek Siwiec, wrote a letter to Viktor Med-vedchuk, then head of Ukraine's presidential administration, concerning the anniversary. Among the suggested actions that Ukraine might take, Siwiec included: erecting monuments, cleaning up and designating the graves of the Poles that were killed, as well as a symbolic action like the one made by German Chancellor Willy Brandt in 1970, when he kneeled before the Monument of Heroes to commemorate the victims of the Warsaw Ghetto destroyed by the Germans in 1944. Wolczuk perceived several serious difficulties that the Ukrainians faced in responding to this request.[31]

In the first place, Ukrainian society failed to reach a consensus on the OUN and UPA. The organizations received very diverse responses, from veneration to outright hostility. The main supporters of these organizations were right and center parties that had support in Western Ukraine, as well as the West Ukrainian public and the Ukrainian Diaspora. Other areas still adhered to the former Soviet perspective that OUN-UPA members were "bourgeois nationalists" and Nazi collaborators. The current debates in Ukraine negate the efforts to condemn or to praise OUN-UPA and render it difficult to respond in any meaningful way to the 60th anniversary of the Volhynia massacres. The year 2003 also preceded a year of presidential elections in Ukraine. Wolczuk maintains that President Leonid Kuchma, who had been in office since 1994, had lost moral credibility as head of state after he was implicated in the killing of an opposition journalist,[32] whereas the opposition contender for president, Viktor Yushchenko, was highly popular in Western Ukraine, where the UPA was venerated. The issue could therefore be used as a political tool to undermine Yushchenko, who might be accused of being a nationalist sympathizer. The second issue was the expectation of the Poles that an apology would be forthcoming, and as a result, they seemed to some to be prepared to demand that their own version of events be accepted wholesale by the Ukrainian side. Seeking an apology in this way would only complicate inter-state relations and have an adverse effect on relations at the societal level, Wolczuk writes.[33]

Pressure on the Polish government comes from right-wing political forces that seek redress for events that have become emblazoned in the historical memory of many Poles, with feelings of anger and resentment that have been simmering for years. In the eyes of many Poles, the events constitute a clear act of genocide at the hands of Ukrainians. In Wolczuk's opinion, the increased tension over the issue forced the Polish government to take the lead and demand an apology in order to offset the demands of the right-wing forces. In this way, however, Poland may have missed an opportunity for reconciliation by focusing exclusively on deaths and the victimization of Poles rather than on the two sets of victims, and the atrocities on both sides. Historians are also not in agreement over the nature of the massacres and have deployed a variety of phrases to describe them, including genocide, ethnic cleansing, mass murder, and the more inoffensive "anti-Polish actions." Wolczuk adheres to the view that the killings had deep historical roots and the violence occurred after a lengthy period of mutual grievances. The Polish case tends to ignore the behavior of the interwar Polish government toward its large Ukrainian minority. Wolczuk feels therefore that an opportunity to put an end to "prejudice and negative stereotypes" may be missed during the 60th anniversary commemoration.[34] Her article offers a perceptive illustration of the main problems and why the issue has persisted in Ukrainian and Polish narratives without any real prospects of resolution.

An angry depiction of the Ukrainian side of these events was authored by Evhen Dudar in an open letter to Polish Prime Minister Leszek Miller in November 2002. The letter was written in response to a statement that there are no Poles today who feel any sympathy toward the Ukrainian Insurgent Army. Dudar maintains that such a statement plays into the hands of Moscow. He wonders whether there is anyone in Poland who recognizes that the UPA had no prospects of conquering Moscow or Warsaw but was solely concerned with defending its own lands from foreign conquerors. An honest Pole whose country had been oppressed by Moscow and Berlin should be more receptive, in his view, to a Ukrainian who was repressed for an even longer period by others, including "Polish chauvinists." Poland, he continues, conducted a policy of colonization with regard to its eastern borderlands and its transplanted colonists constituted the dregs of the Polish nation who would try to steal from others. Two years later these colonists were sent to Siberia, along with Ukrainians, by the new Soviet authorities that had set Ukrainians free from the Polish yoke, but only to impose their own rule. Moscow also "sold" Poland to Hitler, who removed the Bolsheviks from Ukraine then conquered the land himself. Ukrainians had no choice but to take up arms, says Dudar. In fact all the nations that suffered occupation could begin legitimate resistance. However, unlike Ukrainians, they had established state structures, created their own armies, and received international recognition. By contrast, Ukrainians had nothing but "a burning desire for freedom" and implacable hatred toward the occupiers.[35]

Dudar writes that "some of our historians who still worship the Kremlin mother" follow their Moscow masters and mutter about alleged collaborationism of the UPA. This is patently absurd, he says, because the very definition of a collaborator is someone who works or fights on the side of the enemy against one's own government. Yet Ukraine had no government of its own to betray. Moreover, it was those puppet regimes propped up by the imperialists that were collaborationist in nature. The historians who put forward such accusations are collaborators themselves for they serve another state. This is a rather curious mode of argument to make in the period of independence in that it appears to insinuate that those who criticize OUN-UPA are indirectly or directly enemies of Ukraine. Dudar acknowledges that there was some brutality on the Ukrainian side, but UPA soldiers were most ruthless toward themselves with the rule about using the last bullet to kill oneself rather than surrender to the enemy. He tells Miller that "your own AK and Armia Ludowa" troops were also brutal toward Ukrainians, a situation exploited by Stalin. He writes that he knows a Ukrainian from the Lemkiv region who as a child witnessed the arrival of Poles in his native village to carry out Operation Vistula. Everyone was herded into the local church, which was then set ablaze. The Ukrainian was the only one to survive but suffered multiple burns and remained severely disabled for the rest of his life. The perpetrators of this hideous crime might well be alive, he reflects, perhaps they receive a state pension and are considered war heroes. To him it is great paradox that in independent Ukraine those who fought for her independence are neglected, hungry, and often scorned, while its foes are respected heroes who can ridicule opponents with impunity. Dudar asks whether Mr. Miller and his officials have to humor a "red electorate" or whether he is in perennial debt to Moscow.[36]

A more sophisticated analysis is offered by Maksym Strikha, who attended a joint Ukrainian-Polish forum of journalists and experts at Ostrih on the 60th anniversary of the Volhynia events. For Strikha two moments remained in his mind: an OUN veteran who had been in the camps at Kolyma was baffled by the fact that in the Gulag they had sung the same songs and stayed together with AK soldiers. The veteran wondered who was benefiting from their quarrel. The other was a conversation with a Polish intellectual who pondered in a private conversation why Ukraine had not admitted responsibility for the Volhynia tragedy. The Poles had condemned Operation Vistula, Poland was Ukraine's only advocate in discussions with the West (presumably about possible EU membership and others) and yet Ukraine did not even wish to take a step forward and acknowledge the horrors that had occurred six decades ago. Strikha comments that there are no simple answers to such seemingly obvious questions. The Vistula Operation was ordered and carried out by the new government of Communist Poland. This fact made it easier for the Polish Senate, staffed mainly with members of the anti-Communist *Solidar-*

nosc movement, to adopt a resolution condemning the operation. However, a similar resolution failed to find its way through the Sejm despite the best efforts of Ukrainian ambassadors and liberal groups. President Kwasniewski later came forward with a statement condemning the Vistula campaign. By contrast, the Ukrainian government could not take responsibility for the murders in Volhynia because no such government existed. The OUN-M expressed its repulsion toward these events as did the head of the initial UPA, Taras Bul'ba-Borovets'. The highest spiritual authority, Metropolitan Andrii Sheptyts'kyi, also condemned the murders.[37]

Strikha states that although the murders were carried out under the auspices of the Bandera faction, the situation was complex. Lebed', the provisional leader, in the absence of the imprisoned Bandera, refused to support the ethnic cleansing—the statement incidentally runs counter to most other analyses, which maintain that the decision was Lebed's. However, the regional division in Volhynia headed by Klym Savur (Dmytro Klyachkivs'kyi) took the lead in giving the go-ahead for what was a peasant vendetta against the Poles caused by immediate and much older grievances. Strikha therefore asks: who is supposed to apologize for the mass murder of Polish civilians, which clearly did take place? Should it be the state, which to date has not recognized the UPA, the Volhynia inhabitants, or the heirs of the combatants? Even if the current Ukrainian government should take moral responsibility, this step would not receive a positive response from Ukrainians, for the image of Kuchma and his associates had been badly tarnished by the scandal over the murdered journalist. Intellectuals in Ukraine lacked influence and were split into warring camps, and inhabitants of Volhynia and the combatants remain too burdened by the painful memories of the gruesome deaths suffered by Ukrainian women and children at the hands of the Poles. Nevertheless, Strikha feels that an apology would still be the best step in order not to worsen Polish–Ukrainian relations and already prevalent anti-Ukrainian feeling. The Ukrainian elites must take responsibility. The author laments that historians on both sides have yet to free themselves from the mire of past thinking. On the Polish side he cites the "anti-Ukrainian creed" of Eduard Prus in his work "The moons in Beszczady."[38] On the other side is the Communist xenophobic discourse that the Soviets inherited from the Russian Empire, and exemplified in current times by the poet-academician Borys Oliinyk. For these people, writes Strikha, Poles are not Slavic brothers, like Russians and Belarusians, but Catholics, masters, and aggressors.[39]

Strikha reaches the heart of the problem when he writes that some people are afraid of admitting the truth about Ukrainian crimes against civilian Poles, since this admission might impede the process of rehabilitation of the UPA. He believes that rehabilitation would be instrumental in bringing about a change of attitude toward the Volhynia tragedy. Once the UPA is recognized as an official Second World War combatant, then it would be easier for people to admit obvious facts; like any other army of that time, the UPA had its share of murderers and criminals. On the other hand, he concludes, the Polish elite should remember one thing: if the mood of revenge becomes predominant in Poland, it would eventually transform the Eastern Polish border into a border with a new Eurasian commonwealth, whether this latter is some sort of Slavic Union or an organization of regional integration. He feels that this development would not be in the national interests of Poland.[40] In assessing this interesting article, which avoids tarring one side or another, it seems that Strikha is more concerned about national interests than in writing an in-depth study that might benefit historians. His overall goal is to destroy the existing versions of historical narratives, by which one side might traditionally be described as the enemy of the other, as well as the Soviet version—he perceives it as a version that derives from much earlier times in the Tsarist period—by which conflict is the foundation stone for all historical interpretations. In essence, this describes the problem of a new Ukrainian narrative of national history, namely that it has proved difficult for Ukrainian historians to break free completely from the way history was written in the past. The Volhynia tragedy is particularly problematic in that it occurred within a much larger and epic conflict between two totalitarian powers. The destroyed state, Poland, was returned to Europe only following the First World War after more than 120 years of absence from the continent of Europe, while the would-be Ukrainian state experienced only a few weeks of independence in the aftermath of the Russian Revolution.

A response of sorts to Strikha appeared two weeks later in the same journal by Bohdan Oleksyuk, a Volyn resident, and member of the Institute of Open Politics in Kyiv. Oleksyuk reveals that when talking to his fellow Volhynians, he would often hear that prior to 1943-44 Ukrainians and Poles had coexisted happily. Many of them could not comprehend what occurred on 11 July, when Polish settlements were set on fire. There is some speculation that it began on the other side of the Buh River, when Poles burned Orthodox churches and Ukrainian villages. In the summer of 1942, it is known that the German authorities, with the assistance of Ukrainian auxiliary police, began to expel some 200,000 Poles from four districts of the Lublin region. Ukrainians from neighboring territories were settled on the evacuated lands. The Polish underground responded with retaliatory actions in the course of which many

Ukrainians died, while others became refugees and settled in Volhynia with a marked antipathy toward Poles. But why then, Oleksyuk asks, would the massacre have occurred in Volhynia when it originated on the other side of the Buh? It was clear—and here he repeats the familiar line—that the conflict between Poles and Ukrainians could only be to the benefit of the Germans or the Soviet regime. Oleksyuk maintains that a lack of courage prompts some people to seek culprits elsewhere rather than among their own. He recalls the account from a schoolteacher that in one village students at the local school were asked to gather memoirs from witnesses of and participants in the tragic events of 1943–44. But many were unwilling to talk, perhaps because of their strong feelings of guilt. He feels that there must have been a few Ukrainians who rescued their Polish neighbors and provided them with shelter. Such actions could exonerate Ukrainians in the eyes of many Poles. At a Polish cemetery Oleksyuk came across a monument that stated in Ukrainian "Countrymen, rest in peace." He concluded that some Ukrainians considered Poles to be their neighbors and compatriots. However, upon reading the Polish part of the plaque, he realized his mistake. The monument had been erected and written by Poles, not Ukrainians. The new Ukrainian elite, Oleksyuk writes, must be honest and principled when dealing with the issue of Volhynia. Unfortunately, and here he cites the archbishop of the Ukrainian Greek Catholic Church, Lyubomyr Huzar, who stated that there were many thoughtless politicians for whom hatred of the Poles is the essence of being Ukrainian, and their national consciousness cannot transcend such sentiments. Huzar stated that both sides must forgive the other for the evil committed.[41]

Not all agree with such a moderate approach. One of the most prolific historians in Ukraine, Volodymyr Serhiichuk, has devoted two recent books to the Volhynia issue. The first, published in 2000, is a direct response to Wiktor Poliszczuk's 1999 volume on the OUN-UPA.[42] Serhiichuk maintains that land is tied to ethnic groups historically, and the OUN took up arms and fought heroically to preserve the right to inhabit the lands of its members' ancestors. In his introduction, he asserts Ukrainian claims to the lands of Volhynia and Galicia, going all the way back to the period of Kyivan Rus'. During the period of the Second World War, he says, citing Mykola Lebed, the Polish nation was not the enemy; rather the struggle was aimed against the Polish government. The same mode of thinking also applied in the case of Russia. As a historian, Serhiichuk had access to formerly secret archives not seen by the Canadian-based Poliszczuk. He uses these sources to advance his main thesis, which is that wholesale and unjustified massacres of Poles in Volhynia on the orders of the OUN did not occur, and that the entire portrayal of events is based on fabrications by Soviet and Polish authors. These events are encapsulated in the phrase "Polish–Ukrainian armed conflict during the Second World War." He asserts repeatedly that the lands in question were historically Ukrainian, and had been conquered by Poles only in 1349 during a period of weakness of the Galician-Volhynian principality. He comments that even old Polish maps indicate that these territories belonged to "the Ukrainian people." In making these statements, he makes reference to statistics on the ethnic makeup of these regions, but restricts his data to rural areas—most likely because in the urban areas Ukrainians constituted only a small minority.[43]

Serhiichuk raises the question: why did the Poles use force in 1918–19 to prevent the creation of a Ukrainian state in an area in which Ukrainians were the majority population? In his section on the Second World War, he provides information on the close links between the Poles and the German occupation regime in the border regions. Resistance to the occupiers, he writes, came from the Ukrainians who "urged the Poles to join them and direct their weapons against the common enemy," Hitler. But in fact the Poles in general turned their arms against Ukrainians. Poles also feature in his book as close allies of the Bolsheviks, and he cites the formation of a Polish Partisan unit named after Feliks Dzerzhinsky. This friendship led to the escalation of violence in Volhynia, in his view. Ukrainian retaliation was directed against those Polish villages that had become the bases for the "anti-Ukrainian war." He quotes OUN documents which declare that the organization was targeting Polish colonists, most of whom had arrived in the area in the interwar years. Those Ukrainians who did commit atrocities were dealt with summarily by the OUN Security Service (SB), and perpetrators were punished.[44] There are now almost daily reports in the Polish press about Ukrainian atrocities against Poles during the war, writes Serhiichuk, but UPA's policies were directed primarily against the Communist Party and its terrorist armed formations. Concerning the civilian population, the UPA subscribed to the strictest tolerance and humanity. Sometimes the Polish villages provided shelter for the insurgents. The number of Polish victims is not known and could only be established in Serhiichuk's view by a joint Ukrainian–Polish commission. Nevertheless, the removal of Poles from these lands for the most part was not a consequence of UPA's campaigns. Rather the Polish Communist leaders demanded that the Soviet Union accelerate the transfer of the Polish population to former German lands in the west in East Prussia and Pomerania during the bitter winter of 1946.[45]

Serhiichuk returns to the theme in his 2003 book on the "Volhynia tragedy." Once again it is based on information culled from the Ukrainian Central

Archives, and the argumentation and tone of the book are aggressively anti-Polish, and express strong sympathy if not outright support for the OUN and UPA. He compares the "ethnic cleansing" on both sides of the border and from his viewpoint, the Polish cleansing of Ukrainians was incomparably worse than the Ukrainian cleansing of Poles. Until the present, he points out, neither Communist nor Democratic Poland has admitted responsibility for the cruelties carried out by Poles against Ukrainians during Operation Vistula. Supposedly the deported Ukrainians lived comfortably in the houses vacated by Germans, but this is a misleading image in the author's view. As for the massacres of Poles, there are today many Ukrainian cultural figures who think that Ukraine must take responsibility for that tragedy. Serhiichuk is not among them. He thinks it would be more logical to ask Poland for an apology for the crimes carried out against Ukrainians. The book he is writing is partly in response to the monograph by Polish historian Grzegorz Motyka, which he views as very one-sided in its approach.[46] Serhiichuk believes that Polish losses have been grossly exaggerated, and sometimes are cited as being as high as 500,000. Whereas Motyka maintains that the anti-Polish actions of OUN-UPA began in April 1943, Serhiichuk retorts that they occurred on lands populated from earliest times by Ukrainians and on which Ukrainians made up an absolute majority. The OUN liquidated only elements that actively opposed a Ukrainian state, whereas Poles of all political hues were dedicated to the destruction of Ukrainians, including the AK and the Polish underground. Ukrainians, on the other hand, demonstrated in their propaganda of 1943 that they did not want a war with Poles, even though organs such as the Ukrainian Central Committee in Krakow were concerned by Polish massacres of Ukrainians in the districts of Krakow and Lublin, which claimed "hundreds of lives." The Poles were so firmly opposed to Ukrainians, however, that even the Germans co-opted their services.[47] However, the possible connection between ethnic cleansing of Poles and their willingness to work with the Germans is not explored.

Serhiichuk continues by listing a number of villages in which there were Polish police collaborators. UPA leader Klym Savur then allegedly warned them to stop helping the Germans. Whereas the Poles in the book appear to support either the Germans or the Soviet Partisans, the Ukrainians are invariably described as 100% behind Stepan Bandera. The situation deteriorated when a large band of Soviet Partisans arrived in Volhynia. Their Polish supporters were singling out Ukrainians and this was why Ukrainians in Volhynia turned on the Poles. According to the OUN perspective, the Poles had committed the double sin of collaborating with both enemies of Ukrainian interests. Serhiichuk portrays the Polish Partisan leaders as debauched and vindictive and the leader of the Home Army in L'viv as an avowed Communist. In some regions the Germans encouraged the Poles to turn on the followers of Bul'ba-Borovets'. In the summer of 1943 there were many victims on both sides. While Poles suffered the highest casualties in July; the number of Ukrainian victims was higher in October. Was the latter a backlash to the first attack? Serhiichuk does not say. What he does do is try to use statistics to bring down the number of Polish victims by showing that deportations and executions in earlier times had already depleted the Polish community of Volhynia.[48] Finally, when there seems no option but to deal with the fact that the OUN-B ordered the wholesale massacre of the Poles, Serhiichuk reverts again to a 600-year history of conflict marked by Polish duplicity. He therefore maintains that it is time that Poles apologized to Ukrainians for "genocide." But they have not, "and we should not be surprised by that fact."[49] The book uses primary sources selectively to present a partisan version of history that in every instance favors the Ukrainian version of events and denigrates the Poles at every opportunity. It is thus a diatribe rather than an academic work and serves mainly to fan the flames of ethnic conflict.

In similar fashion, a survey of Ukrainian–Polish relations by Serhii Hrabovs'kyi begins by recognizing that both the Polish elites and the population at large are interested in the partnership with Ukraine. They would like to see a democratic Ukraine with a market economy. Therefore in the political climate of Ukraine in 2003, Polish sympathies were on the side of the Ukrainian opposition. However, he feels, the Polish intellectual elite and artists are interested in developing relations only with those Ukrainian counterparts who express pro-Polish sentiment, or adhere to the principles of post-modernism, with its characteristic distancing from questions of nationhood. The attitude of Poles to average Ukrainians is considerably more negative, as these people are usually guest workers, gangsters, and prostitutes. The main historical problems separating the two peoples, in Hrabovs'kyi's opinion are Volhynia, OUN-UPA, the Division Halychyna, and Ukrainian nationalism. The majority of Poles are convinced that the UPA are murderers, arsonists, rapists, and Nazi collaborators, and Ukrainian nationalists belong in the "garbage bin of history." In their view, he writes, the responsibility for the Volhynia events rests 99% with Ukrainians. Poland requires a nonnationalist Ukraine, serene and always ready to acknowledge the influence of Poland on its own history. In this respect he perceives little difference between intellectual Poles and the rest of their compatriots. They are under the delusion, in this author's view, that a non-Ukrainian Ukrainian state can be a reliable partner. However, the only reliable partner would be a Ukraine in which UPA combatants are recognized as heroes, and in which soldiers of the Division Halychyna will receive historical recognition.[50]

Hrabovs'kyi counters traditional Polish attacks on the UPA and Ukrainian nationalism (this concept is left undefined) by pointing out the inconsistency of Polish "nationalists" who make use of the vocabulary and documents of the NKVD and KGB regarding OUN-UPA, but refuse to use these same sources with reference to the Home Army, the non-Communist Polish underground, and the Polish political emigration. He concludes his account with a question: Does Poland aspire to friendship with a Ukrainian state in which the streets are named after Feliks Dzerzhinsky and ruled by the methods of Iron Feliks, or would a better partner for Poland be a Ukraine that descended from the UNR, the country in which monuments to the Petlyura-Pilsudski alliance will be erected?[51] Presumably his statement implies that either Ukraine would be a country that remained under Soviet influence or one based on independent traditions. His article followed closely a joint declaration by the Supreme Soviet of Ukraine and the Polish Sejm on the 60th anniversary of the Volhynia tragedy.[52] Hrabovs'kyi was not the only Ukrainian observer to take exception to this joint statement. Viktor Radionov comments that approving such a declaration was tantamount to demonstrating one's own inferiority vis-à-vis Poland. If such a gesture was needed in order for Ukraine to acquire admission into Euro-Atlantic structures, then the price, in his opinion, was too high. Ukraine could only enter Europe proudly, as a free nation. Radionov speaks of the "unheard of impudence" of the Poles. The groundless demands that Ukraine should apologize and the sluggishness and apathy of Ukrainian politicians led to a negative reaction in Volhynia and Galicia. The people were in his view incensed at the kowtowing to Warsaw and to the new efforts to accuse Ukrainians of all sorts of crimes and to shift the blame "onto our people."[53]

Radionov continues with heightened invective. He asserts that one reason why a joint-declaration could be adopted was because of a so-called "fifth column" in Ukraine. While his organization, the OUN, was picketing the Polish Embassy with slogans such as "Volhynia is Ukrainian land!" and "OUN and UPA are our heroes!", Maksym Strikha, to Radionov's dismay, wrote in an earlier issue of *Ukrains'ke slovo* that for centuries, Galicia and Volhynia belonged to both Ukrainians and Poles, and that these lands had become ethnically Ukrainian only as a consequence of the postwar deportations carried out by Stalin and Beria. Radionov is emphatic: Volhynia and Galicia have always been Ukrainian lands, and this fact has been proved conclusively by historians like Hrushevs'kyi and others. No knowledgeable historian would write such nonsense about a common land.[54] His diatribe here and in an earlier article in the same venue provoked a response from Bohdan Oleksyuk, who comments that Radionov did not understand what sort of guilt Ukrainians had to repent for during the struggle for independence. What do we wish to justify, Oleksyuk wonders? Is it the cleansing from Ukrainian lands of the Polish population by means of slaughter of civilians, including women, children, and the elderly? Radionov represents in his view a tendency to talk only "about our own victims." In fact, the joint declaration indicated a growing awareness of Ukrainian victims on the Polish side of the border.[55] These points are echoed by Viktor Zamyatin writing in *Den'* who cites the editor of *Gazeta Wyborcza*, Adam Michnik, that it would be disastrous, with regard to the Volhynia issue, if chauvinistic anti-Ukrainian forces in Poland and their anti-Polish counterparts in Ukraine took the initiative. Both nations to some extent suffer from the "innocent victim syndrome."[56]

Summary

This chapter has surveyed some of the recent debates about controversial events in Ukrainian–Polish relations, many of which remain in the memory of people and have the potential to foster differences between the two countries. The focus has been exclusively on those narratives that have appeared in Ukraine. Those in Poland, as well as a number of new books on issues such as Volhynia, are of interest but are peripheral to this study, even though they have contributed to the debate and responses from the Ukrainian side. Two key issues have arisen with regard to the construction of Ukrainian national history: the first is context. As some Ukrainian writers have noted with justification, it is impossible to treat the Volhynia massacres in isolation; they need to be examined within the context of—at least—recent history. On the other hand, they cannot be ignored, and it seems simplistic to argue, as Radionov does, that they can be justified simply by the fact that Volhynia belonged historically to Ukraine. The opposite line of reasoning incidentally is used by other nationalist writers to avoid responsibility, namely that Ukraine cannot be responsible for these events because no Ukrainian state existed at that time. One surely cannot have it both ways. The second issue, and it surfaces repeatedly in articles, is that what occurred in Volhynia tarnishes irrevocably the image of the OUN and UPA as heroes and liberators of the Ukrainian lands. Snyder has explained such actions by the fact that the UPA consisted, in part, of former Nazi auxiliaries, extremists and fanatics who had already witnessed some of the worst horrors of the war and were now prepared to apply them to the local Polish population.

A distinction may be made between academic and popular writings on Polish-Ukrainian relations. Popular writings have made significant steps in coming to terms with issues like Volhynia and Operation Vistula—as for that matter have the respective governments in recent times. However, the issue is far from resolved, and not least because of the existence of the two neighboring states. The perceived architects of the dilemma—Nazi Germany and the Soviet Union—have long exited the stage. In the case of the latter, the successor nation, the Russian Federation, has never acknowledged any direct inheritance from the Soviet state, which might be considered illogical given its material gains, such as embassies, former party buildings, and the Kremlin itself. For Ukraine, the problem has always been that if one is to construct a national history that includes the struggle for independence in the wartime years—and it is hard to imagine how that history can be constructed without this pivotal period—then all aspects of the history of the OUN and UPA have to be included, both the heroic and the terrible, no matter how difficult this may be for Ukrainian historians to accept. The position is exacerbated by the "complex" of Ukrainians as victims and the fact that the acclaimed representatives of the nation were armed men who wished to cleanse their perceived territories as thoroughly as possible. It is complicated by the decades of monotonous Soviet narratives of OUN-UPA treachery and collaboration, which without doubt has had a lasting influence in many areas of Ukraine. On the other hand, the massacres were largely absent from Soviet narratives until the last years of the USSR—these writings did not wish to single out persecution of Poles just as Soviet accounts of the war years rarely focused on the Jewish Holocaust. In conclusion, one can say that Volhynia has entered the public consciousness of contemporary Ukraine but it sits uneasily with many people. Many would rather choose to forget such events.

Notes

1   Timothy Snyder, *The Reconstruction of Nations: Poland, Ukraine, Lithuania, Belarus, 1569-1999* (New Haven, Connecticut: Yale University Press, 2003), p. 169.
2   Timothy Snyder, "The Causes of Ukrainian-Polish Ethnic Cleansing," *Past and Present*, Vol. 179, Number 1 (2003): 197-234.
3   Cited in N. Karpova, "Vybor," *Pravda Ukrainy*, 4 January 1990, p. 4.
4   A. Veremeichuk, "My obvinyaem natsionalizm," *Pravda Ukrainy*, 11 April 1990, p. 3.

5 V. I. Maslovs'kyi, "Shchto na 'oltari svobody'? Dekil'ka utochen' shchodo viiny 'na dva front.' Yaku vela UPA ta skil'koma nevynnymy zhertvamy oplachuvas' tsey propahandyts'-kyi myf," *Komunist Ukrainy*, No. 7 (July 1991): 72-73.

6 S. Dluskiy, "Tragediya sela Ganachevka," *L'vovs'kaya pravda*, 2 July 1991, p. 3.

7 Evgeniy Guzhva, "Kolodets smerti," *Pravda Ukrainy*, 22 August 1991, p. 3; and 23 August 1991, p. 3.

8 Wiktor Poliszczuk, *Legal and Political Assessment of the OUN and UPA* (Toronto, 1991), pp. 32-38.

9 Nina Romanyuk, and Yurii Mykolayenko, "Vsyaki uryad, yakui vidmovyvsya b vid Zakhidnoi Ukrainy, buv by rozbytyi," *Ukraina moloda*, 11 January 1995, p. 3.

10 Myroslav Paranchak, "Tyahar nespravedlyvosti zhyvuchyi," *Za vil'nu Ukrainu*, 23 July 1998, p. 2.

11 Yan Hasten, "Ne til'ky pro Volyn," *Za vil'nu Ukrainu*, 24 September 1998, p. 2.

12 Koval', *Ukraina v Druhii svitovii i Velykii Vitchyznyanii viinakh*, p. 153.

13 Stanislav Kul'chyts'kyi, "Ukrainski natsionalisty v chervono-korychnevii Yevropi (do 70-richchya stvorennya OUN)," *Istoriya Ukrainy*, No. 5 (February 1999): 6-7.

14 Yaroslav Isayevich, "Ukrains'ko-pol's'ki vidnosyny periodu Druhoi svitovoi viiny: interpretatsii istorykiv i politykiv," *Istoriya v shkolakh Ukrainy*, No. 2 (2003): 39.

15 Ibid., pp. 39-40.

16 Ibid., p. 40.

17 Wladyslaw and Ewa Symaszko, *Ludobojstwo dokonan przez nacjonalistow ukrainskich na ludnosci polskiej Wolynia, 1939-1945* (Warsaw: Wyd. Von borowiecky, 2000).

18 I. I. Il'yushyn, "Do pytannya pro Volyns'ku trahediyu v 1943-1944 rr.," *Ukrains'kyi istorichnyi zhurnal*, No. 3 (2003): 116-117. Presumably the perpetrators were *former* members of the Communist Party of Western Ukraine since that party was dissolved by the Comintern on Stalin's orders in 1938.

19 Ibid., pp. 116-122.

20 Editorial, "Vernut' narodu istoriyu," *L'vovs'kaya pravda*, 18 February 1990, p. 1.

21 S. A. Makarchuk, "Z istorii druhoi svitovoi viiny. Pereselennya polyakiv iz zakhidnykh oblastei Ukrainy v Pol'shchu u 1944-1946 rr.," *Ukrains'kyi istorychnyi zhurnal*, No. 3 (2003): 103-104.

22 Ibid., pp. 104-105.

23 Ibid., pp. 105-108, 110-111.

24 Ivan Vorobel', "Staly zhertvamy kliky Beria-Stalina," *Za vil'nu Ukrainu*, 30 August 1994, p. 2.

25 Petro Kostyk, ""Polymya, shcho nurtuye donyni slida my trahedii sela Sahrybn na Kholmsh-chyni," *Za vil'nu Ukrainu*, 10 September 1999, p. 6.

26 Oleksandra Potichna, "I bratove-lyatky po khrystyyans'ki vyrizaly Ivanovi na hrudyakh khresta," *Za vil'nu Ukrainu*, 30 July 1999, pp. 8-9. See also Peter J. Potichnyj, *Pavlokoma, 1441-1945: istoriya sela* (L'viv and Toronto: Fund for Pavlokoma, 2001).

27 Ibid.

28 V. Danylenko and V. Baran, "Ostanni period Stalinshchyny (suspil'no-politychni rozvytok)," *Istoriya Ukrainy*, No. 12 (March 2000): 1-3.

29 Ibid.

30 Natalya Klyashtorna, "Vyselennya," *Ukraina moloda*, 19 February 2002, p. 11.

31 Kataryna Wolczuk, "The Difficulties of Polish-Ukrainian Historical Reconciliation," paper published by the Royal Institute of International Affairs, London, 2002.

32 Georgiy Gongadze, a journalist for the on-line newspaper *Ukrains'ka Pravda*, was kidnapped and later murdered in 2000. He had written a number of critical articles about the Kuchma regime, which was implicated in the murder by tapes smuggled out of the country by a former bodyguard of the president. See J. V. Koshiw, *Beheaded: The Killing of a Journalist* (London: Artemia Press, 2003).

33 Wolczuk, "The Difficulties of Polish-Ukrainian Historical Reconciliation."

34 Ibid.

35 Evhen Dudar, "Pravda—odna. Vidkrytyi lyst prem'er-ministrovi Pol'shchi p. Lesheku Milleru," *Literaturna Ukraina*, 7 November 2002, p. 1.

36 Ibid.

37 Maksym Strikha, "Asymetrychnist' Volyni," *Krytyka-Komentar*, 5 May 2003; [http://www.krytyka.kiev.ua/comments/Strixa24.html].

38 Prus has been a prolific and hostile analyst of the OUN and UPA and has also authored a biography of Stepan Bandera. I am not acquainted with the cited source. His recent works include *Rycerze zelaznej ostrogi: oddzialy wojskowe ukrainskich nacjionalistow w okresie II wojny swiatowej* (Wroclaw: Atla 2, 2000); and *SS-Galizien: patrioci czy zbrodniarze?* (Wroclaw: Nortom, 2001).

39 Ibid.

40 Ibid.

41 Bohdan Oleksyuk, "Chy musyt' ukrains'kyi natsionalist nenavydity polyakiv? *Krytyka*, 23 May 2003; [http://www.krytyka.kiev.ua/comments/Oleksjuk14.html].

42 Wiktor Poliszczuk, *Bitter Truth: the Criminality of the Organization of Ukrainian Nationalists (OUN) and the Ukrainian Insurgent Army (UPA): the Testimony of a Ukrainian* (Toronto, 1999).

43 Volodymyr Serhiichuk, *Nasha krov-na svoii zemli* (Kyiv: Ukrains'ka vydavanycha spilka, 2000), pp. 1, 3, 7, 18, and 48-49.

44 Ibid., pp. 64, 67-68.

45 Ibid., pp. 78, 85-86.

46 Grzegorz Motyka, *Pany i rezuny : wspolpraca AK-WiN i UPA, 1945-1947* (Warsaw: Volumen, 1997).

47 Volodymyr Serhiichuk, *Trahediya Volyni: Prychynyi perebih pol's'ko-ukrains'koho konfliktu v roky Druhoi svitovoi viiny* (Kyiv: vydavnycha spilka, 2003), pp. 1-15, 20-21.

48 Ibid., pp. 26, 29, 32, 41-43, 52-53, 58-59.

49 Ibid., pp. 74-75, 97.

50 Serhii Hrabovs'kyi, "Yaka Ukraina potribna Polshchi?" *Ukrains'ke slovo*, 24-30 July 2003, p. 5.

51 Ibid. His reference is to the founder of the Soviet Cheka, the Pole Felix Dzerzhinsky, and to the Ukrainian National Republic of 1918.

52 "Volyns'ka trahediya," *Moya bat'kivshchyna*, No. 7 (July 2003).

53 Viktor Radionov, "Vidhomin," *Ukrains'ke slovo*, 4-10 September 2003, p. 4.

54 Ibid. Compare here the attitude of a Canadian of Ukrainian ancestry, Orysia Tkacz, who commented on the Info-ukes internet list that "What was lost in all the discussion re Volyn was—and yes, retribution is ugly, but—this was Ukrainian land. Ukrainians had been ruled and persecuted by the Poles for centuries on this land, serfdom, the pany/lords, the "Pacification," Brigidky, Bereza-Kartuz'ka, Akcija Wiszla later and on and on and on, and finally, as they say in Ukrainian, terpets' virvavsia [it was the last straw]. In this specific case it was

the Poles who were killed. They, particularly, would not/may not have been guilty of anything but this was what happened, in reaction to all that happened before." Info-ukes, History list, 8 November 2003. One could hardly find a better example of a victimization complex being used to justify a wholesale massacre.

55 Bohdan Oleksyuk, "Natsionalizm ne teroryzm," *Ukrains'ke slovo*, 4-10 September 2003, p. 4.

56 Viktor Zamyatin, "Adam Michnik: One must think ahead," *The Day Digest*, 15 April 2003; [http://www.day.kiev.ua/260479/].

CHAPTER 7

WRITING NEW HISTORY IN UKRAINE

Introduction

This chapter examines the emergence of new history in Ukraine, as well as the issue of the rehabilitation of the OUN and UPA, which has been taken on as a goal by the government of President Viktor Yushchenko. The intention is to ascertain the degree to which—after 15 years of independence—Ukraine has changed the way it looks at the recent past, particularly the events cited in this study that are so controversial, painful, and remain in people's memories. It begins with school textbooks, a prime indicator of how a new generation of Ukrainian citizens will perceive its past, and examines the interpretations of the Famine, and those of the Second World War and afterward. It continues with an overview of Ukrainian thinking about the Second World War in general, and the way that this war is commemorated in the country today. In what ways, for example, is this occasion different from that of the Soviet period, when Victory Day (9 May) constituted one of the main holidays in the Soviet calendar? What questions are being raised about the commemoration and to what degree has the Ukrainian government continued past traditions or tried to change them as part of the new image of Ukraine? The later focus of the chapter is devoted exclusively to the issue of the wartime insurgent movement and the most recent debates and narratives in the media and in academic writing.

The discussions have occurred amid a background of profound political change in Ukraine, a period of turmoil and crisis that at the time of writing was far from over. Much has been written about the Orange Revolution of 2004, when mass protests in the streets of Kyiv successfully overturned an official election result that would have seen Leonid Kuchma's Prime Minister, and designated choice as successor, Viktor Yanukovich, elected president. Instead, in a repeated second round, the winner was opposition leader and head of the Our Ukraine party, Viktor Yushchenko. That election was marred by the attempted poisoning of Yushchenko, the intrusion into the campaign of Russian President Vladimir Putin, and an attempted separatist breakaway movement in the eastern regions of Ukraine, particularly the *oblasts* of Donetsk and Luhansk, where the Orange triumph was perceived as the result of Western influence on Ukrainian political life. With the victory of Yushchenko, Ukraine appeared committed to joining the EU and other European structures, as well as the military organization of NATO. In many ways, Ukraine appeared to leave the Russian orbit altogether and embark on a new course under the leadership of Yushchenko, and another pivotal figure in the Orange Revolution, Prime Minister Yulia Tymoshenko. This change of regime, had it remained in place, might have acted to further amend the official conceptions of the past as it appeared to signal that at last the country would rid itself of the problematic legacies of the Soviet period: former Communists in power; corruption at the highest levels of government; oligarchs controlling key commodities; and uncertainty about the national image and future strategies. The inauguration of Yushchenko as president of Ukraine in January 2005 therefore appeared to herald a fundamental shift in Ukrainian politics and outlook.

Some eighteen months later, the new government came unraveled. It took just nine months before the Cabinet headed by Tymoshenko was dismissed as a result of internal bickering and disagreement over policies, particularly the privatization of large companies. Yushchenko acted as an executive-style president and declined to delve deeply into the corruption and misdeeds of his predecessor and his prominent officials. This live-and-let-live policy resulted in a public image as an indecisive leader, and during the parliamentary elections of March 2006, Yushchenko's Our Ukraine found itself in third place. Leading the polls was the Party of Regions led by the once disgraced Yanukovich, who had substantial backing from the wealthy Donets'k oligarch, Renat Akhmetov. Yulia Tymoshenko's Bloc came in a clear second. Four months of wrangling followed as groups sought to put together a ruling coalition. Initially it appeared that an Orange coalition was again feasible and that Tymoshenko would return as Prime Minister. However, the defection of the Socialist Party, led by Oleksandr Moroz, rendered this impossible. Moroz received the position of Speaker of Parliament and joined a new coalition headed by the Party of the Regions, and also featuring as members of the Communist Party of Ukraine. Yushchenko then had 15 days to contemplate the prospect of Yanukovich returning as Prime Minister. Ultimately his Our Ukraine faction joined the new coalition, and Yanukovich, Yushchenko, and Moroz signed a new Declaration of National Unity, by which the signatories agreed to continue the course outlined by the president in the direction of Europe and Yanukovich agreed to abandon his policy of promoting Russian to the status of a second state language. On the issue of NATO, Ukraine decided not to join without a national referendum and the public currently is opposed to membership.

So where does this leave Ukraine? Its position is uncertain and in some ways it seems no further ahead in resolving the problem of regionalism than it has been in the past. In virtually every election for president, Western Ukraine has voted for one candidate and Eastern Ukraine for another. The diametrically opposite attitudes to elections, to policies, and to the historical past have been illustrated in an article by historian Yaroslav Hrytsak, which compares viewpoints in the cities of L'viv and Donets'k.[1] L'viv is Ukrainian speaking, oriented toward Europe, and in the most recent presidential election provided the firmest supporters of Yushchenko; Donets'k is Russian speaking, oriented toward Russia, and the political base of Yanukovich. The situation is not so straightforward, however, because Yanukovich is avowedly pro-Europe, particularly in business dealings. Nevertheless, the comparison is useful because these two parts of Ukraine are also on opposite sides when it comes to constructing a national history and the way in which history should be written. National historians, writers, politicians, and polemicists maintain that modern history includes a genocidal famine, inflicted by the Moscow government on Ukraine, and that the wartime period witnessed a national liberation movement for Ukrainian independence headed by the OUN and UPA. In this perception they have the widespread support of Ukrainians in the West. The opposite view can certainly be found in places like Donets'k. Here the memory of the Soviet period is quite different. Many still deny the existence of the Famine as an act of genocide, ironically, in that this is the territory in which it occurred. There is also a continuing tendency to regard the OUN and UPA as traitors and collaborators. In terms of reanalyzing recent history, however, deep changes have already taken place despite the uncertain political direction of the country, and we will now examine them in turn.

School Textbooks

This survey of school textbooks is not intended to be comprehensive but rather to provide a general overview of what has been written recently in Ukraine about the events under discussion. Many of them either did not appear in Soviet textbooks or, if they did, the narrative was distorted to fit the ideological line prevailing at the time. Clearly there have been some new and innovative approaches to historiography in Ukraine. In an article published in 2000, Oleksandr Marushchenko provides an analysis of such new methods and highlights some of the thinking of the new historiographers, beginning with M. Koval'. It was Koval', says Marushchenko, who maintained the necessity of reevaluating Soviet historiographic approaches to the events of the Second World War in a new and objective fashion. Koval' felt it essential to reanalyze the reasons why the Soviet armed forces were so poorly prepared for the German invasion. Further, he suggested a new interpretation of events in Ukraine in 1943–44, such as the suggestion that Soviet forces "occupied" rather than "liberated" Ukrainian territories during the course of the war. He also wanted a debate on terminology and definitions used to refer to some of the wartime events and some changes in phraseology. For example, should one refer to the period 1941–45 as the Great Patriotic War or the German-Soviet war? The "national liberation" movement in Ukraine should be considered, in Marushchenko's view, as a civil war led by the Ukrainian people against foreign occupants, and this would mean re-periodizing the war beyond the Soviet stereotype.[2]

The article then introduces the views of V. Stetskevych, who authored a book on the Second World War published in Dnipropetrovs'k in 1992. Stetskevych contends that Second World War history should be regarded as part of the history of the Ukrainian people, rather than war history per se. The people, in turn, should be perceived in their entire context, with all political and social divisions rejected. This approach is described as "humanistic" or "anthropocentric." The overall goal is to seek a national ideology orientation that would help to consolidate the nation. In short, Stetskevych proposes to use history for nation-building. I. Pavlenko, on the other hand, carried out a critical analysis of how Soviet historians interpreted the history of the war, and he makes five conclusions. First, Soviet history characterized the Ukrainian national liberation movement as "treacherous," "criminal," and "bourgeois-nationalist." Second, historical writings were of a propagandistic rather than of a research character. Third, the use of archives and other sources was strictly limited. Fourth, the interpretation of available materials was superficial; and lastly the significance and scale of the armed clashes between members of the "national liberation" forces and the Red Army was deliberately played down. A. Podols'kyi's focus is on the Holocaust, and he has suggested that a new, generalized research needs to be undertaken on the fate of Ukrainian Jews during the course of the war. Marushchenko's article also makes brief references to some writings published by members of the Ukrainian Diaspora and states that the efforts of Ukrainian historiographers, both at home and abroad, should be used for a revised version of the history of the Second World War.[3] These ideas have already been fruitfully applied to some of the new textbooks for schools that are appearing in Ukraine, which for the first time are discussing in depth the issues of the Stalin period.

One can begin the survey of textbooks with a short monograph written for students in grade five by Viktor Mysan, the second edition of which was published in 1997, and which has been cited earlier in conjunction with the important article by Nancy Popson.[4] The topics are neatly divided into subject areas and the explanation of events is clear and simple, but also in its own way quite ideological. Mysan devotes five pages to the Famine of 1932–33, writing that peasants joined collective farms "with pain and terror." Those who did not wish to join were labelled *kulaks* and branded as enemies of the people. Millions were sent to Siberia. He writes that the 1932 harvest was no worse than earlier years but special food detachments came to the villages and confiscated everything. There are then two short sections on the same topic. Under the heading "It is interesting to know," Mysan writes that historians to date have been unable to determine the number of deaths from the famine, which is somewhere between 3.5 million and 8–9 million people. The "Holodomor" is one of the worst tragedies of Ukraine. Soviet power kept silence about the existence of the Famine and did not provide any help to the population. It also refused help from abroad. The second section is entitled "Genocide" and seems unrelated to the earlier narrative. It is also ambivalent, stating that the Famine was a black page on the history of Ukraine but that it also affected other former peoples of the USSR. Mysan also describes the Purges and maintains that Ukraine was the worst affected by these also. As in the years of the Holodomor, children suffered the most. The author ends this section as follows: "Remember this! You—the young part of the Ukrainian people. Our people endured famine, were sent to Siberia, perished, and were shot. But they lived and will continue to live!"[5]

Concerning the start of the Second World War, Mysan states that the population of Western Ukraine greeted the Soviet army happily, but the new Soviet order brought the creation of collective farms, a ban on religion, and punished those people who wished to see a free Ukraine. The Bolsheviks were occupiers rather than liberators. Yet "from the first days" of the war the Ukrainian people began to struggle against the plunderers [the Germans] and Partisan units, and underground organizations rose up.[6]

Already the book would surely confuse the average 10-year-old because the author makes no distinction between the Soviet Partisans and the UPA, other than to state that the UPA fought on two fronts until the end of military operations because its members did not want either Fascists or Russian Bolsheviks on Ukrainian lands. Earlier he has provided examples of Ukrainian Partisans so the appellation of Bolshevik clearly does not apply to people like Sydir Kovpak. The apparent confusion is then heightened by the statement that at the end of October 1944, Ukraine was liberated from "Fascist bandits" and 9 May is a day of happiness. Remember this! He tells the pupils, the deaths of millions of people brought this victory. Finally, he adds that for residents of Western Ukraine, the postwar period was complex because units of the UPA actively resisted the Soviet regime. Family members of UPA soldiers were arrested and sent to Siberia and the Far East. For a long time the UPA warriors were known as Banderivtsi, but it should be remembered, Mysan writes, that the insurgents were on their own land and had no wish to give up this territory. They led a liberation war because they protected their lands and families, and did not want to live "under Bolshevik slavery." Once they were defeated, in the second half of the 1950s, Russification was imposed on Ukraine. In the postwar years, many people did not comprehend that it was necessary for Ukraine to build its own independent state.[7] The logical question that arises is that if the Bolsheviks represented slavery then why is 9 May a day of happiness for Ukraine? There is also no clear relationship between the heroic Ukrainian Partisans and the Soviet occupation forces. For the pupils, there is then a considerable gap in their knowledge of Ukrainian history because after the comments on the UPA, the next topic is the Chornobyl disaster of 1986!

F. H. Turchenko has written a new history of Ukraine for the tenth grade that provides a more detailed outline of the 1932–33 Famine. The Famine is described as one of the worst atrocities of Stalinism against the Ukrainian people, and the reason for it is cited as punishment for those villages that refused to accept the new *kolkhoz* system at the start of collectivization. State procurements drained the lifeblood of the villages, and famine arose as a result. The peasants were then too weak physically to carry out spring sowing for 1932. There was also a lack of order on the farms and the peasants were disinterested in working on them. Because of low-quality threshing of the cultivated crop, part of the areas sown perished. All these "unnatural causes" brought about the tragedy of the Ukrainian peasantry, despite the fact that the 1932 harvest was only 12% less than the average for 1926–30. Turchenko cites the 7 August 1932 law about the theft of socialist property. He also describes the extraordinary commissions, headed by Molotov, that were sent into the villages and regions that allegedly sabotaged grain procurements. Attention is paid to the role of P. Postyshev as Stalin's plenipotentiary in Ukraine and the repressions in the Ukrainian Communist Party. The party-state apparatus based in Moscow knowingly doomed peasants to their death before starting to provide some aid in May–June 1933. Turchenko concurs that the number of deaths has yet to be established and that figures are in the range of 3-4.5 million people—a lower range than in many other works. The Holodomor was entirely the creation of the Stalin leadership, in his view. The empty villages were replenished with new settlers who came mainly from Russia.[8] What Turchenko fails to do is address in any way the concept of genocide or to explain the ethnic dimensions of the Famine. There is no indication here of why the regime caused the Famine other than the Ukrainian opposition to collective farms. Thus this interpretation retains something of the original Soviet version of events, at least in the description of collectivization.

The lavishly illustrated history of Ukraine edited by Volodmyr Lytvyn and others leaves no doubt in the reader's mind that the 1932-33 Famine was an organized act of genocide against the Ukrainian people. It is described as a physical assault and an attack on people's consciousness. After the Famine, the authors write, Ukraine in effect became a colony of Moscow. The "genocide" also embraced North Caucasus, the home of over 3 million Ukrainians, with the Kuban and Don regions suffering especially.[9] The book covers the background to the formation of the OUN—though inexplicably it states that the organization arose from the ashes of the UVO and was led by A. Mel'nyk (rather than Konovalets'). The OUN-B is assigned the key role of liberation movement during the war years and there is no mention of its earlier harmonious relations with the Germans. Though there is no reference to the SS Division Halychyna, there is a photograph of its members marching down a street bearing a large swastika flag and carrying SS emblems that is more damning than any text. There are also numerous photographs of key figures on the Soviet side, such as T. Strokach and S. Kovpak. In Western Ukraine after the war, the authors write, the population remembered well the methods of Stalin, Sovietization and repressions, and either joined the UPA or sympathized with it. The insurgency controlled—more or less—some 150,000 square kilometers of territory, and it cites official figures on the number of people arrested and deported. It includes a photograph of the statue of UPA leader Roman Shukhevych in the village Tyshkivtsi (Ivano-Frankivs'k *oblast*), UPA leaflets, and the statue to UPA members from the Bukovyna region in Chernivtsi *oblast*.[10] In this way, the book offers a partial acknowledgement of the Soviet contribution to the war, but adheres firmly to the perspective that the OUN-B and UPA were national liberation movements, from which are excluded the activities of the SS Division Halychyna.

In a more recent account, O. D. Boyko provides a section on the "Causes of the Famine in Ukraine 1932-1933." He points out that historians have failed to reach a consensus on this question. Western historians have a tendency to cite national-political factors. He cites James Mace's explanation that

Moscow wanted to curb the spread of Ukrainian nationalism among the peasantry as this was a threat to its imperial interests. Thus Stalin, Kaganovich, Postyshev, and others planned in Moscow the destruction of the Ukrainian peasants as the most nationally conscious sector and tried to realize this goal in Ukraine by means of the mass famine of 1932–33. This position is supported by Robert Conquest and by French researcher Alain Bezancon who focuses on the planning behind the operation. On the other hand, Boyko writes, some Russian, Ukrainian, and Western historians (V. Danilov, N. Ivnyts'kyi, V. Marochko, N. Werth, and others) consider that the Famine resulted from various social and economic causes, first and foremost the enforced grain procurements that were unwarranted and based on coercive policies in the countryside. Boyko then states his view that the most acceptable position is that of the collective authorship of the monograph "Stalinism in Ukraine" (V. Danylenko, H. Kas'yanov, and S. Kul'chyts'kyi), who have explored the diverse perceptions and analyzed available sources and reached the conclusion that the various hypotheses need to be combined to come up with the correct analysis, that both economic and political factors lay at the root of the tragedy. Still, the researchers have been unable to come up with a firm figure of the number of victims. Conquest cites 5 million deaths; Werth from 4 to 5 million; and Kul'chyts'kyi 3.5 million. The data of V. Tsaplin, on the other hand, indicate 2.9 million deaths in 1933 alone. Many of the deaths could have been avoided had Stalin offered help, this author states.[11]

Turchenko, cited above, together with P. P. Panchenko and S. M. Tymchenko, published another history textbook in 2001, the second part of which covers the period after 1939. The early section of the book deals with the Soviet annexation of Western Ukraine at the outset of the Second World War in September 1939. The authors note that the population of Western Ukraine, hoping that all would turn out well, offered a warm greeting to the Red Army. Soviet propaganda declared that the Red Army had crossed the border in order to forestall a Nazi occupation. In conditions where the population was completely ignorant of the secret agreement between Hitler's Germany and the Soviet Union, this propaganda had a significant psychological impact on local Western Ukrainians. They hoped for a reunion with the "East Ukrainian brothers," and the image of the Soviet soldier as a liberator was enhanced by the longstanding Polish–Ukrainian animosity in the region. The authors point out that many of the omens for the change of ruler were good: the Ukrainian national intelligentsia welcomed the spreading of a network of Ukrainian schools, higher educational institutes switched to the Ukrainian language, and the L'wow Jan Kazimierz University became known as the L'viv Ivan Franko

University. The opera theater began to function in Ukrainian and was renamed the Theater of Opera and Ballet "Ivan Franko." Ukrainian newspapers also began to appear. However, the new authorities also brought with them a system of acute political terror. The NKVD eliminated political parties, including the Prosvita Society, which had been very popular. Its leaders, like many others, were declared "enemies of the people" and imprisoned. Wholesale arrests followed, including of lawyers, bank managers, the leaders of cooperative societies, priests, and middle and richer peasants.[12]

Along with the more prominent officials, the three authors continue, students and pupils of senior classes were also arrested and without any trial they were interned and later deported to the eastern regions of the USSR. This was done to intimidate the population and prevent opposition. The authors describe how the NKVD put 59 members of the OUN on trial, most of whom were students and the youngest only fifteen years of age. Forty-two people were sentenced to death. In 1939–41, 10% of the population of Western Ukraine was imprisoned, and the immediate victims were Poles, but Ukrainians followed soon afterward. This short period of Soviet rule convinced the population, the authors maintain, that its future lay not in integration into the Soviet Union but in the creation of its own independent Ukrainian state. However, the authors provide no evidence for such a claim, which appears premature in the context of this period. The authors mention briefly, with regard to the early part of the German–Soviet war, the creation of a Central Headquarters of the Partisan movement headed by P. K. Ponomarenko in May 1942, and the Ukrainian headquarters under T. Strokach formed in June 1942. There follows a much lengthier section on the OUN, which is dealt with in great detail. The authors do not conceal their disapproval of the OUN-M for its rapprochement with the Germans, or their approval of and respect for the OUN-B under Bandera. They maintain that the OUN-B represented the majority, and that Bandera, not discounting the possibility of cooperation with the Germans, supported the creation of a Ukrainian army and began an active struggle for an independent Ukraine, leaning on the forces of the Ukrainian people.[13]

The main theme therefore is of the OUN-B in the war years. The authors state that the Nazi leadership of Germany, rejecting the concept of Ukrainian statehood, nevertheless agreed to cooperation with the OUN, which they hoped to use in the struggle against the Red Army. They agreed especially to the formation of the *Nachtigal* and *Roland* battalions, which were staffed with Ukrainian nationalists, and were to be deployed for acts of sabotage in the USSR. For its part, the OUN-B considered these formations the nucleus of a future Ukrainian army. There follows a detailed description of the declaration of independence of 30 June 1941, which is portrayed as a heroic act that had the support of Metropolitan Sheptyts'kyi. The Germans responded by dissolving the government formed by Yaroslav Stets'ko and arresting Stets'ko and Bandera. The repressions, the authors write, affected the attitude of the *Roland* and *Nachtigal* battalions, the troops of which refused to carry out German orders. They were thus disbanded and their Ukrainian officers arrested. The OUN began preparing its own armed forces for a struggle with the occupiers and began to spread its underground network. The authors describe the expeditionary groups that accompanied German forces into the major cities of Eastern Ukraine. Reportedly, they had orders to set up civil organizations in each settlement, but their situation was rendered difficult by the refusal of the Germans to support an independent Ukraine. The portrayal of the impact of these groups appears exaggerated. The authors write, for example, that in the Donbas region the expeditionary group organized an independent underground, which led a campaign under the slogans "Down with Hitler! Down with Stalin! Soviet power—without the Bolsheviks!" Presumably the advocacy of Soviet power was offered to assuage a largely non-nationalistic part of the population. According to the authors, the support for Ukrainian independence, especially in Left-Bank Ukraine and Eastern Ukraine, came as a complete surprise to the Germans. The occupants saw with alarm that the leaders and members of the expeditionary groups united not only the local intelligentsia, but also young people, workers, and peasants.[14]

The authors discuss the UPA and what they term "the defense movement in 1943" at some length. They mention that among those executed at Babyn Yar was Olena Teliha, the well-known Ukrainian poetess, and that after November 1941, the occupation regime received orders to arrest and eliminate all leaders and members of the OUN underground. However, coordinated efforts between the OUN and the Soviet underground were hindered by deep ideological differences and both sides would reveal the whereabouts of the other to the Gestapo with tragic consequences. In Western Ukraine, the social basis for the national movement was wider than elsewhere, and members of the OUN were subject to relatively light acts of repression by the German occupiers. Several units of the OUN united under joint leadership in Volhynia and Polissya and received the name Ukrainian Insurgent Army. The date 14 October 1942 is the day of the creation of the UPA. The authors cite approvingly the Partisan raids led by Kovpak, and they provide a figure of up to 220,000 people in Partisan formations and the non-nationalist underground at various times during the war. The formation of the UPA in its OUN-B variant is discussed without detail as to the in-fighting that occurred among the different groups. The conflict that followed is described exclusively in terms of the German–UPA conflict. Hitlerite terror, combined with Soviet sabotage and Partisan formations, as well as Polish military formations made the situation desperate for the Ukrainian inhabitants.[15] Again the link between the Partisans as heroes and Partisans who opposed the national liberation movement requires better explanation. However, it is a sign of the failure to not have developed a clearly delineated theme for pupils, even after ten years of independence. Clearly now the OUN and UPA have been designated as the forces of national liberation, but the attitude taken toward the Soviet forces is uncertain. As yet, it is not uniformly hostile.

In 2002, a new history of Ukraine appeared in Kyiv, edited by H. D. Temka and L. S. Tupchienka. The book provides individual biographical information about the leading figures of the Ukrainian national movement, which is depicted as a response to Polish assimilation policies and the "repression" of 800 villages in Eastern Galicia from the spring of 1930 onward. Dmytro Dontsov is not assigned biographical space but is described as the main ideologue of the OUN. The biography of Bandera is detailed for the period from his membership of the Ukrainian Military Organization (UVO) in 1929 until he became leader of the Revolutionary Wing of the OUN at its Second Congress in 1941. The next statement pertains to 1947 and his election to the military wing of the OUN, leading the armed struggle of the Ukrainian national underground movement against Soviet power. Bandera's writings, it is stated, supported the concept of Christian revolutionary-liberation nationalism and the independence of Ukraine. Mel'nyk is listed as heading the moderate wing of the OUN after its split in 1940, with nothing of note cited for his activity between 1941 and 1959. The authors write that on the eve of the Second World War both wings oriented themselves in different ways toward political and military assistance from Germany. The leaders of the OUN were guided by Dontsov's formula that Ukraine would liberate itself in the shadow of a German invasion of the Soviet Union. The German people from 1918 to the end of the 1930s were respected in Ukrainian lands as representatives of enlightenment and sophisticated behavior—a statement that might reflect the relatively civilized military occupation of Ukraine in the later months of the First World War. What the authors presumably are trying to do is limit the damage of Ukrainian links with Hitler's regime on the part of the nationalists. Thus on 14 April 1941, Andrii Mel'nyk wrote a letter to Hitler in which he suggested that the German leader create a Ukrainian state under German protection extending from the Danube and Carpathians, to the Caspian Sea, the mountains of the Caucasus, and including Crimea, Bessarabia, half of the Voronezh and Kursk *oblasts* and part of Belgorod *oblast*! Mel'nyk projected that Ukraine would border Kazakhstan on the Volga River, while the Russian Far East could be colonized by Japanese settlers. He promised to join his forces with those of Hitler and the wing of the OUN under Bandera.[16]

Temka and Tupchienka then outline Stets'ko's aborted attempt to form a Ukrainian government in L'viv, which is portrayed as an independent action rather than one in which the Ukrainians openly solicited the support of the Germans. A laudatory biography of Stets'ko is included. Hitler's response to the Ukrainian declaration of independence was rapid, the authors state, and on 5 July, the same day that Stets'ko formed his government, Stepan Bandera was arrested in Krakow and four days later Stets'ko and 300 OUN activists were detained, many of whom were later executed. They describe another abortive attempt to set up a Ukrainian national government in Bukovyna on 1 July 1941 after the Romanian army had left this region at Stalin's request. The Germans subsequently turned down requests for cooperation from Mel'nyk and others in July. The role of the expeditionary groups in Kyiv and other cities is highlighted and the authors express regret that the members of the two wings of the OUN were unable to unify. This book devotes unusual attention to the UPA established by representatives of the exiled UNR government under Taras Bul'ba Borovets'. In the summer of 1941, the text reads, Borovets' formed the UPA-Polis'ka Sich with some 6,000 men. It attacked the retreating Red Army and helped the Germans to transfer production facilities and raw materials to the Reich. The Germans disbanded the unit on 16 November 1941, but as the military situation changed, a new treaty between the German commanders and the UPA was signed on 23 November 1942. Simultaneously in 1942, the authors note the treaty between the OUN-B and OUN-M, made in order to enable the two wings to combine actions against the Germans, Polish nationalists, Soviet Partisans and bandit groups made up of Red Army deserters. From 9 April, the OUN-B had begun negotiations with Borovets' about a common political platform based on Bandera's ideas, which included elimination of the Polish population. The conflict that followed during the OUN-B's enforced takeover of the UPA from Borovets' is well described, as well as the open fighting between the OUN-B Security Service, on the one hand, and the OUN-M and the UPA-Polis'ka Sich on the other. Borovets', the authors write, turned himself in to the Germans following the murder of many of his colleagues by the OUN-B Security Service.[17]

The book's coverage of the Volhynia massacres is short but balanced, and includes a comment from Kubiiovych that "If the OUN-B-UPA continues to

conduct war against six enemies, they will lead Ukraine to the grave." It highlights the assaults on sixty Polish settlements on 11–12 June 1943 on the orders of the OUN-B. In civil war situations, some 40–50,000 people from both
sides were killed in the conflict with the Poles. Also, during 1943 the OUN
conceived of the idea to ask the West to defend Ukraine, based on the model
by which the Japanese ruled the Philippines. There follows a detailed account
of the formation of the SS Division Halychyna which, the authors note, came
after the formation of two Latvian SS Divisions and one Estonian SS Division, the creation of the Russian Liberation Army under Vlasov, and military
units of other Soviet peoples. The initiative for the Ukrainian Division came
from Galician governor Otto Waechter, and had the support of Kubiiovych's
Ukrainian Central Committee, which provided unanimous backing. However,
since there were some Germans who held a negative attitude toward such an
enterprise, a decision was made not to permit the creation of an all-Ukrainian
army, but merely a regional Galician unit led by the SS. The officer corps was
also mixed German and Ukrainian. Prior to its creation, both the UPA and
the OUN had a negative attitude toward it. The Division's military actions and
its transformation in 1945 into an exclusively Ukrainian force under General
P. Shandruk are elucidated carefully. When the war ended, the British refused
to repatriate the Division troops and they were given permission to settle in
Britain. The final section devoted to the war is occupied with the Soviet–UPA
conflict. The malevolent and ruthless role of N. S. Khrushchev, First Secretary of the CPU, is explained in more intricate detail than in most sources,
particularly his application of mass terror in Western Ukraine. The authors
also note that the number of mass arrests far exceeded the actual figures for
UPA insurgents and therefore the majority of those killed or arrested must
have been "peaceful citizens."[18]

The authors conclude this remarkably candid outline in the following way.
They write that the end of the German–Soviet war, and the victory over Fascist
Germany and Imperial Japan failed to bring peace and calm to Ukraine. The
OUN-B had no hope of overcoming the powerful Soviet Union and therefore its
uprising was doomed to failure. In turn, in terms of turning the world against
Soviet power and its ideology, the narrative states, the nationalists also did not
succeed, despite their brave examples in the conflicts that lingered. But the vicious vendetta of the Soviet authorities against the population of Western
Ukraine erased any positive aspects of the changes brought by Soviet rule. A
regime which brought industrialization, a cultural renaissance, the eradication
of illiteracy, and a strengthening of Ukrainian culture. But they all came at a
very high price. They were impeded by Sovietization, and the malevolence and

colonial behavior of the new rulers deeply alienated the population.[19] This explanation for disaffection in Western Ukraine, combined with the comments about the ideological and military failure of the OUN-UPA struggle, provides a much more realistic perusal of Ukraine in this pivotal period than do most of the new histories. Indeed, one could posit that the brutality of Soviet rule—or as it is sometimes described: the period of the second Soviet occupation—was more likely a conduit to later demands for independence than the insurgency of the UPA. What Temka and Tupchienka stress is that the mass arrests and deportations embraced a broad section of the population, much of which had no part in the military conflict. All too often the insurgency and popular disaffection for the Soviets are accepted as one and the same thing, with the UPA depicted as the manifestation of such discontent.

A book that appeared in the same year by V. D. Mironchuk and H. S. Ihoshkin devotes space to the subject of Ukrainian nationalism, and of what it comprised. The authors date the impact of nationalism in Western Ukraine to the 1920s, and analyze the role of the Ukrainian Military Organization (UVO). The OUN's formation under Konovalets in 1929 is discussed. The authors write that OUN ideology was based on "integral nationalism," which put feeling above reason, national interest above individualism, and was dedicated to achieving Ukrainian independence by all possible means. At this time totalitarian tendencies developed in many European countries. However, Ukrainian integral nationalism cannot be compared with Italian or German Fascism since it developed in an environment in which governmental structure was lacking. The OUN began with acts of terrorism and the movement was only strengthened by Polish acts of repression that followed the assassination of Interior Minister Bronislaw Pieracki in June 1934. However, the murder of Konovalets' in Rotterdam in May 1938 left the OUN leaderless on the eve of one of the most decisive periods in European history. The Nazi–Soviet Pact that followed in August 1939 and the secret Soviet–German Treaty of 28 September 1939 are described as cynical acts as the two powers were happy to carve up Polish territory. Nevertheless, the authors questionably add, workers in Western Ukraine were delighted to welcome the Red Army initially because they saw the unification of the region with the Soviet Union as protection against Germany.[20] The statement echoes official Soviet propaganda of the time, and most recent accounts posit that the welcome to the Soviet forces signaled relief at the end of Polish rule and/or support for the reunion of Ukrainian ethnic territories.

The penultimate book in this general survey appeared under the authorship of an editorial team led by M. O. Skrypnyk. Like Mironchuk and Ihoshkin, the team refuses to accept official Soviet excuses for signing the pact with Hitler. If this pact is to be properly evaluated, one author writes, it meant an end to attempts to create a bloc of anti-Fascist states. True, it may have been an attempt of the Soviet Union to avoid a war with Germany, but the protocols, which were kept secret for fifty years, place the USSR on the same moral level as Nazi Germany and can be qualified as an agreement between two aggressors. The OUN is introduced as one of the most influential forces in the territory of Western Ukraine with the goal of establishing an independent Ukraine. The author, however, makes a clear and partial delineation between the two branches that emerged in 1940. While both relied on Germany to accomplish their main goals and felt it inevitable that Germany would be victorious in its eastern conflicts—thus allowing for the creation of a Ukrainian state—the OUN-M offered unconditional support. The OUN-B, on the other hand, considered the alliance with Germany to be temporary, as it regarded Germany, along with the USSR, as enemies of Ukrainian independence. Repression of the OUN-B began after Germany demanded that the Act of Independence be annulled. In similar fashion, the UPA is described as a massive popular movement that included all Ukrainian partisan formations, including the OUN-M. The UPA took it upon itself to protect the local population from the anarchy imposed by the occupiers and from German conscription of foreign labor. An open armed struggle with the Fascists began in February 1943 and had such scope that the Germans were obliged to bring in 10,000 troops to try to crush the uprising. As whole areas came under UPA control, the Soviets also panicked and moved their own forces into the area, resulting in conflict between the UPA and Soviet Partisans. The Polish issue is limited in this book to a brief comment about associated casualties and deaths of peaceful residents because of their ethnicity.[21]

The Soviet–UPA conflict receives extensive attention. In general, the authors are favorable to the goals of the UPA and, like others, they condemn the barbarity of the Soviet regime in the early postwar years, singling out Khrushchev as the worst culprit. This book gives a good indication of the massive scale of operations, with the Soviet side deploying more than 200,000 soldiers and officers, and both sides using brutal methods, provocations, and indulging in bestial acts that fostered mutual enmity, hatred, and deep divisions in West Ukrainian society. The book, more than other sources, takes into consideration the historical background of the occupied region, with local popular customs, strong religious beliefs among the population, and a traditional local way of governing the area that was completely unlike that in the rest of Ukraine. These people, it is stressed, had nothing in common with the Soviet

way of life. As the Soviet front line moved westward, UPA's task was to prevent Soviet control over Western Ukraine, and it established Ukrainian government structures in a territory of over 150,000 square kilometers while conducting widespread armed actions in 1945. Many UPA leaders perished in the
conflict that followed, eventually forcing the UPA to change its tactics and
resort to underground guerrilla warfare, avoiding overt confrontation and rely-
ing on ambushes and sudden attacks. In consequence, "tens of thousands" of
military personnel and Soviet employees lost their lives, while the Soviet side
responded with mass repressions. After the death of Shukhevych in 1950, veterans of the resistance could not expect any reconciliation on the part of the
government. The authors condemn Soviet methods, which they say only made
the situation worse. In May 1945, while the whole world was celebrating the
victory over Fascism, Khrushchev was in L'viv meeting local *oblast* leaders
and the NKVD at a secret venue to discuss the coming crackdown, which
would see the arrests of villagers, OUN family members, representatives from
the intelligentsia, and Greek Catholic priests. Over 500,000 Western Ukrainians would be deported. The active operations ceased but, the authors emphasize, the authorities failed to stop passive opposition in this region.[22]

   We return finally to the textbook by Boyko, cited above with reference to
the Famine of 1932–33. In his comments on the Famine, Boyko essentially
takes a moderate line, outlining the various perspectives and then stating that
they need to be combined to provide the most accurate perspective. On the
OUN and the UPA he is less equivocal. They are regarded as the main organs
of liberation that were turned on both totalitarian state: Nazi Germany and
the Soviet Union. Boyko accepts that from July 1944, on the initiative of the
OUN-B, the movement evolved in a democratic direction. He acknowledges
that there was an agreement of non-aggression between a small part of the
UPA located in the hills on the German side of the front, and the Wehrmacht,
but adds that the step was compelled by the situation of the respective sides in
July 1944. OUN-UPA actively strived to take on the role of a "third force" in
the war in order to attain Ukrainian independence. The book contains a section on the "struggle of the OUN-UPA with the Soviet machine of repression," the title of which provides a good indication of the contents but does
not differ fundamentally from other recent sources in its general line. Boyko
then includes a section on Operation Vistula that is unusually detailed, and is
outlined under the heading "Mass repressions of the Soviet regime against the
population of Western Ukraine." Operation Vistula, he writes, was the conclu-
sive stage of the process of resettlement of the Ukrainian population from the
territory of Zakerzonnya (Lemkivshchyna, Posyannya, Pidlyashshya, and

Kholmshchyna), organized by the USSR and the temporary government of Poland. The author divides the process into three stages: the first, of "voluntary resettlement," from September 1944 to August 1945; the second, of "forced deportation," from September 1945 until August 1946; and the third, Operation Vistula, from April to July 1947. The first stage saw the removal of 81,000 residents, and the second 482,000. The third was a response to the assassination at the hands of the UPA of Polish Deputy Minister of Defense, K. Swierczewski. The "repressive action" was coordinated with the NKVD and the Czechoslovakian army, which blocked the southern and eastern borders of Poland. According to Polish figures, says Boyko, 140,500 people were deported, 3,800 of whom were interned in the Jaworzno camp, and over 650 were killed.[23]

From the books surveyed at all levels of the school and university system of Ukraine, it can be seen that the narrative of events critical to the history of Ukraine in the 20th century, which can be called decisive in the formation of a national history, has changed radically from the Soviet period. However, the change, though fundamental, appears to be still in process and is not simply a case of what was right in the past is now wrong. On the Famine, for example, there does not appear yet to be a very clear narrative and issues such as its origins and whether or not it constituted an act of genocide—a statement that would be accepted in Ukrainian circles of North America as no longer meriting discussion—have yet to be resolved. The consensus on the emergence of the OUN is that it reflected the political environment of the time and the harsh political conditions of interwar Poland. Most sources make a distinction between the pro-German line of the OUN-M, and the more tactical position of the OUN-B. Historians seem to go out of their way to try to show that the OUN-B formed an alliance with the German army for its own purposes. In doing so, they have a tendency to start the story with 30 June 1941 and to ignore the earlier and close cooperation between the OUN-B and certain elements in the Hitler government, particularly the German army and intelligence forces. The Nazi–Soviet Pact is treated in unanimous fashion as a cynical action on the part of the Stalin regime, though there is disagreement as to why one of its consequences—the warm welcome given to the Soviet invaders of Western Ukraine—occurred. The formation of the UPA is regarded as the beginning of a long liberation struggle. Some authors frown upon the attempt to eliminate the Poles of Volhynia, others see it as part of a mini-war in which both sides suffered. The leadership of the OUN-B in UPA's struggle is an accepted fact, as is the heroism of that struggle. The general histories place that contest in the context of the quest for an independent Ukraine that was successful in 1991. Despite the inconsistencies in the narrative, and despite some of the horrors and depravity carried out by both the Soviets and the UPA, it is possible to perceive the future emergence of a very clear narrative of liberation that would examine the evolution of modern Ukraine from a struggle that took place in a relatively small and alienated part of the modern country.

Reviewing the Issue of the OUN and the UPA

Even before the end of the Soviet period, the question of rehabilitation of the OUN and UPA had surfaced. The 28th Congress of the CC CPU in December 1990 condemned such attempts which, it claimed, were being promoted by the Rukh, the Ukrainian Republican Party, the Ukrainian National Party, and the Union of Ukrainian Youth. The Second Congress of Rukh had resolved to rehabilitate OUN-UPA. The Communist Congress, on the other hand, expressed its anger at attempts to organize celebrations and liturgies, and to rename streets and squares, and erect monuments to Bandera, Shukhevych, and other nationalist leaders. The Congress resolution acknowledged that among the insurgents were a lot of duped and intimidated, as well as unjustly repressed people. Nevertheless, it added, this is no reason to present followers of Bandera as part of a national-liberation movement or as strugglers against Stalinism, which the Congress condemned "resolutely," along with the violent anti-popular reprisals with which it was associated by this time. But such condemnation could not excuse the terror against the public that had been unleashed by the nationalists. People who had brought fear, grief, and death could not be reconstituted as national heroes. The Communists refused to permit the rehabilitation of OUN-UPA combatants who shed innocent blood, served the Fascists, and committed war crimes.[24] The issue soon became a talking point because of the rapid renaming of streets and buildings in Western Ukraine. Thus the Rivne city council decided to rename Lenin Square as Independence Square and Lenin Street as Cathedral Street in the summer of 1991. One author declared that this was not the first attempt to create anti-Communist hysteria to defame the cause of Lenin and that every action was geared to the revival of nationalism and the political rehabilitation of OUN-UPA. How could this policy be countered? This writer suggested that older people and war veterans should tell children "the truth about the past," young people should be advised to ask their elders about the bloody atrocities of nationalists and fascists, and all honest people should put their "houses in order" before "lies get the better of reason."[25]

On the other hand, in Western Ukraine, the sentiments were quite different. Thus Mykola Porovs'kyi, a parliamentary deputy from Rivne *oblast*, draws
attention to the problem of rehabilitating participants in armed resistance
against German Fascism who fought in UPA units. That the insurgents attacked the Germans is indisputable, he claims, and he suggests that UPA
members that cannot be accused of fighting against the Soviet army should be
rehabilitated.[26] Another author writes that it is impossible to root out from the
memory of Western Ukrainians their slain parents, brothers, and sisters. He
calls for reconciliation and understanding of such sentiments. One way to do
this, in his view, would be to erect a monument to all Ukrainians who perished in different historical periods, which could be a monument "of national
reconciliation."[27] Ukraine's main literary weekly informed its readers in early
1992 about the creation of an All-Ukrainian Brotherhood of former UPA soldiers. Its first assembly was held in Ivano-Frankivs'k, and the newspaper reis-
sued its appeal to young people, which purported to explain the past misinter-
pretations of the UPA as a hostile force in Ukraine.[28] In the spring of the same
year, an editorial in this newspaper states that "we" have learned the truth
about many things: about the so-called reunion with Russia, the Central Rada
of 1917–18, the wars that followed the revolution, the affair of the Union for
the Liberation of Ukraine, and the enforced Famine of 1932–33. Now, says
the writer, it is time to study the emotional pages in the history of the liberation phenomenon: OUN-UPA. October 1992 would mark the 50th anniversary of the founding of UPA, so the newspaper planned to acquaint its readers
with many names and events connected with the UPA struggle "against the
enslavers of Ukraine." It began by publishing writings of one of the best-
known publicists of the Diaspora, R. Rakhmannyi, originally issued as a brochure in London in 1984.[29] The excerpts duly appeared in nine issues of the
newspaper between 7 May and 16 July 1992.

The anniversary of the official creation of the UPA was the occasion for a
speech by the Ukrainian Minister of Culture, Larysa Khorolets', which was
published in *Literaturna Ukraina*. She begins by declaring that at the next
stage of the strengthening of Ukrainian statehood "we bow our heads" to
those upon whom Ukraine called for its defense at a time of great turmoil. She
evokes images of past heroes, such as Ivan Mazepa, Taras Shevchenko, and
the Sich Sharpshooters, and then adds that on the eve of the first anniversary
of the declaration of Ukrainian independence everything that is related to the
history of the Ukrainian Insurgent Army returns to our official narrative of
history. Under the new "democratic conditions," the attitude to UPA's role in
the Second World War is changing. Historians have not yet shed light on all

aspects of this heroic formation, but already Ukrainians could be confident that with the assistance of foreign historians, a revised, unbiased version of UPA history can be written. This would be undertaken in the name of historical justice, and it would not try to diminish the sacrifices of those Ukrainians who fought against the Germans in the Red Army. People should not be upset with those who do not recognize the UPA because for a long time "an alien spirit" was directing the way that people think, Khorolets' said. After the Second World War, insurgents were left alone to fight the mightiest army in the world. Today people must express their debt to the victims of this fratricidal war, during which the Ukrainian nation lost its most active stratum. The task therefore is to recognize every single person who fought for Ukraine, and Khorolets' took the opportunity to single out the role of women in the UPA as nurses, messengers, cooks, and sometimes even combatants. These people sacrificed love and family lives for the struggle to create a Ukrainian state. She then makes reference to the dead mothers of the graying old men who were listening to her speech, mothers that could not stop the "hate machine" created by the leaders in Moscow and Berlin that operated on the blood of Ukrainian people. Ukrainians ended up fighting on both sides, but all should be regarded as martyrs, and as a mother, she says, she did not know who possessed the moral right to judge such people.[30]

Khorolets' passionate speech seemed to herald a new era in the evaluation of Ukraine's recent past: the government's recognition of the place of the UPA as a heroic army dedicated to Ukrainian independence. Changes, however, did not come as rapidly as anticipated, even with allies in high places such as the Minister of Culture. Yurii Shapoval recalls that in August 1992 in Kyiv there was a scientific conference to commemorate the 50th anniversary of the UPA. The speeches of veterans and scholars continued for two days and Shapoval recognized clearly how difficult it was to deal with the history of the insurgents—a complex scientific and political problem for post-Communist society. In reality, people who declare their profession to be a fighter for nationalism and are labeled as traitors and fascists cannot be declared national heroes overnight. He also recognizes that it would be dangerous to idealize the history of the UPA as some historians have started to do. What is required is understanding and elucidation of those facts that have been consciously suppressed. This would provide an opportunity for an objective appraisal of the history of the UPA.[31] Meanwhile at the regional level, progress seemed to be discernible. In 1995, for example, the L'viv *oblast* government recognized the UPA as a combatant in the Second World War and participant in the national liberation movement as freedom fighters for Ukraine. Nevertheless, the deputies of the L'viv government considered that after 11 years of independence, members of the UPA were still outcasts in society. Why was this? One author set out to explain the reasons through the concept of the "national idea," i.e., nationalists in Ukraine make up a minority of the population. Almost 70% of ethnic Ukrainians, he writes, have a very low level of ethnic consciousness and on the level of ideas they are thoroughly Russified. They do not understand why it is necessary to have an independent Ukraine, nor do they feel impelled to protect Ukrainian statehood. For the most part they identify themselves not with Ukraine and Ukrainian culture, but with the Soviet Union and a culture that is Russian or Soviet.[32]

How do such people relate to the OUN and UPA? The author writes that they oppose the rehabilitation of these organizations because allegedly Ukrainian nationalists were in the service of the Nazis; they killed innocent civilians; and they attacked Soviet army units. He will have none of it. The OUN, he writes, was always independent of the Germans other than a mild form of collaboration that occurred until the summer of 1941, which was dictated by tactical requirements. The UPA fought the Germans. He also refutes the charge that the UPA killed innocent civilians, which he dismisses as Communist propaganda directed at "ignorant" people in Central, Southern, and Eastern Ukraine. The best retort to such fabrications, he writes in a strained form of logic, is that the UPA is least liked in those areas where there was no nationalist insurgency. As for the third charge, he has less concern about it other than to note that UPA's opposition to Soviet rule is the main reason why it has not been rehabilitated. Yet the Soviet army, and today's Soviet veterans, were not protecting Ukraine but rather were fighting for its destruction and the success of Russian colonial policies and NKVD terror.[33] Remarkable in this narrative is the casual dismissal of the views of a majority of Ukrainians as a result purely of ignorance (and implicitly stupidity) and Russian influences. In turn, the perspectives of a part of the Western Ukrainian population are used as representative of what all of Ukraine should be thinking. One view is wrong; the other is correct. Those who think in a mistaken way are either Russified or "Little Russians." This outlook matches exactly that of Viktor Koval' who writes that the UPA saved Western Ukraine from a disastrous calamity, and that the UPA has done the most for the national honor of Ukraine, which it rescued from captivity. Therefore wherever Ukrainians live they will remember "the proud name of UPA."[34]

In the 1990s, writers often differed in their assessment of the impact of the campaign to restore the memory of the OUN and the UPA in Ukraine. Even though the Ukrainian government had established a commission to investigate the question, profound cleavages remained in Ukrainian society. One Rukh activist and former UPA member, who was depicted as living in poverty not far from Luts'k, commented in 1998 that the attainment of a Ukrainian state has not affected the issue substantially. People go "where the wind blows" and although Ukraine has its own army; it does not hold prayers, as in UPA. He recalls that among the Communists in the Soviet period there were many good people, because in their hearts they had remained Ukrainians. He calls for forgiveness and reconciliation between the UPA and Soviet Partisans, or Red Army soldiers. Yet he cannot comprehend why former NKVD members whose task it was to destroy insurgents should be living well and receiving pensions today, whereas those who conceivably are about to be rehabilitated "by history and the state" receive nothing.[35] Poliszczuk, on the other hand, perceives the physical and spiritual transfer of UPA ideology to Ukraine, along with a "rebirth of OUN fascist ideology." He notes that the Rukh leader Ivan Drach, described as a democrat, contributed R1,000 for the construction of a monument commemorating the UPA in Rivne, and describes the physical arrival in Ukraine of emissaries of the OUN abroad, such as Taras Hunczak, former editor-in-chief of the journal *Suchasnist'*, created by Mykola Lebed. A nationwide conference of Ukrainian nationalists occurred in 1992, and the OUN newspaper, *Ukrains'ke slovo*, had relocated from Paris to Kyiv.[36]

OUN-UPA in 21st Century Ukraine

Entering the 21st century it might have been feasible for historical narratives to have advanced beyond the Soviet/nationalist perspectives or that history could be divorced from politics and the impact of political thinking and political views on past events. Yet the divisions of Ukraine in terms of their regional perceptions of the past have remained. There are also contrasting opinions as to how the country should proceed in reassessing the past. Kul'chyts'kyi, for example, has called for an objective and thorough examination, applauding the establishment of the government commission, and arguing that no black-and-white vision should be acceptable in evaluating the matter.[37] Writing in *Za vil'nu Ukrainu*, Iziaslav Kokodnyak, on the other hand, believes that the population of Ukraine has to be rendered nationally conscious, and that the Ukrainian state must become national in content, not just in name. He advocates the dissemination of "nationalist myths" that would supplant Soviet imperialist myths concerning UPA crimes against their own people. The nationalist myths would permit the psychological unification of

Western and Eastern Ukraine. In order to achieve such harmony, organizations of the nationalist variety must "impose their will" on the organs of state and the mass media, making use of the ample evidence of UPA's two-front war during the Second World War. The figure of Roman Shukhevych, in his view, would be the ideal instrument for the construction of a nationalist myth.[38] This idea is quite unusual in that the author is not seeking accuracy or "historical truth," the terms that usually enter the rhetoric, but the adoption of new propaganda and myths.

Another writer who joined the OUN in 1931 calls on the Ukrainian Supreme Soviet to recognize the OUN and UPA as combatants in the Second World War, and to grant participants the honorary rank of officer in the current Ukrainian army corresponding to the rank of company commander in the UPA. UPA veterans should receive pensions in the region of Hr 1,000 (approximately US$200) per month, and those in need should be provided with an apartment and the same benefits enjoyed by Soviet war veterans. He proposes that such a law covering all these points should be adopted before 14 October (2000), and on that day—the anniversary of the official founding of the UPA—the decorations to former soldiers should be distributed at a ceremony.[39] Roman Serbyn, a Diaspora historian, continues this same line of thought, but feels that the creation of a commission to study the UPA actually casts suspicion on the organization. He says that no special investigation is needed because the role of the UPA is well-known, and that there is a double standard in operation since no commission has been established to study the activities of the Red Army and Soviet Partisans. Like most supporters of the UPA, he describes it as the only organization that fought both Nazi Germany and Soviet power. Ukraine today, he writes, is divided into three camps: adherents of the UPA; opponents of the UPA; and "pragmatists" who are willing to recognize only those insurgents who fought against the Germans. In the latter category is to be found the head of the Union of Veterans, Ivan Gerasimov, a Russian who has lived in Ukraine since the 1940s and is nostalgic for Soviet times, as is evident from the pictures of Stalin and Soviet military veterans hanging in the residence of the Union.[40]

Serbyn then elaborates on his comments with reference to modern-day Ukraine. Gerasimov was the editor of a *Book of Memory*, and in the preface he has written that "OUN and its armed formations developed and fought as mercenaries of Fascist Germany against the countries of the anti-Hitler coalition, and established themselves as Fascist collaborators." According to Serbyn, President L. D. Kuchma was a supporter of such views. The key problem here was that Kuchma had linked Ukrainian statehood directly to the victory of the Red Army, since this victory signified a return to Ukraine of a Communist regime that had committed crimes against the Ukrainian people. Another trend in Ukraine is typified by Academician Petro Tron'ko, a former Red Army officer who took part in the removal of the Germans from Ukraine. Tron'ko seeks a compromise, namely granting the status of "veterans" to those insurgents who confined their activities to fighting against Fascism. To Serbyn such a solution, despite its appeal to academics and government officials, is unacceptable because it is unethical. Instead he calls for unity and the recognition of UPA. Moreover, he goes further. Those Ukrainians who continue to object to the recognition of UPA veterans "of all the sons and daughters of the Ukrainian people"—placed by fate on opposite sides of the fronts in the Second World War—must bear the huge burden of responsibility "before their own conscience and before history." He wonders whether such people will find the power to cast aside someone else's burden and join in celebrating the 10th anniversary of the freedom for which they fought.[41] This appeal, published in Ukraine from an academic who is a leading member of the Canadian Ukrainian community, was one of the strongest to date, but it also followed the dictum that there is a single, correct version of the past that all right-thinking Ukrainians need to adopt. Yet it would be unusual if the history of any organization that operated on the fringes of the Second World War, and for the most part was confined geographically to one corner of Ukraine, could really fall into the category of being well-known in terms of its history.

From a different perspective, some people were irked by the way historians who wrote in the Soviet period appeared willing to change their opinions. On the pages of *The Day Digest*, for example, Ivan Khmil devotes his attention to Stanislav Kul'chyts'kyi, an historian he incorporates into the title of his outburst "Hucksterish circumlocutions of the OUN-UPA apologists." In order to undermine Kul'chyts'kyi he begins by attacking his credentials, noting that his candidate's dissertation was in the field of economics, and that one of his main research papers from the past was entitled "The economic development of Soviet Ukraine." But since Ukraine became independent, writes Khmil, Kul'chyts'kyi has changed with the political wind and taken positions that are antithetical to what he wrote in the Soviet period. Khmil writes that the new interpretations of OUN-UPA are "one-sided." However, attention should be paid in his view to the study of the OUN by A. Kentii, in which he writes that the Ukrainian nationalist movement was created from political groups that earlier had been closely associated with Germany and its allies. Kentii is also cited for his comment that OUN-UPA was always careful not to direct its attacks against German military installations.[42] The same debate found its way into current politics. On 28 March 2002, a live television debate was held on Kyiv's 1+1 station between Communist leader Petro Symonenko and Premier Anatolii Kinakh. During the discussion, Symonenko made reference to the alleged preparation of a presidential decree to rehabilitate the UPA and to the recent decision by the Ivano-Frankivs'k city council to declare the veterans of the SS Division Halychyna "freedom fighters" and accused the Ukrainian government of promoting Fascism. Kinakh responded that the time for such enmity had passed and that only through harmony and mutual comprehension would it be possible for the Ukrainian state to make progress. "A grave is not the place for rallies, it is a place for prayer," he concluded.[43]

The controversial article by Kost' Bondarenko, which has been cited earlier, appeared in the Ukrainian media in the spring of 2002. He focuses initially on the confusion around the various Second World War organizations, commenting that the average citizen was unable to differentiate between the ideas of the OUN, the Halychyna Division, the UPA, *Nachtigal* or *Roland*. Consequently parliamentary deputies try to rehabilitate OUN-UPA, even though these organizations are different and the approach to them cannot be identical. In his view the OUN could be rehabilitated without delay and its contributions to the struggle for independence recognized. Also, by focusing on these two organizations exclusively, the contributions of many others tend to be overlooked among those resistance movements that fought both the Nazis and the Red Army. What is essential in Bondarenko's view is that national history be viewed from the perspective of citizens of Ukraine, rather than people who live in Russia, Poland, or the United States. Also, he maintains, this history should be judged based on "Ukraine's interests, independence, and future." This history has to be founded on archival documents as opposed to memoirs or histories of the Communist Party. The collaboration of nations that had attained statehood should be contrasted with that of nations that had not reached this stage, and the differences between the SS Division, the UPA, and the OUN should be acknowledged to avoid mistakes. Having written such statements, Bondarenko then appears to reverse his views by appending that history should be left to the historians and politics to the politicians.[44] Presumably, then, the historians must keep in mind the national interests of Ukraine, which might also be taken to mean that only Ukrainians or residents of Ukraine could make a meaningful contribution to Ukrainian history.[45]

Since the mid-1990s the Ukrainian government especially has been deeply involved with changing political interpretations of the Second World War and the formation of a new historical narrative applicable to Ukraine. On 10 July

2002, five years after the creation of the State Commission (the task force was under the leadership of Kul'chyts'kyi) for the study of the OUN and UPA by President L. D. Kuchma, it approved a draft law "On the restoration of historical justice toward the fighters for Ukraine's freedom and independence." The Commission's statement was much criticized by members of left-wing political groups, but others defended its position. In general, the period since 2001 has seen the creation of a new narrative that rejects completely the former Soviet version of the war and accepts much, if not all, of the narrative that perceives the OUN and UPA as heroes and freedom fighters. What is notable is that the history produced, as in the past, is based largely on black and white perceptions. In other words, the past is being made to conform to the political needs of the present and the result is a history that, in some respects, is no more objective than it was in the Soviet period, mainly because crimes or mistakes are unacceptable for one's own side.

Thus shortly after the draft law was issued, several articles appeared in the media supporting its main goals in the strongest manner, directing attacks against "Communist myths" about the OUN and UPA. The language employed by the writers often militates against an objective appraisal. For example, Oleh Hryniv, having denounced the "semantic nonsense" of the term OUN-UPA, turns to the issue of war crimes, and says that the biggest question is who is defining the crime, and on this issue he sees a direct lexical link between past Soviet propaganda and current propaganda emanating from the Russian Federation. Both refer to UPA insurgents and Chechen separatists as "bandits." Does this signify, he asks, that anyone opposing Russian domination is a bandit? Even Russian intellectuals think in this way, he feels, and Vladimir Putin called "our great Hetman Mazepa" a villain. Like others, Hryniv blames the population outside Galicia for its lack of enlightenment. He declares that the history of the OUN and UPA should be studied in historical context. The OUN appeared as a reaction to the failure to attain a Ukrainian state in 1918–21. Similar movements appeared elsewhere in a European continent disillusioned with democracy. The UPA was not a German ally, he continues, but an instrument to protect the Ukrainian population from the Germans and Poles who collaborated against Ukrainians, and that is why the UPA attacked Poles in Volhynia. Two final points made by Hryniv are that it should be accepted that Moscow occupied Ukraine after the war, as is demonstrated by the famine that occurred in 1946–47 (the logic of this statement is unclear) and the events of the 1940s–50s were not a civil war, as is often written, but a war between a people and a foreign occupier that made use of Eastern Ukrainians to subdue their compatriots.[46]

A similar tone is adopted in an article by Anatolii Fomenko, who states at the outset that his intention is to comply with the goal of the State Commission and inform the public about the activities of the UPA. He does so by citing the work of one of its main apologists, Volodymyr Kosyk. Fomenko agrees that a majority of Galicians might have welcomed the Red Army in September 1939, but states that their attitude changed after the start of Soviet deportations and reprisals. The NKVD murder of political prisoners in June 1941 is linked directly to what is described as a brief period of nationalist collaboration with the Germans. The nationalists rejected such a program of action immediately once the Germans had refused to countenance an independent Ukraine and arrested OUN-B leaders. The OUN, writes Fomenko, and also following Kosyk, did not collaborate. He cites several German documents that describe the OUN-B as the most dangerous of the anti-German units. He also quotes an OUN document that threatens members with the death penalty for collaborating with the Germans. In Fomenko's view this is sufficient evidence that the OUN never collaborated. Concerning the NKVD-UPA conflict, he takes issue with accusations that the UPA killed civilians. Though some murders were committed, he says, the NKVD killed more people, and often did this under cover and dressed as UPA insurgents. Besides, the UPA fought for freedom and the interests of the Ukrainian people. He emphasizes that it was a multi-ethnic organization comprised of many different nationalities. But in Ukraine, he says, an abnormal situation has existed for 11 years in which those who destroyed the Ukrainian people have enjoyed the status of war veterans and receive benefits, while the "freedom fighters" are deprived of this same status. He concludes with an appeal for unity on the basis of the recognition of UPA.[47]

While the Working Commission was fulfilling its task, the Ivan Franko Drohobych State Pedagogical University held its 6th International Scientific Conference entitled "The National-Liberation Movement in the West Ukrainian Lands in the 1920s–1950s." It was organized by the history faculty of the Drohobych University and L'viv National University, with the participation of Drohobych city council, and invited speakers from Ukraine and Poland. In a public statement about the event, the local political leaders outlined the role of the UPA in the "struggle of Ukrainians for freedom and their own state" and expressed the wish that "the conference will restore historical reality"! By this phrase they signified the recognition of UPA combatants as official participants in the Second World War. Among the papers presented, one by M. S. Savchyn, Dean of the Faculty of History, outlined the essence and the content of the "national revolution of the OUN" in the 1930s, and showed how it developed and changed in the 1940s from "elements of totalitarianism" to democracy. K. H. Kondratyuk, head of the department of the contemporary history of Ukraine at L'viv National University, discussed how the UPA was formed, and the various forms of its struggle against the German occupiers in Volhynia, Polissya, and Galicia. Two other speakers were Volodymyr Serhiichuk (Kyiv) who examined national formations in the composition of UPA, and S. I. Makarchuk (L'viv) who spoke on "Soviet methods of struggle with the OUN and UPA," based on materials from Drohobych and L'viv regions in 1944–45.[48] In this same month of October 2002, *Den'* featured an interview with Yurii Shukhevych, son of the UPA leader, Roman Shukhevych, who was asked why nothing had been done to date to recognize the UPA officially. Shukhevych responded that the attitude toward the UPA had developed over several decades, with a hostile attitude toward everything linked to the struggle for national liberation. The truth would be known within one or two decades, he added, "It must be and it shall be."[49] Implicitly therefore there is a correct version of these events that must be elaborated, and the duty of historians is less to ascertain information than to propagate the new version.

Another conference in October 2002 took place in the village that was the birthplace of Stepan Bandera, Staryi Uhryniv, in Kalush region, Ivano-Frankivs'k *oblast* under the title "UPA as a Phenomenon of National History." It was organized by the Subcarpathian University and the Institute of Ukrainian History, National Academy of Sciences of Ukraine and attended by scholars from Kyiv, Ivano-Frankivs'k, Kryvyi Rih, Ternopil', and Chernihiv, as well as by UPA veterans. Conference participants were greeted by the president of the Ivano-Frankivs'k branch of the Brotherhood of UPA soldiers, Fedir Volodymyrs'kyi, who expressed his certainty that the gathering would contribute to the search for "historical truth about the liberation struggle of the Ukrainian people in the 1930s–1950s and the Ukrainian Insurgent Army." Eight papers were presented and covered such topics as the problems of national history in the 20th century, methodological approaches to the study of the Ukrainian national movement from the 1930s to the 1950s, contemporary national historiography of UPA, and the various stages of the struggle between the "Soviet totalitarian regime" and the insurgents in the postwar period. As the conference ended, participants visited the Stepan Bandera Museum in the village and listened to a talk by Taras Fedoriv, head of the village administration, about the main episodes in the life and career of Bandera. Next the famous local singer Mykhailo Kryven' performed a number of UPA songs that were "received emotionally by the audience." It can probably be assumed therefore that the conference's final recommendations—for intensification of research

directed at "an unbiased portrayal of UPA"—would be somewhat more difficult to attain given the setting and conditions in which this gathering was
held.[50]

In an article on the 61st anniversary of the creation of UPA, Roman Zahoruiko, an UPA veteran, places this event in the context of an age-old Ukrainian struggle against "foreign conquerors-enslavers" of Ukraine, which included
Poles, Romanians, Magyars, Germans, Slovaks, and Russians. The struggle of
the UPA was the most intense of all because of the way it had united the
Ukrainian people. He refers to the insurgency as "the awakening of the spirit
of the nation." The UPA was a phenomenal army made up of "enthusiastic
patriots and idealistic fanatics." It was an army without a state and without a
uniform, and no salary was required for serving in it. As an army, it may have
left something to be desired, but its shortcomings were compensated for by
qualities such as dedication, patriotism, and the commitment of its members.
Sometimes, in his view, literature about the UPA is too romantic: the reality
was a permanent lack of sleep, constant hunger, and always the danger of the
enemy. There was also constant uncertainty concerning who was a friend and
who was an enemy. Insurgents were never sure whether or not someone
would betray them to the NKVD for a financial reward. The heavy casualties
eventually convinced the UPA leadership that the struggle was lost, but
Ukraine was an "El Dorado or Klondike" for which foreign conquerors—very
similar in outlook even though they were opposed to each other—were fighting. The UPA was the "third force" that battled only for freedom and the independence of Ukraine on its native land. He concludes by denouncing the
Ukrainian state that has failed to recognize its heroes: the world has recognized OUN and UPA insurgents as heroes, but the state, like a stepmother,
which acquired independence thanks to the blood shed by these people, does
not.[51]

Zahoruiko's hyperbole, particularly regarding "world recognition" is more
than matched by an article by Yevhen Sverstyuk that appeared in late 2003.
The author analyzes social processes in contemporary Ukraine in the context
of the debates over the status of UPA. The question of who supports recognition and who is opposed, he writes, defines who is who today. Looking into
this historical mirror, everyone can see their own reflection. However, the
whole issue is misguided and senseless, because the phenomenon of the UPA
towers over the debate. The UPA is the "tributary of the river of the Ukrainian
people that flows from primordial foundations. This river was raging during
the times of the Cossacks, and although its flow was at times impeded, it was
always a river of the independence struggle." He cites heroes such as Myroslav

Symchych, whose entire life was a struggle, and who even changed the face of the Gulag, transforming it into a hotbed of resistance to both Stalinism and the criminals in the camps. That, for Sverstyuk, is UPA. But what of those who do not wish to recognize or oppose it? The failure of the Ukrainian government to recognize the UPA is a symptom of the lack of identity of the country's new rulers. They are "spiritually alien and nationally empty post-Communists," whose lives are distant from those of nationally conscious Ukrainians. The achievement of independence, in Sverstyuk's view, was a result of UPA's struggle. He recalls his own career and interrogations during his arrest, and how he would be comforted by remembering the OUN Decalogue while in prison. The idealism of the Ukrainian dissidents of the 1960s, he writes, was motivated by UPA's battles and inherited from the insurgents. It was an honest struggle that could not be controlled by Communist propaganda and repression. People must remember the heroes and victims of the liberation struggle, the article concludes.[52]

Idealizing the UPA in this way served as a contrast to the former Soviet writing that demonized the insurgents, though it may have proved equally unhelpful in the quest for a dispassionate assessment of this organization. *Den'* newspaper focused on this negative image in an article by Serhiy Stepanyshyn, issued to commemorate the 60th anniversary of the conference of captive nations in Eastern Europe and Asia. Stepanyshyn considers that this type of propaganda served to separate people from their historical roots and to consolidate hostile regimes in power. Regarding UPA, he remarks that Bolshevik propaganda never used the correct acronym in the official media but always replaced it with phrases that used the name Bandera, which equated insurgents with an image of a murderer or bandit; or a follower of the Nazis; or a "bourgeois-nationalist," etc. The falsehoods about the UPA and who it served were easily propagated in the Soviet Union and even in Ukraine, since people were completely unaware of the situation in Western Ukraine. To be a follower of Bandera—or Banderite— was the worst designation possible, and was adopted by people in Russia and Eastern Ukraine as a general term to depict Western Ukrainians. To some extent such stereotyping could be advantageous, and Stepanyshyn comments how as a Western Ukrainian being conscripted into the Soviet army, he was treated with some respect and not subjected to the bullying that was the common practice. Yet apprehension about Banderites is still enough to intimidate people and make it difficult for them to accept that insurgents of the UPA deserve the same respect as that accrued to any Second World War veteran. They were not brutes, but rather "heroes who sacrificed their lives for the liberation of their native land from the aggressors."[53]

At the end of the Kuchma era, the issue of full recognition of the OUN and UPA as participants in and veterans of the Second World War had not been resolved. As the narratives illustrate, those supporting such recognition were becoming more insistent in their demands, and the portrayals were linked consistently to a centuries-long struggle for independence on the part of the Ukrainian people. Conversely, those who did not support recognition and those in other parts of Ukraine generally were often branded as ignorant or dupes of Soviet propaganda, and as people who did not know their own history. Aside from some qualified remarks—such as the warning not to romanticize the UPA by the former insurgent—the depiction generally to this point was idealistic and always employed a national, rather than regional background. That comment applies not only to UPA, but also to accounts of the interwar period and the rise of the OUN, the earlier years of the war, and the postwar period. Historical memory takes on a singular and narrow image of selfless warriors fighting only for their native land and independence. In 2004, following the Orange Revolution, the Kuchma regime was replaced by a presidency, won over the course of a frenzied election campaign (eventually entailing three rounds of voting) by the leader of the opposition, Viktor Yushchenko, as noted above. The new government, which began with a remarkable degree of unity and international acceptance of change in Ukraine—particularly a move away from the Russian orbit and toward Europe and Euro-Atlantic structures—immediately faced the question of recognition of the national insurgents. The first summer of the Yushchenko government also marked the 60th anniversary of the Soviet victory in the Second World War. Thus we will examine in turn the narratives around this event and then analyze the attitude of the post-Kuchma government toward the question of recognition and how the issue stands today in contemporary Ukaine.

The Great Patriotic War Commemorations

The issue of the commemoration of the Great Patriotic War is closely linked to the campaign to rewrite the history of what is termed "the national liberation movement" in support of an independent Ukraine during this period. The term "Great Patriotic War" was applied particularly in the Brezhnev period when 9 May became a national holiday in the Soviet Union that, along with 7 November, featured as one of the two most important events in the formation (and legitimization) of the Soviet Union. The phrase has at times perplexed Ukrainian historians, who have used both the German–Soviet War and the Great Patriotic War—and sometimes both together—in the titles of their books and articles. The Great Patriotic War could be portrayed as a phrase that served to unify the Soviet state and to provide a perception that all nations were fighting together to defeat the enemy. By the same token, the arrival of the Red Army and its occupation of the prewar Soviet territories was always depicted as an act of liberation. However, in Western Ukraine the perception was always different, and just as in the Baltic States, the return of the Red Army could be described as another period of occupation: the replacement of one dictator with another, and a form of rule that was equally harsh, if indeed not harsher than that of the Germans. In 2006, in Kyiv, the anniversary witnessed Red Army and UPA veterans—naturally well past their prime—coming to blows in the streets. Though most of the narratives that follow address the need to change the concept of a "patriotic war" to the German–Soviet War, and to reassess what it meant for Ukrainians and residents of Ukraine, it is fair to say at the outset that the question is far from resolved. For some Ukrainians, particularly in the eastern and southern regions, the war remains almost a sacred event. For others, it is an embarrassment, like the grotesque maternal figure with shield and sword that towers over the city of Kyiv, and which still symbolizes a war that was won with the aid of Mother Russia.

In June 1993, Professor Stepan Zlupko raised the question of what the war meant to the Ukrainian people and whether it is fair to term it the Great Patriotic War. For Ukraine, in his view, the term is false. There were millions of deaths, but it was not patriotic because it was not fought in the interests of the Ukrainian people, who performed the role of cannon fodder for the Red Army. Ukrainians in Ukraine, he writes, had no rights before, during, or after the war. True, there was a Ukrainian SSR, but this was a token state and the republican government could not even construct a cinema without the permission of Moscow. According to Zlupko, the Bolsheviks occupied Ukraine with some help from Ukrainian traitors, and began anti-human experiments, which reached an apogee with the "Holocaust" of 1932–33 and the mass destruction of the Ukrainian intelligentsia, along with the vicious reprisals in Western Ukraine. The Soviet Union therefore was not a motherland for Ukrainians, and if it was not a motherland, how is it possible to term the war "patriotic"? He explains the fact that many Ukrainians joined the Red Army by saying that they were deceived. In fighting in the Red Army, they were dying for an alien cause, and many of them had little choice in the matter because they were conscripted by force.[54] The element of compulsion is also brought up by a Western Ukrainian who fought in the Soviet army, Mykhailo

Lytvynchuk. If anything, he is even more forthright than Zlupko. The victory that the Russians are preparing to celebrate, he writes in April 1995 on the eve of the 50th anniversary, was for Ukrainians a repeated enslavement by "the Moscow-Bolshevik hordes." Military boards drafted people aged 17–65 years without concern for their health. He makes reference to Soviet estimates that some 6 million Ukrainians fought in the Red Army and says these sources are silent about the fact that half of them were killed. Soldiers from Western Ukraine who were sent to the front always had to operate in the most dangerous areas, and under the guns of the Soviet security forces. After scouting missions only two to three soldiers returned alive and many older or sick soldiers were executed for desertion for being unable to keep up during long marches.[55]

Concerning his own role in the Red Army, Lytvynchuk comments that the UPA could not accommodate everyone because of the strain on material resources. On the other hand, those who fought in the Red Army did fight for Ukraine against the mortal enemy: Nazism. Lytvynchuk promotes national unity in Ukraine on the 50th anniversary by proclaiming all Ukrainians who fought in the war fighters for Ukraine, regardless of whether they were Soviet soldiers, UPA insurgents, or members of the SS Division Halychyna.[56] Another article that appeared in the same venue nine days later continued the theme under the title "USSR is not a motherland for Ukrainians; hence the Second World War is not the Great Patriotic War for us." The war, writes Yaroslav Tymchyshyn, was unleashed by Nazi Germany with the active assistance of the Soviet Union, an even bloodier regime. These two "anti-human" regimes tried to expand their spheres of influence, capturing new territories and sacrificing entire peoples in their ambitious quests. Liberation from Nazi Germany signified further enslavement for Ukraine by the Bolsheviks. Tymchyshyn's claim that "our motherland is Ukraine" and not the "Moscow Empire" is an attempt to monopolize Ukrainian thinking, since the statement would not be universally accepted in Ukraine. To some extent he recognizes this fact in his statement that unfortunately, many functionaries and scholars are still tied to the tenets of Moscow propaganda and the colonial policy of the "criminal" Communist Party. Obsequiousness is their common characteristic, which is why they cannot stand on their feet proudly and say the words of freedom. Ukrainians have traitors in their midst, in his view, and to accept the USSR as a motherland is to assault the foundation on which the act of independence of Ukraine was based. Victory over German Fascism derived first and foremost from the OUN-UPA and the armed underground that fought both the Germans and the Bolsheviks. The latter brought a holocaust of bloody reprisals and the deportation to Siberia of "tens of millions" of Ukrainians.[57] Tymchyshyn's outburst hardly contributed to a quest for unity among Second World War veterans; rather it sought to divide Ukrainians into those who served in OUN-UPA and the remainder of the population, which included "fifth-column Communists and Socialists" who wished to turn Ukraine into a Moscow colony yet again.

A somewhat more rational analysis is provided by I. Antsyshkin on the 54th anniversary of the end of the war. He attempts to elucidate what holiday is being celebrated in Ukraine. He points out the differences between Ukraine and the West: in the West, people celebrate the end of war whereas in Ukraine, the celebration is of a victory in a Great Patriotic War. Was it great and was it patriotic, he asks, answering his own question that the status of "great" is not really in doubt if measured by the number of victims, the amount of human grief, and the heroism of all the peoples of the USSR, by the shocking errors of the Soviet leadership, and the joy of those who returned home. Yet for Antsyshkin the status of "patriotic" has to be measured by the extent of popular support. The Second World War in the Soviet Union cannot be considered patriotic because nearly one million Soviet citizens served in the *Wehrmacht* police forces. Almost 20 national groups in the USSR were declared to be traitors and deported. Millions of Soviet citizens refused to return home from the Western zones of occupation. Antsyshkin then repeats the familiar dictum of the nationalist perspective, namely that for the Ukrainian people after the bloody Civil War, the Famine of the 1930s, and the deportations of 1939, the war could not be patriotic. The second part of Antsyshkin's article draws attention to the Soviet tendency to diminish the importance of battles fought by the Western allies and their assistance to the USSR. From the Soviet version it seems that the Germans did not fight in the West. He attributes this way of writing to an inferiority complex of the Soviet wartime leadership and their successors. He also notes that the West and the former Soviet republics celebrate on different days, 8 May and 9 May respectively, commenting that the Germans actually capitulated on 8 May to the American General Beddell Smith. However, the USSR celebrated the following day, the date that German capitulation was ratified in Moscow. Today, he concludes, 9 May is the holiday when one can easily renounce the notion of an independent Ukraine and fail to recognize UPA veterans, and instead of being a day of remembrance, it has become a day of hatred.[58]

In 2003, Ukrainian film director Serhii Bukovs'kyi produced a film called "Viina: Ukrains'kyi rakhunok," which represented a fairly balanced account of Ukraine during the Second World War. The film provoked a lengthy critique in the pages of *Ukraina moloda* by Roman Zahoruiko, the former UPA insurgent cited above, who chided Bukovs'kyi for a failure to capture what was termed the "in-depth Ukrainian essence" of the war and how it related to Ukraine and Ukrainians, and specifically why the war yet again separated Ukrainians into different and often hostile groups, as well as the morally correct stand of each group. Zahoruiko considers that only national historians can provide an accurate picture of the war. One could begin, in his view, by educating Ukrainians through interviewing on TV living witnesses to and participants in battles featuring Ukrainians. He is tired of hearing "veterans of the so-called Great Patriotic War." He equates the anti-Ukrainian content of Bukovs'kyi's film with the issue of ownership of the mass media. This film was ordered by Moscow and the pro-Moscow oligarchs around Ukrainian president Leonid Kuchma. Why, he wonders, did the film fail to mention 350 years of "Muscovite occupation" of Ukraine, plans to deport Ukrainians en masse from their homeland in 1944, or the matter of genocide against Ukrainians when Russian generals sent thousands of poorly armed Ukrainian youngsters to their deaths? Zahoruiko then descends into an anti-Semitic diatribe, claiming that the film was part of a Jewish intrigue, alongside Russians and new Ukrainians tied to the Kuchma regime. UPA, he maintains, was the Third Force that fought both the Soviets and the Germans, and a state that fails to recognize its own heroes should be ashamed of itself.[59] Zahoruiko's critique represents a more extreme and intolerant perspective that in some ways resembles the sort of integral nationalism of the prewar and early war years. It does little to assist the goal of rehabilitating the UPA and serves to bolster those in Ukraine who still consider the insurgents as representative of narrow and fanatical national interests.

The Second World War in Ukraine was the subject of a more reflective article in the main historical journal in the spring of 2004. O. E. Lysenko admits that the war remains a problematic factor in contemporary Ukraine, provoking confrontation and agitated reactions in much of Ukrainian society in response to efforts to depart from the established stereotypes of the Soviet past. In his view, such a reaction can be explained by the enduring power of ideas and images internalized by many Ukrainians from the Soviet period. He transfers these perceptions to current social and economic issues—alienation from the government, lack of social guarantees, and a failure to assist Soviet veterans who are now enduring difficult times. These factors only exacerbate the irritation with the notion of rewriting the history of the war. Much now falls on the shoulders of historians to resolve this conflict, says Lysenko. Without doubt the Soviet view was one-sided, as it emphasized some issues and ignored others. The portrayal of the OUN and UPA was exclusively negative because Soviet historiography was a servant of official ideology. Therefore the historian must free his discipline from historical constraints in order to bring about an "objective reconstruction of the past." Scholars must be both objective and apolitical. To date, from the Ukrainian side, Lysenko finds studies and documentary collections on the war years to be unsatisfactory. They reflect the weak contacts with scholars abroad, a lack of opportunity for research in archives, and the legacy of Soviet historical writing. Foreign scholars, on the other hand, are starting to provide innovative approaches to the topic. He proposes that historians should move from the macro-levels of study offered by Soviet history, and move to the micro-history of social groups, families, and individuals. Oral history is an important component that could have a positive impact on such studies.[60]

Lysenko is also concerned about terminology and believes that contemporary historical studies are contaminated by an ideological vocabulary that continues to be used long after its originators—the Communist leaders—have disappeared from the scene. They include terms such as "bourgeois and socialist intelligentsia," "collectivization," "industrialization," "cultural revolution," "socialist realism," and "enemy of the people." Such terms, says the author, obscure rather than reflect reality. Another example is the phrase "Ukrainian–German bourgeois nationalism" because the goals of the German National Socialists and the OUN were not identical, and the former consistently refused to recognize Ukrainian statehood as a legitimate goal. Thus the task for historians is to explore the parameters and characteristics of the dominant ideology, the way in which these are used, mutual influences, how the political apparatus functions, and the degree of its effectiveness. In the West—and Lysenko clearly has a very high opinion about historical writing in developed capitalist countries—most historians accept the emancipation of ideology from class or social structure, and refuse to treat ideology as the totality of ideas contained by human minds. Rather ideology affects different spheres from scientific knowledge, to religion, and everyday behavior.[61] It is fair to say that Lysenko's appeal—at least in terms of current writing in Ukraine about the Second World War—has not been widely taken up because historians or publicists still tend to write in a highly emotional fashion, basing their publications on political history and ideology rather than the microcosmic approach. His suggestions also require a considerable leap from what is clearly a non-objective approach to history, or history as propaganda, as encapsulated by Soviet writing, with the Second World War arguably the most difficult place to start, in revising past views.

One historian who has constantly tried to perform such a task is Yurii Shapoval, in major publications as well as in a lengthy series of articles in *Ukrains'kyi istorychnyi zhurnal* and regular items in the popular media. Shapoval's book *Ukraine in the Twentieth Century: People and Events in Difficult Times* is a serious attempt to include the latest archival findings alongside what is more familiarly known, and he firmly rejects Soviet stereotypes.[62] As the 60th anniversary of the war approached in 2005, Shapoval published an article in which he criticized Ukrainian historiography, which he feels is still dominated by retrogressive narratives that idealize and mythologize the topic and continue to promote the stereotypes of "Brezhnev–Stalin historiography." These self-righteous scholars still reject the story of Ukraine in their narratives about the war, in his opinion. He begins with the statement that by concluding the Molotov–Ribbentrop Pact, the two dictators, Hitler and Stalin, divided Europe. There was no place in their planning for an independent Ukraine. The annexation of Western Ukraine in 1939 should be considered part of this conspiracy, and therefore one cannot praise the Soviet regime and Stalin for unifying Ukrainian lands, as is sometimes the case. In 1940–41, he adds, about 320,000 people were deported from Western Ukraine to remote regions of the USSR and thousands of prisoners and POWs were executed in 1941, just as the Soviet–German war started. Hence two totalitarian systems were in operation during the war, and Ukraine suffered under both of them. He also questions the term "Great Patriotic War," which he maintains is an artificial and ideological term. The population during wartime was not monolithic as this term implies. There were at least three different groups: those in the Red Army by force or conviction, those who fought against the Communists, and the silent majority that was prepared or obligated to conform to the different regimes.[63]

Shapoval then examines Ukraine's situation in more detail. At first—and he cites a comment by Demyan Korotchenko, the Second Secretary in the Ukrainian party leadership from 1939—a majority of the civil population tried to adopt itself to the occupation regime. Others realized that freedom would not come from either the Kremlin or Berlin. Thus when Stets'ko announced Ukraine's independence on 30 June 1941, it was not an action taken by German collaborators, but a reflection of the thinking in Ukrainian society. In Shapoval's view, this is why the so-called liberation of Ukraine in 1944 is a topic that should be revisited: "no such liberation took place." True, the Nazis had been expelled from Ukrainian territory, but another war was beginning in the western regions that would last until the mid-1950s. Shapoval remarks that there were two Holocausts that took place in Ukraine during the war: the first

was the total extermination of the Jews; the second was the systematic elimination of the Slavic population: Ukrainians, Russians, Poles, and Belarusians.
But Stalin in his view was no liberator, and even when the Red Army crossed
the Polish border, the leader's goal was to capture Poland's industrial installations rather than free political prisoners in Nazi death camps.[64] His article fits
well with the new narrative that could be termed "nationalist" and seeks to
replace the former Soviet version of events. The difficulty, and it is evident
even in this short article, is that the new version does not fit easily into a
straightforward narrative. As we have seen, the declaration of independence
of 30 June 1941 was a controversial event that was not accepted widely in
Ukraine or by Ukrainians living outside Soviet borders. Moreover, it occurred
at least in the belief that the Germans might accept the situation, as is evident
from the tone and contents of the first communiqués of Stets'ko and his companions.

The same issue has perplexed Canadian historian Roman Serbyn, as revealed in an interview conducted in Montreal in June 2006 (which covers several topics, including the Famine of 1932–33), and published in *Den'* newspaper the following month.[65] Serbyn reveals that he was visiting Ukraine in the
year prior to the 50th anniversary of the end of the Second World War and
felt that it was "outrageous" that Ukraine should find cause to celebrate the
exchange of one tyrant for another, particularly as the Stalin regime accounted for more deaths in Ukraine than Hitler. He conducted inquiries as to
the origins of the phrase "Great Fatherland War" but no one was interested.
He notes that the term was coined on the first day of the war and appeared in
print in an article in *Pravda* the following day. In his view it constitutes a myth
that this was a patriotic war, based on three premises: first, the unity and patriotism of the peoples of the Soviet Union; second, that Ukraine was liberated by the Red Army; and third, that the Soviet people were victorious. However, in his view there was no freedom in Ukraine and the Red Army cannot
be considered as "the real victors." Serbyn discusses the choice of 9 May as
the official Victory Day, and Stalin's toast to the Russian people in late May
1945, at which time he cited the other nationalities of the USSR as cogs in the
machine without which the leaders could not attain victory. He notes that the
holiday was restored by Brezhnev in 1965, and angrily condemns the "metal
monstrosity of a woman warrior" on the right bank of Kyiv's Dnipro River,
and comments that independent Ukraine simply accepted both the holiday
and its accompanying myth. The interviewer, whose pro-UPA sympathies are
evident, then wonders why this myth is still extant when the UPA and the Division Halychyna lack official recognition in independent Ukraine. Serbyn

reels off a list of organizations that have promoted the "myth" that includes the CPSU, Red Army veterans, the Russian Orthodox Church in Moscow, ethnic Russians, and Ukrainian Russophones. He maintains that the concept of the "Great Fatherland War" is impeding unity between Ukrainians who took part in the war in three different military units: the Red Army, the UPA, and, especially, the Division Halychyna.[66]

In May 2005, an article by Lyudmyla Shanhina provides the results of a survey in Ukraine by the Razumkov Center (the number of respondents is not cited) on attitudes to Victory Day. She reports that 86% of Ukrainians intended to celebrate Victory Day, 10% did not, and 4% had not decided. Of those surveyed, 60% regard 9 May as the day of victory over Nazi Germany; and 51% think that the victory was won by the Soviet Union; whereas 9% feel it was won by the countries of the anti-German coalition. 21% consider the date a day of commemoration for war heroes, and for 10% it is a day of mourning for war victims. The survey makes several distinctions in the number of celebrants: 91% in the eastern regions of Ukraine compared to 65% in the west; up to 90% in the age group over 40 intended to celebrate Victory Day compared to 79% in the range of 18 to 29 years. For the younger generation, the day is considered part of history rather than one affecting one's family personally (43% versus 11%). For those over sixty, however, the respective figures are 20% and 35%. In this respect the survey was unable to determine any regional differences. The survey then asked: what kind of war was the Second World War for Ukraine? The results were as follows: 59% felt it was a just war waged by the Soviet people against foreign aggressors, an opinion held by only 31% in the western regions, but 65% in Central and Eastern Ukraine, and 68% in the south. Just 14% consider the war one of two totalitarian states on the territory of Ukraine (the figure is 27% in the west). A reported 49% consider the war a "just war of the Soviet people" and among older respondents that figure rises to 68%. Finally, 67% of those surveyed believe that Nazi Germany was responsible for starting the war (50% in the west); 1% blame Western countries; and 19% think all participants were equally responsible (30% in the west).[67]

How should one evaluate these results? In the first place, the questions are somewhat limited and it would have been interesting to know the attitude of respondents to the various Ukrainian military units in the war. However, the results indicate that independence in Ukraine has not brought a radical change of perspective, a situation that Serbyn has also surmised. Implicitly at least they signal a negative attitude to the recognition of OUN-UPA, and likely there would be even less inclination to recognize the veterans of the Division

Halychyna as official participants in the war. The view of the war as Soviet and one that served to unite the people of Ukraine remains in place for most residents, and even in the western regions it embraces a major portion of the population. Where Western Ukraine differs significantly from the other regions is in its perception of the war as a "just" one. Such an attitude would surely be less likely in a region that commemorates the OUN and UPA heroes through statues, museums, and street names. The Razumkov survey is startling in its illustration that the attitude to the war of the younger generation does not differ radically from that of the older generation. Thus the difference in perception is regional rather than generational. The problem in general with commemoration of the war is that whether or not one blames official propaganda and myths long perpetuated by a now defunct regime, a large proportion of the population currently accepts this perspective and refuses to change its attitude to the war. What one has to ask therefore is whether the new version being proposed, with recognition of OUN-UPA and even the Division Halychyna as combatants alongside the Red Army, will be just as rigid and propagandistic in its own way. Will the outcome be a rational discussion of the war, or will it simply replace the original (Soviet) victors with a new version that can be incorporated into the national history of Ukraine (UPA as the main heroes), the sort of interpretation that has slowly begun to be included in school textbooks?

Notes

1 Yaroslav Hrytsak, "On the Relevance and Irrelevance of Nationalism in Ukraine," Second Annual Stasiuk-Cambridge Lecture, University of Camridge, England, 20 February 2004.

2 Oleksandr Marushchenko, "Ukraina v Druhii svitovii viini: istoriohrafichni doslidzhennya 90h rokiv," *Istoriya v shkoli*, No. 5-6 (2000): 2-4.

3 Ibid.

4 Nancy Popson, "The Ukrainian History Textbook: Introducing Children to the 'Ukrainian Nation'," *Nationalities Papers*, Vol. 29, No. 2 (2001): 325-350.

5 Viktor Mysan, *Opovidannya z istorii Ukrainy* (Kyiv: Heneza, 1997), pp. 174-179.

6 Ibid., pp. 179-181.

7 Ibid., pp. 188-190.

8 F. H. Turchenko, *Novitnaya istoriya Ukrainy: Chastyna persha 1917-1945* (Kyiv: Heneza, 1998), pp. 246-249.

9 Volodymyr Lytvyn, Valerii Dmolii, and Mykola Shapovatyi, *Ilyustrovana istoriya Ukrainy* (Kyiv: Al'ternatyvy, 2001), p. 174. Lytvyn, a politician, former Speaker of Parliament, and close ally of former Ukrainian president Leonid D. Kuchma, has been accused of violating copyright laws and plagiarism in his writing. See, for example, Hryhor'ii Nemyrya, "Sim mi-

fiv abo sproba 'koryhuval'noho presynhu?'," *Dzerkalo tyzhnya*, No. 3, (26 January-1 February 2002): [http://www.zn.kiev.ua/nn/show/378/33632].

10 Ibid., pp. 189, 204-205, 217, and 226.

11 O. D. Boyko, *Istoriya Ukrainy* (Kyiv: Akademvydav, 2003), pp. 398-399.

12 F. H. Turchenko, P. P. Panchenko, and S. M. Tymchenko, *Novitnaya istoriya Ukrainy*, Part 1: 1939-2001 (Kyiv: Heneza, 2001), pp. 5-8.

13 Ibid., pp. 8, 25.

14 Ibid., p. 27.

15 Ibid., pp. 28-29, 40-41.

16 H. D. Temka and L. S. Tupchienka, ed., *Istoriya Ukrainy: Posibnyk* (Kyiv: Akademiya, 2002), pp. 308, 341-342.

17 Ibid., pp. 342-344.

18 Ibid., pp. 345-348.

19 Ibid., p. 349.

20 V. D. Mironchuk and H. S. Ihoshyi, *Istoriya Ukrainy* (Kyiv: MAUP, 2002), pp. 215-216, 221-222.

21 M. O. Skrypnyk, et al, *Istoriya Ukrainy: nachal'nyi posibnyk* (Kyiv: Tsentr navchal'noi literatury, 2003), pp. 240-241, 251-253.

22 Ibid., pp. 262-263.

23 Boyko, *Istoriya Ukrainy*, pp. 479-480, 505-507.

24 "O popytkakh politicheskoy rehabilitatsii OUN-UPA: rezolyutsii XXVIII s'ezda Kompartii Ukrainy," *Pravda Ukrainy*, editorial, 19 December 1990.

25 V. Lutsenko, "Demokratychna metushnaya," *Nadnipryans'ka pravda*, 7 August 1991, p. 2.

26 Cited in *Visti z Ukrainy*, No. 27 (1991): 1.

27 A. Boita, "U skhidnii Ukraini-dobri lyudy, a v zakhidnii-lyshe zlochyntsi," *Visti z Ukrainy*, No. 34 (August 1991): 1-2.

28 "Pershyi zbir soya…v UPA," *Literaturna Ukraina*, 6 February 1992, p. 7.

29 Editorial, *Literaturna Ukraina*, 16 April 1992, p. 1.

30 Larysa Khorolets', "Heroyam slava!" *Literaturna Ukraina*, 13 August 1992, p. 2.

31 Yurii Shapoval, "Skazaty vsyu pravdu: do 50-richchya UPA," *Literaturna Ukraina*, 1 October 1992, p. 7.

32 Volodmyr Yavors'kyi, "Yakshcho derzhava ne pustyi zvuk," *Za vil'nu Ukrainu*, 18 May 1993, p. 2.

33 Ibid.

34 Viktor Koval', "Ukrains'ka Povstans'ka Armiya: dovidka Instytutu istorii AN URSR dlya Komisii Verkhovnoi Rady Ukrainy z pytan' bezpeky vid 1 lypnya 1991 roku," *Ukraina i Svit*, No. 37 (2-8 October 1996): 10.

35 Nina Romanyuk, "Ya istymu lushpaiky, aby Ukraina bula!" *Ukraina moloda*, 2 September 1998, p. 6.

36 Wiktor Poliszczuk, *Bitter Truth: The Criminality of the Organization of Ukrainian Nationalists and the Ukrainian Insurgent Army* (Toronto, 1999), pp. 27, 370-372.

37 Stanislav Kul'chyts'kyi, "Ukrains'ki natsionalisty v chervono-korychnevii Yevropi (do 70-richchya stvorennya OUN)," *Istoriya Ukrainy*, No. 5 (February 1999) 6-7.

38 Iziaslav Kokodnyak, "50 rokiv bezsmertiya," *Za vil'nu Ukrainu*, 3 March 2000, p. 3.

39 Roman Rytiak, "Za shcho my skorodyly spysamy vorozhi rebra?" *Za vil'nu Ukrainu*, 28 July 2000, p. 4.

40 Roman Serbyn, "'Tretya syla' v p'yatomu kuti," *Ukraina moloda*, 21 June 2001, p. 4.

41 Ibid.

42 Ivan Khmil, "Hucksterish Circumlocutions of the OUN-UPA Apologists," *The Day Digest*, 9 October 2001; [http://www.day.kiev.ua/268044/].

43 Cited in *RFE/RL Newsline*, 28 March 2002.

44 Kost Bondarenko, "Istoriya, kotoruyu ne znaem ili ne khotim znat'?" *Zerkalo nedeli*, 25 March–5 April 2002.

45 Serbyn makes essentially the same point in his June 2006 interview. Roman Serbyn, "Ukraine should abandon Soviet-era myths," *The Day Digest*, No. 25 (25 July 2006), [http://www.day.kiev.ua/103]. This article is discussed below.

46 Oleh Hryniv, "Zatavrovani abreviaturamy," *Ukraina moloda*, 30 August 2002, p. 4.

47 Anatolii Fomenko, "Pravda pro UPA," *Ukraina moloda*, 10 October 2002, pp. 4–5.

48 Information provided by V. P. Futala, *Ukrains'kyi istorychnyi zhurnal*, No. 2 (2003): 145.

49 Yuri Kril, "Yuri Shukhevych: the Truth about UPA will be known," *The Day Digest*, 15 October 2002; [http://www.day.kiev.ua/259602/].

50 O. E. Lysenko and O. V. Marushchenko, "Vseukrains'ka naukova konferentsiya 'Ukrains'ka povstans'ka armiya—fenomen natsional'noi istorii," *Ukrains'kyi istorychnyi zhurnal*, No. 1 (2003): 147–149.

51 Roman Zahoruiko, "Zezlamnyi hin do voli," *Ukraina moloda*, 14 October 2003, p. 10.

52 Yevhen Sverstyuk, "Tsyu riku ne zahatyty," *Ukraina moloda*, 20 November 2003, p. 6.

53 Serhiy Stepanyshyn, "Nationalist Internationalism: The Conference of the Captive Nations of Eastern Europe and Asia was held sixty years ago," *The Day Digest*, 9 December 2003, [www.day.kiev.ua/].

54 Stepan Zlupko, "Velyka vitchyznyana chy druha svitova?" *Za vil'nu Ukrainu*, 22 June 1993, p. 2.

55 Mykhailo Lytvynchuk, "My voyuvaly ne za imperieyu," *Za vil'nu Ukrainu*, 27 April 1995, p. 2.

56 Ibid.

57 Yaroslav Tymchyshyn, "SRSR ukraintsyam ne batkivshchyna—itzhe druha svitova viina dlya nas ne vitchyzniana," *Za vil'nu Ukrainu*, 6 May 1995, p. 2.

58 I. Antsyshkin, "Velyka: ale chy vitchyzniana?" *Ukraina moloda*, 8 May 1999, p. 4.

59 Roman Zahoruiko, "Istorychne sharlatanstvo," *Ukraina moloda*, 7 May 2003, p. 12.

60 O. E. Lysenko, "Druha svitova viina yak predmet naukovykh doslidzhen' ta fenomen istorychnoi pam'yati," *Ukrains'kyi istorychnyi zhurnal*, No. 5 (May 2004): 3–10.

61 Ibid., pp. 10–13.

62 Yurii Shapoval, *Ukraina XX stolittya: osoby ta podii v konteksti vazhkoi istorii* (Kyiv: Heneza, 2001).

63 Yurii Shapoval, "Ukrains'ka druha svitova," *Dzerkalo tyzhnya*, No. 15, (23 April–6 May 2005).

64 Ibid.

65 Professor Serbyn also delivered the 2005 Shevchenko lecture at the University of Alberta on the same topic in March 2005 and at the VII ICCEES World Congress in Berlin in July 2005 on a panel organized by the author. In his abstract for this paper, Serbyn writes: "To the old founding myth of the Great October Revolution was thereby added a new myth of consolidation. Soon the new holiday became the most popular. It survived the collapse of the USSR in all the republics except the Baltic states. Its existence in Ukraine creates a

paradoxical situation where a state born out of separatism, continues to celebrate a holiday intended to prevent disintegration." ICCEES VII World Congress, *Europe—Our Common Home? Abstracts 2005* (Berlin: Weltkongress 2005), p. 377.

66 Roman Serbyn, "Ukraine should abandon Soviet-era myths," *The Day Digest,* No. 25 (25 July 2006); [http://www.day.kiev.ua/103]. The image of a "fatherland" war is Serbyn's rendition. Usually the reference is either to a patriotic or "motherland" war, hence the female statues in Kyiv and Volgograd (Stalingrad).

67 Lyudmyla Shanhina, "Dva dni do peremohy, abo myr nashomu domu," *Dzerkalo tyzhnya,* No. 17 (7–13 May 2005) [http://www.zn.kiev.ua/ie/show/544/49954/].

CHAPTER 8

ASSESSMENTS

This concluding chapter will be divided into three parts. The first will examine perhaps the most definitive treatment of OUN ideology to date, by historian H. V. Kas'yanov; the second will look at the main findings of the 2004 Government Commission Report on OUN-UPA; and the final section will offer some conclusions on the issues raised in this book—the question of constructing national history in Ukraine, with a focus on the twentieth century and the Stalin years in particular.[1] There is as yet no prevailing narrative, as we have noted from recent school textbooks, but with the passing of time the analyses have become increasingly sophisticated. The two major assessments described below perhaps define the end of a period of inquiry and debate, though the issues discussed are far from dormant. Kas'yanov's article also formed the basis for his contribution to the Government Commission Report. However, since it appeared first in *Ukrains'kyi istorychnyi zhurnal*, it has been discussed separately. It is to some extent a follow-up to an article he wrote six years earlier in the same journal. The assessments have been placed in the conclusion to the book because they offer the perspectives of Ukraine's leading historians. They do not indicate that these views are widely accepted across Ukraine and doubtless there are significant and radical regional variations and opinions. That is not really the point. The historians' perspectives will likely be transferred to school textbooks over time and form the views of new generations of Ukrainian citizens, and as such they are valuable and influential over the long term.

Kas'yanov on OUN Ideology

Kas'yanov's study notes that OUN ideology was far from monolithic even in its early days. He comments that the term used most often to refer to its 1930s version in Western literature is "integral nationalism," and he cites Armstrong's account of the ideological stances that are familiar to most readers: the belief in the nation as the highest value; and the conception that individuals are united in a single, organic entity through their biological characteristics or common historical development. Armstrong also provided other features such as the presence of a charismatic leader and a cult of action, thus war or violence is seen as evidence of the vitality of the nation. Western political scientist Alexander J. Motyl is also cited and outlines other typical features of OUN ideology, including anti-intellectualism, determinism, anti-parliamentarianism, militarism, and federalism. However, Kas'yanov writes, the Ukrainian variant existed alongside a linked but separate variant of totalitarian nationalism associated with Dmytro Dontsov, which he sees as nihilistic and lacking constructive elements. On the other hand, the OUN's integral nationalism, albeit extremist, contained a clear political program and a consistent worldview. Nevertheless, in the 1920s, Dontsov's book *Natsionalizm* had an enormous impact on Ukrainian youth living in Polish Ukraine, and these same people went on to form the basis of the "Krayova OUN." Gradually the OUN moved away from Dontsovian nationalism, and in August 1943, Dontsov's comments concerning the political guidelines of the OUN at the Third Extraordinary Grand Assembly (August 1943) were pointedly ignored. In the late 1940s, Dontsov strongly criticized the revised OUN stance, and following his emigration to North America (he took up residence in Montreal) after the war, he retained some influence among the ZCh OUN. Integral nationalism was thus ultimately abandoned. However, writes Kas'yanov, there was a certain self-deception to this change since the ideological evolution of the OUN-B in the 1960s and 1970s tended to follow the revolutionary orthodoxy of the 1930s linked with Dontsov.[2]

Moving back in time to the formation of the OUN, Kas'yanov cites the various influences behind the movement (the defeat of the Ukrainian Revolution of 1917–21, the political climate in the countries in which the OUN operated, and European intellectual movements of the period). Its first major theoretical periodical was the Prague-based *Rozbudova natsii* and the emergence of a group of intellectual theorists. Not all ideological issues had been resolved by the time of the OUN's creation at the Vienna Congress of January–February 1929 chaired by D. Andriievs'kyi. There were sharp debates in particular between Krayova OUN members and emigrant activists. Krayova OUN members identified closely with the political views of M. Mikhnovs'kyi and Dontsov. However, both sides adhered to the view of the nation as the highest form of social organization, with the state as the ultimate form of the nation's development, a postulate that remained unchallenged until the early 1990s. The OUN anticipated a three-stage process of construction of a

Ukrainian state. Stage one was the phase of "national liberation" when a national dictatorship would be established. Stage two was to be a transitional period in which the head of state prepares the highest legislative bodies with the participation of all organized social groups. Stage three would see stabilization and the creation of a representative body that would appoint the state leader—the highest executive power. Kas'yanov perceives this structure as rather vague and generalized, and several ideologists expressed regret at the lack of definitiveness in the conception. The OUN came to maturity in the 1930s at a time when totalitarian regimes were thriving in Europe and pressure on Ukrainian society was rising both in Poland and the Soviet Union. As a result the OUN ideology became much more radical. Under these circumstances, Dontsov's writings only exacerbated the emotional atmosphere— Kas'yanov does not see them as offering much that was constructive. Dontsovian nationalism lowered the level of political culture of this militant element among the Ukrainian people.[3]

The split in the OUN is seen as tactically rather than ideologically motivated. It also reflected a generation gap and the personal animosities between the two leaders. Both declared as their main goal the creation of a sovereign, united Ukrainian state. However, the Bandera program involved the revolt of not only Ukrainians but other peoples of the Moscow empire. It also espoused an anti-Moscow and anti-Semitic platform, as Jews were seen as the main foundation of the "Moscow Bolshevik regime." In the OUN-B program, in theory, the leader's power would be counterbalanced by collegial bodies, i.e., the Provid (Leadership) and the Velyka Rada (Grand Council). In practice, a personality and leadership cult developed around the figure of Bandera. By the late 1930s, writes Kas'yanov, the general ideological image of the OUN had been formed: radical Ukrainian nationalism manifesting features typical of totalitarianism, anti-democracy, and anti-Communism in a revolutionary movement founded on the principles of action, militant idealism, and voluntarism, and on the priority of national values over pan-human ones. It was a combination of political elitism and social egalitarianism, in Kas'yanov's view, but with special emphasis on the peasantry as the backbone of the Ukrainian nation. Did the platform have anything in common with Italian Fascism and German National Socialism? Kas'yanov observes that in the late 1920s and early 1930s, the OUN ideologists built up analogies and associations with Italian Fascism quite deliberately, and borrowed components of Italian Fascism's political and socio-economic programs, particularly Corporatism. One of the principal differences, however, was that the Ukrainians lacked their own national state. Still the OUN used some symbols of Italian Fascism, and incorporated within its structure an organization that was originally called the Union of Ukrainian Fascists. The OUN cooperated overtly both with Italian Fascists and the German Abwehr, as well as with the German occupation authorities in the early 1940s. Mirchuk, among others, noted that Ukrainian nationalists were sympathetic toward Fascism as an anti-Communist and as a new political and economic movement, but added that Ukrainian nationalism, which dated back thousands of years, had a much longer tradition than Fascism.[4]

Kas'yanov looks briefly at other writers with an OUN background. At least two—Zinovii Knysh and V. Marhanets—perceive Ukrainian nationalism as a product of domestic development rather than outside forces. Roman Ilnytzkyj maintains that some of the most significant components of Fascism and National Socialism were always alien to the OUN (a corporate state, racism, and anti-Semitism), but the movements possessed a similar organizational structure. The statements lead Kas'yanov to editorialize that:

> Remarkably, all these OUN writers, regardless of their faction affiliations, rejected expressly the ideological similarity to Fascism and Nazism to the extent of denying generally known facts, in particular that elements of racism and anti-Semitism, as well as corporatism, were typical of the OUN ideological constructs, especially in the first half of the 1930s.

Such self-deceptive perspectives are contrasted with the writings of Motyl and Ivan Lysiak-Rudnytsky, who respectively noted common features with Italian Fascism and with the agrarian and other parties of economically backward East European countries (Croatia, Romania, Slovakia, and Poland). Rudnytsky is also cited for his comment that Ukrainian nationalism was a genetically independent phenomenon, but clearly influenced by foreign models in the course of its development. Realistically, Kas'yanov concludes that the OUN could hardly have avoided the dominant trends of Italian Fascism and German National Socialism, but one should not equate these movements with the Ukrainian variant. Even the Soviet Union engaged in productive cooperation in economic, military, and political spheres during the 1930s, but the regimes of Stalin, Hitler, and Mussolini are not linked because of this factor. Similarly even antithetical ideologies borrow from each other. Hence the OUN ideology cannot be termed Fascist or National Socialist, in Kas'yanov's view. He ends with a rather angry swipe at those who persist in the habitual and unproductive practice of using ideological clichés, which are now outdated, in current academic and political debates.[5] The targets are not made explicit, but clearly Kas'yanov rejects the stereotyped view concerning Ukrainian nationalists.

Comment

Kas'yanov's rejection seems a reasonable point to make, particularly given the passive role of Ukrainian nationalists prior to the formation of a sovereign state, a time when they were obligated to throw in their lot with the catalysts for change in Europe. Both the Americans and British covertly supported the nationalist insurgency after the war and opened their doors to many of the leaders of this movement so clearly the Western Powers were not unduly perturbed by their past links with the Germans. Yet perhaps the reason for the persistent denigration and labeling of Ukrainian nationalists has been the rather narrow perspectives and conception of the future—and, after 1991, the established—Ukrainian state. In the efforts to reconstruct a national history, there is a marked tendency to idealize Ukrainian nationalism of the 1930s and 1940s and to render adherents ipso facto freedom fighters. One problem is surely the failure to delve deeper into Ukrainian history to find the roots of modern nationalism. As one author has pointed out, many people equate the concept of Ukrainian nationalism exclusively with Bandera, the OUN and UPA, and with Western Ukraine. Yet the birth of this movement long predated Dontsov and can be linked to the periods of rule of the Russian tsars Peter I and Catherine II. Some would go back much further to the period of the Grand Duchy of Lithuania and medieval Polish state.[6] Thus these earlier influences on Ukraine—and we have already witnessed examples in school textbooks—are ritually negated in a conception of development and state-building that is largely (but not solely) confined to the defining events of the twentieth century. The OUN, or more accurately the OUN-B, remains important because of its prominent role outside of Ukraine. Though its political influence in Ukraine is small, and its impact on elections and government minimal, its perceptions of the past, which are largely unchanging, still continue to exert their effect in historical narratives, writings, and in school textbooks. That is why many Eastern Ukrainians have maintained that the Bandera or Western Ukrainian version of history predominates in Ukraine today. Thus the root of the problem lies less in whether 1930s nationalism was Fascist or National Socialist, and more in the lack of historical debate on topics that clearly still need discussion, including those that have been featured in these pages.

The Government Commission Report of 2004

From the early years of independence, a commission comprising several Ukrainian historians was tasked with perusing the activities of OUN-UPA. In February 1993, the Presidium of the Supreme Soviet approved a resolution "On the investigation of OUN-UPA activities," and in June 1994, the Ministry of Justice convoked a council of experts to examine the problem. However, the historians were unable to start work because of a lack of funding. In September 1996, Parliament endorsed a decision to establish a temporary commission that would facilitate the inquiry into OUN-UPA, but it ran into the problem of ideological disagreements among its members. Finally in May 1997, the then president Leonid D. Kuchma ruled that a Government Commission should be created and its working group formed at the Institute of History, Ukrainian Academy of Sciences. It consisted of twenty scholars, many of whom were well-known as leading historians in Ukraine: S. Kul'-chyts'kyi, Yu. Shapoval, A. Kentii, H. Kas'yanov, I. Il'yushyn, and others. It produced a document entitled "Report of the Working Group of the Government Commission for Examining OUN-UPA Activities: Key theses on the OUN-UPA Problem (A Historical Conclusion)." We will examine this document in detail since it reflects the current thinking of Ukraine's most distinguished historians on the issue of the OUN and UPA, and is based on archival materials, as well as the recent publications of some of its members.

The key theses (Historical Conclusions) are divided into fourteen sections, thirteen of which we will outline briefly before offering an assessment.[7] Section 1, "The subject of research," points out that the OUN and UPA were distinct entities that performed different functions, and their titles should not be linked by a hyphen. The problem of OUN-UPA can only be examined as individual entities. Several underground and insurgent structures were established that fought for Ukraine's independence: the Ukrainian Military Organization (UVO) in 1920 (which joined the OUN in 1929); the OUN that operated in Western Ukraine and among the Diaspora since 1929 (splitting into two independent factions under Bandera and Mel'nyk); the Ukrainian Insurgent Army, from 1943 to 1949; and the Brotherhoods of Ukrainian Nationalists—more commonly known under the names of the *Nachtigal* special detachment and the *Roland* organization. Section 2, "Confrontation between Ukrainian nationalists and the Soviet authorities, 1939–1941," makes the important point that Ukrainian historiography often overestimates the scale of the deportations of the population from Western Ukraine by the USSR in 1940–41. Some reference books provide a figure of more than one million people deported. But the actual figure, based on data from Russian archives, did not exceed 192,000, and these people were mainly Polish officials and Jewish refugees. The nationalists were unable in this period to confront the Soviet authorities by provoking a national uprising. That is why, the document states, after the German attack on the USSR, the OUN took the side of the Wehrmacht and engaged in active subversion operations and intelligence in the rear of the Red Army.[8]

Section 3 is concerned with the "situational alliance between Ukrainian nationalists and Hitler's Germany." It notes that relations between both wings of the OUN and the Germans remained virtually problem-free between September 1939 and June 1941. Having no access to Hitler, the nationalists did not know the Germans' plans for Ukraine. After 22 June 1941, acting out of enthusiasm, but without coordinating their actions with German officials, the nationalists seized power in 187 out of 200 districts of Western Ukraine and 26 districts of Right-Bank Ukraine. They set up regional administrations in Ternopil', L'viv, Rivne, Drohobych, Stanyslaviv, and Luts'k. By disarming Red Army units, OUN combatants acquired significant supplies of weapons, ammunition, and equipment. German field commanders were content to synchronize their operations with OUN actions, but German officials at a higher level remained mistrustful. Section 4 deals more specifically with the armed *Nachtigal* and *Roland* detachments. It points out that cooperation between UVO/OUN and the German Abwehr dated back to the period of the Weimar Republic. After Hitler came to power, the "anti-Versailles spirit" of German policy was strengthened. Initially a subversion detachment called the *Bergsbauernhilfe* was formed in mid-September 1939 under the leadership of Roman Sushko. However, German plans for Western Ukraine were abandoned after the signing of the Nazi–Soviet Pact. The Germans agreed to train only several hundred Ukrainian troops which, the nationalists hoped, would eventually form the nucleus of a Ukrainian army allied to the Wehrmacht. Called *Roland* and *Nachtigal* in the code names used by the Abwehr, the units are referred to in Ukrainian documents as *Druzhyny Ukrains'kykh Natsionalistiv* (Brotherhoods of Ukrainian Nationalists). They had the tasks of securing the movement of German forces in Ukraine, disarming Red Army units defeated by the Wehrmacht, and organizing convoy trains carrying POWs and ammunition.

By June 1941, *Nachtigal* was fully staffed with men wearing the Wehrmacht field uniform and included in the special regiment, Brandenburg 800, commanded by Roman Shukhevych with its German contact person designated as Oberleutnant Oberlaender. It entered L'viv on 30 June and occupied all the strategic locations. Yaroslav Stets'ko, deputy chief of the OUN Provid, declared the national independence of Ukraine on L'viv Radio that same night and on the following morning. Members of *Nachtigal* were then granted a week's leave and German police forces took over the main points of the city. After the arrests of Bandera, Stets'ko, and other OUN-B leaders, Shukhevych informed the Wehrmacht Supreme Command that the battalion would no longer be subordinated to the German army. It was then disbanded. Together with the *Roland* battalion, which had remained in Romania, it was united into a single detachment by October. Troops were asked to sign one-year contracts to serve in the guard police and transferred to Belarus to guard bridges over the Berezyna and Dvina rivers. After the expiration of the year, the battalion was dissolved and its troops arrested, though Shukhevych escaped into the underground. Concerning the issue of *Nachtigal* involvement in the massacre of the Polish and Jewish intelligentsia in L'viv on 3–4 July, the working group points out that such accusations have never been proved, citing the acquittal of Oberlaender on the same charges at the Nuremberg Trials. An investigation in Hamburg in 1966, conducted at the request of Poland with reference to the deaths of Polish citizens, established that the SS was responsible for these atrocities.

Section 5 examines Hitler's plans for Ukraine, noting initially that of the two wings of the OUN, the OUN-B acted more confidently as it was operating on Ukrainian land. Before the German attack, the OUN-M addressed the issue of the formation of a Ukrainian state that would extend well beyond the ethnic boundaries of Ukraine, and which anticipated the immigration of Ukrainians in Siberia and the Far East into the new state. OUN-B perceived its relationship to Nazi Germany as one of an ally. It warned Hitler that the German troops would be greeted as liberators in Ukraine, but that attitude would not last unless a Ukrainian state was created. The OUN-B tried to convince the Germans that the creation of an independent Ukraine was in accord with Germany's own interests. Bandera insisted that Ukraine could not be treated in the same way as the puppet states of Slovakia and Croatia because of its size and population. The authors make two qualifying points in their assessment of the German–OUN relationship. First, the leaders of the Third Reich did not consider the Ukrainian nationalists a politically significant force and did not wish to engage in interaction. Second, "we do not know" whether Ukrainian nationalist leaders were sincere when they tried to convince Hitler that they were committed to the New Order in Europe. It is true that the nationalists were willing to collaborate and accept financial and materiel support from the Abwehr. But the Germans offered collaboration only in the form of service, i.e., on an individual basis. The Ukrainians were not found to have been involved in the criminal actions of the German secret services that were revealed at the Nuremberg Trials.

The question of culpability, in the view of the Working Group, must be examined within the context of time. They comment that before September 1939, the Third Reich had not committed the crimes that any civilized human being shudders to think about. They also point out—and its relevance is not immediately obvious—that the accusers should be reminded that it was the Soviet leadership that had signed an agreement on friendship and borders with Germany. The OUN, without doubt, wished to cooperate with Germany, the authors state, and on the German side, Alfred Rosenberg in particular regarded Ukraine as a very important ally. The OUN leaders appear to have known about German plans to divide the Soviet Union, but they did not know that after his initial military triumphs Hitler had decided to introduce his plans for the creation of a Greater Germany that would include Ukrainian territory. These embraced Himmler's grotesque 30-year plan that envisaged the deportation or extermination of almost the entire Polish population, 75% of Belarusians, and 65% of Galician Ukrainians, some 30–45 million people in total. The Working Group comments that Mel'nyk and Bandera were operating in a situation in which war was a fact of life, but they did not realize that in this way they were subordinating the revival of national statehood to the defeat of the Soviet Union by Germany. The main issues are first, in order to strengthen opposition to the USSR by establishing an alliance with the Germans, the nationalists ended up in the anti-Alliance camp; and second, that they sought friendship with a state that had secret plans to colonize their land, but that they had no prior knowledge of the intended borders of Greater Germany.

Section 6 examines the "Akt" of 30 June 1941, which was clearly an attempt at a *fait accompli* on the part of the nationalists. Possibly they perceived this state as subordinate or allied to the Third Reich but, say the authors in another instance of strained logic, they were not collaborators since that notion refers to cooperation between a dominant and subordinate ally. After 22 June 1941, Berlin did not recognize such allies. The authors cite the full wording of the Akt: "The restored Ukrainian state will be engaged in close cooperation with the National-Socialist Greater Germany which, under Fuehrer Adolf Hitler's leadership, is establishing a new order in Europe and the world, and helping the Ukrainian People to break free from Moscow's occupation." The damning phrase was omitted in postwar émigré literature and made the main focus in Soviet accounts. The Germans reacted "in a relaxed manner" at first, but when Bandera refused to retract the Akt and continued to insist on OUN's equal role in negotiations the German attitude changed. Thus the Reichskommisariat Ukraine was established on 20 August 1941, and on 15 September, the security service of the new state sent a report to Berlin, warning that the OUN-B posed a danger to German interests. OUN leaders found themselves in prison, and later in the Sachsenhausen camp, near Berlin. On 25 November, almost five months after Stet'sko's proclamation, German special services disseminated an order that all activists of the Bandera movement should be arrested immediately and executed following a detailed interrogation. Did the nationalists then adopt an anti-German stance? The issue is the subject of Section 7, which concludes that the strategic line of the OUN was a wait-and-see approach: Germany was a foreign occupier but an armed struggle against it was seen as premature. Until the end of 1942, the nationalists believed that the Soviet Union would be defeated in the war, and they did not plan to begin their armed struggle until Germany had exhausted itself as a military power.

The resistance movement appeared in the winter of 1941–42, and according to German reports it consisted of the two wings of the OUN, as well as detachments led by Taras Borovets' (Bul'ba), linked politically to the 1918 Ukrainian government. Among members of the OUN-M, only the faction of O. Olzhych can be considered participants in the resistance, because Andrii Mel'nyk and his associates retained their pro-German stance. Following the resolutions of its Second Conference in 1942, the OUN-B began preparations to deploy its own armed forces in Galicia, Volhynia, and Polissya. In the spring and summer of that year, its actions against the Germans were passive ones, though some rank-and-file units engaged in occasional responses to brutal German actions against the local population. Turning to the formation of UPA—the subject of Section 8—the Working Group exposes the fallacy of dating it from October 1942 as in émigré literature, since that date could only refer to the UPA-Polis'ka Sich unit led by Bul'ba-Borovets'. While it is true that armed units of the UPA began to emerge in Polissya and Volhynia in the autumn of 1942, they had as yet no clear direction. So why was the date 14 October 1942 selected as the founding date of UPA? The Working Group explains that the date 19 November 1942 saw the Red Army's counter-offensive at Stalingrad. By demonstrating that they began to oppose the German occupiers before knowing that Germany would lose the war, and the Allies attain a victory, the nationalists would improve their standing in the eyes of the West. In reality, the UPA undertook no active operations in 1942 since such actions would, indirectly, only assist the cause of the Bolshevik armies.

Section 9 of the Report turns attention to "UPA's anti-Nazi armed operations." It begins with the 3rd OUN Conference held in the L'viv region, which made a final decision to launch an armed uprising. Yet the choice of the key target remains a matter of dispute. At that time, the nationalists perceived three main enemies: the Germans, the Soviet Partisans, and the émigré Polish government structures. Opinions at the conference reportedly differed as to how the UPA should assess its priorities. The local Western Ukrainian OUN leader, M. Stepanyak, favored a large-scale uprising against the Germans and the formation of a national government that could conduct negotiations with the Western allies. The OUN leader in the south-western region D. Klyachkivs'kyi and the OUN military leader Shukhevych, on the other hand, thought the uprising should be directed against the Red Partisans and Poles rather than the already struggling Germans.

By mid-March 1943, Ukrainian police left their barracks on the orders of the OUN-B and headed into the forests with arms and ammunition. By 13 May, Klyachkivs'kyi became the Chief Commander of the UPA and its strength reached 30,000 by 1944. At the 3rd Extraordinary OUN Grand Assembly in Ternopil' region in 1943, chaired by Shukhevych, the slogan adopted was "Let us struggle against the imperialism of Moscow and Berlin." Nevertheless, Stepanyak's suggestion to turn on the Germans was rejected, because the Soviet Union was recognized as the principal enemy. The commander of a Partisan force is cited as reporting that "The nationalists do not engage in subversion. They fight Germans only in those areas in which the Germans terrorize the Ukrainian population and when Germans attack them [the nationalists]." The authors state that in the winter of 1943–44 the OUN and UPA leaders were trying to avoid clashes with the Germans because the front line of the war was now approaching. Several unfruitful efforts were made to negotiate with the German side from March to July 1944 in Ternopil' and L'viv. In July 1944, a Constitutional Assembly of the Ukrainian Supreme Liberation Council (UHVR) took place, with K. Osmak appointed chairman of the presidium and Shukhevych head of the General Secretariat. The UPA was formally subordinated to the UHVR. An order of 22 August 1944 commanded the UPA group West-Carpathians to close the anti-German front. It stated that the Germans were no longer occupying Ukraine and therefore could not be considered a major foe, and recommended that the UPA avoid clashes with Germans or Hungarians. The historians conclude Section 9 by noting that UPA's anti-German actions in 1943 through to mid-1944 did not have strategic importance in the context of the Soviet–German war. Rather they were limited to restricting the occupation regime's authority in the territory of Volhynia and Polissya, the main UPA strongholds.

Section 10 deals succinctly and negatively with the issue of the SS Division Halychyna which, they say, did not have a direct link to the OUN or UPA, even though individual insurgents may have served in the Division. They recount the formation of the Division on the initiative of German governor Waechter, and then they apply some scathing criticism: the émigré intelligentsia was forced to accept the formation of the SS Division because of its dependence on the German administration. They tried to justify their actions by declaring that the military formation would serve "the Ukrainian cause." Some propagandists even went so far as to interpret the SS acronym as "Sichove striletstvo" (Sich Sharpshooters). Yet in the authors' view, the Division was a typical collaborationist formation and had a very negative impact on the Ukrainian cause. The OUN Provid commented at the end of 1943 that the formation of the Division would reflect badly on their efforts to establish themselves as a sovereign political factor, particularly in international eyes. Stalin had wanted its members deported by the Western allies at the end of the war, but the Allies declined on the grounds that its members were, formally, Polish citizens. On the other hand, while the formation of the Division was a serious error, there have been no indications that it was involved in war crimes. Its activities were checked thoroughly and its members were then allowed to reside in the United States.[9] The Division, the Report assures, had nothing in common with the elite SS units that comprised fanatical devotees of Nazi doctrine and were stained with crimes. Rather it resembled other SS divisions in Nazi-occupied territories. There were even two Russian SS divisions, but, it is noted, that fact "is known to hardly anyone."

On the Ukrainian–Polish confrontation (Section 11), the working group notes that both the Ukrainian and Polish intelligentsia collaborated with the German occupiers, while the latter were actively involved in inciting ethnic hostilities in the region. Under conditions of extreme ethnic tension, ordinary Poles and Ukrainians tended to lay the blame for their misfortunes on the rival ethnic group, rather than on the occuping regime that usually appointed members of the groups to serve as officials. After the formation of UPA, the police—hitherto mainly Ukrainian—were made up of Poles. The OUN used this situation as a pretext to ascribe all responsibility to Poles for the confrontation and ordered those serving in the local administration and police to leave their posts. Social factors that fuelled the conflict were no less explosive than ethnic or religious ones. The memory of Polish rule in the interwar period also rankled among Ukrainians. The Volhynia events have been obscured, the report notes, because the Ukrainian–Polish confrontation was never mentioned in Polish or Soviet historiography prior to the late 1980s.

However, the working group notes in particular the responsibility of the so-called Volhynia OUN led by Dmytro Klyachkivs'kyi, as well as the entire insurgent movement, for a massacre that saw not only Polish officials, but Polish women and children ruthlessly butchered. Diaspora scholars generally agree that the Volhynia tragedy constitutes a "dark stain" on the history of the OUN-B and UPA, which cannot be justified or explained. Further, the authors assert, one cannot blame Klyachkivs'kyi alone without laying culpability on the entire insurgent movement. The only way to avoid responsibility was to maintain a silence. Thus Klyachkivs'kyi's name did not even appear in the biographies contained in *Entsyklopediya ukrainoznavstva*. In other regions, however, it was the Ukrainians who suffered the worst losses in the conflict.

Section 12 outlines the confrontation during wartime between Ukrainian nationalists and the Soviet authorities and begins with the issue of whether the UPA can be considered a Second World War combatant given that it fought the Axis powers and the Soviet Union at the same time. If the point of reference is the Soviet Union, which bore the brunt of the fighting against the Germans, then the answer is clearly no. The UPA are not participants for those who regard the conflict as the Great Patriotic War. The OUN's and UPA's hostile attitude toward the Soviet Union prevented them from taking an active role in the conflict against the German occupiers. Khrushchev, in turn, informed Soviet Partisans that the nationalists were Nazi agents (in some cases including people who had been fooled by bourgeois nationalist propaganda) and regarded UPA insurgents as traitors who deserved particularly harsh punishment. This malevolence was reflected in the mass deportations from the region that began as early as 1945. As the front line moved westward, the UPA and OUN developed more active contacts with the Wehrmacht, and as before arms, and ammunition were exchanged for intelligence data. By this time the Germans were prepared to provide the UPA with arms in unlimited quantities and even without payment. Luftwaffe planes delivered military equipment and arms through established air routes. Data listed in the Report on deaths, captures, arrests, and surrender of insurgents in 1944–45 comply with those cited elsewhere in this monograph. The insurgents survived the Soviet onslaught and entered a period of post-war confrontation with the Soviet authorities—the subject of Section 13.

Section 13 deals with probably the most critical issue in terms of healing deep rifts in Ukrainian society. The war was over and the Soviet authorities tried to impose their rule on a recalcitrant region, particularly on occasions such as the elections to the Supreme Soviet of the USSR in 1946. The UPA called on the population to boycott the elections and threatened those who participated in them. Moscow in turn mounted an operation called the "great blockade." Over 3,500 regular army units, NKVD troops, and punitive battalion soldiers were deployed in the western regions between January and April 1946. They blocked off the insurgents' access to villages during the winter months but failed to eradicate them. The UPA divided into smaller groups and began to use ambushes as the main form of attack. The authorities frequently offered amnesty to those who gave themselves up. On 28 May 1946, the Report states, Ukrainian Minister of the Interior T. Strokach declared that a decisive defeat had been inflicted on the insurgents. However, he was obliged to add that a few fanatics continued the struggle. Why did they fight under such conditions? The Report cited a comment from the wife of Shukhevych. She told the insurgent commander that he had no transport and that he and his troops would be discovered and shot. He responded: "You know how much I love you. But I love Ukraine even more..." The Soviet offensive was renewed during the period of elections to the Supreme Soviet of the Ukrainian SSR in 1947. In the countryside troops surrounded the polling stations and the Interior Ministry units killed some prominent UPA leaders. Yet even according to Soviet sources, OUN cells and the UPA carried out 272 armed actions between January and March 1947. Therefore the CC CPU issued a resolution on 5 April "On intensifying the struggle against the remaining gangs of Ukrainian–German nationalists in the western regions of the Ukrainian SSR." Military and security service operations increased and over 77,000 people—"gang supporters"—were deported to remote regions of the USSR in 1947. By 1948, Khrushchev reassigned priorities and ordered the MGB to complete the task of eliminating the UPA. Intelligence played a key role and the priority assignment was to infiltrate the underground organizations.

In this period, the UPA exhausted its resources. Soviet operations, deportations, and collectivization of farms all took their toll on the insurgency, the Report notes. The penetration of the UPA by Soviet agents created an atmosphere of suspicion and not infrequently the UPA sections dissolved themselves. On 3 September 1949, Shukhevych issued an order concerning the termination of the military activities of the insurgents and headquarters, and their transformation into OUN-B underground structures. By 1949, the special groups of the MGB were disbanded. The authors suspect that the reason was they had committed criminal actions and had become well-known to the local population. In late 1949, the notorious P. Sudoplatov was sent on a six-month mission to L'viv with a special operational unit assigned to locate Shukhevych. On 5 March 1950, the UPA leader was trapped in the village of Bilohoshcha, near L'viv, and killed. Other key leaders of the movement were eliminated in 1951–52 (R. Kravchuk, I. Lytvynchuk, and P. Fedun [Petro Poltava]). On 23 May 1954, Vasyl Kuk, head of the UHVR General Secretariat, leader of the OUN Provid in Ukraine, and UPA Chief Commander, was captured. After 1954, only isolated actions were conducted by the insurgent movement, which had been practically destroyed. The Report cites a resolution of the CC CPSU of 26 May 1953 "On the political and economic situation in the western regions of Ukraine," which summed up the results of the struggle between 1944 and 1952. I have divided these for convenience and comprehension into several tables below.

Table 1: State "Repressions" in Western Ukraine, 1944–1952

Number of arrested:	134,000
Number of killed:	153,000
Number of deported:	203,000

Table 2: KGB Figures (1957) on Underground Casualties, 1944–1956

Total casualties:	155,108
In Eastern Ukraine:	1,746
Voluntary surrenders:	76,753
Arrests for "nationalist activities":	103,866
Including convictions:	87,756

Table 3: Soviet Casualties, 1944–1953[10]

Total casualties:	30,676
NKGB-MGB:	687
Militia:	1,864
Servicemen of internal forces, border guards, and army:	3,199
Punitive battalions:	2,590
Members of Supreme Soviet:	2
Heads of *oblast* executive committees:	1
Heads of city executive committees:	8
Heads of *rayon* executive committees:	32
Heads of village councils:	1,454
Other Soviet officials:	1,235
Party secretaries (*oblast*, city, and *rayon*):	207
Members of collective farms:	15,355
Workers:	676
Representatives of intelligentsia:	1,931
Children, elderly people, and housewives:	860

Comment: the GCWGR and OUN-UPA

The Government Commission Working Group's Report represents a bold attempt to come to terms with the complex issues surrounding OUN-UPA. Almost every major event has been subjected to debate and diverse interpretations, particularly given that there is almost no middle ground on most issues, and the undermining of the old Soviet version has signified that the version espoused by the OUN in the Diaspora has come to the forefront. Western works on the topic are either very dated—such as the classic monograph of John A. Armstrong[11]—or else they have focused on issues that do not make OUN-UPA the main focus. These include the bold attempt by Andrew Wilson to demonstrate the limited appeal of narrow ethno-nationalism in contemporary Ukraine[12] and Amir Weiner's study of the wartime experience and legacy in the region of Vynnytsya.[13] Such works are ever more necessary to provide a guideline to events that remain so politicized that they are rarely approached dispassionately. But to what extent does the Report cover the main issues? Can it be considered a definitive account? How is it likely to be received in the various parts of Ukraine with their preconceived notions about the OUN and UPA that are largely seen in black-and-white dimensions?

In the first place, the authors of the Report have made every effort to include all relevant information. They do not idealize any of the insurgent or opposition formations, and they cite figures from Soviet archives as part of their source base. In their conclusions, they have tended to exonerate the OUN-B and UPA, and to chastise the OUN-M for its unquestioning allegiance to the Germans, even after the uncompromising nature of Hitler's plans for Ukraine had become apparent. The SS Division Halychyna does not emerge from the survey with much credit and is in fact cited as a collaborating unit, despite the fact that it did not commit war crimes. One key issue surfaces immediately, namely the intentions of the OUN-B and the UPA at various times to work with the German authorities for matters of expediency and in the long-term interests of Ukraine. As Kas'yanov has demonstrated, the OUN-B's ideas were similar in many respects to those of interwar regimes in Central Europe and can be designated loosely as Fascist. In the account by Kas'yanov, and as stated in several other sources, there was also a notable element of anti-Semitism among the OUN leadership. The Report is notably silent on examples of anti-Jewish sentiment that may have manifested themselves in L'viv in the last days of June and early July 1941. The Report also uses ambiguous language when it observes that the UPA should be exempted from responsibility as a collaborator precisely because the Nazis would not tolerate the insurgents in the capacity of a 'warring party' on the Nazi-occupied territories (as part of the Nazi strategy not to tolerate non-German armed formations on the occupied territories, according to the report). Willingness to collaborate should be regarded as an important factor in its own right. Oddly, though the authors stress the need for a broader examination of the war years so that the OUN and UPA actions can be seen in perspective, they tend to examine UPA's struggle purely in a Ukrainian context. Very little is said about the mass collectivization campaign that began in 1948 other than that it cut off UPA's food supply from the villages. It was applied simultaneously (albeit without success in the case of Poland and Hungary) to Eastern Europe and was part of a general Soviet campaign to control this entire region. Also, little is written about the Cold War context and US and British aid to the insurgents. When an insurgent movement has outside assistance, it becomes much more dangerous in the eyes of the occupying power, particularly one as sensitive and neurotic as Stalin's Soviet Union.

Ultimately, the Report does not offer a very clear opinion on the question of recognizing UPA combatants for their participation in the Second World War, and as insurgents struggling for an independent Ukraine. There is a certain sympathy and understanding of UPA's motives and activities, particularly on the issue of Volhynia, where one can say that the section differs significantly from Western interpretations, such as those offered by Snyder or Berkhoff. In fairness, the main author of this section (Il'yushyn) does not condone the ultimatum given to the Polish population by Klyachkivs'kyi and implies that the entire insurgent movement must take responsibility for the massacres of 1943. Other authors, particular those in the West who have written for the Ukrainian media, have tended to offer even more one-dimensional narratives. Serbyn, for example, correctly denounces the continuation of the Soviet myths of the Great Patriotic War but he does not offer concomitant critiques of the insurgent movement. One cannot have it both ways. To their credit, the historians working on the Report have tried to see the events from all angles. They do not try to whitewash the crimes of the insurgents, but try instead to explain how these events occurred. As this was a micro-war, fought within a larger conflict, there is a tendency to attribute blame to the larger powers—to some extent such attribution is justified. However, there is also an element of putting into practice long-crystallized views of a future Ukraine that had developed in the interwar period. In this respect, perhaps the integral nationalism and fanaticism of the late 1920s and 1930s were more influential than the example of the 1918 Ukrainian National Republic.

Assessment

In the summer of 2005, the Ukrainian Minister of Justice, Roman Zvarych, requested that central executive bodies in Ukraine peruse materials advanced by the government commission, put together to examine the activities of the OUN and UPA. The ministry intended to submit a draft proposal to the Cabinet of Ministers that recommended the recognition of the OUN and UPA by the Ukrainian state. Commenting on the work of this commission, in the spring of 2005, Shapoval states that the working group did not want to whitewash or blacken anyone. People seem to comprehend that the OUN and the UPA were struggling for an independent Ukraine rather than against it. However, he adds, the authorities during Kuchma's time did not say this out loud, and neither to date had the Orange leadership. It was time therefore for the government, and first and foremost the president to make his own comments on the topic.[14] On 12 May 2005, immediately following the commemoration of the 60th anniversary of the end of the Second World War in Europe, the president obliged in a live interview that was broadcast on ICTV, New Channel, STB, and Channel 5. As a precursor to this interview, Yushchenko had taken the unusual step of inviting UPA veterans to attend the events in Kyiv for the anniversary. Now he advocated reconciliation between former adversaries in the UPA and the Red Army soldiers, noting that Ukrainians had already forgiven the Germans, the occupiers of their land during wartime, as well as the Poles for the events of Operation Vistula. Why cannot Ukrainians forgive themselves, he wondered? He noted that on the individual level, many combatants had shaken hands and made their peace with each other, for which their offspring would be grateful. Once again, this humanitarian attitude did not extend to veterans of the SS Division Halychyna, as was evident from a response of the president to a question from Donets'k, and he refused to deal with the issue of compensation for UPA veterans and victims of repression, which clearly irked some of the wartime participants.[15]

As a final note on the issue of rehabilitating the OUN and UPA, one can turn to the pages of the *Kyiv Post*, which published a memorable editorial in October 2005. There was an outburst of violence in the streets of Kyiv between the UPA and Red Army veterans, during a protest by the former to demand that it be granted the same benefits that the latter continue to receive. Having discussed the polarized viewpoints, the (unnamed) author writes:

> The horror is that both sides are right, and both sides are wrong. There are no easy answers in this corner of the European nightmare of the twen-

tieth century. This is the sort of situation that any morally salient person can only approach with humility, and a recognition that the ambiguity cannot be expunged. That's why it is a tragedy. The controversy also cuts to the root of the question of independent Ukraine's identity. Is today's Ukraine the descendent of Soviet Ukraine? In that case, honoring the UPA would be inappropriate. Or is it the child of the Ukrainian nationalists, the western guerrilla fighters? Who can say?

The editorial doubts whether providing funds for UPA veterans would resolve the problem, though it feels that the president could provide some sort of compensation that is not directly comparable to that given to the veterans of the Red Army. It ends with the following statement:

> There's no reconciling the Red Army and the UPA—the "Stalinists" and the "Fascists." The best that can be done is not to try, but to paper over the dispute for the sake of social harmony until all these old men are gone taking with them into the grave their terrible history.[16]

Will the problem disappear once the veterans are gone? With the OUN and several other nationalist organizations operating now in Ukraine, it seems unlikely. Indeed the traditions, the memories, stories, songs, and memorabilia of the OUN and UPA have been transferred from one generation to another as though they constitute the only outlook and the only past of Ukrainians from all walks of life. In North America the nationalist organizations continue to be the most influential despite the disparate views, arguments, and disputes that have always existed between different factions. The Famine of 1932–33—known among these organizations today as the Famine-Holodomor or "Genocidal Famine"—is an issue that is directly related. How could Ukrainians be loyal to a state that tried to eliminate them in the millions? It is an unanswerable question.

Notes

1   A book has now been published to accompany this pamphlet. See Stanislav Kul'chyts'kyi, et al, *OUN i UPA: istorychni narysy* (Kyiv: Naukova dumka, 2005).
2   H. V. Kas'yanov, "Ideolohiya OUN: istoryko-retrospektyvnyi analiz," *Ukrains'kyi istorychnyi zhurnal*, No. 2 (February 2004): 30–32.
3   Ibid., pp. 35–36.
4   Ibid., pp. 38–39.

5 Ibid., pp. 39-41.

6 Henadii Sakharov, "Natsionalizm?—Natsionalizm!" 17 August 2006; [http://maidan.org.ua].

7 For a brief overview, see Bohdan Chervak, "Ostatochnu krapku ne postavyv nevblahannyi chas," *Maidan*, 10 June 2005. Part 14, written by H. Kas'yanov, is an abbreviated version of the article discussed above: "Ideolohiya OUN: Istoryko-retrospekytvni analiz," *Ukrains'kyi istorychnyi zhurnal*, No. 2 (2004): 68-82.

8 National Academy of Sciences, Institute of History of Ukraine, "Problema OUN-UPA: Zvit robochoi hrupy istorykiv pry Uryadovii komisii z vyvchennya diyal'nosti OUN i UPA. Osnovi tezy z problemy OUN-UPA (istorychnyi vysnovok)," Kyiv, 2004: [http://www.ukraine-poland.com/u/publicystyka/publicystyka.php?id=3480], and ff.

9 There is an evident error here: the majority of former Division combatants took up initial residence in the United Kingdom.

10 The figures are from a report to the Presidium of the Ukrainian Supreme Soviet by the KGB archival and registration department with the Council of Ministers, Ukrainian SSR, April 1973.

11 John A. Armstrong, *Ukrainian Nationalism* (Littleton, Colorado: Ukrainian Academic Press, 1980).

12 Andrew Wilson, *Ukrainian Nationalism in the 1990s: a Minority Faith* (Cambridge: Cambridge University Press, 1997).

13 Amir Weiner, *Making Sense of War: The Second World War and the Fate of the Bolshevik Revolution* (Princeton: Princeton University Press, 2001).

14 Yurii Shapoval', "Ukrains'ka druha svitova," *Dzerkalo tyzhnya*, No. 15 (23 April-6 May 2005); [http://www.zn.kiev.ua/ie/show/543/49834/]

15 The interview with Yushchenko appeared in *Ukrains'ka pravda*, 12 May 2005, [http://ww2.pravda.com.ua/archive/2005/may/12/efir.shtml].

16 Editorial, *Kyiv Post*, 19 October 2005.

CONCLUSION

Having examined the various opinions through discourses on the Famine, the OUN, and the UPA, and other aspects of Ukraine in the Second World War at different levels, one can offer a few comments first concerning the current state of historical knowledge. Though it is posited that historical truth is elusive and perhaps impossible to ascertain—and for the purposes of writing a national history, somewhat rarely applied—the opening of archives and academic debates provides some enlightenment on the issues under discussion. An outsider will want to know whether the Famine of 1932–33, for example, was an act of genocide; or whether the OUN and UPA committed crimes during the war and afterward; or whether it is possible to construct a new history that draws a line directly through these events to the period of independence, announced by the Ukrainian Parliament on August 24, 1991. Such a construct would create a portrait of persecution (the Famine) followed by a movement for liberation (OUN and UPA) that was ultimately successful through the establishment of an independent Ukraine, removing along the way other agents of political change. The question also arises as to the accuracy of the various narratives or the extent to which school textbooks portray the most widely accepted versions of events from the point of view of scholarly inquiry. Still, any interpretation of events is ultimately subjective, and it is fair to say that for every key issue discussed in this book, there are at least two sides, and sometimes more.

The Famine of 1932–33 remains a controversial topic, despite the plethora of writings and the release of volumes of documents and eyewitness accounts. No serious scholar denies that the Famine took place or that its consequences were catastrophic. However, it may be fair to say that political activism with regard to the issues, including the adoption of resolutions by various governments to recognize it as an act of genocide against the Ukrainian people, has *preceded* the conclusion of the scholarly debate. That may reflect the fact that in the minds of many, the Famine as a genocide is not open to question.

There are two well-known genocides that occurred in the 20th century: the Holocaust of the European Jews in the Second World War; and the elimination of the Armenian population by the Turks during the First World War. The Holocaust is accepted as an act of genocide almost universally and certainly by the academic community. The Armenian genocide, according to writing at the present time, led to increased tension and the death of an Armenian journalist in Turkey. The Turkish government does not accept that there was a conscious decision by Turks to eliminate Armenians. The number of victims in Ukraine was the same or greater than that of the Jewish Holocaust. But did the Stalin regime set out deliberately to resolve the national question in Ukraine by eliminating Ukrainian peasants?

James E. Mace and others have demonstrated that Stalin, Molotov, and others were preoccupied with the political situation in Ukraine, partly because of the levels to which the process of "Ukrainization" had progressed, and also because of suspicion of Polish influences and Polish intentions generally. The Soviet regime at the least knew of the problems that grain requisitions had caused and chose to exacerbate them by extracting all foodstuffs from the starving villages. Nothing was left in reserve. Neighboring republics, such as Belarus and Russia, were hungry but not starving, though one should note a similar situation in the ethnically mixed Kuban, as well as large-scale losses of life two years earlier in Kazakhstan. The key issue revolves around the reasons why the Famine occurred. Here, one has to deal with the fact that the supposition that the Famine was directed exclusively at Ukrainians cannot be accepted unequivocally based on current research by scholars outside Ukraine. Here is perhaps the crux of the matter: aside from the output of Mace, the most authoritative studies have been written by scholars who do not accept the genocide theory.[1] That is not to say that this school of thought is static or that it might not be convinced by new archival evidence illustrating that their conclusions are erroneous. To date, however, these figures have been quite adamant that the sources they have consulted support their conclusions. And, as a result, there is a clear lack of consensus on the Famine that devastated the eastern regions of Ukraine, and which is now approaching its 75th anniversary.

It is also evident that there is a strong political dimension to the diversity of views, which encompasses some of the issues discussed herein. First and foremost is the direct rhetorical link from the Famine, through the events of the war years, the OUN and UPA, to the present independent government of Ukraine. The view of the Famine as genocidal was propagated by émigrés, some of whom identified with the "nationalist" perspective of the Second

World War, and originated—mostly—from Western Ukraine. There are numerous examples of writings in the West, scholarly and otherwise, which condemn their perspective out of hand and regard those who write from the "nationalist" viewpoint as right-wing extremists and sympathizers of the OUN and UPA, the fellow travelers of Nazi Germany, and anti-Communist to a fault.[2] In other words, the sentiment of these writers is that the advancement of the Famine as genocidal emanates from the same sources that would wish to recognize UPA insurgents as veterans of the Second World War. In turn, those who would reject the latter may have some doubts about the former issue. In addition, postwar scholarly writing in the West about the Soviet Union traditionally centered on Russia rather than the non-Russian republics until the recent period.[3] Western higher educational institutions for years neglected the other fourteen republics in the USSR. Even today it is reasonable to state that Russia gets an inordinate amount of attention from scholarly publishers, academics, journalists, and writers, even at a time when Ukraine (for example) is independent, and is a state with a long history, as well as a population and area the size of France. Rightly or wrongly, these scholars helped to determine general views of the development of the Soviet Union, and some are deeply entrenched today, so much so that something as radical as a Famine-Genocide in Ukraine is unacceptable. As noted, the lack of serious scholarly studies by those who think otherwise has perpetuated the situation.

Regarding the Famine, one can say the following: it remained a state secret for 54 years, a tragedy that escaped world attention because of its deliberate concealment by the Soviet regime under Stalin. The prelude was the decision to collectivize villages in the Soviet Union in 1929, a crash campaign that was supposed to be voluntary, but which at the same time was initiated under the slogan: "the liquidation of the *kulaks* as a class." It was the biggest social upheaval to that point in modern history, a "second revolution" that has been well researched by historians in the former Soviet Union and the West. Peasants were divided arbitrarily into rich, middle, and poor, with the former targeted for deportation, and sometimes even executed as common criminals. In practice the campaign removed peasants in all three categories who were opposed to the collectivization campaign. Aside from a brief respite in the spring of 1930, when the government halted collectivization because of the violence that had ensued, collectivization continued at a relentless pace. Stalin wanted the formation of collective farms—artels—that could guarantee grain quotas to the state and supply the rapidly growing towns as well as the Soviet army.

Collectivization was carried out by outsiders, most notably the so-called 25,000ers; volunteers from the urban areas who were sent into the countryside to help create the new farms.[4] Additionally it involved the establishment of Machine-Tractor Stations in each district, ostensibly to lease machinery to the farmers. But in the early 30s, these were of little use to the farmers as they lacked tractors and other equipment. Rather they constituted an additional form of political control over the countryside. With the removal of the so-called *kulaks*, the rural regions were deprived of their better-off farmers, usually the most efficient and skilled leaders of the villages. Peasants destroyed livestock rather than see it collectivized. Sometimes they held "feasts" over several days to consume what they owned. The outcome was a catastrophic decline in heads of cattle over the period of all-out collectivization. Once the collective farms were established, then grain quotas were fixed annually to be given up to the state before the farms were permitted to feed themselves. There was notably a discrepancy between the projected harvest—taken before harvesting—and the actual yield. Most of the main grain-growing areas were Ukrainian or inhabited by Ukrainians, including the republic itself, the Kuban, and the North Caucasus. The Volga region of Russia was also of critical concern, as was the territory of Kazakhstan, which was nomadic, and in which one in three among the population died in 1930-31.

It remains unclear whether 1932 was an especially bad harvest year for Ukraine. Certainly, however, the situation had become critical in agriculture. By August 1932, the infamous decree had been issued that made it a criminal offence for anyone to take so much as an ear of grain from the field before the state quota had been filled. At the third conference of the Communist Party of Ukraine in the summer of 1932, which was attended by Stalin's close associates Vyacheslav Molotov and Lazar Kaganovich, Ukrainian leaders and local officials tried to draw the attention of the Moscow officials to the alarming situation developing in Ukraine. In August of that same year, however, Stalin wrote a letter to Kaganovich in which he expressed his suspicions about Ukrainian peasants while also questioning the loyalty of the Ukrainian party leadership in the capital city of Kharkiv. Stalin maintained that these leaders were still under the influence of the late Symon Petlyura as well as agents of Polish leader Jozef Pilsudski. Stalin wrote that the USSR might "lose Ukraine" and demanded that it be given prompt attention by his officials. One can posit that two problems were linked together by Stalin: on the one hand, he was concerned about Ukraine; on the other, his anxiety also reflected his overriding fear of Poland's intentions, and memories of Polish–Ukrainian collusion in the war against Soviet Russia in 1919-20.

On 22 October, the Soviet regime created Extraordinary Commissions, which began to function in the following month. Pavel Postyshev led the

Commission in the Volga region, Kaganovich the one in the North Caucasus, whereas the one in Ukraine was under the control of Molotov. The Ukrainian commission operated with unusual savagery. First of all it carried out the requisitioning of the grain quota, which had been maintained at the same level as the previous year, even though the harvest gathered was considerably lower. The commission soon ran out of grain, and therefore a new penalty was imposed—the requisitioning of meat and potatoes from those in "debt" for grain procurements. The demand was then transformed into the confiscation of all food supplies accumulated from the new harvest, including sugar, fruits, onions, etc. The stated reason, to cite the Ukrainian party secretary Stanislav Kosior, was "to teach the peasants a lesson." Once the grain had been taken, the peasants on these farms were the first to perish, and once stocks of food had been confiscated then the death toll from starvation rose by dozens of times.

Stalin began to be fearful of the results of his policies. He installed internal military police to prevent starving peasants from crossing the border into Belarus or Russia. He appointed Postyshev as Second Secretary of the Ukrainian Communist Party, but in reality with plenipotentiary powers and answerable only to Stalin. Postyshev and other party officials in Moscow not only took an active part in requisitioning grain from the now-starving peasants, they also began a purge of the Ukrainian leadership. This purge was soon extended from the party to Ukrainian cultural leaders, scholars, and teachers, to remove what were termed "nationalists," "enemies," and unreliable elements. A new round of deportations was also begun. A combination of factors negated any kind of aid or support from the West, including the work of pro-Stalinist journalists, such as Walter Duranty, the *New York Times*' correspondent in Moscow, and the ambivalent attitudes of Western powers to what was occurring in the Soviet Union. Paradoxically the United States established diplomatic relations with the USSR at the height of the Famine. Other countries chose to accept the official version that the "food problems" in the USSR were no worse than those in the West as a result of the Great Depression.

The Famine in the year 1933 was a catastrophe created and implemented by man. It did not have to happen. There is ample evidence that the Soviet leadership was aware of the scale of the disaster but chose to extract food from the already hungry farmers nevertheless. At least 4 million starved to death in what was then the Ukrainian SSR. There were further victims in the Kuban and North Caucasus. Entire settlements were depopulated (including as we have seen in the narratives, those inhabited by non-Ukrainians, such as Jews and Germans), and what seems the most tragic factor of all, there was no source of aid to the families that had been deprived of all sources of food. One can say, as Tauger has demonstrated,[5] that drought and poor harvest contributed to the serious problems that occurred in 1932. But in 1933 there was a tragedy of a vastly different dimension—the thousands of starving became millions, and the region reaped the full effects of Stalin's disastrous collectivization program. The Soviet authorities would later eliminate the witnesses to this tragedy; it would eliminate all those outside Stalin's immediate circle. The Famine would be an event confined to whispers and silent memory. When war broke out in 1941, the population of Ukraine was lower than it had been in 1926; even in the postwar decades that imbalance had not been addressed. The Famine remains a symbol of man's inhumanity to his own kind. But was it premeditated murder of a particular ethnic group? Was it permitted to happen in order to punish the recalcitrant peasants, most of whom happened to be Ukrainian, or to eliminate Ukrainians? The answer is far from clear though that does not diminish the enormity of the event. That there was a national element to official policies seems evident from Stalin's correspondence, but one must ask also to what extent that element simply stood in the path of the ruthless plans of the leadership, just as the nomadic population of Kazakhstan could not be permitted to exist under the circumstances brought about by the mass collectivization of agriculture.

Turning to the OUN and UPA, it is possible to offer a narrative that appears to be justified by current historical inquiry. It might run as follows. Under the difficult conditions of Polish rule that followed the First World War, many politically active Ukrainians chose to abandon democratic parties and reverted to extremism. In the 1920s the Communist Party of Western Ukraine (an autonomous section of the Communist Party of Poland) wielded some influence. However, by the late 1920s and early 1930s, and particularly during the period of Polish Pacification, the Organization of Ukrainian Nationalists (OUN), formed from the Ukrainian Military Organization (UVO), became the most dynamic of Ukrainian organizations, albeit in an underground and illegal format. The OUN was a terrorist organization devoted to attaining an independent Ukraine, and influenced by the Fascist and other authoritarian movements then prevailing in Europe. Although it was not in any way unique for its extremism, the OUN nonetheless represented a polarized political outlook. Following the rift in the organization and its division into the two wings under Bandera and Mel'nyk, the OUN continued, as earlier, to cooperate with different structures of Nazi Germany, the most likely agent of change in Eastern Europe. Following the Nazi–Soviet Pact and the division of Poland, it became clear that the OUN wished to use the anticipated German invasion to bring about political change in the territories populated by ethnic Ukrainians. The same Pact also effectively united Ukrainian territories in one entity (the Ukrainian SSR), other than the western region of Transcarpathia.

With the outbreak of the German–Soviet war, both wings of the OUN co-operated with the advancing German army. A distinction should be made between the OUN-M, which continued its collaboration throughout the war years, and the OUN-B, which broke with the German administration, after the latter's failure to approve the independent Ukraine proclaimed in L'viv on 30 June 1941. The announcement of that state, on the other hand, was premature and not clearly supported by a majority of the population. It is also uncertain how severely Bandera and his followers were treated by the Germans in the initial weeks after the 30 June proclamation. Reports say that the OUN-B immediately began to oppose both the new occupiers and the Soviets appear exaggerated. With the lapse of several months, nevertheless, German intentions had been made plain, and the OUN-B, with its commitment to achieving an independent Ukraine, could no longer cooperate realistically with a former ally. The moderation of its prewar doctrine duly followed at the Third Extraordinary Congress of the OUN of 21–25 August 1943, when the "Fascist" elements of the original program were discarded. By this same date, the OUN-B had been superseded as a military formation by the Ukrainian Insurgent Army, though the ideology remained that of the OUN-B, and the latter served as the guiding force for a campaign that now turned against the Soviet Union and Red Army. The turning point in this supposed transformation of OUN-B thinking was the Battle of Stalingrad, which ended on 2 February 1943, and the subsequent retreat of the German Wehrmacht. To most observers it was clear that Hitler's Eastern campaign was doomed to failure. For Ukrainians, like others such as Lithuanians and Latvians, the only potential source of future aid for their cause was an alliance with the democratic powers of the West.

UPA, in turn, was prepared to take the same gamble. Its activities date from the spring of 1943, once the forces under the influence of the OUN-B had triumphed over the original band following Taras Bul'ba-Borovets'; as well as the OUN-M. Politically, placing the date of its foundation at October 1942 was expedient because it suggested that UPA's beginnings occurred at a time when the Germans were still advancing, and the final victor in the war unpredictable. The notion, widely disseminated today, that the army turned its forces on the two totalitarian enemies simultaneously, is far-fetched. The UPA had two enemies, but the other one was the Polish population in Volhynia and Galicia. This is not to suggest that it cooperated wholeheartedly with the

Germans; rather there were conflicts from the spring of 1943 to the spring of 1944 that were sporadic and largely spontaneous. By the latter date, the two sides agreed to cooperate, a move according to Peter J. Potichnyj (a young participant of the UPA shortly afterward) that was expedient from UPA's perspective. The Germans were losing the war but were still strong enough to deliver powerful counterattacks against the advancing Red Army. Under Klyachkivs'kyi, the UPA initiated an ethnic cleansing of the Polish population of Volhynia that, as we have seen, took up to 60,000 lives. It was conducted with a brutality not seen again in Europe until the civil war in former Yugoslavia in the early 1990s. That statement is not to deny that the UPA membership was varied. It contained non-Ukrainians, former soldiers of the Red Army, and people whose ideological outlook was far from extreme. However, those who led the organization brought about a fanatical insurgent group that paid little attention to humanitarian concepts. Poland responded with attacks on the Ukrainian population that was deported from Poland from 1944 onward.

Once the Red Army returned to the territories inhabited by UPA, the UPA–Soviet conflict escalated to a scale unprecedented in the modern history of Ukraine. It is estimated that the population in this region was around four million (following the drastic reduction of ethnic Poles),[6] and at least 10% of that figure had some association with the UPA according to the figures provided by the Soviet side. Two points can be made here. The first concerns the policies of the USSR toward the reoccupied region: an amnesty that seems to have been well received was followed by brutal repressions carried out by troops of the internal security forces under the leadership of party secretary Nikita Khrushchev. Simultaneously a propaganda campaign attempted to identify the UPA with the German occupiers, as collaborators and traitors. Such tactics escalated the violence. In truth what occurred can be described neither as a civil war nor a war of liberation against a foreign occupier. There were ethnic Ukrainians on both sides and—perhaps more to the point—it was mainly innocent people that wished to remain on the sidelines who became the new victims. It was a war without quarter, without any form of toleration or human decency. Further, from the Soviet perspective, Western Ukraine was not unique. The entire Western borderlands were regarded as politically untrustworthy and in need of large-scale repressions. Many who were not killed or injured were deported, further uprooting the lives of people whose had been disrupted in one way or another for the past fifteen years. The population in short was to be subdued by brutality and force and there was no question that the ruthless German occupation was to be succeeded by an equally savage, long-term Soviet one. It is posited that Soviet tactics were needless following the amnesty and they exacerbated the situation, not least by eliminating the freedom of choice for the occupied population concerning their future.

UPA, reorganized into a military formation under the leadership of Roman Shukhevych, offered little solace, either. Its actions were directed first and foremost at eliminating Soviet security officials and Red Army soldiers, and there is ample evidence of the location and consequences of many of these conflicts. In this sense it could be said to be defending Ukrainian lands against an occupier. On the other hand, its viciousness toward ethnic Ukrainians who opted not to join its ranks, or wavered in such a decision, was also much in evidence. As Timothy Snyder has noted, the UPA may have killed as many local Ukrainians as it did Soviet forces, and to this tragic toll must be added the Polish victims cited above. Retribution in the form of removal of limbs, or the deaths of family members of those who refused support, was common. In a fight literally to the death, there was no room for compromise. From the "killing fields" of Western Ukraine it is rather difficult to determine, in any historical narrative that can make up a modern national history, the heroes and villains. What often surprises is less the violence than how well it was organized and directed. The UPA was fighting in its view the same powers that had persecuted Ukrainians and destroyed their national culture in the 1930s. But it was also fighting its own people, and since 1940, such in-fighting had regularly resulted in butchery, even among people whose political outlook was similar. It epitomized the polarization of political life in Ukrainian territories that were yet to fall under Soviet rule and it is difficult to portray the period other than as the saddest chapter in the long history of Ukrainians.

Many questions remain following the appearance of the various narratives of the late 1980s to 2006. Why, for example, is the Famine-Genocide recognized by Ukrainians in the Diaspora and in Western Ukraine (and Kyiv), but has yet to be accepted very widely in the regions in which it occurred? How does one deal with Eastern Ukrainians, many of whom continue to regard Russian as their first language and the USSR as part of their heritage, and refuse to accept the OUN and UPA as anything other than traitors? Is one conception necessarily more advanced than the other? Can people be blamed for their upbringing or having different perceptions of what Ukraine means and how one interprets one's past? The bard Taras Shevchenko is one of the few figures universally accepted as part of this past. Narratives are changing, but there is as yet no pervasive discourse about the recent period that is acceptable by the broad majority of Ukraine's population. Does it matter? President Yushchenko and his government think that it does, and scholars, intellectuals, and writers have tried vainly to come up with a narrative of historical memory that can be applied to the independent state. Such a text cannot come solely from the Diaspora, which preserved for years its own viewpoint of the Stalin years. That is because one version of events cannot simply replace the former one with a similar and bewildering simplicity of interpretation. Much that happened during the Soviet period may have been bad, but not everything. Ukrainians became literate with an educational level as high as anywhere in the West. The Soviet authorities permitted the veneration of certain figures for their own purposes: Ivan Franko, Shevchenko, and others. Many Ukrainians achieved scientific, economic, and political eminence under the Soviet regime.

Ultimately a national history may be written that embraces the memory and perspectives of all Ukrainians, as well as all peoples who live or lived in Ukraine during the tumultuous and tragic events of the twentieth century.[7] Ukrainians are no different from any other group in having a past that contains bravery and atrocities, and errors and achievements. They are not and should never be perceived solely as victims of one power or the other, as depicted in the sort of writing that can look at the past only in terms of persecution at the hands of Russia or Poland, or—lamentably and unforgivably—to blame the Jews for the Famine of 1932–33. Nor can misdeeds, such as those described above that were committed by UPA, be erased from the national memory. Ukrainians are probably no better and no worse than other peoples in offering a conception of the Second World War that contains more distortions than corroborated facts. That statement would embrace the victors in that war as well as the defeated powers. Like other states, they have as yet failed to deal with these events in a satisfactory manner and there is a possibility that they will never do so, and that the darker aspects will simply be concealed—many have already been forgotten. It would be refreshing and perhaps a form of self-healing, however, if Ukrainians could offer a conception of their recent past that looked at all aspects of these events, recognizing in passing that heroes could be criminals and that—Soviet propaganda aside—the reticence in many parts of Ukraine about the OUN and UPA would appear to be justified.

This book has examined narratives of the events that elicit much emotion and anger, and as such it cannot satisfy everyone. However, that was never the intention. The goal was to illustrate the changes in interpretation and the long, and possibly futile, attempt to construct a national history that might have general appeal to the population and can help to define the modern nation. The complexity is demonstrated by the political situation at the time of writing with a democratic, Western-leaning but fundamentally weakened president, Viktor Yushchenko, and his former nemesis and representative of the Donets'k clan, Viktor Yanukovich, as Prime Minister. Ukraine seems already to be slipping back into the ways of the Kuchma regime, and whether it will ever resurrect again the euphoria generated by the Orange Revolution is a moot point. Yet it is clear that in politics, as in historical memory and the reconstruction of the past, the only solution is some form of compromise. There can be no second-class Ukrainians and no single perception of the past. One cannot "restore historical truth" as one writer demanded, because there is no such thing. But one can examine the past from a multi-dimensional perspective without waiting—as commented in the editorial in the *Kyiv Post*—for all these old men with their bitter memories to die. It is a task on which some Ukrainian historians have embarked and one hopes that it is within this post-Soviet independent state that the question is, to some extent at least, resolved.

Notes

1   I include in this group Mark B. Tauger, R. W. Davies, Stephen G. Wheatcroft, Michael Ellman, Lynne Viola, Moshe Lewin, and perhaps Robert Conquest who seems ambivalent on the question. These scholars have been responsible for an enormous quantity of work on Stalin's policies in agriculture in the late 1920s and early 1930s. See, for example, R. W. Davies and Stephen G. Wheatcroft, *The Years of Hunger: Soviet Agriculture, 1931-1933 (The Industrialization of Soviet Russia)* (Basingstoke, Hampshire: Palgrave Macmillan, 2004).

2   See, for example, Douglas Tottle, *Fraud, Famine, and Fascism: the Ukrainian Genocide Myth from Hitler to Harvard* (Toronto: Progress Books, 1987); and Jeff Coplon, "In Search of a Soviet Holocaust: a 55-Year Old Famine Feeds the Right," *Village Voice*, 12 January 1988.

3   We have cited earlier the foundation of the Ukrainian Research Institute at Harvard University and the Canadian Institute of Ukrainian Studies at the University of Alberta in the 1970s. However, both these institutions were founded with the support and active participation of the local Ukrainian communities. It was relatively rare, for example, to find scholars working on Ukrainian topics in US institutions prior to Ukrainian independence.

4   A classic work on this period is Lynne Viola, *The Best Sons of the Fatherland: Workers in the Vanguard of Soviet Collectivization* (New York: Oxford University Press, 1987).

5   Mark B. Tauger, "The 1932 Harvest and the Soviet Famine of 1932-1933," *Slavic Review*, Volume 50, No. 1 (Spring 1991): 70-89.

6   The figure derives from a personal conversation with John-Paul Himka, Edmonton, Alberta, on 24 January 2007. That total seems plausible. In 1931, the total population of Ukrainian ethnic territories under Polish rule is reported to have been 6.5 million people. See Ivan Teslya and Evhen Tyut'ko, compilers, and Lyubomyr Wynar, ed., *Istorychnyi Atlas Ukrainy* (New York: Ukrainian Historical Association, 1980), p. 154.

7   In this regard, one might cite the critique of representation of the past in the city of Drohobych, Western Ukraine, by the Israeli scholar Shlomo Avineri. Professor Avineri writes: "One can well understand that a new nation-state like Ukraine would be zealous in establish-

ing its identity and claim historical continuity even in areas which, because of their mixed heritage, have been disputed. This is natural: other nations—today much more established—have done the same: who remembers that Nizza was once a Savoyard, i.e. "Italian" town? Yet the historical one-sidedness and falsification so rampant in Drohobycz—as well as in other areas in Western Ukraine—carries with it too many under-currents of the old Bolshevik 1984-like falsifications of history: communism is gone, but the combination of ethno-centric nationalism and Bolshevik ruthlessness remains. One can imagine what is being taught in schools in Drohobycz—and all over Ukraine." Shlomo Avineri, "Airbrushing History in the Ukraine," *Jerusalem Post*, 2 September 2003.

BIBLIOGRAPHY

NEWSPAPERS, JOURNALS, AND PERIODICALS

ABN Correspondence
Austrian History Yearbook
Cahiers du monde russe
Canadian Slavonic Papers
Carl Beck Papers in Russian and East European Studies
Day Weekly Digest
Den'
Dzerkalo tyzhnya (Zerkalo nedeli)
East European Politics and Societies
Europe-Asia Studies
Evreiskiye vesti
Istoriya i natsiya
Istoriya Ukrainy
Istoriya v shkolakh Ukrainy
Istoriya v shkoli
Jahrbuecher fuer Geschichte Osteuropas
Jerusalem Post
Journal of Ukrainian Studies
Komunist Ukrainy
Krytyka
Literaturna Ukraine
L'vovs'kaya pravda
Maidan
Moya batkivshchyna, Moya rodina
Nadnipryans'ka pravda
Ogonyok
Osvita
Past and Present
Pravda Ukrainy
RFE/RL Newsline
Samostiina Ukraina

Slavic Review
Spaces of Identity
Ukraina i svit
Ukraina moloda
Ukrainian Weekly
Ukrains'ka pravda
Ukrains'ke slovo
Ukrains'kyi istorychnyi zhurnal
Visti z Ukrainy
Za vil'nu Ukrainu

SOURCES IN UKRAINIAN AND RUSSIAN

Articles

Andrusiv, Stefaniya. "Khto vin, obdurena zhertva chy svidomyi kat? Pro Yaroslava
     Halana i Halanivs'kyi typ lyudyny." *Literaturna Ukraina*, 3 September 1992, p. 7.
Antsyshkin, I. "Velyka: ale chy vitchyzniana?" *Ukraina moloda*, 8 May 1999, p. 4.
Bazdyuk, Mariya. "Ioho pratsya i borot'ba." *Za vil'nu Ukrainu*, 3 June 1994, p. 2.
Bazelyuk, Mariya. "Chy bude v Ukraini Nyurnberg-2?" *Ukraina moloda*, 12 May 2001,
     p. 4.
————. "Khto vidvazhnyi, nekhai ide z namy." *Za vil'nu Ukrainu*, 28 January 1994, p. 2.
————. "Nevyanuche istoriya OUN." *Za vil'nu Ukrainu*, 13 October 1992, p. 2.
————. "Z rodu Kravtsivykh." *Za vil'nu Ukrainu*," 22 February 1994, p. 2.
————. "Zaplatoyu nam radist' borot'by." *Za vil'nu Ukrainu*, 11 February 1994, p. 2.
Berdnyk, Oles'. "Na rynkakh u Kyevi likari provodyly lektsii." *Za vil'nu Ukrainu*, 2
     October 1993, p. 3.
Bilas, Ivan. "Proty stoyannya: aktsii represyvnoho aparatu totalitarnoho rezhymu
     proty natsional'noho-vyzvol'noho rukhu ukrains'koho narodu." *Literaturna Ukraina*,
     22 October 1992, p. 7.
————. "Proty stoyannya: aktsii represyvnoho aparatu totalitarnoho rezhymu proty
     natsional'noho-vyzvol'noho rukhu ukrains'koho narodu." *Literaturna Ukraina*, 29
     October 1992, p. 7.
Boiko, Ivan. "Ukraintsi i evrei v UPA buly razom." *Visti z Ukrainy*, No. 43 (October
     1991): 6.
Boita, A. "U skhidnii Ukraini-dobri lyudy, a v zakhidnii-lyshe zlochyntsi." *Visti z
     Ukrainy*, No. 34 (August 1991): 1–2.
Bondarchuk, V. "Velichiye oktyarbrs'kikh dnei." *L'vovs'kaya pravda*, 28 February
     1991, p. 2.
Bondarenko, Kost'. "Istoriya, kotoruyu ne znaem ili ne khotim znat'?" *Zerkalo nedeli*,
     29 March–5 April 2002; [http://www.zn.kiev.ua/ie/index/387/].

Brylins'kyi, Dmytro. "Ya perezhyv Holod." *Samostiina Ukraina*, No. 25 (June 1992): 3.

Buhai, M. "Deportatsii naselennya z Ukrainy." *Ukrains'kyi istorychnyi zhurnal*, No. 11 (1990): 21-25.

Chaykovskyi, A. and O. Oliinyk. "ODPU-NKVS i kolektyvizatsiya." *Istoriya Ukrainy*, No. 10 (March 1999): 1-3.

Chemerys, Pavlo. "Nasha plata 'nayvnym'..." *Za vil'nu Ukrainu*, 11 September 1993, p. 3.

————. "Operatsiya Holod." *Za vil'nu Ukrainu*, 28 September 1996, p. 2.

Cherevatenko, Leonid. "Heznanyi voyak." *Za vil'nu Ukrainu*, 10 June 1994, p. 2.

Chervak, Bohdan. "Lehendarnyi Sotnyk." *Ukrains'ke slovo*, No. 37 (September 2003): 1-3.

————. "Ostatochnu krapku ne postavyv nevblahannyi chas." *Maidan*, 10 June 2005; [http://www.maidan.org.ua/].

————. "Volyn' yak Rubikon." *Ukrains'ke slovo*, No. 29 (17-23 July 2003): 1-3.

Chishkun, L. "Ploshchad' Rynok 10, 30 yunya 1941-90 gg." *L'vovs'kaya pravda*, 6 July 1990, p. 4.

Chornomorets', Mykola. "Znavets' istorii." *Ukrains'ke slovo*, No. 35, 28 August-3 September 2003, p. 8.

Danylenko V. and V. Baran. "Ostanni period Stalinshchyny (suspil'no-politychni rozvytok)." *Istoriya Ukrainy*, No. 12 (March 2000): 1-3.

Danylenko, V. M. and M. M. Kuz'menko. "Naukovo-pedahohichna intelihentsiya v roky holodu." *Ukrains'kyi istorychnyi zhurnal*, No. 5 (May 2003): 145-155.

Danylenko, Viktor. "'Ukrainizatsiya' v mynulomu i teper." *Osvita*, 25 June 1993, p. 4.

Demchyna, Yaroslav. "Dolyna smerti." *Za vil'nu Ukrainu*, 16 February 1995, p. 2.

Dem'yan, Hryhorii. "Nasha orhanizatsiya pryznachena buty velykoyu." *Za vil'nu Ukrainu*, 4 February 1994, p. 2.

Dem'yanchuk, Bohdan. "Heroi z tinnyu provokatora." *Ukraina moloda*, 17 April 1992, p. 12.

Dem'yanyuk, Ivan. "Natsionalizm: shlyakh do derzhavnosty chy do ruiny?" *Samostiina Ukraina*, No. 46 (12 December 1992): 3; No. 47 (19 December 1992): 3; No. 48 (26 December 1992): 3.

Deshchyns'kyi, Leonid. "Sluzhyty Ukrains'kii idei." *Za vil'nu Ukrainu*, 17 June 1994, p. 3.

Dluskiy, S. "Tragediya sela Ganachevka." *L'vovs'kaya pravda*, 2 July 1991, p. 3.

Doroshenko, K. "Pamyatnik fashistskim prikhvostnyam." *Pravda Ukrainy*, 25 May 1991, p. 3.

Dovgan', V. "Kem byl Bandera: shtrikhi k politicheskomu portretu." *Pravda Ukrainy*, 13 December 1990, p. 3.

Dovhal', Serhiy. "Dnipropetrovs'k-stolytsa banderivtsiv na skhodi Ukrainy." *Ukraina moloda*, 2 June 1995, p. 10.

Drach, Ivan. "Chy pokaets'ya Rosiya?" In Hunczak, Taras, ed. *Tysyacha rokiv Ukrains'koi suspil'no-politychnoi dumky.*" Vol. 9 (1989-2001): 281-284.

————. "Henotsyd Ukrainy—vyklyk XX stolittya." *Literaturna Ukraina*, 3 September 1992, p. 3.

Dudar, Evhen. "Pravda odna: Vidkrytyi lyst prem'er ministrovi Pol'shchi p. Lesheku Milleru," *Literaturna Ukraina*, 7 November 2002, p. 1.

Duzhyi, Petro. "Borot'ba za derzhavu tryvaye," *Za vil'nu Ukrainu*, 1 January 1997, p. 2.

————. "Vede nas v bii bortsiv polehlykh slava," *Za vil'nu Ukrainu*, 4 February 1993, p. 2.

————. "'Za platayu nam radist' borot'by'." *Za vil'nu Ukrainu*, 11 February 1994, p. 2.

"Engebisty u formi UPA." *Samostiina Ukraina*, 5 December 1992, p. 3.

Fedyk, Ihor. "Vystoyaly; prorvalysya!..." *Za vil'nu Ukrainu*, 14 July 1994, p. 2.

Ferents, Volodymyr. "Ukraintsyam ne do antisemitizmu." *Ukrains'ke slovo*, 11–17 September 2003, p. 5.

Fik, Bohdan "Heneralu Vatutinu vid ukrains'koho narodu." *Za vil'nu Ukrainu*, 18 February 1997, p. 2.

Fomenko, Anatolii. "Pravda pro UPA." *Ukraina moloda*, 10 October 2002, pp. 4–5.

Futala, V. P. "VI Mizhnarodna naukova istoryko-kraeznavcha konferentsiya 'Natsional-vyzvol'ni rukh na zakhidnoukrains'kykh zemlyakh u 20-50-kh rr. XX st." *Ukrains'kyi istorychnyi zhurnal*, No. 2 (February 2003): 145–147.

Gorban', A. "Krovavyye sledy banderovtsev." *Pravda Ukrainy*, 11–12 October 1989, p. 3.

Grigoruk, P. "V otryade znali tol'ko Gracheva," *L'vovs'kaya pravda*, 27 July 1991, p. 4.

Gusev, B. "Kak ono bulo." *L'vovs'kaya pravda*, 30 June 1990, p. 3.

Guzhva, Evgeniy "Kolodets smerti." *Pravda Ukrainy*, 22 August 1991, p. 3; and 23 August 1991, p. 3.

Haivanovych, Ivan. "Ne nazyvaite 'SS'!" *Ukraina moloda*, 30 January 2001, p. 4.

Hasten, Yan. "Ne til'ky pro Volyn." *Za vil'nu Ukrainu*, 24 September 1998, p. 2.

Hayevs'kyi, Borys Kyrylyuk, Fedir and Mykola Obushnyi. "Pravda i domysly navkolo 'naukovo natsionalizmu'." *Osvita*, 22 June 1994, p. 8.

Holovyn, Roman. "Pomsta za smert' Ol'hy Basarab." *Za vil'nu Ukrainu*, 13 February 1999, p. 2.

Horan', Mykhailo. "Chyya pravda, chyya kryvda? Publitsystychnyi rozdum." *Literaturna Ukraina*, 15 January 2004, p. 1.

Horoshko, Myroslav and Volodymyr Dudok. "Lystar ukrains'koho lisu." *Za vil'nu Ukrainu*, 8 September 1992, p. 3; and 10 September 1992, p. 3.

Horovyi, V. M. "Navishcho Banderi p'edestal?" *Komunist Ukrainy*, No. 11 (November 1990): 86–93.

Hoyan, Mykhailo. "Na rodyuchii zemli pomyraly khliboroby." *Ukraina moloda*, 8 September 1998, p. 12.

Hrabovs'kyi, Serhii. "Volyn'skyi 'vuzol': ukrains'kyi vymir." *Ukrains'ke slovo*, No. 28 (10–16 July 2003): 4.

————. "Yaka Ukraina potribna Polshchi?" *Ukrains'ke slovo*, 24–30 July 2003, p. 5.

Hromyak, R., et al. "Vymahaemo pravydyvoi otsinky." *Samostiina Ukraina*, No. 18 (April 1992): 2.

Hryniv, Evhen. "L'vivs'komu 'memorialu'—p'yat' rokiv." *Za vil'nu Ukrainu*, 11 March 1994, p. 2.

Hryniv, Oleh. "Teoretyk Ukrains'koi revolyutsii." *Za vil'nu Ukrainu*, 1 January, 1994, p. 2; 4 January 1994, p. 2; 5 January 1994, p. 2; 6 January 1994, p. 3.

————. "Zatavrovani abreviaturamy," *Ukraina moloda*, 30 August 2002, p. 4.

Hrytsak, Yaroslav. "Shcho nam robyty z nashoyu ksenofobieyu?" *Krytyka*, No. 4 (2005); [www.krytyka.kiev.ua]

Hulyk, Ihor. "Petro Poltava i ioho kontseptsiya ukrains'koho derzhavnosti." *Za vil'nu Ukrainu*, 18 July 1992, p. 2.

————. "Yevhen Konovalets'—za Ukrainu i za ii idei." *Za vil'nu Ukrainu*, 14 June 1991, p. 2.

Hupalo, Larysa. "Vony polehly na Kulebakh." *Za vil'nu Ukrainu*, 7 March 1991, p. 4.

Hvozd', Mykola. "Im surmy ne hraly: do 60-richchya divizii 'Halychyna'." *Ukrains'ke slovo*, No. 27 (2–9 July 2003) p. 5.

Il'yushyn, I. I., "Antipol's'kyi front u boiovii diyal'nosti OUN I UPA (1939–1945rr.)." *Ukrains'kyi istorychnyi zhurnal*, No. 3 (2002): 94–104.

————. "Do pytannya pro Volyns'ku trahediyu v 1943–1944 rr." *Ukrains'kyi istorichnyi zhurnal*, No. 3 (2003): 115–123.

————. "Natsional'no-vyzvol'ni prahnennya ukrains'kykh ta pol's'kykh samostiinyts'kykh syl za chasiv Druhoi svitovoi viiny." *Ukrains'kyi istorychnyi zhurnal*, No. 1 (2003): 82–96.

Isayevich, Yaroslav. "Ukrains'ko-pol's'ki vidnosyny periodu Druhoi svitovoi viiny: interpretatsii istorykiv i politykiv." *Istoriya v shkolakh Ukrainy*, No. 2 (2003): 39.

"Ishlu u bii za svoyu peremohu: do 50 richchya Pershoi Ukrains'koi Dyvizii 'Halychyna' UNA." *Za vil'nu Ukrainu*, 7 August 1993, p. 4.

Ivanova, Ol'ha. "Kotyhoroshko povstans'koho lisu." *Samostiina Ukraina*, No. 38, October 1992, p. 3.

————. "Kto vin, Stepan Bandera?" *Samostiina Ukraina*, No. 15 (April 1992): 4.

————. "Vzhaknimosya i pomolimos." *Samostiina Ukraina*, No. 35 (September 1992): 4.

Kalba, Myroslav. "Hirka-pravda—zlochynnist' OUN-UPA." *Za vil'nu Ukrainu*, 25 June 1996, p. 2.

Karnautska, S. "Portret bez retushi." *L'vovs'kaya pravda*, 8 May 1991, p. 2.

Karpova, N. "Vtoroye ubiystvo: po povody odnoy al'ternativnoi versii." *Pravda Ukrainy*, 15 March 1990, p. 4.

————. "Vybor." *Pravda Ukrainy*, 4 January 1990, p. 4.

Kas'yanov, H. "Ideolohiya OUN: Istoryko-retrospektyvni analiz." *Ukrains'kyi istorychnyi zhurnal*, No. 1 (2004): 29–42; and No. 2 (2004): 68–82.

Kentii, A. "OUN i nimets'ko-pol'ska viina 1939 roku." *Istoriya Ukrainy*, No. 3 (2000): 4-7.

Kharchenko, Tetyana. "Mizh povstantsyamy i chervonymy partyzanamy nemaye niyakoho antahonizmy." *Ukraina moloda*, 20 July 2003, p. 5.

Khobot, P. and L. Kudelia. "Dnepropetrovskiye Banderovtsy." *Za vil'nu Ukrainu*, 20 October 1994, p. 2.

Khorolets', Larysa. "Heroyam slava!" *Literaturna Ukraina*, 13 August 1992, p. 2.

Khramamova, Nataliya. "Rol' Bandery: bez pyshnykh vusiv ta ek'zal'tovanoho patriotyzmu." *Ukraina moloda*, 23 July 1996, p. 8.

Kipiani, Vakhtang "Ukrains'ki natsionalisty na Mykolaivshchyni. Roky 1941-1943." *Ukraina moloda*, 16 April 1998, p. 6.

Kitura, Yaroslav. "Natsional'ni viiskovi tradytsii i s'ohodennya." *Za vil'nu Ukrainu*, 21 April 1994, p. 2.

————. "Stepan Bandera—symvol svobody." *Za vil'nu Ukrainu*, 4 January 1996, p. 2.

Klyashtorna, Natalya. "Vyselennya." *Ukraina moloda*, 19 February 2002, p. 11.

Koinash, Grigoriy. "Etot strashnyi 32-i." *L'vovs'kaya pravda*, 15 May 1990, p. 3.

Kokodnyak, Iziaslav. "50 rokiv bezsmertiya." *Za vil'nu Ukrainu*, 3 March 2000, p. 3.

Kolyara, Yaroslav. "Zustrich mera z voyakamy." *Za vil'nu Ukrainu*, 11 June 1994, p. 1.

Konigsman, Yakov. "Golodomor 1933 goda i upadok yevreiskogo zemledeliya." *Evreiskiye vesti*, No. 17-18 (September 1993): 4.

Kopyt'ko, Oleksii. "Pam'yat ob'ednue Ukrainu." *Ukrains'ke slovo*, No. 36 (4-10 September 2003): 11.

Kostyk, Petro. "Polumya, shcho nurtuye donyni slida my trahedii sela Sahrybn na Kholmshchyni." *Za vil'nu Ukrainu*, 10 September 1999, p. 6.

Kosyk, Volodymyr. "Svoboda dast' nam shans." *Literaturna Ukraina*, 23 January 1992, pp. 3, 8.

Koval', M. V. "Bytva za vyzvolennya Ukrainy." *Istoriya Ukrainy*, No. 16 (2000): 1-4.

————. "Druha svitova viina ta istorychna pam'yat'." *Ukrains'kyi istorychnyi zhurnal*, No. 3 (2000): 3-25.

————. "Druha svitova i Velyka Vitchynyana viina v istorychnii doli narodu Ukrainy." *Istoriya Ukrainy*, No. 7 (1996): 4-5; No. 8 (1996): 4-5.

————. "OUN-UPA v istorii i politytsi rozdumy doslidnyka." *Istoriya Ukrainy*, No. 17 (1997): 3-5; No. 18 (1997): 4-5.

————. "Polityka proty istorii: Ukrains'ka nauka u druhii svitovii viini i u pershi poevoenni roky." *Istoriya Ukrainy*, No. 6 (2001): 5-6.

————. "1941-i rikh. Problemy istorychnoi pam'yati." *Ukrains'kyi istorychnyi zhurnal*, No. 2 (2001): 69-90.

Koval', Viktor. "Ukrains'ka Povstans'ka Armiya: Dovidka Instytutu istorii AN URSR dlya Komisii Verkhovnoi Rady Ukrainy z pytan' bezpeky vid 1 lypnya 1991 roku." *Ukraina i svit*, No. 35 (18-24 September 1996): 9-10.

Kovalyuk, V. "Zakhidna Ukraina na pochatku Druhoi svitovoi viiny." *Ukrains'kyi istorychnyi zhurnal*, No. 9 (September 1991): 30-41.

Krainii, Ivan. "Nevidomyi Yaroslav Stets'ko." *Ukraina moloda*, 1 February 2002, p. 4.
————. "Ostanni z pidzemnoho bunkera." *Ukraina moloda*, 15 November 2002, p. 5.
————. "Sorok chotyry roky strakhu." *Ukraina moloda*, 21 January 1992, p. 7.
————. "Vo im'ya ottsya Andriya Bandery." *Ukraina moloda*, 28 October 1999, p. 10.
————. "Za shcho voyuvala dyviziya 'Halychyna'?" *Ukraina moloda*, 7 February 2001, p. 10.
Kul'chyts'kyi, Stanislav. "Akt 30 chervnya 1941 roku." *Istoriya Ukrainy*, No. 23-24 (June 2000): 6-9.
————. "Den' pamyati zhertv holodomoru." *Istoriya Ukrainy*, No. 46 (2000): 1.
————. "Do otsinky stanovyshcha v sil's'komu hospodarstvi URSS u 1931-1938 rr." *Ukrains'kyi istorychnyi zhurnal*, No. 3 (March 1988): 15-27.
————. "I znovu pro 17 veresnya 1939 roku." *Istoriya Ukrainy*, No. 38 (October 2000): 9.
————. "Iosyp Stalin u nashii istorii." *Istoriya Ukrainy*, No. 9 (1998): 1-3.
————. "Istoriya i chas: Rozdumy istoryka," *Ukrains'kyi istorychnyi zhurnal*, No. 4 (April 1992): 3-10.
————. "Istorychnyi kalendar. Pam'yat pro trydtsyat' tretii rik." *Istoriya Ukrainy*, No. 24 (1998): 4.
————. "Kolaboratsionizm OUN-UPA: derzhavnoi zrady ne bulo." *Ukraina moloda*, 8 December 1999, p. 7.
————. "Kryza kolhospnoho ladu." *Ukrains'kyi istorychnyi zhurnal*, No. 5 (May 2003): 5-25.
————. "Mizh dvoma viinamy (1921-1941 rr.)." *Ukrains'kyi istorychnyi zhurnal*, No. 9 (September 1991): 3-17.
————. "Nerozv'yazani problemy vykladannya istorii u seredni shkoli," *Istoriya Ukrainy*, No. 11 (1998): 1-2.
————. "Pam'yat' pro trydtsyat' tretii." *Istoriya Ukrainy*, No. 24 (June 1998): 4.
————. "Trahediya pysana samoyu istoriyeyu." *Za vil'nu Ukrainu*, 14 October 1997, p. 2.
————. "Ukrainski natsionalisty v chervono-korychnevii Yevropi (do 70-richchya stvorennya OUN." *Istoriya Ukrainy*, No. 5 (February 1999): 6-7.
————. "Ukrains'ka povstans'ka armiya z vidstani 55 rokiv." *Istoriya Ukrainy*, No. 41 (1997): 2-3.
————. Velykyi holod." *Istoriya v shkolakh Ukrainy*, No. 3 (2003): 51-52.
————. "Vitchyzniana istoriya v shkolakh i VNZ Ukrainy: stannie desyatyrichchya." *Istoriya Ukrainy*, No. 15 (2003): 1-6.
————. "Za Ukrainu, za ii volyu." *Ukraina moloda*, 31 August 2000, p. 10.
————. "Zavershal'na storinka Druhoi svitovoi viiny." *Istoriya Ukrainy*, No. 37 (2000): 10.
Kulnyak, Danylo. "Bil'." *Visti z Ukrainy*, No. 32 (August 1991): 7.
————. "Esesivs'ka chy 'Persha ukrains'ka?" Z pryvodu odnoho yuvileyu," *Ukraina moloda*, 3 September 1993, p. 10.

Kushpeta, Omelyan. "Znav ioho osobysto." *Literaturna Ukraina*, 23 January 1992, p. 6.

Kuz'menko, Oleksii. "Na Holod pishly svidomo." *Osvita*, No. 21–22 (1993): 12.

Kuzminets', O. "Stepan Bandera." *Istoriya Ukrainy*, No. 47 (1997): 8–9.

Kyrychuk, Yurii. "Heroichnyi litopys." *Za vil'nu Ukrainu*, 11 July 1996, p. 2.

Kyrylyuk, Vitol'd. "Chas hromadyty kaminnya: rozmova s holovoyu Ukrains'koi asotsiatsii "Holod-33" Lidiyeyu Kovalenko-Manyak." *Literaturna Ukraina*, 6 August 1992, p. 2.

———. "I vdaryat' dzvony pam'yati." *Literaturna Ukraina*, 25 March 1993, p. 1.

Lebed, Mykola. "My znaly-nas chekae Ukraina." *Za vil'nu Ukrainu*, 22 August 1992, pp. 1–2.

Lebedeva, Yu. H. "Zakhidnoukrains'ki zemli u 1920–1939rr." *Istoriya Ukrainy*, No. 16 (April 2001): 9–11; No. 17 (May 2001): 4–6.

Lernatovych, Oles'. "Svityti zoreyu nadiya." *Za vil'nu Ukrainu*, 24 January 1991, p. 4.

Luk'yanenko, Levko. "U lystopadovi zhalobni dni." In Drodets'ka, M.V., ed. *Komu buv vyhidnyi holodomor?* Kyiv: Telesyk, 2003.

Lutsenko, V. "Demokratychna metushnaya." *Nadnipryans'ka pravda*, 7 August 1991, p. 2.

Lysenko, O. E. "Druha svitova viina yak predmet naukovykh doslidzhen' ta fenomen istorychnoi pam'yati." *Ukrains'kyi istorychnyi zhurnal*, No. 5 (May 2004): 3–16.

Lysenko, O. E. and O. V. Marushchenko. "Vseukrains'ka naukova konferentsiya 'Ukrains'ka povstans'ka armiya—fenomen natsional'noi istorii," *Ukrains'kyi istorychnyi zhurnal*, No. 1 (2003): 147–149.

Lytvyn, Mariya. "Povstanskymy stezhkamy." *Literaturna Ukraina*, 18 September 2003, p. 1.

Lyal'ko, Yaroslav. "Vony povernyly nam muzhnist' i natsional'nu hidnist'." *Za vil'nu Ukrainu*, 12 September 1996, p. 2.

Lytvynchuk, Mykhailo. "My voyuvaly ne za imperieyu." *Za vil'nu Ukrainu*, 27 April 1995, p. 2.

Mak, Bohdan. "Polkovnyk Shelest." *Za vil'nu Ukrainu,* 27 April 1996, p. 2; 30 April 1996, p. 2; 4 May 1996, p. 2; 7 May 1996, p. 2; 14 May 1996, p. 2.

Makarchuk, S. "OUN: Metamorfozy voennogo vremeni." *L'vovs'kaya pravda*, 27 November 1988, p. 3.

———. "Volya naroda." *L'vovs'kaya pravda*, 26 October 1988, p. 2.

Makarchuk, S.A. "Pereselennya polyakiv iz zakhidnykh oblastei Ukrainy v Pol'shchu u 1944–1946rr." *Ukrains'kyi istorychnyi zhurnal*, No. 3 (2003): 103–114.

———. "Z istorii druhoi svitovoi viiny. Pereselennya polyakiv iz zakhidnykh oblastei Ukrainy v Pol'shchu u 1944–1946 rr." *Ukrains'kyi istorychnyi zhurnal*, No. 3 (2003): 103–115.

Maksimyuk, P. and G. Slivka. "Ispytannym oruzhiyem pravdy." *L'vovs'kaya pravda*, 20 February 1988, p. 3.

Marchenko, Kateryna. "Mama proty 'chervonoi' valky." *Ukraina moloda*, 26 June 2003, p. 11.

Margolis, Erik. "Zhaduyuchy nevidomyi holokost Ukrainy." *Za vil'nu Ukrainu*, 6 February 1999, p. 2.

Marochkin, Vasyl'. "Trydtsyat' dniv z Mykoloyu Lebed'em." *Visti z Ukrainy*, No. 27 (June 1991): 3.

———. "'Torgsin': Zolota tsina zhyttya Ukrains'kykh selyan u roky holodu (1932–1933)." *Ukrains'kyi istorychnyi zhurnal*, No. 3 (2003): 90–102.

Marochko, Vasyl' I. "Holod u natsional'nykh rayonakh Ukrainy." *Evreiskiye vesti*, No. 15–16 (August 1996): 1–2.

———. "Holodomor v Ukraini: prychyny i naslidky (1932–1933)." *Osvita*, No. 21–22 (1993): 3–9.

———. Kontseptual'ni pidvalyny zakhidnoevropeis'koi ta rosiis'koi istoriohrafii holodomoru 1932–1933 rr. V Ukraini." *Ukrains'kyi istorychnyi zhurnal*, No. 5 (2003): 125–144.

———. "Problemy istorii Ukrainy novitn'oho chasu. 'Torhsyn': zolota tsina zhyttya ukrains'kykh selyan u roky holodu (1932–1933)." *Ukrains'kyi istorychnyi zhurnal*, No. 3 (2003): 90–103.

Marushchenko, Oleksandr. "Ukraina v druhii svitovii viini: istoriohrafichni doslidzhennya 90h rokiv." *Istoriya v shkoli*, No. 5–6 (2000): 2–4.

Maslii, P. "V UPA buly heroi." *Visti z Ukrainy*, No. 42 (October 1991): 4.

Maslovs'kii, V. I. "Shchto na 'oltari svobody'? Dekil'la utochen' viiny 'na dva fronty,' yaku vela UPA, ta skil'koma nevynnymy zhertvamy oplachuvas' tsey propahdandyts'kyi myf." *Komunist Ukrainy*, No. 7 (July 1991): 67–73.

Maslovs'kii, V. and V. Pomogayev. "OUN-UPA: Dokumenty svidetel'stvuyut'." *L'vovs'kaya pravda*, 11 June 1991, p. 2.

Mazorchuk, Vasyl'. "Henotsyd na Chornozemakh." *Osvita*, No. 21–22 (1993): 10–14.

Moroz, Ostap. "Na terenakh Drohobychchyny." *Za vil'nu Ukrainu*, 24 November 1992, p. 2.

Mudryk-Mechnyk, Stepan. "OUN—kermanych nashoi borot'by." *Za vil'nu Ukrainu*, 5 February 1998, p. 2.

Muzychenko, Yaroslava. "Holod proty voli." *Ukraina moloda*, 22 November 2002, p. 4.

———. "Pidruchnyky: istorychni chy isternychi?" *Ukraina moloda*, 18 September 2002, p. 12.

———. "Z choho pochynalasya 'Rodina'?" *Ukraina moloda*, 17 May 2002, p. 5.

Mytsyk, Yaryna. "Holod u Vyshnopoli." *Osvita*, 10 September 1993, pp. 14–15.

National Academy of Sciences, Institute of History of Ukraine, "Problema OUN-UPA: Zvit robochoi hrupy istorykiv pry Uryadovii komisii z vyvchennya diyal'nosti OUN i UPA. Osnovi tezy z problemy OUN-UPA (istorychnyi vysnovok)," Kyiv, 2004: [http://www.ukraine-poland.com/u/publicystyka/publicystyka.php?id=3480].

Nemyrya, Hryhor'ii. "Sim mifiv abo sproba 'koryhuval'noho presynhu?'." *Dzerkalo tyzhnya*, No. 3 (26 January–1 February 2002); [http://www.zn.kiev.ua/nn/show/378/33632].

Ohipko, Rostyslav. "Vybory po-halyts'ky chy front natsional'noi ednosti?" *Za vil'nu Ukrainu*, 24 March 1994, p. 3.

Oleksyuk, Bohdan. "Chy musyt' ukrains'kyi natsionalist nenavydity polyakiv?" *Krytyka*, 23 May 2003; [http://www.krytyka.kiev.ua/comments/Oleksjuk14.html].

———. "Natsionalizm ne teroryzm," *Ukrains'ke slovo*, 4–10 September 2003, p. 4.

Oleksyuk, Mykola. "Rozmova z ubyvtseyu." *Za vil'nu Ukrainu*, 6 March 1993, p. 2; 20 March 1993, p. 2; and 30 March 1993, pp. 2–3.

———. "Ubyvtsya Konoval'tsya vidomyi." *Za vil'nu Ukrainu*, 19 September 1992, p. 1.

———. "Zlovisnyi symvol." *Za vil'nu Ukrainu*, 2 August 1996, p. 2; and 5 August 1996, p. 2.

Palii, Oleksandr. "Chy pidpysuvav Stepan Bandera pakt Molotova-Ribbentropa?" *Ukrains'ka pravda*, 12 October 2006.

Panchuk, M.I. and S.S. Dibrova. "20–30-ti. Dokumenty, fakty, svidchennya." *Komunist Ukrainy*, No. 4 (April 1990): 70–84.

Paranchak, Myroslav. "Tyahar nespravedlyvosti zhyvuchyi." *Za vil'nu Ukrainu*, 23 July 1998, p. 2.

Pasichnyk, Bohdan. "Provokatsiya vyvirenym metodom." *Za vil'nu Ukrainu*, 4 May 1995, p. 2.

Pastukh, Roman. "Dmytro Hrytsai-heneral UPA." *Za vil'nu Ukrainu,*" 20 March 1991, p. 2.

———. "Dva portrety narodnykh heroiv." *Za vil'nu Ukrainu*, 22 December 1998, p. 3.

———. "Enkavedysts'kyi heneral u rukakh u nashykh povstantsiv." *Za vil'nu Ukrainu*, 19 July 1997, p. 2.

———. "Orhanizator hulahivs'koho pidpillya." *Za vil'nu Ukrainu*, 15 June 1991, p. 2.

———. "Rodyna Stepana Bandery." *Za vil'nu Ukrainu*, 13 October 1994, p. 2; 14 October 1994, p. 2; 15 October 1994, p. 2; and 18 October 1994, p. 2.

———. "Sestry Stepana Bandery pereizhdzhayut' do Stryya." *Za vil'nu Ukrainu*, 18 January 1995, p. 2.

———. "Za narod poklaly molodi zhyttya." *Za vil'nu Ukrainu*, 23 December 1995, p. 2.

———. "Zahynu pokynutyi napryzvolyashche svoimy." *Za vil'nu Ukrainu*, 6 May 1993, p. 2.

Patrylyak, I. K. "Do pytannya pro vnesok OUN ta UPA u borot'bu proty natsysts'-kykh okupantiv na terytorii Ukrainy." *Ukrains'kyi istorychnyi zhurnal*, No. 5 (2004): 81–95.

———. "Natsionalistychnyi partyzanskyi rukh na terytorii Zakhidnoi Ukrainy v litku 1941r." *Ukrains'kyi istorychnyi zhurnal*, No. 4 (2000): 113–119.

———. "Viis'kovi plany OUN(b) u taemnii instruktsii Revolyutsiinoho provodu (traven' 1941r.)." *Ukrains'kyi istorychnyii zhurnal*, No. 2 (2000): 127–137.

———. "Viis'kovotvorchi zakhody OUN(b) u lypni-veresni 1941r." *Ukrains'kyi istorychnyi zhurnal*, No. 4 (2001): 126–139.

Pavliv, Bohdan. "I perevernem zaharbnyts'kyi svit: spomyn chlena OUN." *Literaturna Ukraina*, 15 October 1992, p. 7.

Petrushchak, Mykola. "Ednaisya—v borot'bi, kripys'—u viri!" *Za vil'nu Ukrainu*, 7 June 1994, p. 2.

Pisots'ka, Ruslana. "Inodi treba vse zhadaty, shchob vyduzhaty." *Ukraina moloda*, 4 March 2003, p. 5.

Polozhin, Viktor. "Fil'm 'Holod-33' u roboti." *Literaturna Ukraina*, 21 March 1991, p. 6.

"Polupokayanie: Volynskaya tragediya: 60 let spustya." *Moya batkivshchyna, Moya rodina*, No. 8 (August 2003): 4.

Popovych, Myroslav. "Volyn': nashe e ne nashe gore." *Krytyka*, 5 May 2003; [www.krytyka.kiev.ua].

Porovs'kyi, Mykola "Konvoy korovu z soboyu ne veze..." *Visti z Ukrainy*, No. 27 (1991): 1.

Potichna, Oleksandra. "I bratove-lyatky po khrystyyans'ki vyrizaly Ivanovi na hrudyakh khresta." *Za vil'nu Ukrainu*, 30 July 1999, pp. 8-9.

Pozdnyakova, Yelena. "Narodnyi fil'm: Snimayut ukrainskiye kinematografisty o golode 1933 goda." *Pravda Ukrainy*, 13 June 1991, p. 3.

Pryhornyts'kyi, Yurii. "Ivan Oleksyn: Use zhyttya borovsya za Ukrainu. Dyviziya 'Halychyna'. Yak tse bulo." *Literaturna Ukraina*, 18 June 1992, p. 3.

―――. "Shcho ikh velo u dyviziyu?" *Literaturna Ukraina*, 14 January 1993, p. 6.

Radionov, Viktor. "Spiv iz chuzhoho holosu—bezladnyi: do pytannya ukrains'kopol's'koho protystoyannya na Volyni v 1943r." *Ukrains'ke slovo*, No. 28 (10-16 July 2003): 4.

―――. "Vidhomin." *Ukrains'ke slovo*, 4-10 September 2003, p. 4.

Rakhmannyi, R. "Vyznachnyi Akt istorii." *Za vil'nu Ukrainu*, 30 June 1992, p. 2.

Romanchenko, Nikolai. "Plamya." *L'vovs'kaya pravda*, 16 February 1988, p. 3.

Romanets', Dana. "Pochatkom 1937-ho roku v Ukraini stav 1933-i." *Ukraina moloda*, 1 December 2000, p. 5.

Romanyk, Ivan. "Banderivs'kyi chervonoarmiets." *Ukraina moloda*, 12 September 2001, p. 13.

Romanyuk, Nina. "Khoroshyi u vas cholovik. Ot choho vin u tii UPA buv?" *Ukraina moloda*, 12 October 2002, p. 4.

―――. "Vony ishly do lyubovi i myloserdya, a pomyraly zradnykamy i vorohamy." *Ukraina moloda*, 19 May 1995, p. 7.

―――. "Ya istymu lushpaiky, aby Ukraina bula!" *Ukraina moloda*, 2 September 1998, p. 6.

Romanyuk, Nina and Yurii Mykolayenko. "Vsyaki uryad, yakui vidmovyvsya b vid Zakhidnoi Ukrainy, buv by rozbytyi." *Ukraina moloda*, 11 January 1995, p. 3.

Ruchko, Tamara. "A bratyk plakav, prosyv isty..." *Ukrains'ke slovo*," 24-30 July 2003, p. 13.

Rudenko, Ivan. "Trahediya Kozats'koho." *Za vil'nu Ukrainy*, 23 October 1993, p. 4.

Rusak, A. "Perebuvannya dobrovol'tsiv—frantsuziv, khorvativ, ispantsiv, ukraintsiv—
u lavakh vermakhtu i vaffen-SS u 1941-1945rr." *Istoriya Ukrainy*, No. 21-24 (June
2001): 3-7.

Rytiak, Roman. "Za shcho my skorodyly spysamy vorozhi rebra?" *Za vil'nu Ukrainu*,
28 July 2000, p. 4.

Savchenko, M. "70-richchya holodomoru v Ukraini: metodychni porady do provedennya zakhodiv pam'yati zhertv holodomoru 1932-1933 rokiv v Ukraini." *Istoriya
Ukrainy*, No. 3 (January 2003): 17-19.

Savchuk, V. "Ukrains'ke natsionalistychna pidpillya i lehal'ni hromads'ki orhanizatsii
v halychyni u 20-30-kh rr. XX st." *Istoriya Ukrainy*, No. 35 (September 2001): 4-6.

Savel'ev, V. "V poiske istiny: k voprosy o prichinakh goloda 1932-1933 godov na
Ukraine." *Pravda Ukrainy*, 8 July 1989, p. 2.

Serbyn, Roman. "'Tretya syla' v p'yatomu kuti." *Ukraina moloda*, 21 June 2001, p. 4.

Shaikin, Iosif. "Na yuge Ukrainy." *Evreiskiye vesti*, No. 1-2 (January 1994): 6.

Shanhina, Lyudmyla. "Dva dni do peremohy, abo myr nashomu domu." *Dzerkalo
tyzhnya*, No. 17 (7-13 May 2005); [http://www.zn.kiev.ua/ie/show/544/49954/].

Shapoval, Yurii. "Komunistychno-fashysts'kyi 'roman.' Podii 1939 roku ochyma komunistiv todi i teper." *Ukraina moloda*, 22 October 1999, p. 4.

———. "Proloh trahedii holodomoru. III konferentsiya KP(b)U." *Istoriya Ukrainy*,
No. 43 (2002): 1-8.

———. "Skazaty vsyu pravdu: do 50-richchya UPA." *Literaturna Ukraina*, 1 October
1992, p. 7.

———. "Stalinizm i Ukraina." *Ukrains'kyi istorychnyi zhurnal*, No. 8 (August 1991):
30-41.

———. "Ukrains'ka druha svitova." *Dzerkalo tyzhnya*, No. 15 (23 April-6 May
2005); [http://www.zn.kiev.ua/ie/show/543/49834/].

Shatnaya, Etia. "Pod rodnym nebom." *Evreiskiye vesti*, No. 21-22 (November 1993):
15.

Shybyk, Nikolai. "Porkhavka." *Pravda Ukrainy*, 21 November 1989, p. 4.

Shytyuk, M. M. "Problemy istorii Ukrainy novitnoho chasu." *Ukrains'kyi istorychnyi
zhurnal*, No. 3 (2001): 128-142.

Sirs'kyi, Vasyl. "Knyha, yaka vymahaye dyskusii." *Za vil'nu Ukrainu*, 29 July 1994,
p. 2.

Skochii, Pavlo. "Nadislannyi tsar-holod." *Za vil'nu Ukrainu*, 9 April 1998, p. 2.

Slavutych, Yar. "Holodomor buv splanovanyi." *Za vil'nu Ukrainu*, 3 November 1990,
p. 2.

Sluka, Myron. "Kharkivs'kyi 'bandiora'." *Za vil'nu Ukrainu*, 30 January 1999, p. 2.

———. "Palacha k otvetu." *L'vovs'kaya pravda*, 12 March 1988, p. 3.

Snovydovych-Mazyar, Oksana. "To chy byly vony kolaborantamy?" *Za vil'nu Ukrainu*,
8 June 1993, p. 2.

Solomonchuk, Les'. "Povernennya Burlaka." *Za vil'nu Ukrainu*, 24 September 1999,
p. 5.

Solovei, Fedir. "Sumni svyata buly v sorok shostomu rotsi." *Za vil'nu Ukrainu*, 19 January 1991, p. 4.

Sosnyak, Sofiya. "Lyst do Viktora Yushchenka u spravi Volyni." *Ukrains'ke slovo*, No. 31 (31 July–6 August 2003): 5.

Sotnychenko, V. "Reformuvannya kontseptsii zmistu standartiv istorychnoi osvity." *Istoriya Ukrainy*, No. 7 (February 2003): 14–18.

Stakhiv, Evhen. "I v Krasnodoni diyalo natsionalistychne pidpillya." *Ukraina moloda*, 21 August 1992, p. 6.

"Stan'mo pid prapor odyn! Zvernennya do Ukraintsiv do chesnykh hromadyan i patriotiv Ukrainy." *Za vil'nu Ukrainu*, 1 March 1994, p. 1.

Starobohatov, A. V. "OUN u Kharkovi za chasiv okupatsii." *Ukrains'kyi istorychnyi zhurnal*, No. 6 (1999): 81–88.

"Stolychna OUN hotuets'kya do aktsii protestu." *Ukrains'ke slovo*, No. 31, 31 July–6 August 2003, p. 12.

Strikha, Maksym. "Asymetrychnist' Volyni." *Krytyka-Komentar*, 5 May 2003; [http://www.krytyka.kiev.ua/comments/Strixa24.html].

Sverstyuk, Yevhen. "Tsyu riku ne zahatyty." *Ukraina moloda*, 20 November 2003, p. 6.

Syvitskyi, Mykola. "Shche odyn holos v dyskusii...." *Ukrains'ke slovo*, No. 38 (18–24 September 2003): 4.

Tatarenko, Volodymyr. "A koshty peredaty zhertvam..." *Literaturna Ukraina*, 20 June 1991, p. 2.

Tomina, Lyudmyla. "Na poklykh sumlinnya." *Ukrains'ke slovo*, No. 27, 2–9 July 2003, p. 5.

Troshchyns'kyi, V. P. "Proty vyhadok pro tak zvanyi 'antyfashysts'kyi rukh oporu' Ukrains'kykh natsionalistiv." *Ukrains'kyi istorychnyi zhurnal*, No. 5 (1988): 76–87.

Tyma, Petro. "Pol's'ko-Ukrains'kyi konflikt mity, uyavlennya." *Krytyka*, 22 November 2002; [www.krytyka.kiev.ua].

Tymchyshyn, Yaroslav. "SRSR ukraintsyam ne batkivshchyna-itzhe druha svitova viina dlya nas ne vitchyzniana." *Za vil'nu Ukrainu*, 6 May 1995, p. 2.

Valko, L., and T. Huryk. "Viche pam'yati: do 70-richchya holodomoru 1932–1933rr u Ukraini." *Istoriya Ukrainy*, No. 11 (March 2003): 22–25.

Valuev, Yurii. "Bil' Babynoho Yaru." *Visti z Ukrainy*, No. 40 (September 1991): 6.

———. "Popil Babynoho Yaru." *Visti z Ukrainy*, No. 42 (October 1991): 3.

Vashkiv, Ivan. "I stav vin Lehendoyu," *Za vil'nu Ukrainu*, 31 October 1991, p. 2.

Vasyl'chuk, Mykola. "Pobratani z hromom: nova knyha Mykhaila Andrusyaka pro UPA." *Ukraina moloda*, 30 January 2002, p. 6.

Vasylevs'kyi, Panteleimon. "Bii za 'banderivs'ku stolytsu." *Za vil'nu Ukrainu*, 13 January 1995, p. 2.

———. "Heneralu Vatutinu vid ukrains'koho narodu." *Za vil'nu Ukrainu*, 9 May 1997, p. 2.

———. "Tsili-vorozhi heneraly." *Za vil'nu Ukrainu*, 14 October 1997, p. 2.

Vedeneev, D. "Pidpil'na diyal'nist' OUN v Zakhidnii Ukraini u 1939–1941 rr." *Istoriya Ukrainy*, No. 12 (2001): 4–5.

Veremeichuk, A. "My obvinyaem natsionalizm." *Pravda Ukrainy*, 11 April 1990, p. 3.

Veryha, Vasyl. "Im prysvichuvala velyka ideya... Dyviziya 'Halychyna', yak tse bulo." *Literaturna Ukraina*, 25 June 1992, p. 3.

Veselova, O. M. "Vysvitlennya holodu 1932–1933 rr. U zbirnykakh dokumentiv i materialiv." *Ukrains'kyi istorychnyi zhurnal*, No. 5 (2003): 101–125.

———. "Uvichnennya pam'yati zhertv holodu-henotsydu 1932-1933 rr. v Ukraini." *Ukrains'kyi istorychnyi zhurnal*, No. 2 (2004): 50–67.

Vidyans'kyi, S. V. "Ukrains'ke pytannya v mizhvoenni Pol'shchi: osnovni problemy i napryamky naukovnykh doslidzhen' u suchasnii vitchyznyanii istorychnii nautsi." *Ukrains'kyi istorychnyi zhurnal*, No. 2 (2003): 39–55.

Vol'vach, Petro. "Kudy ta homu znykayut' ukraintsi na neosiazhnykh prostorakh imperii?" *Istoriya i natsiya*, 17 June 1993, p. 5.

Vorobel', Ivan. "Ostannii bunker." *Za vil'nu Ukrainu*, 17 October 1996, pp. 2–3.

———. "Staly zhertvamy kliky Beria-Stalina." *Za vil'nu Ukrainu*, 30 August 1994, p. 2.

Vovkanych, Stepan. "Mavzolei—ne tryzna, imperiya—ne vitchyzna." *Za vil'nu Ukrainu*, 19 January 1994, p. 2.

———. "Ne malorosiis'kyi etnos, a derzhavotvorcha natsiya." *Za vil'nu Ukrainu*, 18 January 1994, p. 2

V'yatkovych, V. "Mizhnarodna naukova konferentsiya 'Ukrains'ka povtsans'ka armiya. Do 60-richchya stvorennya." *Ukrains'kyi istorychnyi zhurnal*, No. 2 (2003): 144–145.

Vyshnevs'ka, Halyna. "Trahediya sela Sahryn'." *Ukrains'ke slovo*, No. 31 (31 July–6 August 2003): 5.

Yakovchuk, Petro. "Pam'yatnyk fashystu." *Za vil'nu Ukrainu*, 4–10 July 1993, p. 3.

Yakymovych, Yaroslav. "Z zhertovnym styahom ikh zvytyah." *Za vil'nu Ukrainu*, 21 August 1993, p. 4.

Yatsura, Mykhailo. "Professor Kubiiovych i Dyviziya 'Halychyna'." *Za vil'nu Ukrainu*, 30 September 1995, pp. 1–2.

———. "Vidlunnya zlochynu." *Za vil'nu Ukrainu*, 23 May 1998, p. 2.

Yavors'kyi, Volodymyr. "Vin ne vpadav u vidchai. Vin borovsya," *Za vil'nu Ukrainu*, 22 May 1993, pp. 1–2.

———. "Yakshcho derzhava ne pustyi zvuk." *Za vil'nu Ukrainu*, 18 May 1993, p. 2.

"Yevhen Konovalets': do natsional'noho kalendarya." *Literaturna Ukraina*, 28 May 1992, p. 7.

Zahoruiko, Roman. "Istorychne sharlatanstvo." *Ukraina moloda*, 7 May 2003, p. 12.

———. "Zezlamnyi hin do voli." *Ukraina moloda*, 14 October 2003, p. 10.

Zalyps'kyi, Bohdan. "Zberehty sebe, shchob vykhovuvaty nove pokolonia." *Za vil'nu Ukrainu*, 7 April 2000, pp. 6–7.

Zarechnyi, Z. and O. Lastovets. "Banderovshchina," *Pravda Ukrainy*, 9 August 1989, pp. 3–4; *Pravda Ukrainy*, 9 August 1989, pp. 3–4; 10 August 1989, p. 4; 11 August 1989, p. 3; 17 August 1989, pp. 3–4; and 19 August 1989, p. 3.

"Zayava OUN z pryvodu vidznachennya 60-i richnytsi podii na Volyni." *Ukrains'ke slovo*, No. 29, 17–23 July 2003, p. 12.

Zhyznyak, Ihor. "Natsional'nyi vymir u peredumovi vynyknennya Holodomoru 1932–1933 rokiv v Ukraini." In Drozdets'ka, M. V., ed. *Komu buv vyhodnyi holodomor?* Kyiv: Telesyk, 2003, pp. 18–26.

Zlupko, Stepan. "Velyka vchy druha svitova," *Za vil'nu Ukrainu*, 22 June 1993, p. 2.

———. "Ukraina v svitli nimets'kykh dokumentiv." *Za vil'nu Ukrainu*, 28 June 1997, p. 2.

"Zvit robochoi hrupy istorykiv pry Uryadovyi komisii z vyvchannya diyalnosti OUN i UPA." Kyiv: Institute of History of Ukraine, National Academy of Sciences, 2005.

Zyulkovs'kyi, Marek. "Mist nad Volynnyu." *Ukrains'ke slovo*, 11–17 September 2003, p. 4.

Books

Boyko, O. D. *Istoriya Ukrainy*. Kyiv: Akademvydav, 2003.

Cherednychenko, V. *Natsionalizm proty natsii*. Kyiv: Vydavnytstvo politychnoi literatury Ukrainy, 1970.

Chyrkov, V. M. ed., *Holodomor 1932-33 rokiv yak velychezna trahediya ukrains'koho narodu*. Kyiv: MAUP, 2003.

Hordasevych, Halyna. *Stepan Bandera: lyudyna i mif*. L'viv: Piramida, 2001.

Koval', Mykhailo. *Ukraina v Druhii svitovii i Velykii Vitchyznyanii viinakh, 1939-1945 rr.* Kyiv: Vydannyi Dim Al'ternatyvy, 1999.

Kul'chyts'kyi, S. V. *Holod 1932-1933 rr. v Ukraini yak henotsyd*. Kyiv: Natsional'na akademiya nauk Ukrainy, Instytut istorii Ukrainy, 2005.

Lytvyn, Volodymyr, Smolii Valerii, and Mykola Shpakovatyi. *Ilyustrovana istoriya Ukrainy*. Kyiv: Al'ternatyvy, 2001.

Mironchuk, V. D. and H. S. Ihoshyi. *Istoriya Ukrainy*. Kyiv: MAUP, 2002.

Motyka, Grzegorz. *Pany i rezuny: wspolpraca AK-WiN i UPA, 1945-1947*. Warsaw: Volumen, 1997.

Mysan, Viktor. *Opovidannya z istorii Ukrainy*. Kyiv: Heneza, 1997.

Potichnyj, Peter J. et al. *Litopys UPA*. Toronto: Litopys UPA, 1976–2005, 42 volumes to date.

Potichnyj, Peter J. *Pavlokoma, 1441-1945: istoriya sela*. L'viv and Toronto: Fund for Pavlokoma, 2001.

Serhiichuk, Volodymyr. *Nasha krov-na svoii zemli*. Kyiv: Ukrains'ka vydavanycha spilka, 2000.

————. *Trahediya Volyni: Prychynyi perebih pol's'ko-ukrains'koho konfliktu v roky Druhoi svitovoi viiny.* Kyiv: vydavnycha spilka, 2003.

————. *Ukrains'kyi zdvyh.* 5 vols. Kyiv: 2004-2005.

Shapoval, Yurii. *Ukraina XX stolittya: osoby ta podii v konteksti vazhkoi istorii.* Kyiv: Heneza, 2001.

Shcherbak, Yurii. *Chornobyl'.* Kyiv: Dnipro, 1989.

Skrypnyk, M. O. et al, *Istoriya Ukrainy: nachal'nyi posibnyk.* Kyiv: Tsentr navchal'noi literatury, 2003.

Symaszko, Wladyslaw and Ewa. *Ludobojstwo dokonan przez nacjonalistow ukrainskich na ludnosci polskiej Wolynia, 1939-1945.* Warsaw: Wyd. Von borowiecky, 2000.

Temka, H. D. and L. S. Tupchienka, ed. *Istoriya Ukrainy: Posibnyk.* Kyiv: Akademiya, 2002.

Teslya, Ivan and Evhen Tyut'ko, compilers, and Lyubomyr Wynar, ed., *Istorychnyi Atlas Ukrainy.* New York: Ukrainian Historical Association, 1980.

Turchenko, F. H. *Novitnaya istoriya Ukrainy: Chastyna persha 1917-1945.* Kyiv: Heneza, 1998.

Turchenko, F. H., P. P. Panchenko, and S.M. Tymchenko. *Novitnaya istoriya Ukrainy,* Part 1: 1939-2001. Kyiv: Heneza, 2001.

SOURCES IN ENGLISH

Articles

Aster, Howard. "Reflections on the Work of Peter J. Potichnyj." *Journal of Ukrainian Studies,* Vol. 21, No. 1-2 (Summer-Winter 1996): 223-234.

Avineri, Shlomo. "Airbrushing History in the Ukraine." *Jerusalem Post,* 2 September 2003.

Burds, Jeffrey. "AGENTURA: Soviet Informants' Networks and the Ukrainian Rebel Underground in Galicia, 1944-1948." *East European Politics and Societies* 11, No. 1 (Winter 1997): 89-130.

————. "The Early Cold War in Soviet West Ukraine, 1944-1948." *The Carl Beck Papers in Russian and East European Studies.* Pittsburgh: The Center for Russian and East European Studies, a program of the University Center for International Studies, University of Pittsburgh, 2001.

————. "Gender and Policing in Soviet West Ukraine 1944-1948." *Cahiers du monde russe* 42/2, No. 3-4 (April-December 2001): 279-319.

Commission on the Ukraine Famine. *Report to Congress: Investigation of the Ukraine Famine 1932-1933* Washington, D.C.: Government Printing Office, 1988.

Coplon, Jeff. "In Search of a Soviet Holocaust: a 55-Year Old Famine Feeds the Right." *Village Voice,* 12 January 1988.

Davies, R. W. and Stephen G. Wheatcroft. "Stalin and the Soviet Famine of 1932–33: a reply to Ellman." *Europe-Asia Studies*, Vol. 58, No. 4 (June 2006): 625–633.

Ellman, Michael. "The Role of Leadership Perceptions and of Intent in the Soviet Famine of 1931–1934." *Europe-Asia Studies*, Vol. 56, No. 6 (September 2005): 823–841.

Golczewski, Frank. "Poland's and Ukraine's Incompatible Past." *Jahrbuecher fuer Geschichte Osteuropas*, Vol. 54, No. 1 (2006): 37–49.

Himka, John-Paul. "A Central European Diaspora under the Shadow of World War II: the Galician Ukrainians in North America." *Austrian History Yearbook*, Vol. 37 (2006): 17–31.

———. "Ethnicity and the Reporting of State Violence: *Krakivs'ki Visti*, the NKVD Murders, and the Vinnytsia Exhumation." Paper presented at the Holocaust Workshop, University of Alberta, 15 January 2005.

———. "*Krakivs'ki Visti* and the Jews." *Journal of Ukrainian Studies*, Vol. 21, No. 1–2 (Summer–Winter, 1996): 81–96.

———. "War Criminality: a Blank Spot in the Collective Memory of the Ukrainian Diaspora." *Spaces of Identity*, Vol. 5, No. 1 (2005): 9–24.

Hrytsak, Yaroslav. "On the Relevance and Irrelevance of Nationalism in Ukraine." Second Annual Stasiuk-Cambridge Lecture, University of Cambridge, England, 20 February 2004.

Hunczak, Taras. "OUN–German Relations, 1941–1945." In Joachim Torke and John-Paul Himka, ed., *German-Ukrainian Relations in Historical Perspective,* Edmonton: CIUS Press, 1994, pp. 178–186.

Isaevych, Iaroslav. "Ukrainian Studies—Exceptional or Merely Exemplary?" *Slavic Review*, Vol. 54, No. 3 (Fall 1995): 702–708.

Khmil, Ivan. "Hucksterish Circumlocutions of the OUN-UPA Apologists." *The Day Weekly Digest*, 9 October 2001; [http://www.day.kiev.ua/268044/].

Jilge, Wilfried. "The Politics of History and the Second World War in Post-Communist Ukraine." *Jahrbuecher fuer Geschichte Osteuropas*, Vol. 54, No. 1 (2006): 50–81.

Kril, Yuri. "Stepan Bandera is Back Home." *Den'; The Day Weekly Digest*, 15 October 2002; [http://www.day.kiev.ua/259594/].

———. "Yuri Shukhevych: the Truth about UPA will be known." *Den'; The Day Weekly Digest*, 15 October 2002; [http://www.day.kiev.ua/259602/].

Kul'chyts'kyi, Stanislav. "Skeletons in the closet in the Light of Perestroika." *Den'; The Day Weekly Digest*, 4 December 2001; [http://www.day.kiev.ua/268404/].

———. "Why did Stalin exterminate the Ukrainians?" *Den'; The Day Weekly Digest*, 25 October 2005; [http://www.day.kiev.ua/151228/].

———. "Why did Stalin Exterminate the Ukrainians? Comprehending the Holodomor." *Den'; The Day Weekly Digest*, 1 November 2005; [http://www.day.kiev.ua/151682/].

————. "Why did Stalin exterminate the Ukrainians: Comprehending the Holodomor: the Position of Soviet historians." *Den'; The Day Weekly Digest*, 8 November 2005; [http://www.day.kiev.ua/152116/].

————. "Why did Stalin Rxterminate the Ukrainians?" *Den'; The Day Weekly Digest*, 22 November 2005; [http://www.day.kiev.ua/153208].

————. "Why did Stalin exterminate the Ukrainians? Socioeconomic and national dimensions of the Famine." *Den'; The Day Weekly Digest*, 6 December 2005; [http://www.day.kiev.ua/153901/].

Kuropas, Myron. B. "Free at last! Free at last!" *The Ukrainian Weekly*, 8 December 1991, p.7.

————. "UPA and the Ukrainian Identity Problem." *The Ukrainian Weekly*, 19 June 2005, p. 7.

Kuzio, Taras. "Denial of Great Famine Continues a Decade after the Collapse of the USSR." *The Ukrainian Weekly*, 7 July 2002. [http://ukrweekly.com/Archive/2002/270203/shtml]

————. "Loyal Nationalism in Postcommunist States." *RFE/RL Newsline*, Vol. 7, No. 122, 30 June 2003.

Mace, James. "A Historic Motion." *Den'; The Day Weekly Digest*, 24 June 2003; [http://www.day.kiev.ua/260728/].

————. "Dealing with 1933." *Den'; The Day Weekly Digest*, 12 November 2002; [http://www.day.kiev.ua/259745/].

————. "Denying the undeniable." *Den'; The Day Weekly Digest*, 28 May 2002; [http://www.day.kiev.ua/259000/].

————. "Facing past suffering." *Den'; The Day Weekly Digest*, 28 November 2000; [http://www.day.kiev.ua/266745/].

————. "Is the Ukrainian Genocide a Myth?" *Den'; The Day Weekly Digest*, 25 November 2003; [http://www.day.kiev.ua/261343/].

————. "Remembrance and Justice." *Den'; The Day Weekly Digest*, 28 October 2003; [http://www.day.kiev.ua/261177/].

————. "Truth and Fact." *Den'; The Day Weekly Digest*, 26 November 2002; [http://www.day.kiev.ua/259821/].

Makhun, Serhiy, et al. "History as Taught in the Schools: Time to Decide." *Den', The Day Weekly Digest*, 14 October 2003; [http://www.day.kiev.ua/261121/].

Nykytyuk, Tetyana. "A Candle Lit in Memory and Hope." *Den'; The Day Weekly Digest*, 25 March 2003; [http://www.day.kiev.ua/260363/].

Plokhy, Serhii M. "The History of a 'Non-historical' Nation: Notes on the Nature and Current Problems of Ukrainian Historiography." *Slavic Review*, Vol. 54, No. 3 (Fall 1995): 709–716.

Plyushch, Vasyl'. "Genocide of the Ukrainian People: Artificial Famine in the Years 1931-1933." *ABN Correspondence*, Vol. 25, No. 3 (May–June 1973): 31.

Potichnyj, Peter J., "The Ukrainian Insurgent Army (UPA) and the German Authorities." In Himka and Torke, *German-Ukrainian Relations in Historical Perspective*, pp. 163–177.

———. "Ukrainians in World War II Military Formations: An Overview." In Yury Boshyk, ed. *Ukraine During World War II: History and its Aftermath,* Edmonton: CIUS Press, 1986, pp. 61-66.

Popson, Nancy "The Ukrainian History Textbook: Introducing Children to the 'Ukrainian Nation'," *Nationalities Papers,* Vol. 29, No. 2 (2001): 325-350.

Rodgers, Peter. "Rewriting History in Post-Soviet Ukraine: Contestation and Negotiation of Ukraine's Eastern Borderland." Paper presented at the International Graduate Student Symposium, Centre for European, Russian, and Eurasian Studies, University of Toronto, 17 March 2006.

Rudling, Per Anders. "Organized Anti-Semitism in Contemporary Ukraine: Structure, Influence, and Ideology." *Canadian Slavonic Papers,* Vol. 48, No's. 1-2 (March-June 2006): 81-118.

Serbyn, Roman. "Ukraine Should Abandon Soviet-era Myths." *The Day Digest,* No. 25, 25 July 2006; [http://www.day.kiev.ua/103].

Shapoval, Yurii. "The Famine of 1932-33 in Ukraine: What do we know about it today?" Paper presented at the Ukrainian Youth Centre in Edmonton, Canada, 16 November 2003.

Snyder, Timothy "The Causes of Ukrainian-Polish Ethnic Cleansing." *Past and Present,* Vol. 179, No. 1 (2003): 208.

Stepanyshyn, Serhii. "Nationalist Internationalism: The Conference of the Captive Nations of Eastern Europe and Asia was held sixty years ago." *The Day Digest,* 9 December 2003; [http://www.day.kiev.ua/261419/].

Tauger, Mark B. "Natural Disaster and Human Action in the Soviet Famine of 1931-1933." *Carl Beck Papers in Russian and East European Studies,* No. 1506, 2001.

———. "The 1932 Harvest and the Famine of 1933." *Slavic Review,* Vol. 50, No. 1 (Spring 1990): 70-89.

Tol'ts, Mark. "Skol'ko zhe nas togda bylo?" *Ogonyok,* No. 51 (December 1987): 10-11.

Von Hagen, Mark. "Does Ukraine have a History?" *Slavic Review,* Vol. 54, No. 3 (Fall 1995): 658-673.

Williams, Morgan. "Ukrainian issues joint declaration at the United Nations in connection with the 70th Anniversary of the Great Famine in Ukraine of 1932-1933," *The Action Ukraine Report,* 11 November 2003, [http://www.artukraine.com/famineart/ukr_un_decl.htm.]

Wolczuk, Kataryna. "The Difficulties of Polish-Ukrainian Historical Reconciliation." Paper published by the Royal Institute of International Affairs, London, 2002.

Yurkevych, M. "Organization of Ukrainian Nationalists," *Encyclopedia of Ukraine*; [http://www.encyclopediaofukraine.com/display.asp?AddButton=pages\O\R\OrganizationofUkrainianNationalists.htm].

Zamyatin, Viktor. "Adam Michnik: One must think ahead." *Den'; The Day Weekly Digest,* 15 April 2003; [http://www.day.kiev.ua/260479/].

Books

Anderson, Benedict. *Imagined Communities: Reflections on the Origin and Spread of Nationalism.* London: Verso, 1983.

Armstrong, John A. *Ukrainian Nationalism*, 3rd ed. Englewood, Colorado: Ukrainian Academic Press, 1990.

Berkhoff, Karel. *Harvest of Despair: Life and Death in Ukraine under Nazi Rule,* Cambridge, Massachusetts: Harvard University Press, 2004.

Bociurkiw, Bohdan R. *The Ukrainian Greek Catholic Church and the Soviet State (1939-1950).* Edmonton: Canadian Institute of Ukrainian Studies Press, 1996.

Boshyk, Yury, ed. *Ukraine during World War II: History and its Aftermath.* Edmonton: Canadian Institute of Ukrainian Studies, 1986.

Brown, Kate. *A Biography of No Place: from Ethnic Borderland to Soviet Heartland.* Cambridge, Massachusetts: Harvard University Press, 2004.

Conquest, Robert. *Harvest of Sorrow: Soviet Collectivization and the Terror-Famine.* Oxford: Oxford University Press, 1986.

Davies R. W. and Stephen G. Wheatcroft. *The Years of Hunger: Soviet Agriculture, 1931-1933.* London: Palgrave Macmillan, 2004.

Davies, Norman. *Europe at War 1939-1945: No Simple Victory.* London: Macmillan, 2006.

Dietsch, Johan. *Making Sense of Suffering: Holocaust and Holodomor in Ukrainian Historical Culture.* Lund, Sweden: Department of History, Lund University, 2006.

Dyczok, Marta. *Ukraine: Movement without Change, Change without Movement.* Amsterdam: Harwood Academic Publishers, 2000.

Dzyuba, Ivan. *Internationalism or Russification: a Study in the Soviet Nationalities Problem*, 3rd ed. New York: Pathfinder Press, 1974.

Gross, Jan T. *Revolution from Abroad: the Soviet Conquest of Poland's Western Ukraine and Western Belorussia.* Princeton, NJ: Princeton University Press, 2002.

Halan, Yaroslav. *Lest People Forget: Pamphlets, Articles, and Reports.* Kyiv: Dnipro, 1986.

Heike, Wolf-Dietrich. *The Ukrainian Division "Galicia," 1943-45: a Memoir.* Toronto: The Shevchenko Scientific Society, 1988.

Hobsbawm, Eric. *Nations and Nationalism since 1780: Programme, Myth, Reality.* Cambridge, UK: Cambridge University Press, 1990.

Hunczak, Taras. *On the Horns of a Dilemma: the Story of the Ukrainian Division Halychyna.* Lanham, MD: University Press of America, 2000.

Khrushchev, Sergei, ed. *Memoirs of Nikita Khrushchev.* Volume 1: Commissar [1918-1945]. University Park, Pennsylvania: Pennsylvania State University Press, 2004.

Koshiw, J. V. *Beheaded: the Killing of a Journalist.* London: Artemia Press, 2003.

Kuzio, Taras and Paul D'Anieri, ed. *The Dilemmas of State-Led Nation Building in Ukraine.* Westport, Connecticut: Praeger, 2002.

Kuzio, Taras. *Ukraine: Perestroika to Independence.* New York: St. Martin's Press, 2000.

Liber, George O. *Soviet Nationality Policy, Urban Growth, and Identity Change in the Ukrainian SSR 1923-1934.* Cambridge: Cambridge University Press, 1992.

Littman, Sol. *Pure Soldiers or Bloodthirsty Murderers? The Ukrainian 14th Waffen-SS Galicia Division.* Toronto: Black Rose Books, 2003.

Logusz, Michael O. *Galicia Division: the Waffen SS 14th Grenadier Division 1943-1945.* Atglen, PA: Schiffer Publishing, 2000.

Mace, James E. *Communism and the Dilemmas of National Liberation: National Communism in Ukraine, 1918-1933.* Cambridge, Mass: Harvard University Press, 1983.

Marples, David R. *Stalinism in Ukraine in the 1940s.* London: The Macmillan Press, 1992.

Martin, Terry. *The Affirmative Action Empire: Nations and Nationalism in the Soviet Union, 1923-1939.* Ithaca and London: Cornell University Press, 2001.

Molchanov, Mikhail A. *Political Culture and National Identity in Russian-Ukrainian Relations.* College Station, TX: Texas A & M University Press, 2002.

Motyl, Alexander J. *The Turn to the Right: the Ideological Origins and Development of Ukrainian Nationalism, 1919-1929.* Boulder, CO: East European Monographs, 1980. Distributed by Columbia University Press, New York.

Nahaylo, Bohdan. *The Ukrainian Resurgence.* Toronto: University of Toronto Press, 1999.

Peterson, D. J. *Troubled Lands: the Legacy of Soviet Environmental Destruction.* Boulder, Colorado: The Westview Press, 1993.

Poliszczuk, Wiktor. *Bitter Truth: the Criminality of the Organization of Ukrainian Nationalists (OUN) and the Ukrainian Insurgent Army (UPA): the Testimony of a Ukrainian.* Toronto, 1999.

———. *Legal and Political Assessment of the OUN and UPA.* Toronto, 1997.

Potichnyj, Peter J. ed. *English Language Publications of the Ukrainian Underground: Litopys UPA.* Vol. 17, Toronto: Litopys UPA, 1988.

———. *Litopys UPA: Underground Journals from Beyond the Curzon Line: 1945-1947.* Vol. 16, Toronto: Litopys UPA, 1987.

Potichnyj, Peter J. and Evhen Shtendera, ed. *Political Thought of the Ukrainian Underground: 1943-1951.* Edmonton: CIUS Press, 1986.

Serbyn, Roman and Bohdan Krawchenko, ed. *Famine in Ukraine, 1932-1933.* Edmonton, Canadian Institute of Ukrainian Studies, 1986.

Seton-Watson, Hugh. *Language and National Consciousness.* Oxford, UK: Oxford University Press, 1981.

Smith, Anthony D. *Myths and Memories of the Nation.* Oxford, UK: Oxford University Press, 1999.

Snyder, Timothy. *The Reconstruction of Nations: Poland, Ukraine, Lithuania, Belarus, 1569-1999.* New Haven, Connecticut: Yale University Press, 2003.

———. *Sketches from a Secret War: a Polish Artist's Mission to Liberate Soviet Ukraine.* New Haven, Connecticut: Yale University Press, 2005.

Subtelny, Orest. *Ukraine: A History.* 3rd. ed., Toronto: University of Toronto Press, 2000.

Suny, Ronald G. *The Revenge of the Past: Nationalism, Revolution, and the Collapse of the Soviet Union.* Stanford, California: Stanford University Press, 1993.

Taylor, Sally J. *Stalin's Apologist: Walter Duranty, the New York Times' Man in Moscow.* New York: Oxford University Press, 1990.

Torke, Hans-Joachim and John-Paul Himka, eds. *German-Ukrainian Relations in Historical Perspective.* Edmonton and Toronto: Canadian Institute of Ukrainian Studies Press, 1994.

Tottle, Douglas. *Fraud, Famine, and Fascism: the Ukrainian Genocide Myth from Hitler to Harvard.* Toronto: Progress Books, 1987.

Varvartsev, Nikolai N. *Ukrainian History in the Distorting Mirror of Sovietology.* Kyiv: Naukova dumka, 1987.

Velychenko, Stephen. *Shaping Identity in Eastern Europe and Russia: Soviet-Russian and Polish Accounts of Ukrainian History, 1914-1991.* New York: St. Martin's Press, 1993.

Viola, Lynne. *The Best Sons of the Fatherland: Workers in the Vanguard of Soviet Collectivization.* New York: Oxford University Press, 1987.

Wanner, Catherine. *Burden of Dreams: History and Identity in Post-Soviet Ukraine.* University Park: Pennsylvania, 1988.

Weiner, Amir. *Making Sense of War: the Second World War and the Fate of the Bolshevik Revolution.* Princeton: Princeton University Press, 2001.

Wilson, Andrew. *The Ukrainians: Unexpected Nation.* Cambridge, UK: Cambridge University Press, 2000.

―――. *Ukraine's Orange Revolution.* New Haven, Connecticut: Yale University Press, 2005.

―――. *Ukrainian Nationalism in the 1990s: a Minority Faith.* Cambridge, UK: Cambridge University Press, 1997.

Yekelchyk, Serhy. *Stalin's Empire of Memory: Russian-Ukrainian Relations in the Soviet Historical Imagination.* Toronto, University of Toronto Press, 2004.

―――. *Ukraine: Birth of a Modern Nation.* New York: Oxford University Press, 2007.

INDEX